Mount Horeb Church

Minute Books, 1841-1923

An Anthology of
Church and Family History

(Jefferson County, TN)

Mount Horeb Church, 2016

Compiled by Hazel Timblin Townsend
2016

Please direct all correspondence and orders to:

www.southernhistoricalpress.com
or
SOUTHERN HISTORICAL PRESS, Inc.
PO BOX 1267
375 West Broad Street
Greenville, SC   29601
southernhistoricalpress@gmail.com

ISBN #0-89308-501-4

Printed in the United States of America

Dedication

To the memory of my Aunt and Uncle,
Marguerite Justus Rankin and Roy Marshall Rankin
of White Pine, Tennessee,
who worked tirelessly to preserve the Rankin stories
through their research and written information.

Contents

Acknowledgments

Thanks go to many people, but first I am indebted to Manuela Connatser who started my interesting journey by giving me two old session minute books of Mount Horeb Presbyterian Church.

Thank you to Steve Cotham, Manager of the Calvin M. McClung Historical Collection of the East Tennessee Historical Center, for locatimg the typed manuscript copy of Volumes I-III of the Mount Horeb Church Session Minutes. He copied Volume II and borrowed the original books to microfilm. I'd also like to thank that unknown person who transcribed and typed all three volumes in 1940. What a gift that was.

I thank Donna Turner for the old 1805 family Bible that belonged to Jennet Bradshaw and Thomas Rankin II of Dumplin Valley. It was found in the former Knoxville home of Faye Rankin, granddaughter of Christopher Houston Rankin. The family record has the births, marriages, and deaths of their children. This confirmed the death date of Thomas II as August 3, 1821.

A huge debt of gratitude goes to my Uncle Roy Marshall Rankin, son of Frank Walter Rankin and grandson of Christopher Houston Rankin. His interest in the Rankin family history inspired me. His research on the Thomas Rankin II line for the First Families of Tennessee is on file in the McClung Collection. The East Tennessee Historical Society published information about *First Families of Tennessee: A Register of Early Settlers and Their Present-Day Descendants* (Nashville, TN: Ambrose, 2000).

I'd like to thank Bob Jarnagin, the Jefferson County Historian, for locating the history and pictures of Mount Horeb School collected by Don Barbee in the Jefferson County Archives Office in Dandridge and the early Rankin deeds.

A thank you to Kathy Underwood for donating the Rankin papers to the Hamblen County Historical Society of Morristown, published in 2016 as *The Lost Rankin Papers, Jefferson Co., TN, 1824-1866*. I appreciate their willingness to share this information at the 2016 Rankin Clan Reunion and the additional help from Lynda Raitala.

Thanks go to Dr. Melanie Thomas Hodgson, Secretary of the Rankin Clan Reunion, for finding information about the speakers and programs for each year.

My thanks and gratitude go to many writers (known and unknown) who have preserved the family stories and information down through the years, including: William Rankin, Sr., Nathaniel Hood Franklin, Reva Rankin Hammer, Jack Brown Franklin, Jean Bible, Martha Lou Coile, Mary Ruth McMurray Crawford, Eva Elizabeth Blackburn McMurray, and Clara Bettis Zirkle.

Many thanks go to my cousins who typed and proofread various parts of the book: Helen H. Rankin Hall, Jeanyne Cole Rankin, Marjorie Anne Rankin Peterson and Marilyn Rankin Clark.

A big thank you goes to our daughter-in-law, Barbara Lefferts Townsend, who helped with the overall organization and editing of the book and our son, Walter Rankin Townsend, who gave technical support. A huge thanks goes to my husband, D. Earle Townsend, Jr., for his encouragement, patience and technical support.

Preface

A surprise e-mail arrived in February 2013 that started an avalanche. I did not know the writer, but I knew what she was talking about. She had found two church session books and wondered if I was interested in having them. Of course I was! They were the long lost Session Minute Books for the Mount Horeb Presbyterian Church in Dumplin Valley, Jefferson County, Tennessee, the church that my ancestors helped organize in 1841. The little country church no longer has a congregation, but the Rankin Clan meets annually in the old church for a day of remembering.

After transcribing the two books, I felt there should be another book between them. The Civil War period was missing. At the 2014 Clan Reunion, I mentioned the books and also my thoughts about a third book. No one had a suggestion. In early 2015, someone suggested checking the McClung Historical Collection of East Tennessee History Center in Knoxville. I talked with the Manager but he didn't know anything about the church or information they might have. However, he said he would check and get back to me. He called and said he had found a typed manuscript of all three books! He agreed to send a copy of the second volume and asked to borrow the two original books so that he could make a microfilm copy of them.

At the 2015 Clan Reunion, a newcomer said she wanted to show me something after the meeting. It was an old family Bible that belonged to my great-great-great grandparents, printed in 1805. This was one of the settler families in Dumplin Valley, Jennet Bradshaw (1772-1824) and Thomas Rankin II (1764-1821). Their descendants were active in the organization and work of the Mount Horeb Church.

There was a Mount Horeb School at the same time the church was organized and both met in the same building for about 10 years. A group from Hamblen County Genealogical Society visited our 2016 Rankin Clan Reunion. They published some old Rankin papers stored in a leather pouch that had been passed down for generations. They were John D. Rankin estate papers and included a list of students in his subscription school during the winter of 1826-1827. His father was Thomas Rankin II. The school on John's farm was in Dumplin Valley and predated the Mount Horeb School.

Three Rankin brothers—Samuel, Richard and Thomas, with John Bradshaw—settled near the headwaters of Dumplin Creek around 1786. The Mount Horeb Presbyterian Church was organized on a hill above the headwaters in 1841 with a charter membership of sixty-seven people. The little church closed its doors about 1925 but the Rankin Clan wanted to keep the stories alive. In 1948, the first Rankin Clan Reunion was held and has continued every year since then.

So what was I to do with all of this information? Publish it, of course! I found an interested publisher, Southern Historical Press in Greenville, South Carolina. Now future generations can have information and stories to read about the little country church in Dumplin Valley and her people who scattered around the world.

Chapter 1

Introduction

By the time the children of the early pioneers of Dumplin Valley were adults, there were enough people to organize more churches. John Bradshaw had ten children. There were thirty-two children among the three Rankin brothers—Thomas (thirteen), Richard (twelve), and Samuel (seven). Hopewell was the first Presbyterian Church in Jefferson County, organized in 1785 in Dandridge, but by 1841 people wanted a church closer to their homes in Dumplin Valley.

The men and women mentioned in the Mount Horeb minutes and stories were Scots-Irish Presbyterians. Their faith was strong. They believed the Bible and they taught it to their children. Many homes had one large Bible that was read to the family often. Many learned to read from studying the Scriptures. Education was important. The family recorded births, marriages and deaths in the Bible for safe keeping.

Train up a child in the way he should go: and when he is old, he will not depart from it. (Proverbs 22:6 KJV) This verse was a strong guideline for many families. The children were taught many things, but the most important was passing on their faith. Baptisms are listed in the session books. Later the same names are on the church membership rolls and some in leadership positions.

Paul's words to Timothy could be said to many of the children who were in the Mount Horeb Church. *When I call to remembrance the unfeigned faith that is in thee, which dwelt first in thy grandmother Lois, and thy mother Eunice; and I am persuaded that in thee also. Wherefore I put thee in remembrance that thou stir up the gift of God, which is in thee by the putting on of my hands. For God hath not given us the spirit of fear; but of power, and of love, and of a sound mind. (II Timothy 1:5-7 KJV)*

Many of these children grew in faith and followed it through good times and bad. They did have some very rough times when they found themselves in the middle of a war zone with troops of both sides roaming over their farms in battle or in search of food. The aftermath of the Civil War was also very difficult for all of the families in Jefferson County. Some families lost loved ones, while others felt alienated from family and friends. Many left the area and joined the westward movement.

They obeyed the great commission. They became leaders in their homes, churches, community, our country, and around the world. *Go ye therefore, and teach all nations, baptizing them in the name of the Father, and of the Son, and of the Holy Ghost: Teaching them to observe all things whatsoever I have commanded you: and, lo, I am with you always, even unto the end of the world. (Matthew 28:18-20 KJV)*

Look for the men and women who followed this command in the record and stories. Read between the lines to look a little closer at some of the families who were the strong leaders of faith in this community. Do you know anything more about their children, grandchildren and on down to their descendants today? Have these same characteristics continued down through the generations?

Chapter 2

The Big Picture

This chapter presents an "at-a-glance" preview of *Mount Horeb Church Minute Books* to set the stage in four sections: You will be introduced to:

- **the families and leaders of the community,**

- **the actual locations of their homes, churches, cemeteries, and monuments which you can visit today,**

- **a timeline of historical events surrounding these events in East Tennessee, and**

- **the original sources for the stories and records, and where they may be found today.**

By including snapshots of "Who," "Where," "When," and "What" we are talking about, it is my hope that history will come alive, connections will be made, and stories will continue to be told and added to this collection.

Who: People

Marguerite Justus Rankin and Roy Marshall Rankin, 2007
Celebrating their 65th Wedding Anniversary

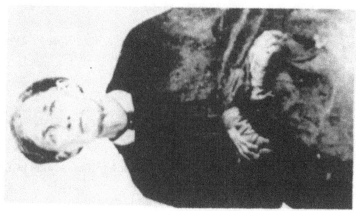

Frances George "Fanny" Gilbraith Rankin

Christopher Rankin

Lieut. Samuel E Rankin

Rev. John T. Rankin

Catherine Ruth Franklin & Christopher Houston Rankin, circa 1874

Benjamin Francis Franklin & Lucinda Harriett Rankin, circa 1870

Catherine Ruth Franklin Rankin was the daughter of Benjamin F. Franklin and Lucinda Harriett Rankin Franklin.

Christopher Rankin and Frances George "Fanny" Gilbraith Family 1892
The empty chair was for Christopher who died July 1, 1881.

1892 Christopher Rankin family: Sam E., Martha Jane, Charlotte L, Nancy E., Sarah M., Leanna, Christopher Hodson, Jim Tom, Andrew W., Frances, Huldah, John Fain, Joseph M.

John Franklin Newman and Mary Jane Corbett Family, Circa 1900

Andrew J. & Lillian W. (Alexander) Newman, Martha G. Newman, Zorado F. Newman, Joseph P. & Martha M. (Baker) Newman,
Daniel H. & Lula (Smith) Newman; Front-Dorman O. Newman (son of Andrew J.), John Franklin & Mary Jane (Corbett) Newman,
Lula J. Newman, Lillie C. Newman, John C. Newman.

Frank Walter Rankin and Lula Belle Sharp Family, 1929

Family of Lula Belle Sharp and Frank Walter Rankin, White Pine, TN, 1929
Frank Walter, Roy Marshall, Lula Belle, Ralph Everett, Helen Kathleen, Lynn Boyd,
Beulah Belle, Stanley Lee, Frank Earle, Ross Wayne

`Where: Places

Dumplin Valley Area Home Sites, Jefferson County, Tennessee
Marked by Roy Marshall Rankin, 2000

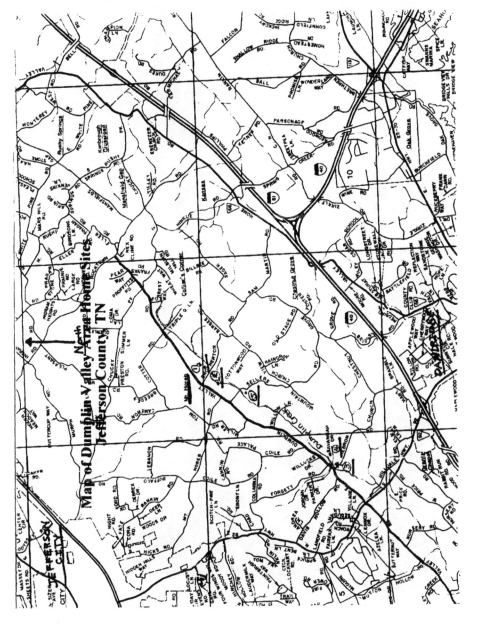

Home Sites

Christopher Rankin House with Family, 1892

Coile-Sheddan Store, Mount Horeb Community

Schools

Mount Horeb School, Rear View &
Church Cemetery, 1916

Mount Horeb School, Dumplin Valley
front view, 1945

Churches

Hebron Presbyterian Church on Hebron Church Road

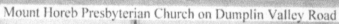

Mount Horeb Presbyterian Church on Dumplin Valley Road

Rankin Clan Reunion

Dumplin Valley Road   Clan Reunion Sign

Bob Pennington, Piper, Dumplin Valley 1989

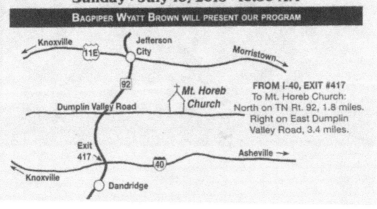

69TH ANNUAL RANKIN CLAN REUNION
Sunday · July 10, 2016 · 10:30 AM

BAGPIPER WYATT BROWN WILL PRESENT OUR PROGRAM

FROM I-40, EXIT #417
To Mt. Horeb Church:
North on TN Rt. 92, 1.8 miles.
Right on East Dumplin
Valley Road, 3.4 miles.

Rankin Clan Reunion
Fiftieth Anniversary Signature Quilt
Made by Joy Hammer Bemis, 1998

Rankin Clan Reunion

Gov. Lamar Alexander 1983

Roy M. & Lynn B. Rankin 1987

Wanda & Joe Newman 2013

Melanie Thomas Hodgson 2013

Cemeteries and Monuments

Cars parked near location of Mount Horeb School

Mount Horeb Cemetery, Pioneer Monument, 2009

THIS TABLET WAS ERECTED IN 1930 BY
CHRISTOPHER HOUSTON RANKIN
COURTLAND THALES RANKIN ATTY.
REV. JOHN GRANT NEWMAN D. D.
MRS. ALMYRA - RANKIN - McMURRAY
MRS. ROZEE - RANKIN - TAYLOR
FRANK WALTER RANKIN
HARRY JAY RANKIN
SAM HULL RANKIN

Pioneer Monument Donor Plaque

Pioneer Monument Plaque

First Settlers Monument in Dumplin Valley
Mount Horeb Cemetery, Erected 1930

June 2001 -- THE FOLLOWING CORRECTIONS SHOULD BE MADE
ON THE TABLET BELOW:

THOMAS RANKIN (I) 1724-1812   MARRIED ISABELLA CLENDENIN
OF PA AND SETTLED IN THAT STATE.

SAMUEL 1758-1834   MARRIED   SAMUEL RANKIN 1758-1834
WILLIAM 1759-1833   MARRIED
ISABEL   MARRIED   JANE ISABELLE PETTY
MARY   MARRIED   SARAH MOORE
                              ROBERT McCUISTION
                              ANDREW McCUISTION

Revolutionary Cemetery
Dandridge, Jefferson County, Tennessee

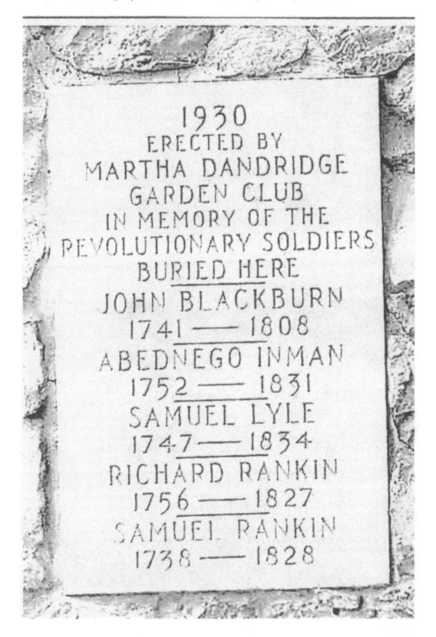

Revolutionary Cemetery, Dandridge

Thomas Rankin II (1764-1821), Headstone

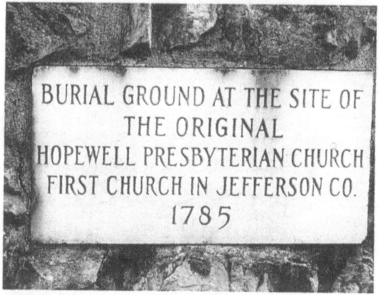

When: Timeline

Overview

The historical timeline was included to show where the events in the church or in the family stories fit into the historic context. History was made in East Tennessee.[1]

Timeline of Events Affecting East Tennessee

Compiled by Hazel Timblin Townsend

1750s	First permanent settlements began in what is now Tennessee.
1769-1771	Both North Carolina and Virginia claimed the area known now as East Tennessee.
1771	Watauga Association formed in what is now the northeastern corner of Tennessee. Pemberton District, in southwest Virginia, formed.
1775	Revolutionary War began with England.
1776	United States declared Independence. Presbyterian ministers Charles Cummings and Joseph Rhea came from Virginia to what is now East Tennessee, part of Hanover Presbytery, Synod of New York and Philadelphia. Col. Christian's forces assembled from the Watauga settlement to fight the Indians as far west as present day Sevier and Blount Counties. A provisional peace was reached with the Indians.
1777	Washington District, North Carolina (later Tennessee). Samuel Doak licensed by Hanover Presbytery to minister to Watauga and Holston settlements in NC/TN.
1779	Cumberland Settlements in what is now the Nashville, Tennessee area. Jonesboro, NC/TN settled. Battle of Augusta, Virginia.
1780	Battles of Charleston and Camden, South Carolina. Battle of Kings Mountain in North Carolina. Rev. Samuel Doak began Salem Church and school, congregations at Mount Bethel and also Carter's Valley.
1781	Americans won the battle at Cowpens, South Carolina and lost Guilford Courthouse in North Carolina. Americans and France defeated British at battle of Yorktown, Virginia. General Charles Cornwallis surrendered at Yorktown, Virginia.
1782	Rev. Samuel Doak established New Bethel Church at the fork of the Watauga and Holston Rivers in North Carolina (later Tennessee).
1783	Rev. Samuel Doak incorporated Martin Academy, later became Washington College, "the first literary institution west of the Alleghenies."
1784	State of Franklin organized in what is now East Tennessee.
1785	Hopewell Presbyterian Church in Dandridge organized, first church in Jefferson County. Abington Presbytery organized for western Virginia and North Carolina west of the mountains (Tennessee), attached to the new Synod of the Carolinas.

---

[1] Information taken from the following sources: Billie R. McNamara, *Guide to Genealogical and Historical Research in Jefferson County, Tennessee*, copyright ©1995; Vera Wilson Gilmore, *Presbytery of Union 1797-1976*, Published by The United Presbyterian Church in the USA, Presbytery of Union, Knoxville, TN, 1976; Sandra S. Wilson and Dennis L. Snapp, *Broken Hearts Broken Lives, Jefferson County, Tennessee, 1860-1868*, Published by Restore Our Country, 1986; Judy Jacobson, *History for Genealogists*, Genealogical Publishing Company, Baltimore, Maryland, 2009.

1786	Transylvania Presbytery organized in Kentucky. Eusebia and New Providence Churches organized by Rev. Archibald Scott in what is now Blount County. Richard Rankin and John Bradshaw settled on the headwaters of Dumplin Creek about this time. Richard's brothers, Samuel and Thomas, probably followed in the the next year or two.
1787	Westminster Presbyterian Church founded by Rev. Robert Henderson about 10 miles northeast of Dandridge in Leadville. Later Westminster Church moved to White Pine, Tennessee.
1789	State of Franklin reunited with North Carolina. This area became part of the Southwest Territory South of the Ohio River.
1792	June 11, Jefferson and Knox counties formed by an ordinance of Governor Blount.
1793	Town of Dandridge established in Jefferson County.
1794	Rev. Hezekiah Balch founded Greeneville College on part of his farm. Rev. Balch remained president and professor until his death in 1810. Later this became Tusculum College, Greeneville, TN.
1796	June 1, Tennessee became the 16th state of the United States.
1797	Union Presbytery organized by the Reverends Hezekiah Balch, John Cossan, Samuel Carrick, Robert Henderson and Gideon Blackburn.
1802	Washington Church organized by Rev. Samuel Carrick. in "Grassy Valley," now Corryton, near Knoxville.
1804	St. Paul's Church organized by Rev. Robert Henderson at Flat Creek. Later church was moved to Morristown. Another account states it began in 1787.
1817	Synod of Tennessee organized.
1818	Second Presbyterian Church of Knoxville founded by Rev. Isaac Anderson.
1819	Tennessee Synod approved Isaac Anderson's plan to open a "Southern and Western" Theological Seminary. Later it became Maryville College in Maryville.
1826	New Market Presbyterian Church organized by Rev. John McCampbell. John D. Rankin had a subscription school on his plantation Dec. 6 to Feb. 20, 1827.
1841	Mount Horeb Church organized by Union Presbytery and met in the Mount Horeb log school house.
1842	Land for the Mount Horeb school, church and cemetery deeded in February for that purpose by Richard Duffield Rankin and Richard Ammon Bradshaw, sons of the first settlers.
1851	Additional land was deeded to the Mount Horeb church and school by Richard Duffield Rankin and Richard Ammon Bradshaw. The first church meeting house was constructed.
1853	Concord Presbyterian Church organized about ten miles west of Dandridge.
1860	Mount Horeb Presbyterian Church closed because of the impending war.
1861	Abraham Lincoln sworn in as President of the United States. Tennessee withdrew from the Union and joined Confederate states. Union sympathizers in East Tennessee objected strongly. In Strawberry Plains a train of Confederate troops and a group of pro-Union locals exchanged gunfire. Confederate troops stationed along the railroad to Knoxville at Strawberry Plains, New Market and Mossy Creek. Attempts were made to burn railroad bridges and some succeeded. Confederate units were organized in Jefferson County.

1862	Confederate Conscription Law passed. Union Army controlled Kentucky. Many Unionists went to Kentucky. Some men captured and imprisoned for trying to flee to Kentucky. Jefferson County became a police state.
1863	Spring of 1863, Richard Rawlings Bradshaw wounded and died at seige of Vicksburg. In June, Union General Ambrose Burnside sent Col. William P. Sanders to Jefferson County, near Strawberry Plains. His troops destroyed the East Tennessee & Virginia Railroad bridge across the Holston River, cutting the Confederate supply line to Knoxville. Burnside established headquarters near Morristown. He had 22,750 men between Loudon and Bulls Gap. East Tennessee was under Federal control after two years under the Confederates army. General James Longstreet, Confederate, drove Burnside and troops back to Knoxville. The siege of Knoxville began on November 17. However, Longstreet didn't know the French Broad River flowed into Knoxville but the local farmers did. Supplies of grain, livestock and other foods were floated down the river on small boats and rafts. The siege lasted two weeks. In December, Longstreet withdrew and moved east along the northern border of Jefferson County. On December 14, the Burnside troops (Union) were defeated at Bean Station and went back to Knoxville. On December 20, Longstreet crossed Holston River, camping along the railroad between Morristown and Russellville. Troops raided the local homes and fields for food. The battle on December 29 was fought between Morristown Road and the railroad. More than 500 men were killed, wounded or missing. Union troops held Mossy Creek. Elsewhere there were Union victories at Gettysburg, Pennsylvania and Vicksburg, Mississippi. The Confederates won the Battle of Lookout Mountain near Chattanooga, Tennessee.
1864	The weather turned bitterly cold on January 1, falling to 29 degrees below zero. The residents and both armies were in crises. No one was prepared. Anything that would burn was used to provide warmth, including buildings and fence rails. Animals were freezing to death. There was no way to get supplies from Knoxville. The rivers were frozen and the railroad bridge over the Holston River was not finished until January 15. Both armies raided the countryside to survive. On January 17 the battle of Dandridge was fought under the leadership of Union Brig. Gen. Samuel D. Sturgis, commanding the Cavalry Corps, Army of the Ohio, and Lt. Gen. James Longstreet leading the Confederate troops. The attempt by the Union troops to take Dandridge failed. They retreated to Knoxville, arriving on January 19. After crossing the river on the new railroad bridge, they burned it so that the enemy troops couldn't follow. Jefferson County was again under Confederate control. Smallpox broke out early in the year, which further complicated things. As the western war was winding down, soldiers on both sides were sent closer to their native area, including soldiers from Jefferson County. In August the Union troops at Strawberry Plains were ordered to re-establish control of the area. First Lt. Samuel E. Rankin of Mount Horeb was in the Ninth Tennessee Cavalry, Company B of the Union forces. More than half of this unit came from Jefferson County. Similar numbers were in many of the units on both sides. This meant kinsman and neighbors were fighting each other. There were many skirmishes and battles throughout that year. Control of Jefferson County changed seven times within a year. Confederate soldiers harassed and killed John "Black Jack" Newman in his front yard. Samuel McMurray died in Galatin, Tennessee in the U.S. Army. Elsewhere, the Union army took Atlanta and Gen. Sherman marched across Georgia and the Carolinas.

1865	Dr. William Thomas Rankin was a war casualty. After the occupying armies moved out, there was a period of lawlessness. Deserters on both sides and other men took advantage by breaking into private property and stealing, or harassing and beating the owners. Confederate States surrendered.
1866	Mount Horeb Church began holding services again.
1868	Bethel Presbyterian Church of Dandridge organized.
1874	Hebron Church organized by members of Mount Horeb Church who had withdrawn. Hebron remained in Union Presbytery, Northern Presbyterian. Mount Horeb Church reorganized under Holston Presbytery, Southern Presbyterian.
1875	Current Mount Horeb church building erected. Hebron Church building completed and dedicated on September 19, 1875. Christopher Houston Rankin was the builder.
1902	July 6, agreement ratified by contending members of Hebron and Mossy Creek Churches to unite with Mount Horeb Church. New officers elected in Mount Horeb.
1905	Repairs made to stove and windows of Mount Horeb Church.
1906	Repairs made to the roof of Mount Horeb Church.
1911	June 2, Mount Horeb Congregation voted to move members and property to Presbyterian Church U.S.A., Northern Presbyterian denomination.
1913	Mount Horeb Church repaired and remodeled.
1923	Apr 8, last recorded Session meeting of the Mount Horeb Church.
1925	Mount Horeb Church closed.
1930	August 15. Dedication of Pioneer Monument at Mount Horeb Church Cemetery.
1948	July 11, first meeting of the Rankin Clan Reunion in the Mount Horeb Church.
1982	Reunion of the denominations of the United Presbyterian Church U.S.A. (northern) and the Presbyterian Church U. S. (southern). Union Presbytery and Holston Presbytery joined to become Holston Presbytery.
1986	Holston Presbytery deeded the Mount Horeb Church building to the Rankin-Bradshaw Properties, Inc.
2011	Mount Horeb Church building had major repairs—foundation, roof, and paint.

What: Original Sources

Overview

What happened to these original documents after the book was written? They were donated to various historical libraries and archives.

The two original session minute books, Volumes I and III were donated to the Presbyterian Historical Society in Philadelphia, Pennsylvania.

The old 1805 Bible of Jennet Bradshaw and Thomas Rankin II was given to the McClung Historical Collection along with the Christopher Houston Rankin Bible and the following items: deed information, the 1884-1888 Mount Horeb Sunday School Roll Book, Mount Horeb Sunday School Secretary's Record March 2, 1922-March 25, 1923, *Presbytery of Union* by Vera Wilson Gilmore, and 'This and That' newspaper column by Jean Bible from the *Standard Banner* (Jefferson City, Tennessee, November 21, 1974).

The microfilm of the Mount Horeb Minute Books and Sunday School Roll Books made by Steve Cotham, McClung Collection Manager, is part of the McClung Collection in Knoxville, Tennessee. The film includes most of the information mentioned above except the Bibles.

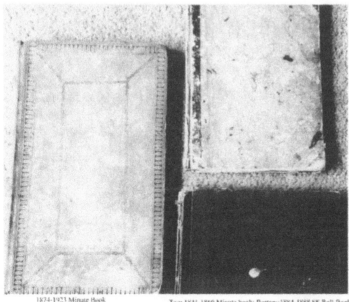

1805 Bradshaw-Rankin Bible

1874-1923 Minute Book   Top: 1841-1860 Minute book; Bottom:1884-1888 SS Roll Book   1827 John D. Rankin Pouch

View of Dumplin Valley from Mount Horeb Church, 2013

Flyleaf in the 1841 Mount Horeb Minute Book

November 30ᵗʰ 1841
The Session of Mount Horeb church
Met, and elected Wᵐ Rankin clerk
of Session, & Christopher Rankin
Treasurer
Wᵐ Rankin, Clk

Page One in the 1841 Mount Horeb Minute Book

Page. 1.

November 20th. 1841. By order of the Presbytery of Union the Revd. John McCampbell organised a church at the School house near R. D. Rankins by ordaining four Elders. Viz

William Rankin.
Richard Bradshaw
Christopher Rankin and
John Newman Junr.

} Elders.

Also at the same time five persons who were chosen to act as trustees. Viz)

William Rankin.
William Massengill Sr.
Richard D. Rankin.
Josiah C. Rankin.
& James Newman.

} Trustees

In the organising of this church the following members in full communion in Hopewell and New Market churches fell within the bounds of this church.
Viz;

Page Two in the 1841 Mount Horeb Minute Book

Hopewell Church

Jane Massengill
Susan P. Massengill
Joseph C. Bradshaw
Sarah Bradshaw
Richard Bradshaw
Lydia Bradshaw
Nancy Ann Bradshaw
Richard H. Bradshaw
Jane Bradshaw
John P. Bradshaw
Elizabeth M. Bradshaw
Thomas R. Bradshaw
Margaret Bradshaw
Jane Rankin
Richard D. Rankin
Mary Ann C. Rankin
Aaron B. Rankin
Aaron Newman
Cassandra Newman
James Rankin
James Newman
Isabella Newman
Joseph R. Newman
Nancy C. Newman
Mary Newman
Josiah C. Rankin
Christopher Rankin

Frances Rankin
William Rankin
Eliza J. Kimbrough
Lucinda Rankin
Joseph McCuistian
Rachel McCuistian
James McCuistian
Isabella Wells
Mary C. Wells
John H. Franklin
Benjamin H. Franklin
Mahulda Newman
~~Total 39~~
Lucinda H. Franklin

Total 40

Page Three in the 1841 Mount Horeb Minute Book

New Market
John Newman Sr
Elizabeth Newman
... Ann Newman
Sophia E. Newman
Louisa H. Newman
Elenor Newman
Blair Newman
Margaret Newman
Aron Newmander
Isabella Newman
Catherine Newman
Thomas I. Newman
Margaret Newman
John Newmander
Jane Newman
William M. Newman
Catherine E. Newman
Mary C. Newman
Mary A. Newman
Aron Newman
John C. Newman
Eliza C. Newman
James H. Hammel
Elizabeth Hammel
Mary Ann Hammel

Berg. Mitchell
Elizabeth Mitchell
Total 27.
Added since the Organisation of this church
Mary W. Easterly
Curion Bowles
Eliza beth Mc...
Moses Easterly
Margery Rankin
Thomas Rankin Sr
Mary M. Rankin
Patrick M. Rankin
Aron A. Newman
Louisa I. Rankin
Catherine E. Hammel
Sarah M. Newman
Wm Goss
Susan Rankin
Plesant Bowes
William B. Mayingill
Aron A. Hammel
Mary Newman
Jane Rankin
Rebecca Ann Jacobs
Nancy ... Goss
John W. Wallas

History of Mount Horeb Church, 1860
1841 Mount Horeb Minute Book, Page 178
By William Rankin, Clerk

178

History of Mt. Horeb Church

Mount Horeb church in Jefferson County Tenn
was organized by the Rev. John McCampbell he
acting by order of Union Presbytery on the 20th
day of November AD 1841 By ordaining four
elders viz Richard Bradshaw William Rankin
Christopher Rankin and John Newman jun.
There were 67 members, taken from Hopewell and
Newmarket churches. The James M. Gass was chosen
their minister and continued to have charge of said
church for five years as stated supply. Since the
Rev. M. Gass left the Rev. Nathaniel Hood has had
the charge of the church as stated supply assisted
a part of the time by the Rev. William Harrison.
They would tell further that in the year 1858 in the
month of April Joseph C. Bradshaw Elias
Alexander and Patrick M. Rankin were elected
and ordained as additional elders in the church

April 7th 1860   William Rankin

Page Three in the 1874 Mount Horeb Minute Book

Mount Horeb E. Tenn.
May 30" 1874

We the undersigned being, or desiring to become members of the Presbyterian Church and believing that it will be for the glory of God and for the good of our community, to have a Presbyterian church organized at or near Mt. Horeb, Jefferson County, Tennessee, and desiring said Church to be in connection with "Holston Presbytery", and Synod of Nashville" of the Presbyterian Church in the United States, do hereby petition the proper authority of said Holston Presbytery to aid us, at as early a day as practicable in effecting said organization according to the rules and usages of said Presbytery

Jos. C. Bradshaw
Andrew Bradshaw
Catherine E. Newman
John P. Bradshaw
Sarah J. Bradshaw
Florence O. Wixom
William P. Bradshaw
Mary L. Bradshaw
F. J. Bradshaw
R. D. Rankin
Nancy D Bradshaw
Harriet J Bradshaw
Sarah E Bradshaw
Michael H. Bradshaw
John H. Bradshaw
Nancy J Franklin
Thomas J. Bradshaw
Cinaerietta C. Bradshaw
John C. Bradshaw
Emma Bonachaw
Jane Massingill
Tyaia Franklin

Susan Dirkle
Mary J. Dirkle
James Truman
Rebecca McGhee
E.R. McGhee
Hugh J Newman
Trimanda Truman
Joseph R. Bradshaw

Page Four in the 1874 Mount Horeb Minute Book

4

The commission of Holston Presbytery consisting of Rev Messrs William Harrison, A Wilson, A.C. Snoddy and Elder S. N. Fain met the above petitioners at Mt Horeb on Saturday 30 May 1874 and proceeded to the organization of the church by the election of the following officers, viz –

Elders	Deacons
R. D. Rankin	Hugh A Newman
James Newman	William P Bradshaw
John P Bradshaw	
J. C. Bradshaw	
John W. Bradshaw	

Joseph C. Bradshaw being a Ruling Elder in the Presbyterian church, signified his acceptance of the office. James Newman & John P Bradshaw having accepted the call to the office of Ruling Elder, also William P Bradshaw accepted the office of Deacon, were regularly set apart and Rev A C Snoddy proposed the questions and Rev A W Wilson offered the ordination prayer – Rev William Harrison conducting the services.

John P Newman
Clerk of Session

Jan 14 1874 — R. D. Rankin having accepted the office of Ruling Elder was regularly ordained, him, John McDaniel presiding.

John P Bradshaw Clerk

Aug 15 1874 — Session met and was opened with prayer by Rev John Daniel the Moderator. Elders present J C Bradshaw R. D. Rankin James Newman John W Bradshaw and J P Bradshaw. Joseph C Bradshaw was appointed delegate & R D Rankin alternate to attend the presbytery of Holston to convene at Rutledge Sept 24 1874

John P Bradshaw
Clerk of Session

Chapter 3

Stories of the Mount Horeb Community

Overview

Various original stories were found and included to help tell the story of the Mount Horeb Presbyterian Church and her people. If you read only the minutes, which are often repetitive and only business, it is hard to fit families and events together.

How do we learn our family stories? We hear the same stories told over and over by members of our family. We are fortunate when the stories are written down. *Mount Horeb Church Minute Books, 1841-1923* demonstrates this through a collection of stories and historical records written on various occasions spanning almost 200 years. While some stories include the same events, each represents a unique audience and time period in the history of this community. So listen carefully to what each one is telling us and you will discover a new fact or point of interest. Someday it will be your turn to tell the family stories to the younger generations!

1826: John Rankin School

by Hamblen County Genealogical Society
The Lost Rankin Papers, Jefferson Co. TN. 1824-1866 [2]

A leather pouch containing old papers preserved in the Rankin family came down to Kathy Underwood. She presented it to the Hamblen County Genealogical Society. It contained estate records and receipts of various members of the John D. Rankin extended family. It also had a record of a subscription school that John Rankin, son of Thomas Rankin II, taught in the winter of 1826-1827. Education was very important to Scots-Irish Presbyterians. They believed everyone should be able to read the Bible for themselves. This would have preceded the Mount Horeb School but in the same vicinity, probably closer to where the Hebron Presbyterian Church is now located. To date no other record of this school has been found. John's wife, Ruth McGuire, died in 1827 and John died in 1828.[3]

---

[2] Hamblen County Genealogical Society, P. O. Box 1213, Morristown, TN 37916. Book published in 2016.

[3] John D. Rankin (1792-1828), son of Thomas Rankin II (1764-1821) and Jennet Bradshaw (1772-1824), married Ruth McGuire on February 13, 1815. They had four children—Lucinda Harriet (1815-1893), Catherine Ruth (1817-1860), Patrick McGuire (1818-1902), and Thomas (1824-1849). John D. Rankin was related to the two men who donated land for the Mount Horeb School and Church. Richard Duffield Rankin was a first cousin and a second cousin. Richard Ammon Bradshaw was an uncle and a first cousin once removed. Richard Ammon Bradshaw and Jennet Bradshaw were children of John Bradshaw (1743-1818) and Nancy Agnes "Annie" Clendenin. (Hazel Timblin Townsend Records)

Contained in the Pouch

Articles of agreement made conseeded [*sic*] and agreed upon between John Rankin of the one part and the under-named subscribers of the other part (Witnesseth) that the said Rankin for the consideration of the sum herein after mentioned agrees to teach a school at the school house on his plantation for the term of sixty school days; wherein he will as health and circumstances may permit attend regularly to common school time and will teach reading, writing and arithmetic to the best of his skill and abilities endeavoring to observe good rules regulations and restrictions. The school to consist of at least 18 scholars and to commence on Tuesday the 5th of December 1826.

We the subscribers for the schooling of our children agree to pay said Rankin two Dollars for every scholar admitted to each of our names, which may be discharged with six bushels of corn delivered at said Rankins house. We also agree to furnish wood and water sufficient to accommodate the school. In witness whereof we have hereunto set our names and respective numbers. This __ Day of November 1926.

Sub. Names[4]

Eleanor Line (Cline?), Paid in full	1
Joseph Churchman	1
George Wray, Paid eight shillings, paid 9s more	2
A. H. C. (?) McSpadden, Paid all	2
Richard Bradshaw[5] Paid	4
John Darr, Paid	2
John Newman[6] Paid	4
Paid Falton (?) Brooks, Paid	2
Blair Newman	2 / 4

Time Sent

Names on roll list	Time Total
R Bradshaw[7]	260
J Newman[8]	237
J Darr	153
M McSpadden[9]	137
Falton (Fallon?) Brooks	116
W Y Line (or Cline ?)	40
Joseph Churchman	64

---

[4] Subscriber names, usually a parent of child or children.
[5] Probably Richard Ammon Bradshaw (1788-1872), son of John Bradshaw (1743-1818) and Nancy Agnes "Annie" Clendenin (1748-1823).
[6] Probably John Newman, Sr. (1782-1865).
[7] Probably Richard Harden Bradshaw (1815-1863), son of Richard Ammon Bradshaw and Lydia Prigmore.
[8] Probably John Newman, Jr. (1811-1864), son of John Newman, Sr. (1782-1865) or John "Black Jack" Newman (1800-1864), son of Aaron Newman, Sr. (1772-1870) and Catherine Blair.
[9] Possibly Milton Harris McSpadden (1806-1846), son of Samuel McSpadden and Nancy Harris.

George Wray	112
Blair Newman[10]	50
Richard Rankin[11]	14
Anderson Coiles	25
James Rankin [12]	20
Henry Haggerd	11

The school began according to articles which was on the 5th Day of December 1826. The school finished on Saturday the 24th day of February 1827 according to agreement. Witness John Rankin

Feb. 20th 1828 George Wray owes 7s on the article

1860: Mount Horeb Presbyterian Church

by William Rankin

Mount Horeb church in Jefferson County Tenn. was organized by the Rev. John McCampbell, he acting by order of Union Presbytery on the 20th day of November AD 1841 by ordaining four elders viz. **Richard [Ammon] Bradshaw, William Rankin, Christopher Rankin and John Newman Jun'r**. There were 67 members taken from Hopewell and New Market churches. The Rev. James H Gass was chosen their minister and continued to have charge of said church for five years as stated supply. When the Rev. Mr. Gass left, the Rev. Nathaniel Hood has had the charge of the church as stated supply minister and part of the time by the Rev. Nathaniel Harrison. They state further that in the year 1854 in month of April **Joseph C. Bradshaw, Elias Alexander and Patrick M. [McGuire] Rankin** were elected and ordained as additional elders in the church. [13]

---

[10] Probably Blair Newman (1798-__), son of Aaron Newman, Sr. (1772-1870) and Catherine Blair.
[11] Possibly Richard Duffield Rankin (1800-1890), son of Richard Rankin (1756-1827) and Jennett "Jane" Steele.
[12] Probably James Eaton Rankin (1816-1893), son of Jane Isabelle "Ibbie" Rankin, daughter of Samuel Rankin (1758-1834) and Jane Isabelle "Ibby" Petty.
[13] This history was written at the end of the 1841-1860 Mount Horeb Minute Book. See Original Records.

1876: Hebron Presbyterian Church History

by Nathan Hood Franklin
Compiled by Jack B. Franklin, 1974 [14]

Mount Horeb Presbyterian Church of Jefferson County, Tennessee was organized by order of Union Presbytery by Rev. John McCampbell on the 20th day of November 1841 by ordaining four Elders, viz: Richard Bradshaw, William Rankin, Christopher Rankin and John Newman jun. with a membership of sixty seven, forty taken from Hopewell Church at Dandridge and twenty seven from New Market.

Rev. James S. Gass supplied the pulpit for the first five years after which Rev. Nathan Hood took charge and continued as stated supply until in 1864 at times assisted by Rev. William Harrison.

In April 1858 there were three additional Elders elected and ordained, viz: Joseph C. Bradshaw, Elias Alexander and Patrick M. Rankin.

After Rev. Nathan Hood ceased his labors, the pulpit was vacant for a short time, being occasionally supplied by Rev. James A Griffis.

In January 1866 Rev. William H. Lyle was called and took charge of the church and continued as stated supply until December 22, 1867 when he was called to the pastorate and was installed in the spring following, in which relations he continued until 1871 when the pastoral relation was dissolved, after which the church was without a minister till February 1873 when Rev. Isaac A. Martin was engaged and continued for two years as stated supply; during which time there had been an election for three additional Elders, which resulted in the election of Samuel E. [Edwin] Rankin, John G. [Gass] Rankin and N. H. [Nathaniel Hood] Franklin. John G. Rankin declining to serve. S. E. Rankin and N. H. Franklin was [sic] ordained January 4, 1874, after which a dissatisfaction arose and a goodly number withdrew and organized two other churches, one in connection with the Southern Presbyterian Church and one in connection with the Cumberlain [sic] Presbyterian Church.

In April 1874 at a meeting of the officers of the church it was thought advisable to sell the old house of worship, it being inconvenient to the majority of the church membership then existing and a committee was appointed to confer with the Southern Brethern [sic] to whom they proposed selling, which committee succeeded in selling the old house and all property belonging thereunto for two hundred dollars.

Preparations were immediately commenced for building a new house three miles below the old site which was completed in the autumn of 1875. In the meantime a petition was sent to Presbytery to drop the old name Horeb and insert Hebron which was granted.

---

[14] Jack B. Franklin, *The John M. Franklin Family, Jefferson County, Tennessee*, Memphis, TN, 1974, pp. 114-117. Information found in Session Book 1 of Hebron Presbyterian Church.

On September 19, 1875 the new house of worship was dedicated. Sermon by William B. Rankin of Greenville assisted by Rev. E. N. Sawtell and Isaac Emory.

The Eldership consisting of Christopher Rankin, Elias Alexander, Samuel E. Rankin[15] and Nathan H. Franklin. Christopher Rankin being the only one of the original Elders living at the time. Benjamin F. Franklin, James T. [Thomas] Rankin, Samuel E. [Edwin] Rankin, George S. [Samuel] McGhee and Benjamin Franklin, Jun. were elected Trustees.

Members belonging at this time were Elias Alexander, Thomas T. Alexander, Emma Alexander, Inez Bell, David Cokenour, Mary A. [Rankin] Cokenour [1837-1909], Martha J. [Lea] Davis, Benjamin F. Franklin [Sr.], Lucinda H. [Rankin] Franklin, Thomas P. Franklin, Benj. [F.] Franklin, jun., Nathan H. Franklin, Margaret C. Franklin, Sarah E. [Emily Corbett] Franklin, Mary E. Franklin, Isaac A. [Anderson] Franklin, George [W.] Franklin, Lucinda A. Franklin, Rachel I. Gass, Mary A. McMurry, James M. [Moore] McMurry, William N. [Newton] McMurry, George S. [Samuel] McGhee, Susan A. [Adeline Rankin] McGhee, Almira [Minerva] McMurry, Samuel B. [Blair] Newman, Nancy E. [Elizabeth Rankin] Newman, Mary E. Newman, David G. Newman, James Rankin, Julian Rankin, Frances [George "Fanny" Gilbraith] Rankin, Susan Rankin, Sarah J. F. Rankin, Elizabeth C. Rankin, Samuel E. [Edwin] Rankin, [15] Christopher Rankin, Sarah L. Rankin, John Fain Rankin, Christopher H. [Houston] Rankin, Catherine R. [Ruth Franklin] Rankin, Samuel Doak Rankin, James T. [Thomas] Rankin, Mary A. C. Rankin, Mary E. Rankin, Alexander Porter Rankin, Mary A. Rankin, Charlotte I. [Isabel] Rankin, William E. Rankin, Elizabeth Rankin, Joseph W. [Wilson] Rankin, Joseph M. H. [Marshall Hood] Rankin, Andrew N. [Nelson] "Andy" Rankin, Jennet Steele Rankin, Belanda [sic] V. [Belle] Rankin,[16] Martha M. Rankin, James L. [Lafayette] Rankin, Andrew A. H. Rankin, Samuel T. L. [Thomas Luther] Rankin, Leonadas S. [Smith "Lon"] Rankin, William M. [Melvin] Rankin, Huldah I. [Iantha] Rankin, Mahalah Sivels, Thomas N. Williams.

In November 1875 Rev. E. N. Sawtell was engaged to preach for one year which has not yet expired.
    April 1st 1876

N. H. Franklin, CK.

The only session books which are now known are two volumes which are now held by the present Clerk of the Session of Hebron Church. The first three pages of Book 1 [of Hebron] has the above quotation which was written by N. H. Franklin, Clerk of the Session at the time Horeb moved to the new location and present location, and at the time that name was changed to Hebron Church. It is fortunate that the Clerk took time to write a brief history of the church dating it back to the time of its inception in November 1841. This is especially true since the old session books have been lost, and if they are now in existence, the writer has not been able to locate them. I recall seeing

---

[15] Samuel Edwin Rankin was the son of Christopher Rankin.
[16] Probably Bellvada "Belle" Victoria Rankin (1858-1934), married Orville Meigs Carson (1872-__) in 1893.

at least one Session Book that was used in the old Mount Horeb Church and I have some notes taken from the book about 1941.

Nathan Hood Franklin was born October 27, 1849, at the home place built by his father, Benjamin Frances Franklin. This house has just recently been torn down by the present owner, Ben P. Seahorn, and the place is located on the old Dandridge-New Market Pike and just over the hill and just south of Hebron Presbyterian Church.

From the records at Hebron, Nathan Hood Franklin joined the Mount Horeb Presbyterian Church on January 4, 1866. This dates before the present Hebron Church was organized and built and before the name was changed. Also, predating the Hebron Church, the record shows that N. H. Franklin was ordained a Ruling Elder of Horeb Church on August 4, 1874, a year before the new church was dedicated. N. H. Franklin died on December 12, 1923 and the following entries in the Session Book are of interest.

Hebron, Nov. 11, 1923
Session met and was opened with prayer by the Moderator.
Present: Benjamin Franklin, Dr. J. M. Caldwell & I. A. [Isaac Anderson] Coil.
It was reported that N. H. Franklin, Clerk of Session for nearly 50 years, was very sick. Since Mr. Franklin had witnessed all ordinations in the church for the past 50 years, it was voted to postpone the ordination of the new officers till November 25th, hoping that Mr. Franklin would be able to be present at that time.
Minutes read & approved. Session closed with prayer.
N. H. Franklin, Clerk
Per. R. O. Franklin, Mod.

Hebron, Nov. 25, 1923
At a congregational meeting, which was opened and closed with prayer, John N. McMurray and Mark Roy Rankin were ordained to the Eldership of this church, and John A. [Andrew] Coil, Elmer B. Zirkle, and Benjamin W. [Wallace] McMurray were ordained as Deacons.
R. O. Franklin, Mod.

Hebron, Dec. 23, 1923
Session met and was opened with prayer by the Moderator.
Present: R. O. Franklin, Mod., Benjamin Franklin, I. A. Coil, John M. [Moore] McMurray and [Mark] Roy Rankin.
The following was presented and adopted; and a copy ordered to be spread on the Minute Book of this church, also a copy to be sent to the bereaved family.
"Whereas; It hath pleased Almighty God to call unto himself our Beloved Clerk of Session, Nathan Hood Franklin, and
Whereas; We know that the Almighty Father doeth all things well, we, therefore humbly submit to this dispensation of His Holy Providence.

In his death, which occurred on December 12, 1923, we lost a beloved co-worker of firm convictions, of strong faith, of consistent Christian Character, and of warm devotion to the church.

His record as Clerk of this Session is most unusual. On Jan. 10, 1874, he was elected to this sacred office and served continuously until the day of his death – lacking but 29 days of half a century of service as Clerk of this Session. His records were well kept, having been critized [sic] but four times by Presbytery during the 50 years, and these criticisms were but minor ones.

As a Session, we render sincere thanks to Almighty God the "three score and ten years," plus four, given him to live – for the two score and ten years in this Session, and for the stamp of genuine Christian manhood that marked his entire life.

As a Session, we extend to the bereaved family our sincerest sympathy."

Upon motion, John M. McMurray was elected Clerk of this Session. Minutes approved. Closed with prayer.

R. O. Franklin, Mod.

From every indication in reviewing the Session Books, it appears that Nathan Hood Franklin served the Hebron Presbyterian Church long and well. Apparently he was very active in the work of the church during his entire lifetime. J.B.F.

1927: Mount Horeb School

by Eva Elizabeth Blackburn McMurray
Presented by Mary Ruth McMurray Crawford[17]
Adapted by Hazel Timblin Townsend

I was a student at the Mount Horeb School from 1933-1934 term through the 1939-1940 term[17] Harriette Seahorn was my first teacher.

The school was a two-room school. The lower four grades were usually in one room. This room had a stage. The other room was for the other grades. There were two small rooms as you entered the school. These were later made into a kitchen and library.

The rooms were heated with a pot belly stove. Some of the older boys would serve as janitors and would come early to build the fires. At times when it was really cold we would have our lessons sitting around the stove. Everyone had to walk to school. No school buses. We brought our lunches, usually wrapped in a newspaper or in a "poke."[18] Later they did have a kitchen and served hot meals.

---

[17] Mary Ruth McMurray Crawford, daughter of John McCampbell McMurray and Louella Ruth "Ella" Caldwell McMurray.

[18] A "poke" is a paper bag.

The water was carried from the McMurray spring.[19] Usually two of the older boys would walk to the spring and carry the water back. At first we had a bucket and dipper that everyone drank out of, then we got a big cooler type container and it had a spout that we could turn on to get water.

We had two outhouses. The back of the building had a long porch across the whole building. This is where we kept the water cooler. The porch faced the fence of the [Mount Horeb] graveyard. On days that they had a funeral we couldn't play on that side of the building and we had to be very quiet while the burial was taking place.

Recess time was fun. We would play baseball, basketball, running games marbles, Ante Over, Ring Around the Roses, tag, relay races, Simon Says, Whoopee-and-Hide, handkerchief, etc. We had very little equipment to play with. One year I remember we would crack out walnuts at recess time. We sold them and bought some balls with the money. This was more fun than playing. We would cross over the fence and crack the walnuts on big rocks. Joe Myers was janitor at this time and this was one of his projects.

As far back as 1785, two men, William Bradshaw[20] and Richard Rankin, being young men each with a wife and child, left the Genesee Valley with other relatives in the state of Pennsylvania. They moved to the white settlement on Limestone in what is now Washington County, Tennessee. Bradshaw and Rankin left their families in Limestone and came through the dense wilderness looking for a location to open up a home for themselves. They found two fine springs, one at the head of Dumplin Creek, now the property of Richard Brotherton, the other a fourth of a mile down the creek, now owned by the McMurrays. From the pioneer Bradshaw five generations have sprung up, none of them living here now. The Rankins are in almost every state of the union.

When these two pioneers decided their location, they went to work to build a house for each, using logs they could handle. After the houses were completed, they cleared a two-acre plot for each. When this was cultivated and fenced, their crops were planted. They had never said anything about how the houses and land should be divided until this was done. Then Rankin said to Bradshaw, "As you are a little my senior, I will give you a choice." Bradshaw took the house that is now Mr. Brotherton's as it had the coldest spring.

When this was done, they returned to Limestone to move their families down. On their return they found that the buffaloes had broken in and devoured the whole crop. Also, Bradshaw's spring had run dry as it does in long dry spells. Just to show you how lonely it must have been for them, Bradshaw came back before Rankin and they had only one rooster with their chickens. When Rankin came he had several roosters. Bradshaw had never known their rooster to crow until it heard Rankin's crow and answered them!

---

[19] The house next to the Mount Horeb Church was the home of Benjamin Wallace "Ben" McMurray (1882-1966) and Eva Elizabeth Blackburn McMurray (1886-1952). Their three children were Mildred Joy McMurray Rankin, Myra Elizabeth McMurray Felknor and Harriett Jeannette McMurray Blackburn.

[20] William Bradshaw is an error. John Bradshaw (1743-1818) was the settler at the headwaters of Dumplin Creek according to the monument in the Mount Horeb Cemetery. John had a son named William (1778-__).

The home of Mr. Brotherton is at the head of Dumplin Creek—so named because during the war soldiers were making dumplings along the creek when the kettle was overturned, spilling the "dumplins" into the creek. The home of Mr. Brotherton is the oldest building in the community; a part of it being over a hundred and fifty years old.

One little item of interest is that part of the meadow on the creek bottom, just below the McMurray house spring, has never been plowed for over a century.

The name Mount Horeb was taken from the Bible for the Church; therefore, the post office, school and vicinity were called the same.

The Mount Horeb Church was organized by order of Union Presbytery in an old log school house on November 20, 1841 with Rev. John McCampbell receiving the membership (sixty-seven) and ordaining four elders. Rev. James H. Gass supplied for five years. The Rev. Nathan Hood had charge for a number of years. At that time those who wished to commune at the sacrament of the Lord's Supper were required to have tokens to present before they were allowed to receive it. These were round metal pieces about the size of a dime.

The first real church was built in 1851. It was 85 feet long and 45 feet wide. This was torn down and another church built in 1875. In 1875 a goodly number of these members withdrew and organized two other churches: Hebron and Lebanon. In 1875 the old church building, and all property belonging to it, was sold to the Southern Presbyterian Church Presbytery. The building was remodeled in 1913.

By March 1925, the membership became so small it was thought best to discontinue services. Then Horeb and Hebron were united.

Lebanon Church was organized in 1874 and is still active with a large Sunday School and preaching services once each month.

The first school building was a log cabin built in 1841. A large school building was built in 1861. This burned on October 15, 1888. Another building was built in 1889, which is the present building. It was remodeled in 1925. We have a very good elementary school with the eight grades and two teachers.21

The first grave in the Mount Horeb Cemetery with a marker is of a child in 1842. As we know for a long time the cemetery had a neglected appearance. But in 1926 it was incorporated. It is now very much improved in appearance.

The son of Mr. John Pad Rankin was the first to be buried in Lebanon Cemetery in 1876.

---

[21] Mildred Joy McMurray Rankin tells this story in her autobiography: Mother [Eva Elizabeth Blackburn McMurray] boarded with Aunt Effie [Effie Blackburn Franklin] and Uncle Mac [Mack Calvin Franklin] when she was teaching "subscription school" at Mount Horeb. At this time my Father [Benjamin Wallace McMurray], who lived near the school and Mount Horeb Presbyterian Church, started courting my mother and soon married her, July 29, 1908…In the fall of 1916 Grace Brotherton stopped by to take me with her to the one room Mount Horeb School. Mr. Homer Edwards was principal and the teacher. We all sat at two-seater desks on benches with our feet and legs dangling. When it became time for a specific class to recite, Mr. Edwards would call those in that grade to come forward and sit on the front bench for their lesson…Only six grades were taught at Mt. Horeb. After completing the sixth grade, I went to Oakland School. I rode my sorrel pony Prince to school. ("Mildred Joy McMurray Rankin Autobiography," 1988)

There is one store. This store was first owned by Mr. J. J. [John James] Coile and Mr. J. G. Rankin. It was built about 1869. It is now known as Sheddan Store, Mr. Joe Sheddan owner. Mount Horeb's first post office was in the store building for a number of years. Mount Horeb has had rural delivery since 1901.

Thirteen ministers were reared in Mount Horeb. One T. T. [Thomas Theron] Alexander was a missionary to Japan for twenty-five years. He died in Honolulu. His body was cremated and his ashes were sent to Maryville for burial. He and his wife were the first missionaries to go out from Maryville College. Other ministers are as follows: Rev. John M. [McNitt] Alexander, Rev. Mac [Melville McElvain] Rankin, Rev. Henry [Harrison] Newman,[22] Rev. Tom [Rankin] Bradshaw, Rev. Harvey [Smith] Bradshaw, Rev. O. D. [Oakley D.] Bradshaw, Rev. W. H. [William Harris] Lyle, Rev. Joe [Wilson] Rankin, Rev. Charlie Newman, Rev. Frank [Ashley] Bradshaw, Rev. Ernest Bradshaw, Rev. Beecher Mathes. Other ministers who lived here were Rev. A. [Alexander] J. Coile and Rev. S. A. Coile.

There have been twenty-one college graduates and eight college students. There was one University graduate, one physician, one Senator, two world war soldiers and a number of high school graduates.

The president of our club at this time was reared at Mount Horeb.

The original of this article may have been written by Mrs. B. W. McMurray[23] and presented by Mary Ruth McMurray Crawford.

Notes handwritten on the typed document:
"Probably written 1927-1928 when Home Demonstration Club Dandridge, Jefferson County became federated." [24]

Oldest grave in Mount Horeb Cemetery is that of William Massengill, b. 12-23-1782; d. 6-17-1852.

Paragraph below was written on the page with three photos of the Mount Horeb School School:

The first school building was a log cabin built in 1841. A larger school building was built in 1861 and burned October 15, 1888. To quote from a talk given by Clara (Bettis) Zirkle at the 1952 Rankin Reunion: "Years ago the old school house burned to the ground one cold wintery day. We small children were very frightened. Professor Hicks sent us a safe distance away so the older students could salvage the desks, books,

---

[22] Rev. Henry Harrison Newman was Superintendent of the Monroe Harding Home, Nashville, TN from 1902-1908.

[23] Eva Elizabeth Blackburn McMurray (1886-1958), wife of Benjamin Wallace "Ben" McMurray. Mary Ruth McMurray Crawford was daughter of John McCampbell McMurray and Luella Ruth Caldwell.

[24] Probably written about 1927-1928 when the Dandridge Home Demonstration Club became federated. This original history is included by Don Barbee in the *Mt. Horeb School 1841-1958*, Jefferson County Archives Office, Dandridge, Tennessee. Used with permission.

dinner baskets, wraps and what not. During the next few days the Elders, Deacons, and Board of Education met and arranged to finish the school term in the Mount Horeb Church. Accordingly, the church benches were piled high at the back and come Monday morning, the desks had been installed. School opened in the church and closed the last day of March. On the closing day, the patrons were invited to be present at the closing exercises."

Many of the teachers had names familiar to the area, such as Brotherton, McMurray, Zirkle, Graham, Blackburn and Sheddan. The school closed in 1958 due to consolidation and the building was torn down.

1930: Monument to Early Settlers

by Roy Marshall Rankin
Adapted by Hazel Timblin Townsend, 2016

The monument to the early settlers of Dumplin Valley is located in the Mount Horeb Church Cemetery on Dumplin Valley Road in Jefferson County, near the headwaters of Dumplin Creek. Just inside the cemetery gate behind the church is a bronze tablet dedicated to the four pioneer settlers.

Christopher Houston Rankin erected the marker with financial help from descendants of these four pioneer families. In 1930 four girls, representing each of the pioneers, unveiled the tablet at its dedication. They were Isabelle Moore McMurray,[25] Cleva Ward Rankin,[26] Phyllis Daphne Rankin,[27] and Charlotte Bradshaw Stoner.[28]

Richard Rankin and John Bradshaw were the first settlers to come to the Dumplin Valley area about 1786. They came from the Limestone, Tennessee area, cleared land, planted crops, and returned home to bring their families to what is now Jefferson County. The other two Rankin families following soon. Thomas came from the present Timber Ridge area of Greene County.

The following material is excerpted by Hazel Townsend from the information recorded in the "Program of Unveiling of Tablet to Memory of Pioneer Settlers of Dumplin Valley, Tennessee," August 15. 1930. The service was held in the Mount

---

[25] Isabella Moore McMurray (Peck), daughter of John McCampbell McMurray, fifth generation descendant of Richard Rankin.

[26] Cleva Ward Rankin (Cox), daughter of Isaac Lafayette Rankin, sixth generation descendant of Samuel Rankin.

[27] Phyllis Daphne Rankin (Lintz), daughter of Sam Hull Rankin, fifth generation descendant of Thomas Rankin II.

[28] Charlotte Bradshaw Stoner (Bruce), daughter of Marshall C. Stoner, sixth generation descendant of John Bradshaw.

Horeb Presbyterian Church, Jefferson County, Tennessee. The Marker was erected in memory of Richard Rankin, Samuel Rankin, Thomas Rankin and John Bradshaw.

The speech, "The Rankin Tribe," was given by Rev. Hubert S. Lyle, President of Washington College, grandson of Jane Wright Rankin and Dr. John P. [Pickney] Mathes of Strawberry Plains. Jane was the daughter of Thomas Rankin II (1764-1821) and Jennet Bradshaw.

The Rankin Tribe

Today we are thinking and talking about the Rankin Tribe. It is a mark of good intelligence on the part of a person or people to get acquainted with their ancestors and to know their characteristics, their physical, mental, and spiritual qualities and also to know their achievements. It certainly is a mark of devotion, after learning their various characteristics, to endeavor to appreciate their lives and their efforts to the extent of following them in all good things.

In order to know this Rankin Tribe it is necessary that we go back to Old Scotland about 380 years ago to get started. The Rankin Tribe is pre-eminently Scotch. Later, they came to Ireland and became Scotch-Irish. They had all the qualities and characteristics of the Scotch-Irish. The most of them had big families. Many times there were a dozen children. They loved their homes.

In the second place they loved the Church and they loved the Bible. They were essentially religious. Usually they were Presbyterian in their faith.

In the third place, these people loved liberty. They were opposed to anything like religious or political oppression. They resisted with all their souls everything that seemed to them to have tyranny in it. The Scotch-Irish people settled the eastern part of the United States. The Southern Appalachians are full of Scotch-Irish. They are often stiff and angular…They are people of strong convictions.…

The Rankin family never cared very much for popularity in the eyes of the world. Consequently, they have never obtained great worldly fame. They have belonged to what is known as "the middle class" of people. They have been lovers of freedom. They have been sturdy people. They have had sterling qualities of character and have had high ideals and convictions. They have lived well and rendered splendid service both to the Church and State. David Rankin, of Tarkio, Missouri,[29] has been rated as one of the most advanced farmers in the United States. Josiah Emmons Rankin,[30] who lives here in Mount Horeb community, was one of the finest local farmers in the way of taking care of and developing the soil.

The Rankin family has produced a great many ministers, doctors, lawyers, dentists, merchants, mechanics, teachers, college presidents, nurses, dress makers, etc., all doing their part as Christian citizens should do. The family of Richard Rankin was noted for

---

[29] David Rankin, son of William Rankin and Elizabeth Gross Rankin, born 1825 in Sullivan County, Indiana, died 1910 in Tarkio, Atchison County, Missouri. He was the largest farmer in the U.S.A, with 24,000 acres in Missouri and 6,000 in Iowa. (David Rankin, *David Rankin, Farmer*, Garst and Thomas Hybrid Corn Company, c1978. A reprint of the 1909 edition printed in Tarkio, Missouri; *Ancestry.com; Genealogy.com*.)

[30] Josiah Emmons Rankin (1815-1893), son of Thomas Rankin II and Jennet Bradshaw.

the production of preachers. The family of Thomas Rankin II was noted for the production of farmers. It has been said that William Rankin was 50 years ahead of his day in the matter of barn building. Samuel Rankin's daughters were especially noted as textile workers and were masters of the loom. John Bradshaw raised up mechanics. His son Richard [Ammon] Bradshaw (1788-1872) was a cooper who made vessels equal to that of the best that were made in his time. He was complimented as having planned a church 50 years ahead of his day and age.

The Rankin family produced church members and church officers for the Lebanon Cumberland Presbyterian Church here in this community, the Mount Horeb Presbyterian Church, the Hebron Presbyterian Church, the Hopewell Presbyterian Church at Dandridge, and for the New Providence Presbyterian Church at Maryville under the shadow of Maryville College. It is said that Rankins furnished over 40 elders for churches and 32 ministers.

It is said that Uncle [Richard] Duffield Rankin and his father who lived here in this community held family worship in the same house for more than 100 years. It is no wonder that the Rankin family produced church members, and Christian citizens who were a bulwark to the Church and to the State....

First, let us think of Rev. John Rankin[31] who was born in 1793. I do not know where he first saw the light but I think it was here in this Mount Horeb Community and perhaps was in the very house where Duffield Rankin lived his life and where family worship was conducted for over 100 years by father and son. This Rev. John Rankin received some of his education from Rev. David Ware at Dandridge. Later he was a student at Washington College under Rev. Samuel Doak, the Founder of the College, and graduated with the class of 1816, the same class in which Dr. J. G. M. Ramsey, the noted historian, graduated. There is a memorial window at the Presbyterian Church at Washington College commemorating the life and work of this Rev. John Rankin. He was known as the Martin Luther of the Slavery Movement. Also, he has been called the manager of the "underground railroad." His mother was Jane Steele of Virginia and it is said that he received his inspiration from her for making his life effort to abolish slavery in the United States. He had 9 sons and 4 daughters. He was licensed to preach by Holston Presbytery in Tennessee. He did not want to bring up his children where slavery existed and so he moved from Tennessee to Ohio very soon after he graduated from Washington College. He became pastor of the Church at Ripley, Ohio, where he remained 44 years....

The Rev. John Rankin was a brilliant man, a man of great ability, and a man of strong convictions. He was very happy in his married life with Jean Lowry[32] whom he obtained at Washington College....

The second man of note and interest whose life is an inspiration is Rev. Thomas T. Alexander.[33] His name was not Rankin but his mother was a Rankin, the daughter of

---

[31] Rev. Rankin's full name was John Thomas Rankin (1793-1886), son of Richard Rankin (1756-1827) and Jennett Steele, grandson of Thomas Rankin I and Isabella Clendenin.

[32] Jean Lowry's full name was Jane Gilfillen "Jean" Lowry. Her parents were Adam Lowry and Julia Doak.

[33] The parents of Rev. Thomas Theron Alexander, Sr. (1850-1901) were Elias Alexander, Sr. and Jane Rankin.

Duffield Rankin who lived for 90 years in the same house here in this Mount Horeb Community, the house in which family worship was conducted for over 100 years. Thomas T. Alexander was thus a grandson of Duffield Rankin. He grew up in the community. He graduated from Maryville College. Just when he was graduating from Maryville College he received a call from three different churches to become their pastor. Also, he was asked to engage in journalistic work.

He turned aside from all of these opportunities of service in the Kingdom of God and went with his bride who was Miss Emma Brown, the daughter of Rev. William B. Brown, to Japan to be a foreign missionary. In the days of his going it was a great journey. It was like going around the world never to return again. It was cutting loose from home and friends with little hope of returning. Thomas T. Alexander did a remarkable work both in preaching and along the lines of Christian Education in the Sunrise Kingdom. He came home on furlough [twice]....

I have mentioned a few of the Rankin tribe. There were hundreds of them. They stood for things that were noble and true. They stood for God and the Church and the Bible and for Righteousness. They stood for liberty, good government, and law and order. They stood against all kinds of oppression. Those of us who still live may well study this Rankin tribe, its ideals and its great personalities. There is much to inspire us. There is much that we should take into our own lives and transmit into action and conduct. Let us follow in their footsteps. Let us live unselfishly. The descendants of the Rankin family are erecting a marker to commemorate their history. The best marker that any and all of us can erect is to take their principles and their example into our own hearts until they become the controlling factor in our lives. They trod the humble walks of life but they kept their eyes fixed on God and eternity. Those of us who claim them as ancestors can do no better than to do as they did.

Monument

This Tablet is to Commemorate the Memory of

Richard Rankin 1756-1827	Samuel Rankin 1758-1828
Thomas Rankin 1762-1821 [34]	John Bradshaw 1743-1818

Four Pioneer Settlers of Dumplin Valley
Genealogy of the Rankin Family

Generation 1

Alexander Rankin, born in Scotland, had three sons, two were martyrs to their religion. Of these one was killed on the highway. The other suffocated in a smokehouse where he had taken refuge to escape from his pursuers. The third brother, William, together with his father and family escaped to Derry County, Ireland, in 1688. William and his father, Alexander Rankin, were participants in the siege of Londonderry, which took place in 1689.

---

[34] This is an error. The dates for Thomas Rankin II should be 1764-1821.

Alexander Rankin's name is signed to the "Petition of Thanks to Almighty God," and William, King of Orange, for his timely assistance in raising the siege in August, 1689.[35]

Generation 2

William Rankin had three sons. Adam, born in Scotland, 1699. John and Hugh born in Ireland.

Adam and Hugh came to America in 1721, landing in Philadelphia, PA, and settled in Chester County. Hugh was killed in a mill accident. Adam married Mary Steele.

Generation 3

John Rankin married Jane McElwee, in Ireland, came to America in 1727. He had two sons, Thomas and Richard, and eight daughters. Richard married a Miss [Mary Agnes] Douglass and settled in Augusta County, VA.

Generation 4

Thomas Rankin 1724-1828[36] married Isabel Clendon of PA and settled in that state. Their children were:

John	1754-1825	married Martha Waugh
Richard	1756-1827	married Jennett Steele
Samuel	1758-1826	
William	1760-1834	married Sarah Moore
Thomas	1762-1821	married Jennett Bradshaw
James	1770-1839	married Margaret Massey
Jane		married William Gillespie
Margaret		married Samuel Harris
Ann		married Lemuel Lacy
Isabel		married Robt. McQuiston
Nancy		married Samuel White
Mary		married James Bradshaw[37]

---

[35] The following information was found in Ireland by Hazel Townsend in 2006 in the National Library in Dublin. Is this the same Alexander Rankin? In the book *Fighter's of Derry*, by William R. Young (1932, Eyre and Spottiswoode, London), the following three Rankin men are mentioned:

(#342) LIEUT. RANKIN, defender, served all through the defence, and is referred to by "Londeriados" in his description of the Pennyburn sortie of the 21ˢᵗ April, viz.:-- "Lieutenant Rankin hewed the Irish down And in that battle gained much renown."

(#343) ALICK. RANKIN, possibly the above, was a signer of the address to King William after the relief.

(#344) JOHN RANKIN was among the signers of the Corporation's Commission of 1690.

... The family have for generations been closely connected with the city and county, where many of the name are still to be found.

[36] Some errors. Dates for Thomas Rankin I should be 1724-1812. His son John's might be 1754-1829.

[37] James Bradshaw (1799-___) married Mary Rankin, daughter of John Rankin and Martha Jane Waugh and granddaughter of Thomas Rankin and Isabella Clendenin. (*Tennessee Family Bible Records, Volume II,* Compiled & Indexed by Stephenie H. Tally-Frost, Printed by Printing & Lithographing, 4606 Lamont, Corpus Christi, Texas, 1970.)

Thomas Rankin of Generation 4, was a Captain in the Revolutionary War. His four eldest sons were privates in said war.

Donor Plaque

The names on the donor plaque are Christopher Houston Rankin,[38] Courtland Thales Rankin (Att'y),[39] Rev. John Grant Newman (D.D.);[40] Mrs. Almyra Rankin McMurray,[41] Mrs. Rozee Rankin Taylor,[42] Frank Walter Rankin, Harry J. Rankin,[43] and Sam Hull Rankin,[44] all Jefferson County natives. Six of them lived all their lives in Jefferson County. They were first cousins, father and sons or brothers and sisters. They spent time visiting among families near them and those farther away maintained close contacts with Jefferson County relatives.

Correction Plaque

June 2001 – The following corrections should be made on the tablet below:

Thomas Rankin (1) 1724-1812	married Isabella Clendenin of PA and settled in that state.
Samuel 1758-1834	married Jane Isabelle Petty
William 1759-1833	married Sarah Moore
Isabel	married Robert McCuistion
Mary	married Andrew McCuistion

Roy Marshall Rankin discovered family records that were not available in 1930. In 2001 he added another tablet above the original plaque to correct several errors. The following information is from Roy's research.

The death date and burial of Thomas Rankin I (1724-1812) have had various dates and locations recorded. Roy concluded that he was buried somewhere in the Revolutionary Cemetery in Dandridge, Tennessee, as are many others with unmarked graves.[45] Adding to the belief that Thomas Rankin (I) was buried in the Revolutionary (Hopewell) Cemetery is the family connections with the Presbyterian churches. Thomas Rankin (I) was first a ruling elder in Pennsylvania, and later a ruling elder in the Timber Ridge Presbyterian Church in Greene County for fourteen years after he and his family came to Tennessee. He moved to Jefferson County in 1800 and was a member of the Hopewell Presbyterian Church. Thomas Rankin (II) (1762-1821) was a member and ruling elder in the Hopewell Church at the time of Thomas Rankin (I)'s death.

---

[38] Christopher Houston Rankin was the son of Christopher Rankin and grandson of Thomas Rankin II.

[39] Courtney Thales Rankin was the son of Lieut. Samuel Edwin Rankin and grandson of Christopher Rankin.

[40] Rev. Dr. John Grant Newman was the son of Samuel Blair Newman and Nancy Elizabeth Rankin. Nancy was rhe daughter if Christopher Rankin.

[41] Almyra Minerva Rankin McMurray, wife of James Moore McMurray, daughter of Richard Duffield Rankin and granddaughter of Richard Rankin (1756-1827).

[42] Rozee Amanda Rankin Taylor, sister of Sam Hull Rankin, both children of Samuel Edwin Rankin

[43] Frank Walter Rankin and Harry J. Rankin, sons of Christopher Houston Rankin of White Pine, Tennessee.

[44] Sam Hull Rankin, son of Samuel Edwin Rankin and Sarah Lorinda Lyle. His wife was Chlorice N. Bible.

[45] *Stories in Stone, Jefferson County Cemeteries, Vol. II*, Templin and Henderson.

Organized in 1785, the Hopewell Presbyterian Church was the home church for Dumplin Valley residents until 1841 when Mount Horeb Church was organized and forty Hopewell members transferred their memberships.

The assumption has been that the Old Revolutionary Cemetery of the old Hopewell Presbyterian Church in Dandridge was the burial ground for many early residents of the area. The original Hopewell Church was located there. This was the first church in Jefferson County, built in 1785. There are about sixty plots with uninscribed fieldstones. Many people in the area regard this as the cemetery of their ancestors who lived in Jefferson County around 1800. None of the Dumplin Valley cemeteries were established until later. The general assumption is that Thomas Rankin died in 1812 and that he and his wife were buried in this cemetery. The stone marked "T R" is probably his marker. [See picture of stone in photo section.]

Roy M. Rankin found this information concerning Samuel Rankin.[46] He owned land on the south side of Dumplin Creek when he came as a pioneer settler. One corner of his land met a corner of brother Thomas' (1762-1821) land near the present location of Hebron Church Road.[47] Samuel was born September 1758 in Pennsylvania and died in Jefferson County December 13, 1834. He fought in the Revolutionary War as a member of the Cumberland County Militia, PA. He was in the Battle of Cowpens, South Carolina and at Yorktown, Virginia for the surrender of Cornwallis.[48] Samuel Rankin is buried in the Old Revolutionary Cemetery (Old Hopewell) in Dandridge. He and four other Revolutionary War soldiers are named on the monument erected by the Martha Dandridge Garden Club in 1930. The other names on the monument are John Blackburn, Abednego Inman, Samuel Lyle, and Richard Rankin. Samuel Rankin was a member and elder in the Hopewell Presbyterian Church but the exact dates are not known. There are no existing Hopewell records earlier than 1816. Samuel Rankin married Jane Isabelle (Aunt Ibby) Petty in Pennsylvania. They had five daughters and two sons—Lucy, Isabelle, Elizabeth "Betsy" [Whittington], Sarah "Sally" [Lockhart] (1804-1883), Mary, John, and Thomas.[49]

William Rankin's grave marker is given in the history of the *Timber Ridge Church*, p. 102, 125: (Old marker) "In memory of Wm. Rankin died December 13, 1833 [misread tombstone, should be 1838], age 75. (New marker) William Rankin born

---

[46] The 1996 research information by Roy M. Rankin is included in records for Samuel Rankin, son of Thomas Rankin I (1724-1812), for the *Tennessee First Families* in the McClung Collection, Knox County Library, Knoxville, TN.

[47] Part of Samuel's land (110 acres), deeded to James Rankin 9 Oct. 1821, recorded in Jefferson County Deed Book Q, 1 October 1825.

[48] *Pennsylvania Archives, Second Series, Vol XIII, page 187; Fifth Series, Volume IV*, pages 494, 725; *Sixth Series, Volume II*, pages 129, 131, 258, 396.

[49] Richard Duffield Rankin (1800-1890), son of Richard and nephew of Samuel Rankin (1758-1834), lived his entire life on Dumplin Creek. In *The Magill Family Record*, by Robert M. Magill, published in 1907, Richard Duffield has written early facts about the Rankins of his family and community. In this history he says: "Samuel, born 1760, Presbyterian; farmer; was on American side at the Battle of Cowpens; settled in Jefferson County...Uncle Samuel, a farmer and teamster, had five daughters and two sons. Both sons died before their father."

January 27, 1759, died December 3, 1833, (Tennessee) Wagoner Continental Line, Rev. War." William and Sarah Rankin are the oldest graves in the cemetery.[50]

In the *Roster of Soldiers and Patriots of the American Revolution Buried in Tennessee*, 1974, the following information is given: William Rankin (born 1-27-1759 Cumberland Co., PA, died 12-12-1833 Greene Co.), buried Timber Ridge, Greene Co., Pvt. - Teamster - Q.M. VA, Pvt. then Q.M. of wagons under Q.M. Hunter - Col. Carrington - Gen. Stuart. Served in Battles of Hot Water, Jamestown, Siege of York. Age 76 - 1832 pension list - Greene Co., TN; 1834 P.L.W. Married 8-29-1787 Sarah Moore born July 1763, died 10-9-1850. Children: Thomas, born 7-13-1788, married Jane Shields; Peggy born 1-1-1790; John born 4-10-1792; Anthony born 8-23-1794; Isabella born 8-30-1796, married John Wear Wilson; William Jr., born 3-23-1799; Jane born 11-17-1801, married Nathaniel Magill; David born 2-10-1804, married Margaret Wilson.[51]

A letter written by Mary Rankin McCuistion[52] on May 8, 1834 from Meesville, TN, was located by William T. McCuistion of Bellingham, Washington. The letter is to her son and his wife, Thomas and Mary McCuistion. (Spelling is as it was in the letter. No punctuation.)

"Tennessee State, Roan County, May 8, 1834. Deir Son and Daughter I take my pen to inform you of my trouble and distress on the 24 of April last your Father deceast this life he was taken sick in the last of January last and in March he took a getherin in his head and broak and run out of both ears he then took a cough and spit up a considerable quantity of flame he got weaker and weaker till the 24 of April last he deceast and was beried on the 25 at Esq. Longacre My near and deir children it is a trying thing to part with a companion or at least to describe it is out of the question We are all well at present and hoping through the blessing of all Mighty God these few lines will find you all well Robert and his family is all well and Stanley and Jane [Spradling] lives close to me and is all well Rebecca David and Andrew is well and sends their best complements to you and yours So no more at present but remains your affectionate mother till death separates us Mary McCuistion" (NOTE: Does not mention Catherine and James.)[53]

---

[50] Roy M. Rankin of White Pine, TN read the tombstones at the Timber Ridge Church and feels the birth date is 1760 and the death date is 1838.

[51] Reference: DAR #181774; A 1.

[52] A list of Dismissions in the Hopewell Session Book lists the following family unit: "Andrew McCuistion and wife Mary, Catherine McCuistion, Thomas McCuistion, Robert McCuistion, Rebecca B. McCuistion, Jane Liles and Sally Grace, all on certificate, March 1827." (Roy M. Rankin)

[53] Copy of letter in Public Library, Dandridge, TN in *Tennessee Family Bible Records, Volume II*, Compiled & Indexed by Stephenie H. Tally-Frost, Printed, 1970.)

1952: Rankin Clan Ministers and Missionaries

by Clara Bettis Zirkle
Rankin Clan Reunion, July 13, 1952

This Dumplin Valley has in it three churches – Horeb, Lebanon, and Hebron. Our ancestors were devout Christians, for which we are all deeply grateful. The sense of obligation that comes from a family tradition of community service and good citizenship is something worth keeping and passing on.

In my youth the greater part of the families bore the names Bradshaw, Rankin, Franklin, and Newman. Miss Kate Newman married Mr. Will McMurray. Miss Almira Rankin married Mr. [James] Moore McMurray. That brought a new name into the valley. Many of the former names are gone, but some of the members of the Moore-McMurray family still live on their mother's ancestral acres.

I am the daughter of John Anderson and Mary Rankin Bettis. Our home was near Lebanon Church. Both of my parents died in 1888. It has been a long time since I have stood up here before an assembled group in Horeb Church.

Years ago the old school house burned to the ground one cold wintry day. We small children were very frightened. Prof. Hicks sent us a safe distance away so the older students could salvage the desks, books dinner baskets, wraps and what not. During the next few days the elders, deacons, and the Board of Education met and arranged to finish the school term here in this church. Accordingly the church benches were piled high here at the back and come Monday morning, the desks had been installed. School opened here and closed the last day of the following March. On closing day the patrons were invited to be present at the closing exercises. I remember that four members of my spelling class had an equal number of head marks. A prize had been offered for the one receiving the most head marks. Zorada Belle Carson, Henry Bradshaw, Anna Belle McGhee, and Clara Bettis had an equal number. We were called up front here to receive the prize. We surely earned that dollar, for we were required to stand here not one day but five days. To miss a word was a tragedy in our young lives. I can't remember the part the other students played...but I do remember that the older girls' boy friends had given them silk handkerchiefs with the presidential candidate's pictures on them. We small girls were envious.

When you think back and realize how many ministers grew up in this valley and went out to give of their best to the Master, you just know that their parents were God-loving and taught their children Christian principles. These ministers labored both at home and in foreign lands. Rev. Thomas and Rev. John [McNitt] Alexander were sons of Elias Alexander. Rev. Thomas and his wife were sent by the Board to Japan. Rev. John [Alexander] taught Bible for many years in Maryville College. Two sons of Josiah [Emmons] and Mary Gass Rankin were Rev. Joe and Rev. Mack Rankin. Rev. Joseph "Joe" died and his fiancée, Miss Cora Bartlett, went alone to Persia and worked in that field until retirement. Rev. Mack [Melville McElvain] Rankin devoted his life to work here in the states. Mr. & Mrs. John L. [Leonard] Coile moved from this community to

Tusculum College to educate their children. Two ministers came from their family – Rev. S. A. [Samuel] Coile and Rev. A. J. [Alexander] Coile. Rev. S. A. Coile served Tusculum several terms as president. The youngest daughter of the John L. [Leonard] Coile, Mary [Isabel], married Dr. Thomas [Samuel] Rankin, who from graduation until retirement taught in Tusculum College. Their son, Raymond [Coile], who is now president of Tusculum College, will speak to you later today.

George Silvius, son of Mr. and Mrs. John Silvius, was a member of the Lebanon Church. He took his degree from Tusculum College. His pastoral work was spent largely in churches in Ohio. Rev. Ernest [Neal] Bradshaw, son of John Calvin and Leanna Rankin Bradshaw, Rev. Frank [Ashley] Bradshaw, son of Thomas and Cindrella [Caldwell] Bradshaw, Rev. Harvey [Smith] Bradshaw, son of Richard Bradshaw and Fanny [Frances Jane Berry] Bradshaw, were all three members of this church and went out into the world from this valley to preach Jesus Christ and his love for all mankind.

Rev. John Grant Newman, son of S. B. [Samuel Blair] and [Nancy] Elizabeth Rankin Newman, spent some of his earlier years teaching in Maryville College and also preaching. Later he was called to Philadelphia and served his church there for many years. He is now its pastor emeritus. James Wallace Willoughby, is a missionary to Beirut, Lebanon.[54]

Rev. Ben Houston Rankin, son of [James] Thomas and Frances Lockhart Rankin, was in my age group. His work was confined largely to Presbyterian churches in Indiana. Once when my husband was a commissioner to the General Assembly at Winona Lake, Indiana, I accompanied him and we visited with Ben often during that week. Also at that time I met a Mrs. McCauley, a returned missionary from Japan, who spoke highly of the work done by the Alexanders in Japan. So you see the influence of this Christian training in our valley has gone far.

The mother of another missionary once lived a mile or so up the valley. Miss Rebecca [Catherine] Massengill[55] married Henry [C.] Tipton and moved over into the Mossy Creek valley where they reared a family. Their son, William [Henry], married Nelle Roberts of Talbott. They were sent out to China by the Baptist Board of Missions. Robert Franklin, son of Robert and Mary Cline Franklin, was also a missionary. He and I were students together at Maryville College. Rev. [John Grant] Newman, Rev. Ben Rankin, and Rev. Robert Franklin were all members of Hebron Church. Another minister just across yon mountain was Rev. Beecher Mathis, son of Rev. Alfred Mathis. He came home to visit his father one summer and was invited to preach here in Horeb church. That June morning he read for his scripture lesson the 144th Psalm and chosed with the 12th verse of the lesson for his text. It reads, *"That our sons may be as plants grown up in their youth; that our daughters may be as cornerstones, polished after the similitude of a palace."* He emphasized Christian training in the home, God's goodness and love for us, the Golden Rule and the old virtues. When my sons and daughters came into our home, I took that verse as a goal.

---

[54] Son of John Wallace Cunningham Willoughby and Martha "Mattie" Rankin Willoughby.
[55] Rebecca was the daughter of William Massengill, Sr. and Jane M. Nicholson Massengill.

1974: This and That

by Jean Bible
Standard Banner, Jefferson City, Tennessee[56]
November 21, 1974

It often happens that historical articles, because of their very concern with getting down the correct facts and figures, make rather difficult and occasionally dull reading to the average person not intimately connected with the subject. For that reason, little human interest stories relayed through earlier generations to today's and interspersed with the factual material usually enliven such writing.

Thanks to several of you, I have had the opportunity to read a number of church histories done in this fashion by members or a minister. Taken largely from church records, most of them also include recollections of stories told by grandparents or other old-timers. Today's story of one of these, Mount Horeb, also includes the founding of the community. The material comes from a history of the church, done by Elizabeth McMurray (Mrs. Edward) Felknor, and a copy of an old record pertaining to the history of Hebron Church furnished me by Jack Franklin.

Back in 1785, two young men, William Bradshaw[57] and Richard Rankin, each with a wife and child, left Pennsylvania along with other relatives for the "wilds of East Tennessee," to make their homes. Their first stop was Limestone, to what is today Washington [Greene] County. But, once settled, the pioneer urge was still not satisfied, and the two men left their families in Limestone and headed down in the direction of even more dense wilderness around Dumplin Creek.

There they found two excellent springs whose location appealed to them. One was at the head of the creek (later named Dumplin) on what is now the property of Miss Grace Brotherton. The other was a quarter of a mile down on land that belongs to Mary Ruth McMurray Crawford (Mrs. Tom) today. No sooner said than done, once site was selected, the two went to work to build their rustic cabins of such logs as they could cut and handle. The next move was to clear a two-acre plot of new ground near each house, fence it in and plant their crops.

Then and only then was any mention made of whose house was whose. They must have been close friends, because with no further discussion, Rankin said to Bradshaw, "As you're a little my senior, I'll give you first choice." Bradshaw took the Brotherton place since it had the coldest spring. This decision arrived at, they went back to Limestone to move their families down to the new homes.

Returning, they found that a herd of roving buffalo had broken in and devoured their crops. Not only that, but Bradshaw's spring had gone dry, but not so with the pioneer spirit of the two. They stayed and formed the nucleus of the later Mount Horeb community, church, post office and school.

---

[56] Permission was granted by the *Standard Banner* editor for Hazel Townsend to include this article.
[57] Error. Should be John Bradshaw, not William, according to the Monument, as well as records of Hazel Timblin Townsend and Roy Marshall Rankin.

Here Elizabeth adds a quaint little story that shows how isolated the families were – even the chickens got lonely. Bradshaw had preceded Rankin on the return trip, bringing with him one rooster and several hens. When Rankin arrived with several roosters, it was said to be the first time Bradshaw's lone rooster had crowed since leaving Limestone.

Back to the community named for the Biblical Mount Horeb, its church was organized by order of Union Presbytery in an old log house on November 20, 1841. Rev. John McCampbell received the membership of 67 members and ordained four elders. Of the 67, 40 came from the Hopewell Presbyterian Church at Dandridge and 27 from New Market. Rev. James H. Gass supplied for five years, followed by Rev. Nathan Hood, who had charge for several years. The first actual church building was erected in 1851, and was 85 feet long and 44 feet wide. In 1875, it was torn down and another church built.

About this same time a good many of the members withdrew and organized two other churches, Hebron and Lebanon. The old church with its land was sold to the Southern Presbyterians. It was remodeled in 1913, but by March, 1925, membership had decreased to such an extent that services were discontinued and Mount Horeb and Hebron were united.

An interesting note about the communion services when the church was organized was that those wishing to partake of the sacrament or "Lord's Supper" were required to have small metal tokens about the size of a dime.

A monument that wraps up the story of four of Mount Horeb's early settlers for posterity was erected in its historic old cemetery in 1930. It was unveiled by four descendants: Isabelle Moore McMurray, daughter of John M. [McCampbell] McMurray and fifth generation descendant of Richard Rankin; Cleva Ward Rankin, daughter of Isaac Lafayette Rankin and sixth generation descendant of Samuel Rankin; Phyllis Rankin, daughter of Sam Hull Rankin and fifth generation descendant of Thomas Rankin; Charlotte Stoner, daughter of Marshall C. Stoner and sixth generation descendant of John Bradshaw. The tablet commemorates the following four: Richard Rankin, 1756-1827; Samuel Rankin, 1758-1828; Thomas Rankin, 1762-1821, John Bradshaw, 1743-1818.

1976: Hebron Presbyterian Church History

by Martha Lou Coile
Condensed by Vera Wilson Gilmore, 1976[58]
Jefferson City, Tennessee

The history of the Hebron Church dates back to 1841 with the founding of the Mount Horeb Church, and its relationship with earlier churches is very close.

Hopewell Presbyterian Church, the parent church of Hebron, is the oldest church in Dandridge, the second oldest town in the state. Hopewell was organized in 1785, eight years before the town was established. Jefferson County, which lies between the French Broad and Holston rivers, was formed by an ordinance of Governor Blount on June 11, 1792, simultaneously with Knox County. Records show that settlers arrived, cleared the ground and planted crops soon after the mountains were first crossed. Dumplin Valley was settled as early as any section in Jefferson County, Richard Rankin and William Bradshaw[59] having come down the valley from Pennsylvania in 1785.

One hundred and fifty years ago the distance between Dandridge and New Market was much greater than today by virtue of the mode of travel. That, more than anything else, was the reason for organizing a church at New Market. About March 1819, the Reverend John McCampbell, Stated Supply at Hopewell, began preaching services and in 1826 organized the New Market Presbyterian Church, under the direction of Presbytery.

On November 20, 1841, forty members from Hopewell and twenty-seven members from New Market were organized by Union Presbytery into the Mount Horeb Presbyterian Church, meeting in an old log schoolhouse. The Rev. John McCampbell received the members and ordained four elders. The first church building was constructed in 1851.

During the Civil War and the years of reconstruction, the times were troubled in this area. The majority of the population in East Tennessee was favorable to the union, however, neighbors fought against neighbors, families were divided, cousin fought against cousin, brother against brother, and even son against father. Emotions ran high because each faction fought for principles in which they strongly believed. Such feelings and animosities did not quickly subside and unfortunately were brought into the church. Mount Horeb was no exception. The Rev. Nathan Hood was minister at the outbreak of the war. He was a Southern sympathizer, and is said to have prayed from the pulpit for the success of the Confederacy. Tradition says he petitioned the Almighty that the East Tennesseans who left to join the Union forces might die and their bones

---

[58] Martha Lou Coile, *The Hebron United Presbyterian Church, 1875-1976*, Publisher Tom Gentry, Standard Publishing Company. Vera Wilson Gilmore included portions in *Union Presbytery 1791-1976*, The Synod of the South, The United Presbyterian Church in the U.S.A.

[59] Error. Should be John Bradshaw, not William Bradshaw, according to the records of Hazel Townsend, Roy M. Rankin and the Monument to the Settlers in the Mount Horeb Church Cementery.

"decorate and grow white on the top of Cumberland Mountain." He left the church in 1865 before the end of the war.

In 1874 the division and dissatisfaction among the members resulted in a number of withdrawals from the church. The officers and members sent a petition to the Presbytery of Union:

Whereas: two ruling elders and a goodly number of the members of Mount Horeb Church have withdrawn therefrom and have been organized into two separate churches, one in connection with the Southern Presbyterian Church, the other in connection with the Cumberland Presbyterian Church, and whereas, the church and congregation of Mount Horeb now existing are engaged in erecting a new house of worship at a point near four miles distant from the old house of worship.

There, the undersigned ruling elders and members of Mount Horeb Church would respectfully petition the Presbytery to drop from the roll of churches the name of Mount Horeb and insert instead the name Hebron.

Presbytery granted the request and the name was changed. The old church property was sold to the officers of the Southern Presbyterian congregation.

Dedication services for the new church building were held September 19, 1875, with the Rev. William B. Rankin of Greeneville officiating. On the same day the Session—Christopher Rankin, Elias Alexander, Samuel Rankin and Nathan Franklin— held its first meeting under the new name. Three new members were received, making a congregation of sixty-four. The following Sunday, the Sunday School superintendent organized classes from the sixty-two church and family members present. The first deacons were elected in 1878. The Rev. Eli N. Sawtell was installed as pastor and served Hebron Church fourteen years.

The Hebron Church building was completed in the autumn of 1875 from plans largely drawn up by Benjamin F. [Francis] Franklin. It was built by C. H. [Christopher Houston] Rankin, assisted by several other members. T. P. [Thomas Patrick "Pad"] Franklin planed and paneled the back of the pulpit and made the pulpit furniture. Members planed the lumber and laid the floor. Jimmy Rankin dressed most of the lumber for the seats and Benjamin Franklin built them and designed the windows. C. H. Rankin built the rooms at the entrance, including the paneled doors. Henry Dannis plastered the church and Bob Bogle built the spire.

The whole building was a joint effort, and it stands today as a memorial to the foresight, the ability and dedication of this group.

2000: Mount Horeb Presbyterian Church History

by Roy Marshall Rankin

In the 1780's the first settlers began to locate in the area that is now Jefferson County. By about 1785, three Rankin brothers, Samuel, Richard and Thomas, with John Bradshaw had settled on the headwaters of Dumplin Creek very near the present location of Mount Horeb Church. These families had recently come from Cumberland County, Pennsylvania, to the Washington/Greene counties territory of North Carolina/Tennessee.

The Mr. Horeb Presbyterian Church was organized November 20, 1841, by the Presbytery of Union with a charter membership of sixty-seven. Forty of the members came from Hopewell Presbyterian Church at Dandridge which was organized in 1785. Twenty-seven members of the new church came from the New Market Presbyterian Church which had been organized in 1826 with many of its members transferring from Hopewell to New Market at that time.

The Mount Horeb Presbyterian Church was organized with four elders being ordained. The elders were Richard [Ammon] Bradshaw (1788-1872), William Rankin [Sr.] (1796-1871), Christopher Rankin (1809-1881), and John Newman, Jr. The Rev. James H. Gass served as minister for the first five years. In 1858 three additional elders were elected and the Rev. Nathan Hood was minister at that time. The three new elders were Joseph C. Bradshaw, Elias Alexander and Patrick M. [McGuire] Rankin.

The first meetings were held in a log schoolhouse and the first church building was built in 1851. The land for the church, schoolhouse and cemetery was deeded to the Church of Mount Horeb by Richard D. Rankin and Richard [Ammon] Bradshaw.

Part of the land was transferred in February 1842 and additional land in the February, 1851. The present building was erected in 1875 and remodeled in 1913.

An entry in the Hebron Church record states that:

"A goodly number of the members have withdrawn therefrom and have been organized into two separate churches, one in connection with the Southern Presbyterian Church, the other in connection with the Cumberland Presbyterian Church."

The name of Mount Horeb Presbyterian Church was changed to Hebron Presbyterian Church by the Presbytery of Union on September 8, 1874, at the request of the church session.

The 1851 Mount Horeb Church building and location were sold to the Southern Presbyterians in 1874 for the sum of $200.00. The Southern Presbyterian members continued to use the Mount Horeb Church building until 1925. In March of 1925 the membership was very small and the decision was made to close the church. At that time Hebron and Mount Horeb members were again united as one congregation.

In 1986 Holston Presbytery deeded the Mount Horeb Church to the Rankin-Bradshaw Properties, Inc. and extensive repairs were made.

The Mount Horeb Church has been the home of the annual Rankin Clan Reunion since its inception in 1948. The reunion is held the second Sunday in July at 10:30 a.m.

2000: Rankin Heritage from Dumplin Valley

by Roy Marshall Rankin
Adapted by Hazel Timblin Townsend

This Rankin family material was prepared for the Rankin Clan Reunion of 2000 at Mount Horeb Church. My hope is to make a connected story of Rankin families, relatives, and neighbors who moved into East Tennessee to become the earliest Dumplin Valley settlers, and to include some family information and activities of the next fifty to one hundred years near Dumplin Creek.

Why did these ancestors come to the frontier area of the country with its dense forests and canebrakes? The Revolutionary War was over. There was no religious persecution. Many of the community were of similar Scots-Irish background.

Most of you have heard the family story that Alexander Rankin was born in Scotland, married Maria there and escaped to Ireland in 1688 with their son William and family to avoid further religious persecution. Alexander died in Ireland in 1689.[60]

William (1658-1720) was born in Scotland, married Dorothy Black there and died in Ireland. His two brothers were martyrs to their faith in Scotland.

Hugh and Adam, (first and third sons of William) came to Philadelphia, Pennsylvania in 1721 and settled in Chester County southwest of Philadelphia.[61] Adam was born in Scotland in 1688 and Hugh was born in Ireland in 1692.

William's son John (cir 1690-1749) married Jane McElwee (cir 1689-1719) in Ireland, came to Pennsylvania in 1727, and died in Lancaster County, Pennsylvania. Most, but not all of the East Tennessee Rankins came from this Thomas Rankin I line.[62]

James (1711-1795), son of Adam, lived in the western Pennsylvania area. Adam's daughter Esther married William Dunwoody (Dinwiddie) and had ten children. Some of them came to Greene County and then to Blount and Jefferson counties, Tennessee. Adam's son William (1723-1792),[63] born and died in Pennsylvania, married Mary Huston and had eight children whose families were widely scattered in Virginia, North Carolina, Kentucky, and Tennessee. Most of those in Tennessee from this line came to Greene County and later some came to the Sequatchie Valley.

---

[60] Alexander Rankin's death date is uncertain. Maria Rankin, presumed to be his wife, is named in the estate settlement of Alexander in 1703. Administration of the estate of Alexander Rankin was granted to his widow, Maria Rankin, 12 Feb 1703 as recorded in the *Prerogative Administrations Intestate to about 1800* in Betham's Abstracts listed in the "Genealogical Manuscript 259" at the National Archives in Dublin, Ireland. (Vol. 42, 1A, shelf 44-13, page 126, entry 356) "Rankin Alex'r Sergt. Lord Dongals Regt.--To Maria-the Wid. Act Rec'd day of 12 February 1703." This document does not give his death date.

[61] Chester County (one of the three original counties of Pennsylvania) was in the southeastern part of Pennsylvania and extended west for an undetermined distance.

[62] A clarification note is in order here. We have used I, II and III designations after the Thomas Rankin names for years but it is not part of the original Thomas name. It is much easier to use than the birth and death dates.

[63] Records give various birth dates for William Dunwoody Rankin as 1723 and 1726. Jenne Renkin's "Genealogy of Rankin & Renkin Descendants of Adam Rankin of Pennsylvania, 1663-1974," a direct desendant, has 1726. (Unpublished copy in PA State Library, Harrisburg, PA)

Richard, Thomas and possibly Elizabeth (b. cir 1726), children of John, were born in Ireland. Richard married Mary Agnes Douglas in Pennsylvania and moved to Augusta County, Virginia, near Staunton, between 1776 and 1779. Rankin history there indicates other Rankins were probably in the area before Richard arrived. Within a few years this became a stopover point for the Rankins and other Pennsylvania families on their way south. The families often left in a group, traveled the Great Wagon Road down the Virginia Valley on their way to East Tennessee and North Carolina.

Jane Rankin, daughter of David Rankin (1817-1894) of Greene County wrote the following information. "The Moore's, the Galbreath's, and Rankin's all started from Pennsylvania together and the Rankin children became sick in the fall in Virginia. The Moore's, the Bradshaw's and Galbreath's came on to Tennessee and the Rankin family came the next spring and settled above the Moore's." There is no information to identify which families were involved but it is very interesting about the movement pattern.

After the Revolutionary War, many veterans were able to get East Tennessee land grants or buy land at a very low price. At that time a farmer could buy a hundred acres for twenty-five dollars. Thomas Rankin I (cir 1724-1812) and his four oldest sons – John (1754-1829), Richard (1756-1827), Samuel (1728-1834) and William (1760-1838)[64] --served in the Revolutionary War.

Thomas Rankin I, born in Ireland in 1724, died in Jefferson County, Tennessee in 1812. He married Isabella Clendenin in Pennsylvania before 1754. Real estate records there show that Thomas Rankin I sold farm land in Cumberland County, Pennsylvania in 1779. The deed was recorded in 1780. William Rankin, the fourth son of Thomas I, in his Revolutionary War pension application states that "in June 1780 his father, Thomas Rankin I, and family moved to Augusta County, Virginia, near Staunton." I do not know how long they stayed in Virginia but they moved to Greene County from that stop. The next official record of Thomas I is the 1783 Greene County Tax List with his name on it.

Some, but not all, of Thomas I and Isabella's children moved to Greene County. Thomas, Isabella and those of his family with him settled in the Timber Ridge area of Greene County about six miles west of Greeneville. Thomas I was an elder in the Timber Ridge Presbyterian Church from 1786 until 1800 when he "moved west" according to the church session book. This moving west was the time he came to Jefferson County where he and Isabella joined their family members already there. The Timber Ridge area became a settlement with many Rankins as shown by the church cemetery list.

It is very hard to trace family movements in 1780 by records that we expect to find in our courthouses today. Many legal records of today didn't exist on the frontier at the time of early East Tennessee settlement. At that time Tennessee was still part of North Carolina, almost twenty years before Tennessee became a state in 1796. These settlers were people "West of the Allegheny Mountains" and their political life still faced the government of the State of Franklin (1784-1788) and later the Territory South of the

---

[64] Alternate dates for William Rankin are 1759-1833. Alternate dates for John are 1754-1825.

Ohio River. Jefferson County was formed in 1792. Some of the early East Tennessee legal records belonged to these governing entities and were never transferred to the current government in Tennessee. Many early land deeds cannot be found, particularly when they were between family members because they were never recorded. These were known as "pocket deeds" and sometimes recorded many years later when the property was sold outside the family.

Three of Thomas Rankin I's sons were the pioneer settlers of Dumplin Valley -- Richard, Thomas II and Samuel. John Bradshaw [65] is the fourth settler honored on the tablet in the Mount Horeb Church Cemetery.

Richard Rankin (1756-1827) was the second child of Thomas I and Isabella Clendenin Rankin. He came to Tennessee with his wife Jane Steele Rankin and they had one child, a son, at that time. One record has Richard coming directly to Greene County, North Carolina on January 8, 1786. Other records have Richard coming to Dumplin Creek from the present Limestone area near the Washington and Greene County line. In early Tennessee history this county line changed more than one time. The Greene County arrival date could have referred to either location, since all the area was still part of North Carolina. The 1786 date may fit better as the arrival time in what is now Jefferson County. [66]

John Bradshaw (1743-1818) was the fourth Dumplin Valley settler with the three Rankin brothers. No record of his arrival in Tennessee has been found. Family connections and other sources seem to indicate that he was from Wales. He may have settled in Pennsylvania or Virginia, but in an area where the Rankins lived. It also seems probable that Bradshaw lived in the Limestone area near Richard Rankin. The family story that Richard and Bradshaw came to Dumplin Valley to clear land, build houses and plant a corn crop seems to fit the Limestone location. After planting the crop, they returned home to bring their families to Dumplin Creek. When they arrived, they found that the buffalo had eaten the corn crop, resulting in very short rations through the winter months. Richard had given Bradshaw, who was an older man, his choice of the two springs where they would build their houses. When the families arrived at their new homes, they found that the Bradshaw's spring was dry. The Bradshaw location is now known as the Brotherton place on Mountain View Road, about a quarter of a mile from the door of the Mount Horeb Church. The Richard Rankin property joined Bradshaw

---

[65] 1787 Deed from North Carolina to John Bradshaw, 200 acres on head of Dumplin Creek, Book 1, page 253. 1791 Deed from North Carolina to John Bradshaw, 475 acres, Dumplin Creek, Book 2, page 408. 1795 Deed from North Carolina to John Bradshaw, 200 acres, above head of Dumplin Creek, Book 5, page 474.
[66] 1791 Deed from North Carolina to Richard Rankin, Grant #944, 300 acres, Dumplin Creek adjacent to Bradshaw, Book 8, page 411. 1795 Deed from North Carolina to Richard Rankin, Grant #1327, 110 acres, Dumplin Creek Book 5, page 493. 1803 Deed from George Gordon to Richard Rankin, 75 acres, out of 750 acre grant, Book 5, page 13. 1815 Deed from George Gordon to Richard Rankin, 175 acres, out of 750 acre grant, Book N, page 187. 1799 Deed from Thompson Grisham to Richard Rankin, 200 acres from NC Grant #1342, Book D, page 348. 1816 Deed from State of TN to Richard Rankin, Grant #4011, 10 acres, Book 4, page 528. 1816 Deed from State of TN to Richard Rankin, Grant #4012, 10 acres, Book 4, page 522. 1822 Deed from State of TN to Richard Rankin, Grant #12968, 6 acres, Book 6, page 561.

just down the creek. Today a fifth generation descendant of Richard Rankin lives on part of the original farm.

Samuel Rankin (1758-1834) was the third child of Thomas I and Isabella Rankin. Samuel married Jane Isabelle Petty in Pennsylvania. I have not seen any date for their arrival in Tennessee, but it seems probable that he was in the Timber Ridge area near his father and other family members. Samuel and Thomas II apparently came to Dumplin Valley from the Timber Ridge location within a year or two after Richard Rankin and John Bradshaw settled there. Samuel Rankin owned land on the south side of Dumplin Creek joining the Thomas II land near the present Hebron Church Road. [67]

Thomas Rankin II (1762-1821) had land grants and other land on Dumplin Creek at the present Dumplin Valley Road and Hebron Church Road about two and a half miles down the creek from Richard Rankin. [68] Thomas II married Jennet "Jane" Bradshaw in Greene County in 1789 (Jefferson County was organized in 1792) and they reared all their thirteen children in Dumplin Valley. "Jane" was the daughter of John Bradshaw (1743-1818) and Annie Agnes Clendenin of the early Dumplin Valley settlers. [69]

After Thomas II's death, much of his land passed to his son, Christopher. In May 1875 some of this land was deeded to the trustees of the Hebron Presbyterian Church.

There is no doubt that the Rankin families became the predominant population of Dumplin Valley. They moved from the valley toward Dandridge and Mossy Creek (Jefferson City since 1901). In 1885 Christopher and his wife Frances Galbreath Rankin had seventy-one descendants from their fifteen children. Somebody certainly had to move somewhere! From about this time and until 1920, many Rankins moved to the new frontiers as the United States developed westward. They became leaders in their communities and professions, and many contacts with faraway cousins are still maintained today.

Why did our ancestors hunt a new frontier? Some lessons learned by our ancestors are still just as good for us today. They learned that what was good for them was also good for the others who made up the community. The complete meaning of sharing was never better understood and expressed than in the frontier community.

---

[67] 1804 Deed from Thomas Rankin to Samuel Rankin, Tract on waters of Dumplin Creek, Book F, page 241. 1814 Deed from Christopher Hanes to Samuel Rankin, 300 acres, Page N, page 94. 1914 Deed from Christopher Hanes to Samuel Rankin, 30 acres, Book N, page 95. 1815 Deed from James Rankin to Samuel Rankin, 149 acres, part of two NC Grants to Thomas Rankin, Book N, page 185. 1817 Deed from State of TN to Samuel Rankin, 100 acres assigned from George Gordon, Book 4, page 668.

[68] 1791 Deed from North Carolina to Thomas Rankin, Grant #926, 150 acres, Dumplin Creek, Book 2, page 407. 1792 Deed from North Carolina to Thomas Rankin, Grant #1048, 400 acres, N/S Dumplin Creek, Book 2, page 404. 1795 Deed from John Shields to Thomas Rankin, 200 acres on both sides of Dumplin, Book C, page 168. 1795 Deed from John Shields to Thomas Rankin, Sr., 100 acres on both sides of Dumplin Creek, Book C, page 177. 1815 Deed from Christopher Hanes to Thomas Rankin, 200 acres on NW side of head of Dumplin Creek, Book N, page 210. 1817 Deed from State of TN to Thomas Rankin, Sr., 30 acres on Dumplin Creek, Book 4, page 583. 1817 Deed from State of TN to Thomas Rankin, Sr., 30 acres on Dumplin Creek, Book, 4, page 583. 1822 Deed from State of TN to Thomas Rankin, 20 acres Dumplin Creek, Book 6, page 432.

[69] See the Bradshaw-Rankin Bible information in this book.

2001: Dumplin Valley's Original Rankin Home Sites

by Roy Marshall Rankin
Presented at the 2002 Rankin Clan Reunion
Edited by Hazel Timblin Townsend, 2016

I am frequently asked, "Where were the locations of the homes of the original Rankin family settlers in Dumplin Valley?" I have made several trips down the valley with relatives pointing out these locations. A map of the area in Chapter 2 shows how closely the present Dumplin Valley Road follows Dumplin Creek, but at the time of the original settlement, the log cabins and barns were nearer the creek.[70] I think the first road/trail along the creek was the Great Indian Warpath which entered present-day Jefferson County on the eastern edge at the mouth of Long Creek and the Nolichucky River, continued through the county in a southwesterly direction to the present Jefferson-Sevier County line. The Warpath followed Long Creek to its head waters, crossed two or three ridges not far from South Chucky Pike through Finley's Gap and turned southwest again toward the head of Dumplin Creek following it into Sevier County.

It is interesting to note that this is the same route that Col. Christian's three-month expedition followed in 1776. They had started from Virginia to fight the Indians as far west as present day Sevier and Blount Counties. A provisional peace was reached with the Indians, and Col. Christian's forces, who were assembled from the Watauga settlement, North Carolina and Virginia volunteers, returned home.

The first two of the Dumplin Valley pioneer settlers were John Bradshaw (1743-1818) and Richard Rankin (1756-1827). They probably lived near present-day Limestone, Tennessee area (Greene County) for a short time before coming to Dumplin Creek about 1786. They came to the valley to clear land, plant crops, and build log cabins. Having done that, they returned home to move their families to the Dumplin Valley location.

The John Bradshaw (1) location was the present-day location of the Brotherton house on Brotherton Road, about a quarter mile from Mount Horeb Church. The Richard Rankin property was just down the creek joining the Bradshaw land with both houses being built near a spring. (2) The men worked together, making places for the two families, but not having decided which would be their own home. Richard Rankin, the younger of the two men, gave Bradshaw his choice of locations. John Bradshaw chose the upper place that is now the Brotherton property. I understand that part of the present Brotherton house is of log construction and may be one of the oldest houses in Jefferson County still in use. The log section is not being represented as the Rankin-Bradshaw construction though. The family story tells that when Bradshaw and Rankin

---

[70] Numbers on the map in "Places" section, Map of Dumplin Valley, indicate the original homesites: (1) John Bradshaw, (2) Richard Rankin, (3) Thomas Rankin (II), (4) Samuel Rankin, (5) Zirkle/Rankin House.

returned with their families later in the season, Bradshaw's spring had gone dry and the buffalo had eaten the corn crops.

Richard Rankin settlement location and part of the land is still owned and farmed by Mary Ruth (McMurray) and Tommy Crawford on the south side of Dumplin Valley Road and west of Mount Horeb Church. Mary Ruth is a fifth-generation descendant of Richard Rankin. The location of the first log cabin home was very near the present John McMurray house which is about two or three hundred yards south of Dumplin Valley Road and an eighth of a mile west of Mount Horeb Church.

The third and fourth of the pioneer settlers were Samuel (1758-1834) and Thomas II (1762/64-1821),[71] younger brothers of Richard Rankin. They came from the Timber Ridge area of Greene County about six miles west of Greeneville, Tennessee. Their father and mother, Thomas I and Isabella Clendenin Rankin, were in Greene County by 1783 with his name on the tax roll. The younger members of their family came to the Timber Ridge home with them, but older sons were already married. Samuel, already married to Jane Isabella Petty, appears to have settled near the other members of his family, and Thomas II and Samuel came to Dumplin Valley from the Timber Ridge area a year or two after Richard Rankin and Bradshaw.

Thomas II settled on Dumplin Creek in the southeast quadrant of the Dumplin and Hebron Church Road intersection. (3) He owned land on both sides of Dumplin Creek and of Hebron Church Road. Thomas also has a land grant dated 1792 for land adjoining Richard Rankin two miles upstream. Often the land grants do not locate the original homestead, as they were made several years after the homes were established. Later Thomas II acquired much more land at the Hebron Road location, and, at his death, much of this land went to his son Christopher. It is reasonably easy to identify this location for Thomas II as the bounds are referenced to the Hebron Church Road.

Hebron Church was built in 1875 on land donated by Christopher Rankin, but the road was an important route soon after the Dumplin Valley settlement was made. It was the primary road from Dandridge, the county seat, and Mossy Creek (Jefferson City after 1901). The road came from Dandridge past the west end of the Dumplin Creek settlement, moved slightly west after crossing the creek and continued north along today's Davis Hollow Road to the Flat Gap area. The road branched there with one leg going to Mossy Creek and the other going west to New Market.

Samuel Rankin owned land on the south side of Dumplin Creek which at some point joined the southern boundary of the Thomas (II) property. (4) I do not know just which way his property extended or how much property he owned there.

There is another house in Dumplin Valley that was not built until at least two generations after the settlement but has an interesting history. It has been known as a "Rankin House" since about 1900. It was a "Zirkle House" for more than fifty years before that. The house is located on Sellers Road which goes south of Dumplin Valley

---

[71] The birth of Thomas Rankin II is 1764 in *Jefferson County.Tennessee Genealogy.net* transcribed by Doris Kinser Fountain, (Family Bible Records, <http://jefferson.tngenealogy.net> from original transcriber W. A. Lyle, of Jefferson County, 1937, published by the Works Progress Administration under the title Jefferson County Bible Records), Bible of Patric M. Rankin of Mt. Horeb, published: 05 July 2008 on TN GenWeb.

Road about seven-tenths of a mile west of Mount Horeb Church. The brick house is on the west side of Sellers, south of Dumplin Creek. (5)

Benjamin Zirkle married Susan [Ruth] Pennywit in Virginia in 1838. They came to Jefferson County and lived in a two-room house where two or three children were born. The present brick house was probably built in 1844 by slave labor. Benjamin Zirkle died in 1890, but his estate was not settled until 1898. A granddaughter, Virginia Zirkle, received part of the property and was married to Rev. A. T. [Arthur Tappan] Rankin in 1898. They bought another part of the property after their marriage which included the house. Tappan lived in the house until his death in 1947. It was during this time that the house became a "Rankin House." [72]

Tappan and Virginia's oldest daughter, Adnah, married Ivel Large, lived in the house, took care of Tappan, and farmed the property. The next owners were the fifth child of Tappan and Virginia, Evelyn Louise. Evelyn married V. York Leedy. After York's death, the house and farm were sold at auction and bought by Mary Rankin, the widow of Robert Ward Rankin, who was the oldest son of Tappan and Virginia. Mary lived in Knoxville and owned the house for about four years and made some repairs to it. Mary sold the house to D. L. Thomas, outside the family, and there have been two or three subsequent owners since then.

---

[72] Rev. Arthur Tappan Rankin was the son of John Gass Rankin and Adiadne Jane "Adna" Lyle. Virginia Elizabeth Zirkle was the daughter of George Adam Zirkle (son of Benjamin Zirkle) and Florence Obalma Wisdom. Arthur and Virginia married in 1898. Their children were an infant daughter born and died in 1899, Adnah Florence, Robert Ward, Kent K., George Gass, Evelyn Louise, and John Wisdom. Adnah married Ival Large. Evelyn Louise married V. York Leedy.

2016: History of the Rankin Clan Reunion

by Dr. Melanie Thomas Hodgson
Hazel Timblin Townsend

The Mount Horeb Church on East Dumplin Valley Road in Jefferson County has been the home of the annual Rankin Clan Reunion since its inception in 1948. The reunion is held the second Sunday of July at 10:30 a.m. followed by a picnic lunch on the grounds.

The following minutes are of the first Rankin Clan Reunion on July 11, 1948:

The Rankin Reunion was held on July 11, 1948, at 10:30 a.m. at the Mount Horeb Presbyterian Church. The program began with a song by the audience, "Come, Thou Almighty King." After this song the opening prayer was presented by Mr. I. L. [Isaac Lafayette "Fate"] Rankin. At this point, a suggestion was made that there be a presiding Officer and Recording Secretary elected for the remainder of the Program. Mr. I. L. Rankin was elected as Presiding Officer, and Miss Wanda [Faye] Rankin was elected as Recording Secretary by acclamation. These officers took charge and the remainder of the program was presented.

Reading "The House by the Side of the Road" - Lillian Rankin

Talk "What It Means To Be A Rankin" - Mrs. Ina Rankin

Solo "Ninety and Nine" - Rev. John Tullock

Talk "Rankins" - Mr. Sam Hull Rankin

Dr. J. O. Rankin took over at the conclusion of the program and talked to those present on the subject "Rankin Clan".

The program was adjourned for two hours for the purpose of eating lunch. The lunch was spread in the Mount Horeb school house.

After lunch, the program was resumed. Mr. I. L. Rankin presented to the audience the names of persons that were appointed to hold a place on the committee in preparation of the Rankin Reunion of 1949. The names of these persons and committees are as follows:

ARRANGEMENTS: Time, place, speakers, program

Mr. Sam Hull Rankin, Mr. John McMurray, Mrs. John McMurray, Mr. I. L. Rankin, Mr. Pierce Rankin

SOCIAL: Hospitality (Greet and Register people) – Food

Mrs. Evelyn Leedy, Mrs. Mary McCampbell, Mrs. Lula Harding, Mr. Luke Rankin, Mr. Ira M. Davis

ENLISTMENT AND PUBLICITY

Miss Annabelle McMurray, Mr. Sam Hull Rankin, Mrs. Hubert Rankin [Elizabeth Geneva "Dixie" Landrum] , Mr. Ralph Rankin

After the businesses was taken care of in the afternoon session, Dr. J. O. Rankin, again spoke on the history of the Rankin family. At the close of his talk the Reunion adjourned to meet on the date set by the committee, July 10, 1949, and was dismissed.

Signed: I. L. Rankin, Chairman, Wanda F. Rankin, Secretary

In 1952 a picture was presented to the Clan that was given by Dr. J. O. Rankin of Hayti, Missouri, who attended the first Rankin Reunion in 1948 and passed away in 1951.[73]

After a few years the afternoon session was discontinued and the program was concluded by noon. Apparently lunch was eaten only the first year in the old school house. For several years it was set-up in the school yard. After that it was under the giant oak tree beside the church. After it died, the tables were set-up in the grove of trees behind the church.

In 1986 the Hebron Church deeded Mount Horeb to the Rankin Clan. The by-laws and deed were drawn up by an attorney in Jefferson City and the deed was transferred to the Rankin-Bradshaw Church Properties, Inc. Members of the board of Directors were Robert W. "Bob" Rankin, David Jones, Chris Davis, David Rankin and Melanie Hodgson.

About 1987 the tradition started to have a piper play while the Rankin Clan gathered. Some of the pipers have been Bob Pennington of Knoxville, TN; Robert Rankin, Jr., of McAllen, TX; Kelly Shipe, Choral Music Director of Jefferson County High School; and Wyatt Brown, a student at St. Andrew's University, NC.

In 1998 Joy Hammer Bemis donated a quilt memorializing the 50th Anniversary Clan Reunion. The 70½" x 78" quilt is made of muted brown plaids and muslin. Almost all of the squares have someone's signature and how they are related to the Rankin clan. The squares are machine sewn together and the whole quilt is hand quilted. The quilt is usually displayed at the reunion and kept safe in someone's home.

In 1998 John Rankin of Gastonia, North Carolina, shared his research about our Scottish Heritage. His presentation included Caledonian Values, Scots' Family Tapestry, four core Scots' ethnic groups including Scots'-Irish, the Scots and Scots' Irish in North Carolina. John painted a symbolic picture using 6,000 surnames woven together to suggest rivers and lochs, firths and fields, moors and mountains. The various sept names swirl about the much larger names of each of the hundred clan chiefs. The 32" x 48" framed print hangs in the church.

In 2010 the "Building Restoration Fund" was started. The foundation and the under pinning of the building needed restoring, as well as new paint and roof.

"Morning Has Broken" has opened the service for many years. "Church in the Wildwood" is sung during the service. The hymn written by Jeremiah E. Rankin, "God Be with You," traditionally closes the service. The first time it closed the service was in 1949.

The Secretaries through the years have been Wanda Faye Rankin Thomas, Miss Florence Evelyn Gass, Dorothea Leedy, Mrs. Mary Ruth [McMurray] Crawford, Mrs. J. [John] Maurice Cate [Frances Emily Newman Cate], Mrs. David Newman, Marilyn Rankin, Martha Watkins, Anita Fielden, Dr. Melanie L. Hodgson.

---

[73] Townsend believes it is the picture of the Clansman playing bagpipes that still hangs in the church.

The pianists over the years have included Carroll [Anderson Coile] Brotherton (Mrs. Quince David Brotherton), Mildred Joy McMurray Rankin (Mrs. Ralph Everett Rankin), Jane Nichols, Mrs. J. W. Ellis, Tanya Thomas.

Thanks go to the Ira M. and I. Chris Davis family for keeping the church and grounds in good shape for so many years.

Information about the Rankin Clan Reunion can be found at our website at <http://www.Rankinreunion.org>, thanks to Carol Titus, our web-mistress.

Chart of Reunion Presidents and Speakers

Year	President	Speaker	Topic
1948	I. L. Rankin	Ina Rankin Trentham and Sam Hull Rankin; Dr. J. O. Rankin, Prof. at University of TN	"What It Means to Be a Rankin" and "Rankins"
1949	I.L. Rankin	Sam Hull Rankin	"From Father's Shoulders"
1950	Pierce Rankin	David Lintz	"Rankin History"
1951	Luke Rankin	Henry Rankin	"Rankin History"
1952	Joe Rush Rankin	Mrs. Clara Bettis Zirkle Dr. Raymond Rankin, President of Tusculum College	"Ministers and Missionaries of the Rankin Clan", No program title given
1953	Roy Rankin	Roy Rankin	Talk on William B. Rankin
1954	George Rankin	Richard Rankin	"Rankin's settling in Tennessee in 1786"
1955	Bruce Rankin	Orton L. Duggan, retired scout executive	"Our heritage and Responsibility for Christian Citizenship"
1956	Andrew L. Alexander	Commodore B. Fisher, professor of history, Maryville College	"A Crowd of Witnesses"
1957	R. Ward Rankin	Dan Rankin	"What it means to be a Rankin"
1958	Nancy Newman Jones	Reverend W. R. Simmons, pastor of New Market and Hebron Presbyterian Church	"Open the Gates to the Temple"
1959	Lyle Rankin	Dr. Carl T. Vance, a Rankin Clansman and Professor of Education at Carson Newman College	"Cornerstone of Unity Faith and Loyalty"
1960	Ira M. Davis	1. Mabel Rankin Ellis 2. Rev. David W. Profitt, Maryville, TN, Past Moderator of Presbyterian Church USA 3. Robert and Myra Rankin Fielding, Brazil, South America	1. About Rankin Reunion 2. "The Present Generation's Obligation in Light of Its Heritage" *Proverbs 22:1* 3. Missionaries on leave
1961	Bob Holsaple	Ed Bettis of Knoxville	No program title given

1962	David H. Newman	Wallace R. Burroughs and Cousin Herber Rankin	No program title given and Report on his trip to England to visit the Rankin's there
1963	Mrs. Bruce (Dorothy) Rankin	John J. Duncan, Mayor of Knoxville	No program title given
1964	George Rankin	Orton L. Duggan	No program title given
1965	F. Earle Rankin	1. Marilyn Rankin 2. Edward S. Bettis	History of the Rankin Name Worship Message
1966	Robert Holsaple	Andrew Smith	"Sacred Experience of Families"
1967	Robert Fielden	Dr. Joe Chapman, Professor of Biology at Carson Newman College	"A Great Name and Family"
1968	Chris Davis	Reverend Pritchett	"Building a World"
1969	Bob Rankin	Bedford Bird	"Family Ties"
1970	Gary Fielden	Harold Beard	No program title given
1971	Jim Rankin	Robert Fielden	No program title given
1972	Tom Sawyer	Dr. Bill Blevins	"Religious Significance of Eating"
1973	Judy Rankin	Martin Spangler	No program title given
1974	George Rankin	Lamar Alexander	"Heritage and Characteristics of the Rankins"
1975	David Jones	Dr. Hayden Laster	No program title given
1976	Dan Rankin	W. E. Fitzgerald	"The Importance of Family Life"
1977	Chris Davis	Dr. R. R. Turner	No program title given
1978	Lena Beth Cate	Martin Spangler	"The Psalms"
1979	Myra Fielden	Doug Goddard	No program title given
1980	Bob Rankin	Jim Ronalds, from the American Cancer Society	No program title given
1981	Jim Rankin	Bishop Jesse L. Dunn	"Importance of the Family Unit"
1982	Luey Rankin	Rell B. Smith, Jr.	"John Rankin, son of Richard and Isabella Steele Rankin"
1983	David Rankin	Gov. Lamar Alexander	"Heritage of Lamar Alexander"
1984	Nancy Jones	Anna Blackburn McSpadden	"Ancestors of the Blackburn and Rankin's – How They Came to America and Settled the Land"
1985	Chris Davis	Roy Rankin	"Rankin Clan's Scotch and Irish Background"
1986	Dan Rankin	Dr. Ted Rankin	"Heritage of the Rankin Family Dating Back to the 1200's"

1987	Roy M. Rankin	Jack Franklin, Attorney, Memphis, TN	"Presbyterian Churches in the Jefferson County Formed in 1792"
1988	Bob Rankin	Keith J. Honaker, Knoxville	"How to Tell Your Family Stories"
1989	Ted. L. Rankin	F. M. "Pete" Rankin, Jr., Tyler, TX	"Family Roots"
1990	Linda A. Rankin	Robert C. Rankin, McAllen, TX	"Research in the Scottish Ancestry of the Rankins – Rankins as Bagpipe Players"
1991	Frank E. Rankin, Jr.	Michael J. Rankin	"Rankin History – Talents in Writing Poetry and Musicians"
1992	Michael J. Rankin	Roy and Marguerite Rankin of White Pine, TN	"History of the Mount Horeb Church and Dumplin Valley Area"
1993	Douglas H. "Doug" Rankin	No Speaker	
1994	F. Wayne Rankin	No Speaker	
1995	David M. Rankin	Cherel Henderson, Adm. Assistant, East TN Historical Society	"Cemeteries and How They Exemplify the Sum of All the People Who Have Gone Before Us"
1996	Linda A. Rankin	Linda A. Rankin	Planning for 50th Reunion
1997	Chris Davis	Lamar Alexander, Sec. of Education and 2nd term Governor of Tennessee	50th Rankin Clan Reunion
1998	Hazel Townsend	John Rankin, Gastonia, NC	Searching for Scottish Roots
1999	David M. Rankin	David Jones, Mayor of Dandridge, Tennessee	"The Last Will and Testament of Thomas Rankin"
2000	Wayne Rankin	Roy M. Rankin	Dumplin Valley's Original Rankin Home Sites
2001	Bob Rankin	Judy Rankin, Utah	Memories of the Reunion, What Does It Mean to Be a Rankin?
2002	Katherine Rankin Alexander	Bill Bothamley, California	The Rev. John Rankin, Abolitionist
2003	Jim & Tom Rankin	Hazel Timblin Townsend, Greenville, SC	Music in the Rankin Clan in Scotland
2004	Judy Rankin Hansen	Lowell Jones, retired director (27 years) of Berea College Appalachian Center	Author of several books on mountain humor and Appalachian religions.
2005	Jimmy Gass	Bob Jarnagin, Dandridge's Unofficial Historian	Great Warpath Trail Through Dumplin Valley
2006	Carol Jean Rankin	Martha Hess, Maryville College Registrar	How things had changed and stayed the same in Liberal Arts Education

2007	Karma McNew	Jeff Daniel Marion, Former Carson-Newman Professor, Author and Poet	He shared several poems and prose that he had written over the years.
2008	Dan Rankin, Jr.	Dr. Ted Rankin, Longview, Texas	Brothers Alexander and William Rankin Moving to America Because of Fear of Attack on Their Families[74]
2009	Nancy Rankin Smith	Joe and Wanda Newman, Asheville, NC	"Two of Us" Traditional Music with Joe and Wanda
2010	Walter Rankin Townsend	Hazel Timblin Townsend, Greenville, SC	Discovering Backgrounds for Our Rankin Roots
2011	David Jones	Bob Jarnagin, Dandridge's Unofficial Historian	Rankin Family Businesses and Farms
2012	Stanley Walter Timblin	Bob Jarnagin, Dandridge's Unofficial Historian	Early migration of clans— Ireland to Scotland, Scotland back to Ireland, then to PA and TN
2013	Kent Rankin	Joe and Wanda Newman, Asheville, NC	They shared many enjoyable songs
2014	Jason Rankin	Jason Rankin	A paper that was written by John Shedden in 1959, about Cort Rankin.
2015	John Rankin	Bob Markli	"A nation founded on Christian principals and the importance of our heritage"
2016	Dan Rankin, Jr.	Wyatt Brown, Piper	Bagpipes
2017	David Rankin		

---

[74] Was this referring to the father Alexander Rankin and son Willliam fleeing Scotland to Northern Ireland or the three brothers Adam, Hugh and John Rankin leaving Ireland and coming to Pennsylvania, or another Alexander and William?

Chapter 4

Session Minutes

Overview

The initial reason for this book was to preserve and share the information from two lost Session Minute Books. Baptism and birth records, as well as marriage and death records were in these old books, November 20, 1841 to April 30, 1860 and May 30, 1874 to April 1923. When a transcribed copy of all three volumes was found, the second book was included.

You will notice that the books are transcribed as best as they could be read from the spelling and punctuation used. Many names and some words had variations of spelling. Often the script was hard to decipher. The format of the information depended upon the Clerk of Session at that particular time. Most of the charts were spread across two pages. By using smaller print, these charts were reduced to one page to make them easier to follow. The plus symbol beside some names was in the original for some unknown reason.

The 1940 typed manuscript was transcribed by an unknown person from the original handwriting. A few dates and names appeared to be incorrectly transcribed. For some of these the correct information is in square brackets.

To preserve the order of the books, the original page numbers are in square brackets. The numbers in the round bracket are page numbers of the typed manuscript. In a few instances pages are moved to make it easier for today's reader to follow, such as keeping some of the baptism rolls together. These Registers are listed in the Index.

Square brackets are used to indicate additional information added to the original by the author. Initials were frequently used instead of given names. When initial and names could be verified, the given names were added in square brackets. Names are indexed with the full name when known. Married females are indexed under their maiden name and under their married name with the maiden name included.

Words or names were often written the way they sounded to the listener. For instance, the name of the same person may be spelled several different ways, depending on the Clerk of Session. Examples are Almira, Almyra; Barbee, Barby; Catharine, Catherine, Katherine; Clendenin, Clindenin, Clendon; Coil, Coile; Darr, Dorr; Ernest, Earnest; Galbreath, Gilbraith; Harden, Hardin; Harvey, Hervey; Jolly, Jolley, Jollay; Massie, Massey; Massengil, Massingill; Mathis, Mathes, Mathas; McCuiston, McCuistion, McQuiston; McMury, McMurry, McMurray; Neal, Neil; Shadden, Sheddan, Shedden; Tittsworth, Titsworth; Wilson, Willson, etc. In some cases, the current common spelling in square brackets.

Volume I (1841-1860)

Contents

A list of members page 1st & onward
The business of Session page 13 and onward
Form No. 1, 1st page 192 and onward
Form No. 2nd page 206 and onward
Some Thing on page 178 and onward

Session Minutes

November 20, 1841
The session of Mount Horeb church met and elected Wm. Rankin[75] clerk of Session, and Christopher Rankin Treasurer.
[signed] Wm. Rankin, Clk.

[Page 1] November 20th 1841.
By order of the Presbytery of Union the Rev'd John McCampbell organized a church at the School house near R. D. [Richard Duffield] Rankin's by ordaining four elders, viz.
   Elders: William Rankin
      Richard [Ammon] Bradshaw
      Christopher Rankin and
      John Newman, Junr.

Rebecca Massengill married Henry Tipton

Also at the same time five persons who were chosen to act as trustees, viz.
Trustees: William Rankin
   William Massengill, Sr.
   Richard D. [Duffield] Rankin
   Josiah E. [Emmons] Rankin & James Newman

---

[75] William Rankin, Sr. (1796-1871), son of Thomas Rankin II (1764-1821) and Jennet Bradshaw (1772-1824). William, Christopher (1809-1881) and Josiah Emmons (1815-1893) are brothers. Richard D. Rankin, son of Richard (1756-1827) (brother of Thomas II) and Richard Ammon Bradshaw (1788-1872), son of John (1743-1818) are cousins. James Newman (1798-1879) married Isabella Rankin (1800-1886), sister of William, Christopher and Josiah E. Rankin. James and John Newman, Jr. (1811-1864) were brothers.

In the organizing of the church the following members in full communion in Hopewell and New Market churches fell within the councils of this church. Viz.

[Page 2]

Hopewell Church

Jane [Nicholson] Massengill	Isabella [Rankin] Newman
Susan P. Massengill	Joseph R. [Reece] Newman
Joseph C. Bradshaw	Nancy C. Newman
Sarah [Grizzle Blackburn] Bradshaw	Mary Newman
Richard Bradshaw	Josiah E. Rankin
Lydia Bradshaw	Christopher Rankin
Nancy Ann Bradshaw	Frances Rankin
Richard H. [Harden] Bradshaw	William Rankin [Sr.]
Jane [P. Rawlings] Bradshaw	Eliza T. Kimbrough
John P. [Prigmore] Bradshaw	Lucinda [Harriet] Rankin
Elizabeth T. [Tymanda] Bradshaw	Joseph McCuistion
Thomas R. [Rankin] Bradshaw	Rachel McCuistion
Margaret [Blackburn] Bradshaw	James McCuistion
Jane Rankin	Isabella [H.] Bettas
Richard D. Rankin	Mary E. Bettas
Mary Ann C. [Carol Woods] Rankin	John H. Franklin
Aaron B. [Bogue] Rankin	Benjamin F. [Francis] Franklin [Sr.]
Aaron Newman	Mahulda Newman
Cassandra [Branner] Newman	Lucinda H. Franklin
James [Eaton] Rankin	Total 40
James Newman	

[Page 3]

New Market

John Newman Sr.	William M. [Milton] Newman
Elizabeth [Ashmore] Newman	Catherine E. Newman
Nancy Ann Newman	Mary C. Newman
Sophia C. Newman	Mary A. Newman
Louisa H. Newman	Aron [Aaron] Newman
Elenor Newman	John C. Newman
Blair Newman	Eliza C. Newman
Margaret Newman	James H. Hammel
Aran [Aaron] Newman, Jur.	Elizabeth Hammel
Isabella Newman	Mary Ann Hammel
Catherine Newman	Benj. Mitchell
Thomas I. Newman	Elizabeth Mitchell
Margaret Newman	Total 27
John Newman	
Jane Newman	

[Page 3] **Added since the organization of the church**

Mary B. Easterly	Sarah M. Newman
Euinice Bowles	Wm. Gass
Elizabeth McCuistion	Susan [Kimbrough] Rankin
Moses Easterly	Plesant Vance
Margery Rankin	William P. Massengill[76]
Thomas Rankin, Jr.	Aron A. Hammel
Mary M. Rankin	Mary Newman
Patrick M. Rankin	Jane Rankin
Aron A. Newman	Rebecca Ann Jacobs
Louisa J. Rankin	Nancy Ann Gass
Catherine E. Hammel	John W. Bettas

[Page 4]

Jesse A. Newman	George W. Wright
Samuel B. [Blair] Newman	Lydia J. [Lidea Jane] Newman
Samuel T. Bettas	James H. Newman
Andrew C. [Carroll] Newman	Eliza Rankin
Andrew P. Newman	Margaret J. Malcom, E. Eaton
Albert M. Newman	Charles T. Jolly, Robert P. Eaton & Eleanor[77]
Thomas W. Nance	Nancy Jane Bradshaw
Charles C. Newman	Emily White Gass
James Cox+	Catharine Emiline Bradshaw
Rachel Cox+	James T. Rankin
David Barbee	Florence Thomas
Mary Jane McCuistion	Lydia P. Bradshaw
Eliza Newman	Stephen R. [Roten] Bradshaw
Mary A. [Lockhart] Newman	Robert P. Eaton
James E. Loyd	Eleanor C. Eaton
Ann Franklin	James H. Darr
Eglantine Isabella Newman	Adaline Gass
Elijah – a man of colour	Polly Ann McMurray
Hannah – a woman of colour	Sarah Newman
Vina – a woman of colour	Elias A. Alexander
Thomas Jacobs	Joseph A. Malcom
Elizabeth Jacobs	Mary W. Malcom
Rebecca A. Jacobs	Mary D. Bradshaw
William Masengill	Martha A. Bradshaw
Richard R. [Rawlings] Bradshaw	William H. Lyle
George G. Vance	John F. Newman
Mary A. E. [Ann Emily] Kelly	Martha M. [Matilda] Newman
Julyann Rankin	

---

[76] Dr. Massengill's full name is thought to be William Porter Massengill (1819-1875), the son of William Massengill, Sr. (1782-1852) and his first wife Deborah Chisholm (1786-1837). (Records researched on *Ancestry.com* by Townsend.)

[77] E. Eaton, Charles T. Jolly, Robert P. Eaton and Eleanor were written in a different handwriting between Margaret J. Malcom and Nancy Jane Bradshaw as if they had been added later.

[Page 5]

Nancy E. Rankin	Margaret A. Jolly
Mary E. Rankin	Mary E. Jolly
Elizabeth C. Rankin	Barsheba W. Talbott
Frances J. Perry	Harriet J. Bradshaw
David G. [George] Newman	Sarah G. Alexander
Isabella of colour	Sarah J. Rankin
+David Ashmore	Mary A. Rankin
+Polly Ashmore	John Mc. Rankin
+Harriet Ashmore	John Rankin
John Patton	Daniel H. [Hardin] Bradshaw
Edy Patton	John C. [Calvin] Rankin
Nancy Emily Rankin	Lydia J. [Jane] Zirkle
Aaron B. [Bogue] Rankin	Ellen L. Rankin
Marjorie [Lockhart] Rankin	Isabella E. Newman
Samuel Funk	Isabella Rankin
Elizabeth Funk	Samuel McMury
Susan Zirkle	Mark T. Rankin
Alexander Rankin	John F. Rankin
Mary J. Rankin	Albert M. Meadowes
Andrew T. Gass	John J. Newman
Delila Rimmer	Thomas J. Bradshaw
Cadelia [Cordelia] F. Mountcastle	William Rankin [1796-1871]
David C. Cockenour	James A. Barby
Gideon W. Newman	Mary A. C. Newman
Sarah C. Zirkle	John G. Rankin
Orlena E. [Eglentine] Bradshaw	Thomas P. Franklin
Edward A. Bradshaw	Daniel Meadows
William M. Bradshaw	Margaret J. Newman
Samuel E. Rankin	

[Page 6]

Margaret E. Rankin	Martha J. Rankin
Mary E. Cline +	Thomas C. Lyle
Darthula J. [Jane] Bettis	William A. Bowers
Margaret S. Newman	Jonathan L. Newman
George W. Newman Jr.	Pleasant J. [Jackson] Bettis
Minerva A. Newman	Mary S. Zirkle
Elizabeth C. Rankin	George A. [Adam] Zirkle
Joseph H. Cline +	Sarah A. Rankin
Mary A. Cline +	Laura A. Franklin
George W. Newman, Senr.	Anderson – a man of colour
Daniel L. [Lyle] Bettis	Madison Newman
Hugh A. Newman	John V. Richards
Richard A. Newman	Senora E. Shadden
Henry O. Newman	~~Thomas C. Shadden~~
Silas J. A. [John Anderson] Newman	Nancy C. Lyle
Patrick L. [Lafayette] Newman	Sarah A. Vance

William F. Newman	Mary E. Newman
John W. Newman	Thomas C. Shadden
Samuel H. Franklin	William H. Newman
William T. Rankin	Alexander Rimmer
Martha E. Newman	John Talbott
Campbell Franklin	Benjamin C. [Casper] Newman
Joseph W. Shadden	Mary [Louise] Lyle
Rachel L. Shadden	David C. Gass
Matilda E. Newman	Thomas Newman
	William P. Masengill

[Page 7]

Martha J. Newman	Margaret Mathis
Nancy J. Newman	George A. Mathis
Harriet Malinda Rankin	John Jolly
William A. Mathis	Rufus E. Carson+
	Harriet D. Carson+

[Pages 8-12 blank]

[Page 13] March 20, 1842

The Session met and constituted by prayer. Members present [Rev.] James H. Gass, Richard Bradshaw, William Rankin, Christopher Rankin and John Newman.[78]

And after examination, received Moses Easterly as a member on profession of faith in Christ. Also his wife Mary B. Easterly, by certificate.

Concluded by prayer.

William Rankin, Ck.

April 15, 1842

Session met & constituted with prayer. Members present J. H. Gass, Wm. Rankin, Richard Bradshaw, Christopher Rankin & John Newman.

They proceeded to examine Margery Rankin on experimental[79] religion and received her as a member.

Concluded by prayer.

William Rankin, Clerk of Sess.

April 16, 1842

Session met and constituted by prayer. Members present Jas. H. Gass, [page 14] Richard Bradshaw, Wm. Rankin, Christopher Rankin and John Newman

and received by letter Mrs. Eunice Bowles as a member.

Concluded by prayer.

Wm. Rankin Ck.

---

[78] Session members are indexed the first and last time they are listed as present or absent in the minutes and when they were given a responsibility.

[79] "based on experience" (*Webster's Seventh New Collegiate Dictionary*, Based on Webster's Third New International Dictionary, G. & C. Merriam Company, Publishers, Springfield, Mass., U.S.A, 1965.)

April 17, 1842
Session met. Constituted with prayer. Members present; Jas. H. Gass, Wm. Rankin, Christopher Rankin, John Newman, and Richard Bradshaw and proceeded to examine and receive the following persons on profession of their faith in Christ. Viz. John Rankin Junr., Mary M. Rankin, Aron [Aaron] A. Newman, Patrick M. Rankin, Louisa Jane Rankin, Cathrine E. Hammel, Sarah M. Newman.
Concluded by prayer.   William Rankin

May 22, 1842
Session met and constituted with prayer. Members present. James H. Gass, Richard Bradshaw, John Newman, Christopher Rankin, & Wm. Rankin and after examining William Gass on experiential allegiance received him as a member
[Page 15] Concluded by prayer.   Wm. Rankin, Ck.

October 9th 1842
Session met. Constituted with prayer. Members present Jas. H. Gass, Wm. Rankin, Richard Bradshaw, Christopher Rankin and John Newman
  and examined Susan Rankin on experiental religion after which they received her as a member.
Concluded by prayer.   Wm. Rankin, Ck.

October 11, 1842
Session met. Constituted with prayer. Members present James H. Gass, Richard Bradshaw, Wm. Rankin, John Newman & Christopher Rankin
  and examined the following persons on experiential religion, viz. After which they were received as members, viz. John D. Morrow, Plesant Vance, Wm. J. J. Blackburn, Julia A. A. Edgan, Pearson Blackburn, and Julia Edgan went to Hopewell church.
Concluded by prayer.   Wm. Rankin, Ck.

[Page 16] October 12, 1842
Session met. Constituted by prayer. Members present Jas. H. Gass, Richard Bradshaw, William Rankin, Christopher Rankin & John Newman
  and examined and received as members on profession of their faith in Christ the following persons, viz. Aron [Aaron] A. Hammel, Mary Newman, Phebe Ann Eliza Biddle, and Jane Rankin. Miss Biddle went to Westminster Church.
Concluded by prayer.   Wm. Rankin, Ck.

October 13, 1842
Session Met. Constituted by prayer. Members present: Jas. H. Gass, Richard Bradshaw, Wm. Rankin, Christopher Rankin, John Newman
  and examined Rebecca Ann Jacobs, Nancy Ann Gass, John W. Bettas on experimental religion after which they received them as members.
Concluded by prayer.   Wm. Rankin, Ck.

October 14, 1842
Session met. Constituted with prayer. Members present Jas. H. Gass, Richard Bradshaw, Wm. Rankin, Christopher [Page 17] Rankin and John Newman and received on examination the following persons, viz. Jesse A. Newman, Samuel B. [Blair] Newman, Andrew C. Newman, Andrew P. Newman, Samuel T. [Thomas] Bettas, Albert M. Newman, Thomas W. Vance.
Concluded by prayer.   Wm Rankin, Ck.

October 15, 1842
Session met. Constituted with prayer. Members present. Jas. H. Gass, Wm. Rankin, Richard Bradshaw, Christopher Rankin, John Newman and examined on experimental religion Finly Childers & Charles C. Newman after which they were received as members. Childers was transferred to New Market church.
Concluded with prayer.   Wm. Rankin, Ck.

October 16, 1842
Session met. Constituted by prayer. Members present. James H. Gass, Wm. Rankin, Richard Bradshaw, Jn. Newman and Christopher Rankin and examined an experimental religion James Cox and his wife Rachel Cox and David Barbee. After which they received them as members.
Concluded by prayer.   Wm. Rankin, Ck.

[Page 18] November 5, 1843
Session met. Constituted by prayer. Members present. [Rev.] Jas. H. Gass, Richard Bradshaw, John Newman, Christopher Rankin and examined Mary Jane McCuistion on experimental religion after which they received her as a member.
Concluded by prayer.   Wm. Rankin, Ck.

New Market, Apl. 26, 1844
Examined and approved thus far.
Fielding Pope, Md., Moderator of Union Pbyr.

October 21st 1848
Session met. Members present Nathaniel Hood, Richard Bradshaw, John Newman, Christopher Rankin and William Rankin and examined Mary A. [Lockhart] Newman on experimental religion after which they received her as a member into the church.
                              William Rankin, Clerk

[Page 19] October 22nd 1848
Session met. Members present Nathaniel Hood, Richard Bradshaw, John Newman, Christopher Rankin & William Rankin and examined James E. Loyd on experimental religion after which they received as a member in the church.
                              William Rankin, Clerk

New Market. April 12, 1849
Examined, and approved thus far.
James H. Gass, Moderator of Union Presbytery

August 26th 1849
The Session met. Members present Nathaniel Hood, Richard Bradshaw, John Newman, Christopher Rankin & William Rankin and examined the following persons to wit Ann Franklin, Eglantine Isabella Newman, Elijah a man of colour, Vina and Hannah women of colour on experimental religion after which they were received as members in the church.

William Rankin, Clerk

[Page 20]
Eusebia Church, April 12, 1850
Examined and approved thus far, Nath'n Hood, Moderator of Union Presbytery

May 26th 1850
The session of Mount Horeb church met. Members present Nathaniel Hood, Richard Bradshaw, Christopher Rankin, John Newman and William Rankin and examined the following named persons on experimental religion after which they were received into the church as members. William Masengill sen,[80] Richard R. [Rawlings] Bradshaw, George G. Vance, Mary A. E. [Ann Emily] Kelly

William Rankin, Clerk

October 27th 1850
The Session of Mount Horeb church met. Members present Nathaniel Hood, Richard Bradshaw, John Newman, Christopher Rankin and William Rankin. And after considering on the standing of the church members made the following decisions to wit [page 21] whereas Susan P. Carson, Eliza P. Kimbrough, and Samuel T. Bettis having connected themselves with other churches are discontinued as member of Mount Horeb church. And whereas Pleasant Vance and David Barbie members of Mount Horeb church having discovered that they have no religion and having requested their membership to be discontinued. Therefore resolved that their request be granted.

William Rankin, Clerk

November 17th 1850
The Session of Mount Horeb church met members present Nathaniel Hood, Christopher Rankin, John Newman, Richard Bradshaw and William Rankin and examined Lydia J. [Lidea Jane] Newman and James H. Newman on experimental religion and being satisfied they have experienced a change of heart they were received as members into the church.

William Rankin, Clerk

---

[80] Sen. is the abbreviation for senior. Sr. is used in the indexing of this book.

November 14th 1850
The Session met present N. Hood, Rich'd Bradshaw and Christopher Rankin examined Eliz. Rankin and Margaret J. Malcom on experimental religion and received them into the church.

William Rankin, Clerk

[Page 22]
May 26th 1851
The Session of Mount Horeb church met members present Nathaniel Hood, Richard Bradshaw, John Newman, Christopher Rankin and William Rankin and on information received Charles T. Jolly, Robert P. Eaton and Eleanor C. Eaton into the church they having been previously examined by a called session on Holston river near the mouth of Panther Creek.

William Rankin,
Clerk

May 24th 1851
The Session of Mount Horeb church met members present Nathaniel Hood, John Newman, Richard Bradshaw, Christopher Rankin & William Rankin and examined Nancy J. Bradshaw, Emily W. Gass and Catharine E. [Emeline] Bradshaw on experimental religion after which they were received as members into the church.

William Rankin, Clerk

August 7th 1851
The Session of Mount Horeb met members present Nathaniel Hood, Christopher Rankin, John Newman, Richard Bradshaw and William Rankin and proceeded to examine the following persons on experimental religion after which they received them as members into the church. To wit. James T. Rankin and Florence Thomas.

William Rankin Ck.

[Page 23]
November 27th 1851
The members of Mount Horeb church met members present Nathaniel Hood, Richard Bradshaw, Christopher Rankin and John Newman and examined Lydia P. Bradshaw and Stephen R. [Roten] Bradshaw on experimental religion after which they received them as members into the church.

William Rankin, Clerk

Mount Horeb Church, Apl. 2, 1852
Examined and approved up to the present date.
John McCampbell,
Mod. of the Pres. of Union

[Page 24]

August 22nd 1852

The Session of Mount Horeb church met members present Nathaniel Hood, Richard Bradshaw, John Newman, Christopher Rankin and William Rankin and the session examined James H. Darr on experimental religion and he was received as a member into the church.

William Rankin, Clerk

Examined in Presbytery April 1, 1853 thus far & approved.
William Minnis, Mod.

November 20th 1853.

The Session of Mount Horeb church met members present Nathaniel Hood, John Newman, Richard Bradshaw, Christopher Rankin and William Rankin and they examined Sarah Newman on experimental religion and received her into the church.

William Rankin, Clerk

February 26th 1854

The session of Mount Horeb met members present Nathaniel Hood, Richard Bradshaw, Christopher Rankin and William Rankin and whereas the name of Dr. William P. Massengill through over sight or neglect has not been recorded as a member of the church & [Page 25] he having made a profession at St. Pauls church perhaps in October 1842. Resolved that his name be recorded back to correspond with the above date near as practicable.

William Rankin, Clerk

Examined & approved this for March 25, 1854.
G. S. White, Mod. of Pby. of Union

April 9th 1854

The Session of Mount Horeb church met members present Nathaniel Hood Moderator, John Newman, Christopher Rankin, Richard Bradshaw and William Rankin and proceeded to examine and received into the church the following named persons. Viz. Mary D. Bradshaw, Martha A. Bradshaw, William H. Lyle, John F. [Franklin] Newman, Martha M. Newman, Nancy E. Rankin and Mary E. Rankin.

William Rankin, Clerk

October 4th 1854

The Session of Mount Horeb met members present Nathaniel Hood moderator, John Newman, Richard Bradshaw and Christopher Rankin and examined the following persons on experimental religion and received them into the church Elizabeth C. Rankin, Frances J. [Jane] Berry, David G. [George] Newman & Tabitha a woman of colour.

William Rankin, Clerk

[Page 26] Thus far examined & approved with the exception specified.
March 29, 1855, G. S. Whtle, Mod'r of Pres.

September 2nd 1855
The session of Mount Horeb church met members present Nathaniel Hood moderator, John Newman, Christopher Rankin and William Rankin and constituted by prayer and examined Nancy E. Rankin on experimental religion and received her as a member of the church. Concluded by prayer.
                                         William Rankin, Clerk

March 22nd 1856
The Session of Mount Horeb church met and constituted with prayer
present Reverend Nathaniel Hood, Moderator, Elders: Richard Bradshaw, John Newman, William Rankin, Christopher Rankin
By motion William Rankin was appointed a member to presbytery to meet in Washington church on the 4th day of April next. [page 27] Miss Margaret J. Malcom being charged by common fame of improper conduct that is the breach of the Seventh commandment and it appearing to the satisfaction of the Session that the charge is true. Therefore Resolved that Miss Margaret J. Malcom be and hereby is suspended from all the privileges of the church untill the charge be fully investigated. Concluded with prayer.   William Rankin, Clerk

Washington Ch. Apr. 5th 1856
Examined and approved thus far.
Nath'l Hood, Mod'r

August 31st 1856
The Session of Mount Horeb church met members present. Nathaniel Hood Moderator, Richard Bradshaw, Christopher Rankin, John Newman, and William Rankin. Examined Mary J. Rankin on Experimental religion after which they received her into the church as a member.
                                         William Rankin, Clerk

Examined & approved thus far.
Wm. Minnis, Mod'r

[Page 28] May 3rd 1857
The Session of Mount Horeb church met and constituted by prayer members present Nathaniel Hood Moderator, John Newman, Richard Bradshaw, Christopher Rankin and William Rankin and Examined Delila Rimmer on experimental religion and received her as a member into the church and concluded by prayer.
                                         William Rankin, Ck.

May 30th 1857

The Session of Mount Horeb church met members present Nathaniel Hood Moderator, Richard Bradshaw, Christopher Rankin, John Newman and William Rankin and constituted by prayer and examined the following persons in the faith in Christ and received them into the church. Viz. Cadelia [Cordelia] F. Mountcastle and Andrew T. Gass. Concluded by prayer.   William Rankin

January 16th 1858

The session of Mount Horeb met and constituted by prayer. Members present Nathaniel Hood moderator, John Newman and Richard Bradshaw and examined the following persons on experimental religion and received them into the church that is David C. Cockenour, Gideon W. Newman, Sarah C. Zirkle, [Page 29] Orlena E. Bradshaw, Edward A. Bradshaw, William M. Bradshaw, Samuel E. Rankin, Margaret A. Jolly and Mary E. Jolly. Concluded by prayer.
William Rankin Clerk

January 17th 1858

The Session of Mount Horeb church met and constituted by prayer members present Nathaniel Hood moderator, William Rankin, Richard Bradshaw and John Newman and examined the following persons on experimental religion and received into the church as members that is Harriet J. Bradshaw, Sarah J. [Jane] Alexander, Sarah J. Rankin, Mary A. Rankin, John Mc. Rankin, John Rankin, Daniel H. Bradshaw, John C. Rankin, Lydia J. Zirkle, Ellen L. Rankin, Isabella E. Newman, Isabella Rankin, Samuel McMurry, Mark T. Rankin, John F. [Fain] Rankin and Mary H. Hood and concluded with prayer. Mary H. Hood fell to Hopewell church.
William Rankin Clerk

January 14th 1858

The Session of Mount Horeb church met and constituted by prayer members present Nathaniel Hood moderator, Richard Bradshaw, William [Page 30] Rankin, John Newman and examined the following persons on experimental religion Viz. Albert M. Meadows, John J. Newman, Thomas J. Bradshaw, William Rankin, James A. Barby, Mary A. C. Newman, John G. [Gass] Rankin, Thomas P. Franklin, Daniel Meadows, Margaret J. Newman, Margaret E. Rankin and received them into the church. Concluded by prayer.   William Rankin Clerk

January 19th 1858

The Session of Mount Horeb church met and constituted by prayer members present Nathaniel Hood moderator, John Newman and William Rankin and examined Mary E. Cline, Darthula J. Bettis, Margaret S. Newman, George W. Newman Jr. and Minerva A. Newman on the profession of their faith in Christ and received them into the church and concluded by prayer.
William Rankin, Clerk

January 20th 1858
The Session of Mount Horeb church met and constituted with prayer members present Nathaniel Hood moderator, John Newman and William Rankin and proceeded to examine the following persons on experimental religion and received them into the church [Page 31] that is Elizabeth C. Rankin, Joseph H. Cline, Mary A. Cline, George W. Newman sen., Daniel L. [Lyle] Bettis, Hugh A. [Alexander] Newman, Richard A. Newman, Henry O. Newman, Silas J. A. [John Anderson] Newman, Patrick L. [Lafayette] Newman, William F. Newman, John W. Newman, Samuel H. Franklin and William T. Rankin concluded by prayer.   William Rankin Clk.

January 21st 1858
The Session of Mount Horeb church met and constituted by prayer member present Nathaniel Hood moderator, William Rankin, John Newman and Richard Bradshaw and examined the following persons on experimental religion and received them into the church Viz. Martha E. Newman, Campbell Franklin, Joseph W. Shadden, Rachel L. Sheddan, Matilda E. [Elizabeth] Newman, Martha J. Rankin concluded by prayer.
William Rankin Clerk

January 22nd 1858
The Session of Mount Horeb met and constituted by prayer members present Nathaniel Hood moderator, Richard Bradshaw, William Rankin and John Newman and examined the following [Page 33] the following persons on experimental religion and received them as members of the church Viz. Thomas C. Lyle, William A. Bowers, Jonathan L. Newman, Pleasant J. [Jackson] Bettis, Mary S. Zirkle, George A. [Adam] Zirkle concluded with prayer.
William Rankin, Clerk

January 23nd 1858
The Session of Mount Horeb met and constituted by prayer members present Nathaniel Hood moderator, William Rankin, Richard Bradshaw, and John Newman and proceeded to examine as to their faith in Christ and on their faith received them as members into the church Viz. Sarah A. Rankin, Laura A. Franklin, Anderson a man of colour. Concluded with prayer.
William Rankin, Clerk

January 24th 1858
The Session of Mount Horeb church met members present Nathaniel Hood Moderator, John Newman, Richard Bradshaw and William Rankin and constituted with prayer and examined on experimental religion and received them into the church Viz. Maddison (sic) Newman, John V. Richards, Senora [Page 33] E. Shadden, Nancy C. Lyle, Sarah A. Vance, Mary E. Newman, Thomas C. Shadden, William H. Newman, Alexander Rimmer, John Talbott and Benjamine C. [Casper] Newman concluded by prayer.   William Rankin Ck.

February 21st 1858
The Session of Mount Horeb church met and constituted by prayer members present Nathaniel Hood moderator, Richard Bradshaw, John Newman and William Rankin and examined the following persons on experimental religion and received them into the church that is Mary [Louise] Lyle and David C. Gass concluded by prayer
William Rankin Ck.

March 21st 1858
The Session of Mount Horeb church met and constituted by prayer members present Nathaniel Hood moderator, Richard Bradshaw, Christopher Rankin and John Newman and proceeded to examine Thomas Newman on experimental religion after which they received him into the church as a member. Concluded by prayer
William Rankin
Clerk

Examined & approved.
Rockford, March 27, 1858,
F. [Fielding] Pope, Mod. Pby. of Union

[Page 34]
September 19th 1858
The Session of Mount Horeb church met and constituted by prayer. Members present Nathaniel Hood moderator, Richard Bradshaw, John Newman, Christopher Rankin, Elias Alexander, Patrick M. Rankin, Joseph C. Bradshaw, and William Rankin and Examined Martha J. Newman and Nancy J. Newman on experimental religion and received them into the church concluded by prayer.
William Rankin,
Stated clerk

April 2nd 1859
The Session of Mount Horeb church met members present Nathaniel Hood Moderator, John Newman, Patrick M. Rankin, Elias Alexander, William Rankin, Joseph C. Bradshaw and Christopher Rankin. Whereas Elizabeth Newman and Louisa H. Newman, having left our church and connected themselves with the Baptist church, Resolved that their names be dropped as members of Mount Horeb church. Further that Thomas R. [Rankin] Bradshaw's name be dropped he being a minister of the gospel.
William Rankin, Clerk

[Page 354]
Examined & approved thus far. April 16, 1859
Wm. Minnis, Moderator

September 4th 1859

The Session of Mount Horeb church met and constituted by prayer members present Nathaniel Hood moderator, John Newman, Christopher Rankin, Elias Alexander, Joseph C. Bradshaw, Patrick H. Rankin and William Rankin and examined Harriet Malinda Rankin on Experimental religion after which they received her as a member into the church concluded by prayer.

William Rankin, Clerk

Examined & approved thus far
St. Pauls Ch., April 13, 1860
C. C. Newman Mod.

[Blank from page 36 to 177]

[Page 178]

History of Mount Horeb Church

Mount Horeb church in Jefferson County Tenn. was organized by the Rev. John McCampbell, he acting by order of Union Presbytery on the 20th day of November AD 1841 By ordaining four elders viz. Richard Bradshaw, William Rankin [Sr.], Christopher Rankin and John Newman Jun'r. There were 67 members taken from Hopewell and New Market churches. The Rev. James H Gass was chosen their minister and continued to have charge of said church for five years as stated supply. When the Rev. Mr. Gass left, the Rev. Nathaniel Hood has had the charge of the church as stated supply minister and part of the time by the Rev. Nathaniel Harrison. They state further that in the year 1858 in month of April Joseph C. Bradshaw, Elias Alexander and Patrick M. Rankin were elected and ordained as additional elders in the church.

April 7th 1860

William Rankin Ck.

[See copy of original in photo section, Original Documents.]

Membership Roll

Form No. 1st

Name	When received	How received	Baptized	Dismis-sed	Sus-pended	Excom-muni-cated	Restor-ed	Died
Moses Easterly	March 20, 1842	On exam	In infancy					
Margery Rankin	April 15, 1842	On exam	Adult					
Mary B. Easterly	March 20, 1842	By letter						
Eunice Bowles	April 16, 1842	By letter						
Thomas Rankin Jr.	April 17, 1842	By exam	In Infancy					
Mary M. Rankin	Do	Do [81]	Do					
P. M. [Patrick McGuire] Rankin	Do	Do	Do					
Aron A. Newman	Do	Do	Do					
Louisa J. Rankin	Do	Do	Adult					
Catherine C. Hammel	Do	Do	Apr. 17, 1842					
Sarah M. Newman	Do	Do	Do					
Wm. Gass	May 22, 1842	Do	May 22, 1842					
Susan Rankin	October 9, 1842	Do	Octo. 9, 1842					
Plesant Vance	[Oct] 11, 1842	Do	Octo. 11, 1842					
[Dr.] William P. Massengill (inserted)	October 11, 1842	By certificate						
Aron A. Hammel	[Oct] 12, 1842	Do	[Oct] 12, 1842					
Mary Newman	Do	Do	Do					
Jane Rankin	Do	Do	In infancy					
Rebecca A. Jacobs	Octo. 13, 1842	Do	Do					
Nancy Ann Gass	Do	Do	Do					
John W. Bettas	Do	Do	Adult					
Jesse A. Newman	Oct. 14, 1842	Do	Oct. 14, 1842					
Saml. B. [Blair] Newman	Do	Do	Infancy					
Saml. L. Bettas	Do	Do	Oct. 14, 1842					

---

[81] "Do" is abbreviation used for Ditto.

[Pages 194-195]   No. 1st

Name	When received	How received	Baptized	Dismis-sed	Sus-pend-ed	Ex-com-muni-cated	Restored or Died
Andrew C. [Carroll] Newman	Oct. 14 1842	On exam-ination	In infancy				
Andrew P. Newman	Do	Do	Do				
Albert M. Newman	Do	Do	Do				
Thomas W. Vance	Do	Do	Oct. 14, 1842				
Charles C. [Coffman] Newman	Oct. 15, 1842	Do	In infancy				
James Cox	Oct. 16, 1842	Do	Oct. 16, 1842				
Rachel Cox	Do	Do	Do				
David Barbee	Do	Do	Do				
Elizabeth McCuistion	Novem'r 8th 1842	By letter					
Mary J. McCuistion	Nov. 5, 1843	On exam-ination	Nov. 5, 1843				
Moses Easterly and Elizabeth Easterly	June 18th 1844			By letter			
Berry Mitchell[82] and Elizabeth Mitchell	Nov. 15th 1844			By letter			
Isabella Newman, now Malcom [Mrs. Alexander R.][83]	Novem 4th 1844			By letter			
Elisa Newman	May 2nd 1846	By Letter					
Jane Rankin	January 17th 1846			Dismis-sed			By death
Lucinda Rankin	June 14th 1846			Dismis-sed			Died
Katherine E. Loyd late Hamill [Mrs. James E. Loyd][84]	April 27th 1847			By Letter			
Rebecca A. Jacobs	May 9th 1847			By letter			
Mary E. Bettis and Sarah M. Bettis now Mary & Sarah Coil	May 16th 1847			By letter			
Margaret Bradshaw				died			May 28th 1847
Aaron B. [Bogue] Rankin	Novem'r 28, 1847			By letter			
Margery [Lockhart] Rankin	Novem'r 28, 1847			By letter			

[82] This may be Berry or Benjamin Mitchell. It is very difficult to read in the original book.

[83] Virginia Carlisle d'Armand, *Jefferson County Marriages Records 1792-1870*, TN, Knoxville, 1983, p. 174.

[84] Ibid., page 95.

Eunice Bowls	Jan 2, 1848			By letter			
Mary A. [Lockhart] Newman	October 21st 1848	On exam-ination	By immersion in Baptist church				

[Pages 196-197]
Form No. 1

Name	When received	How received	Baptized	Dismis-sed	Sus-pended	Excom-muni-cated	Restored or Died
James E. Loyd	October 22nd 1848	Examina-tion	In Infancy				
James Cox and Rachel Cox	October 1st 1848			By letter			
Thomas Rankin	August 13th 1849						Died
James H. Hamel	Sept 30th 1849			By letter			
Elizabeth Hamel	Do			By Do			
Aaron A. Hammel	Do			By Do			
Mary A. [Ann] Hammel	Do			By Do			
James E. Loyd	Do			By Do			
Ann Franklin	August 26th 1849	Examina-tion	In Infancy				
Eglantine Annabelle Newman	Do	Do	In Do				
Hannah of colour	Do	Do	In Do				
Vina of colour	Do	Do	Adult				
Elijah of colour	Do	Do	Adult				
Thomas Jacobs	May 26th 1850	By letter					
Elizabeth Jacobs	Do	Do					
Rebecca A. Jacobs	Do	Do					
William Masengill	May 26th 1850	Examina-tion	Adult				
Richard R. [Rawlings] Bradshaw	Do	Do					
George G. Vance	Do	Do					
Mary Ann Emily Kelly	Do	Do	In Infancy				
Julyann Rankin	August 4th 1850	By letter					
George W. Wright	August 28th 1850	By letter					
James McCuistion	August 26th 1850			By letter			

Pages 198-199]

Name	When received	How received	Baptized	Dismissed	Suspended	Excommunicated or restored	Restored or Died
Susan P. Carson	October 27th 1850				Suspended		
Eliza T. Kimbrough	Do				Do		
Samuel T. Bettis	Do				Do		
Pleasant Vance	Do				Do		
David Barbee	Do				Do		
Lydia J. Newman	November 17th 1850	On examination	In Infancy				
James H. Newman	Do	Do	Do				
Eliza Rankin	November 18th 1850	Do	Do				
Margaret J. Malcom	Do	Do	Do				
Lydia P. Bradshaw	Nov. 27th 1851	On examination	In Infancy				
Stephen R. [Roten] Bradshaw	Do	On Do	In Do				
James T. Rankin	September 7th 1851	On examination	In Infancy				
Florence Thomas	Do	On Do	Adult				
Nancy J. Bradshaw	Sept 8th 1851	On Examination	In Infancy				
Emily W. Gass	Do	On Do	In Do				
Catharine E. Bradshaw Catharine Emiline Bradshaw	Do	On Do	In Do				
Robert P. Eaton	May 17th 1851	On Examination	In Infancy				
Charles T. Jolly	Do	On Do	In Do				
Eleanor C. Eaton	Do	On Do	In Do				
George W. Right [Wright]				Died			October 24th 1857
William Masengill				Died			June 17th 1852
James H. Darr	August 22, 1852	On Examination	Adult				
John C. Newman				By letter Oct 10, 1852			
Elisa Newman				By Do			
Mary Newman				By Do			
Elisa H. Newman				By Do			
Sarah M. Newman				By Do			

[Pages 200-201]

Name	When received	How received	Baptized	Dismissed	Sus-pended	Excom-municated or restored	Restored or Died
Adaline Gass	Septem'r 26th 1852	By letter					
Mary A. E. [Ann Emily] Kelly				Died			July 12th 1853
Polly Ann McMurray	May 10th 1852	By letter					
Lydia Bradshaw				Died			October 20th 18 __ 85
Sarah Newman	Nov. 20th 1853	On Exam-ination					
Aaron Newman and Cassander [sic] [Branner] Newman his wife				Mar 14 1852 joined new church at Tuckahoe			
Elias Alexander	April 9th 1854	Certifi-cate					
Joseph A. Malcom	April 9th 1854	By Do					
Mary W. Malcom	April 9th 1854	By Do					
Mary D. Bradshaw	April 9th 1854	Exam-ination	In infancy				
Martha A. Bradshaw	Do	On Do	In Do				
William H. Lyle	Do	On Do	In Do				
John F. [Franklin] Newman	Do	On Do	In Do				
Martha M. [Gilbraith] Newman	Do	On Do	In Do				
Nancy E. Rankin	Do	On Do	In Do				
Mary E. Rankin	Do	On Do	In Do				
Elizabeth C. Rankin	Oct 8th 1854	Exam-ination	Infancy				
Frances J. Berry	Do	On Do	In Do				
David G. Newman	Do	On Do	In Do				
Isabella of colour	Do	On Do	Adult				
David Ashmore	July 16th 1854	Certifi-cate					
Polly Ashmore	Do	By Do					
Harriet Ashmore	Do	By Do					
Joseph A. Malcom				Died			March 7, 1855

---

[85] Impossible to read in Minute Book 1.

[Pages 202-203]

Name	When received	How received	Baptized	Dis-missed	Suspend-ed	Excom-municated or restored	Restored or Died
John Patton	May 6th 1855	Certifi-cate					
Edy Patton	May 6th 1855	Certifi-cate					
Nancy E. Rankin	Septem'r 2nd 1855	Examina-tion	In Infancy				
Magaret J. Malcom					Mar 22nd 1856		
William P. Massengill				July 7th 1856			
Aaron B. Rankin	July 6th 185[6]	On Cer-tificate					
Marjora [Lockhart] Rankin	July 6th 1856	On Do					
Samuel Funk	August 3rd 1856	On Do					
Elizabeth Funk	August 3rd 1856	On Do					
Susan Zirkle	August 17th 1856	On Do					
Mary J. Rankin	August 31st 1856	Exam-ination	Adult				
Andrew T. Gass	May 30th 1857	Exam-ination	In Infancy				
Alexander Rankin	May 24, 1857	Exam-ination	In Infancy				
Delila Rimmor	May3rd 1857	Exam-ination	In Infancy				
Cadelia [Cordelia] F. *Mountcastle*	May 30th 1857	Exam-ination	Adult				
Isabella E. McGuire	May 10th 1857			On cer-tificate			
Margaret Newman				Aug 19, 1857			Died
Lydia J. Newman				Oct 5th 1857			Died[86]
Delila Remmer				Dec 28th 1857			Died
David C. Cockenour	Jan 16th 1858	Exami-nation	Adult				
Gideon W. Newman	Do	Do	In Infancy				
Sarah C. Zirkle	Do	Do	Do				

---

[86] Lydia J. Newman died Oct. 28, 1857, *Find A Grave*, http://www.findagrave.com/cgi-bin/fg.cgi.

Orlena E. Bradshaw	Do	Do	Do					
Edward A. Bradshaw	Do	Do	Do					
William M. [Minnis] Bradshaw	Do	Do	Do					
Samuel E. [Edwin] Rankin	Do	Do	Do					

[Pages 204-205]
Form No. 1

Name	When received	How received	Baptiz-ed	Dismis-sed	Suspend-ed	Excom-municated or restored	Restored or Died
Margaret A. Jolly	Jan 16th 1858	Exam-ination	In Infancy				
Mary E. Jolly	Do	Do	Do				
Harriet J. Bradshaw	Jan 17th 1858	Do	Do				
Sarah J. [Jane] Alexander	Do	Do	Do				
Sarah J. Rankin	Do	Do	Do				
Mary A. Rankin	Do	Do	Do				
John Mc. Rankin	Do	Do	Do				
John Rankin	Do	Do	Do				
Daniel H. Bradshaw	Do	Do	Do				
John C. Rankin	Do	Do	Do				
Lydia J. Zirkle	Do	Do	Do				
Ellen L. Rankin	Do	Do	Do				
Isabella E. Newman	Do	Do	Do				
Isabella Rankin	Do	Do	Do				
Samuel McMurry	Do	Do	Do				
Mark T. Rankin	Do	Do	Do				
John F. Rankin	Do	Do	Do				
Albert M. Medows	Jan 14, 1858	Exam-ination	Adult				
John J. Newman	Do	Do	Do				
Thomas J. Bradshaw	Do	Do	In Infancy				
William Rankin [Jr.]	Do	Do	Do				
James A. Barby	Do	Do	Adult				
Mary A. C. Newman	Do	Do	Do				

[Pages 204 a & b inserted pages]

Name	When received	How received	Baptized	Dismissed.	Sus-pen-ded	Excom-municated or restored	Restored or Died
Elizabeth W. Bradshaw				January 14, 1860			Died
Rufus E. Carson	June 5th 1861	On cer-tificate					
Harriet D. Carson	June 5th 1861	On cer-tificate					
John H. Franklin				July 27th 1861			Died
George W. Newman				July 28th 1861			Died
Elizabeth Franklin				Septem'r 17th 1861			Died
John Jolly	At Dripping Springs	Exam-ination					
William Rankin [Jr.]				Died			May 29, 1862
Aaron Newman				Died			June 11th 1862
Harriett Malinda Rankin				Died			June 12th 1862
Adeline Gass				Died			July 1862
Joseph McCuistion				Died			December 24th 1862
Richard H. [Harden] Bradshaw				Died			Dec 31st 1862 [Jan 7 or 17, 1863][87]
Jane [Rawlings] Bradshaw				Died			[Feb. 14. 1863][88]
Orlena E. Bradshaw				Died			April [7] 1863

[Pages 204 c & d inserted pages]

Name	When received	How received	Baptized	Dismis-sed	Sus-pended	Excom-municated or restored	Restored or Died
John G. Rankin	Jan 18th, 1858	Exam-ination	In Infancy				
Thomas P. Rankin	Do	Do	Do				
Daniel Medows	Do	Do	Adult				
Margaret J. Newman	Do	Do	Do				
Margaret E. Rankin	Do	Do	In Infancy				
Barsheba W. Talbott	January 17th 1858	On Cer-tificate					
Mary E. Cline	Jan 19th 1858	Exam-ination	In Infancy				
Darthula J. Bettis	Do	Do	Adult				

---

[87] *Find A Grave.* Find A Grave. http://www.findagrave.com/cgi-bin/fg.cgi
[88] Ibid.

Margaret S. Newman	Do	Do	Do				
George W. Newman, Junr	Do	Do	In Infancy				
Minerva A. Newman	Do	Do	Adult				
Elizabeth C. Rankin	Jan 20th 1858	Examination	In Infancy	-			
Joseph [Henry] Cline	Do	Do	Do				
Mary A. [Ann Sina Newman] Cline	Do	Do	Do				
George W. Newman Sen	Do	Do	Do				
Hugh A. Newman	Do	Do	Do				
Daniel L. Bettis	Do	Do	Adult				
Richard A. Newman	Do	Do	Do				
Henry O. Newman	Do	Do	Do				
Silas J. A. [Silas Anderson] Newman	Do	Do	Infancy				
Patrick L. Newman	Do	Do	Do				
William F. Newman	Do	Do	Do				
William T. Rankin	Do	Do	Do				
John W. Newman	Do	Do	Adult				
Samuel H. Franklin	Do	Do	Do				
Martha E. Newman	Jan 21st 1858	Examination	Adult				
Campbell Franklin	Do	Do	Do				
Joseph W. Shadden	Do	Do	Do				
Rachel L. Shadden	Do	Do	Do				
Matilda E. Newman	Do	Do	In Infancy				
Martha J. Rankin	Do	Do	Do				
Thomas C. Lyle	January 22nd 1858	Examination	Adult				
William A. Bowers	Do	Do	Do				
Pleasant J. Bettis	Do	Do	Do				
Nancy Ann Alexander	Jan 22nd 1858			Certificate			

[Pages 204 e & f inserted pages]

Name	When received	How received	Baptized	Dismissed	Suspended	Excommunicated or restored	Restored or Died
Jonathan L. Newman	Jan 22nd 1858	Examination	In Infancy				
Mary S. Zirkle	Do	Do	Do				
George A. [Adam] Zirkle	Do	Do	Do				
Sarah A. Rankin	Jan 23rd 1858	On Examination	In Infancy				
Laura A. Franklin	Do	Do	Adult				

Anderson a man of colour	Do	Do	Do				
Madison Newman	Jan 24th 1858	Exam-ination	In Infancy				
John V. Richards	Do	Do	Do				
Senora E. Shadden	Do	Do	Do				
Benjamin C. Newman	Do	Do	Do				
Nancy C. Lyle	Do	Do	Adult				
Sarah A. Vance	Do	Do	Do				
Mary E. Newman	Do	Do	Do				
Thomas C. Shadden	Do	Do	Do				
William H. Newman	Do	Do	Do				
Alexander Rimmer	Do	Do	Do				
John Talbott	Do	Do	Do				
Mary [Louise] Lyle	February 21st 1858	Exam-ination	Adult				
David C. Gass	Do	Do	In Infancy				
Nancy Ann Alexander			Jan 22nd 1858				
Thomas Newman	March 21 1858	Do	In Do				
William P. Massengill	September 5, 1858	Certifi-cate					
Martha J. Newman	September 19th 1858	Examina-tion	Adult				
Nancy J. Newman	September 19th 1858	Examina-tion	In Infancy				
Andrew P. Newman				Oct 31st 1858			
Manerva A. Newman				Oct 31st 1858			
Robert P. Eaton				March 6th 1859			
Nancy C. Hood				April 2nd 1859			
Thomas R. [Rankin] Bradshaw				April 2nd 1859			
Elizabeth Newman				April 2nd 1859			
Louisa H. Newman				April 2nd 1859			
Erasmus H.[Harvey] Cline	July 17th 1859	Certifi-cate					
Juliet E. [Emily] Cline	July 17th 1859	Certifi-cate					
Phebe A. Armintrout	July 17th 1859	Certifi-cate					
Harriet Malinda Rankin	September 4th 1859	Examina-tion					

[Pages 206-207]
Form No. 2

Children Baptized

Name	Born	Baptized	Presented by whom
May 1, 1842			
Hariet Eliza Gass	March 17, 1841	May 1, 1842	By [Rev.] J. H. [James] & Malinda [Blackburn] Gass
Edward Alex'r Bradshaw	Nov'r 7, 1841	Do	Joseph C. & Sarah [Grizzle Blackburn] Bradshaw
Benjamin Casper Newman	Oct. 30, 1841	Do	Aron [Aaron] & Casandra [Branner] Newman
Mary Jane Rankin	Nov. 29, 1841	Do	Aran B. [Aaron Bogue] & Margery [Marjary Copin Lockhart] Rankin
Mary Elizabeth Pasterly	Nov. 14, 1842	Do	Moses Pasterly & wife Mary
George Washington Newman	Sept. 4, 1839	Do	Mary [Ann Nicholson] Newman
Silas John Anderson Newman	Nov. 8, 1841	Do	Wm. M. [Milton] Newman & wife Mahulda [Henry]
Wm. Thomas Rankin	Sep. 26, 1849 (1839? in pencil)	Do	Josiah E. Rankin & wife [Mary Emma Gass]
Nancy Emily Rankin	Decb. 21, 1841	Do	Do
May 22, 1842			
John [Patrick "Pad"] Rankin	Jan. 7, 1842	May 22, 1842	P. M. [Patrick McGuire] Rankin & wife Jane [Louisa Jane Lockhart]
John Rankin Franklin	Jan. 24, 1842	Do	Benjamin F. [Francis] Franklin & wife Hariet
Isaac Nelson Rankin	Dec. 18, 1837	Do	James [Eaton] Rankin
Elizabeth Catherine "Kate" Rankin	May 12, 1839	Do	Do
Wm. Erskine Rankin	Aug 'st 14, 1841	Do	Do
David Rankin	Aug'st 26, 1842	Oct. 2, 1842	R. D. Rankin & wife Mary [Mary Ann Carol Woods]
Wm. Mathew Cox	July 7, 1840	Oct. 16, 1842	Jas. Cox & wife Rachel
Mary Ann Cox	Feb. 15, 1842	Do	Do
Martha Jane Rankin	Sep. 19, 1842	Nov. 14, 1842	Christopher Rankin & wife Frances [George Galbraith] Rankin
John Douglas Cox	Feb. 12, 1839	Dec. 30, 1842	Jan's Cox & wife Rachel
Hariet Jane Bradshaw	April 8 1843	Sep. 4, 1843	Richard H. [Harden] Bradshaw & wife Jane [Jane P. Rawlings]
Thomas Patrick Franklin	May 30, 1843	Nov. 6, 1843	B. F. Franklin [Benjamin Francis] & wife Hariet [Lucinda Harriet Rankin]

[Pages 208-209]   No. 2

Name	Born	Baptized	Presented by whom
Nancy Rankin	March 15, 1843	November 5, 1843	Aron B. [Aaron Bogue]& Margery Rankin
Joseph Reece Bradshaw	November 1st 1843	May 6th 1844	John P. [Prigmore] & Elizabeth W. [Rawlings] Bradshaw
Orlena Eglentine [Clementine] Bradshaw	October 2nd 1843	Do	Thomas R. [Rankin] & Margaret Blackburn Bradshaw
Arthur Alexander Newman	September 1st 1843	Do	Aaron & Cassandra [Branner] Newman
William Rankin [Jr.]	November 12th 1843	Do	William & Susan [Kimbrough] Rankin
Theodora Frelingeuysen Gass	[not given]	September 2nd 1844	[Rev.] James H & Malinda Gass
Nancy Jane Newman	March 17th 1844	Do	Mary Ann Newman
Mary Ann Rankin	April 28th 1844	Do	Christopher & Frances [George Galbraith] Rankin
John Gass Rankin	November 28th 1843	Do	Josiah E. & Mary M. [Emma Gass] Rankin
Isabella Rankin	September 12th 1844	November 4th 1844	Richard D. & Mary A. [Ann Carol Woods] Rankin
Mary Ann Rankin	June 1st 1843	May 5th 1845	Patrick M. [McGuire] & Louisa J. [Lockhart] Rankin
Sarah Jane Rankin	November 30th 1844	Do	Patrick M. [McGuire] & Louisa J. [Lockhart] Rankin
William Minnis Bradshaw	August 20th 1844	Do	Joseph C. & Sarah G. [Grizzle Blackburn] Bradshaw
Daniel Hardin Bradshaw	July 12th 1845	September 21st 1845	John P. & Elizabeth W. Bradshaw & Elizabeth W. [Rawlings] Bradshaw
Lydia Timanda Bradshaw	December 11th 1844	October 5th 1845	Richard H. [Harden] & Jane [P. Rawlings] Bradshaw
Hugh Alexander Newman	November 19th 1843	May 4th 1846	William M. [Milton] & Mahulda [Henry] Newman
James Anthony Newman	December 26th 1845	Do	Do
John Calvin Rankin	February 23rd 1844	Do	James [Eaton] Rankin
Alexander Porter Rankin	November 12th 1845	Do	William & Susan [Kimbrough] Rankin
Sarah Malinda Rankin	April 7th 1846	June 14th 1846	Christopher & Francis [George Galbraith] Ranki
Isabella Elizabeth Newman	May 2nd 1846	July 5th 1846	James & Isabella Newman
Ellen Leander Rankin	November 23rd 1845	September 7th 1846	Josiah E. Rankin & Mary M. [Emma Gass] Rankin
Benjamin [Francis] Franklin, [Jr.]	June 30th 1845	September 7th 1846	Benjamin F. [Francis] & Lucinda H. Franklin
Elizabeth Clindinon Rankin	October 30th 1846	December 20th 1846	Richard D. & Mary A. [Ann Carol Woods] Rankin

Sarah Elizabeth Bradshaw	September 2nd 1846	April 25th 1847	Richard H. [Harden] & Jane P. [Rawlings] Bradshaw
Lydia Jane Zirkle	March 5th 1843 [Feb. 5, 1844][89]	Do	Benjamin & Susan [Susannah Ruth Pennywitt] Zirkle
George Adam Zirkle	March 12, 1846	Do	Do

[Pages 210-211]   No. 2

Name	Born	Baptized	Presented by whom
John Calvin Bradshaw	January 9th 1848	April 30th 1848	Joseph C. Bradshaw & wife [Sarah Grizzle Blackburn]
Frances Leanna Rankin	September 14th 1847	April 30th 1848	Christopher Rankin & wife [Frances George Galbraith]
William Porter Masengill Bradshaw	October 15th 1847	September 10th 1848	John P. Bradshaw & wife [Elizabeth W. Rawlings]
Sarah Amanda Rankin	September 15th 1847	October 23rd 1848	James [Eaton] Rankin
Harvey Anderson Rankin	January 5th 1848	Do	James [Eaton] Rankin
Margaret Elizabeth Jane Newman	April 14th 1848	Do	William M. Newman & wife Mahulda [Henry]
Sarah Aminda Carolina Campbell Rankin	January 2, 1849	February 25th 1849	Richard D. Rankin & wife [Mary Ann Carol Woods]
Sarah Isabella Sinea Newman	January 24th 1849	April 30th 1849	Joseph R. [Reece] Newman & wife [Mary A. Lockhart]
Maria Elizabeth Newman	November 7th 1845	August 27th 1849	Aaron Newman & wife [Cassandra Branner]
Margaret Juliet Newman	December 29th 1847	August 27th 1849	Aaron Newman & wife [Cassandra Branner]
Charlotte Isabella Rankin	April 2nd 1849	August 27th 1849	Christopher Rankin & wife [Frances George Galbraith]
Martha Ann Rankin	November 18th 1847	August 27th 1849	Josiah E. Rankin & wife [Mary Emma Gass Rankin]
Harriett Malinda Rankin	December 17th 1846	Septem'r 16th 1849	Patrick M. [McGuire] & wife [Louisa J. Lockhart] Rankin
Patrick Thomas Rankin	July 22nd 1849	Septem'r 16th 1849	Patrick M. [McGuire] & wife [Louisa J. Lockhart] Rankin
John William Massengill Bradshaw	January 4th 1850	May 27th 1850	Richard H. [Harden] Bradshaw & wife [Jane P. Rawlings]
Oliver Hood Newman	April 12th 1850	Do	Joseph R. [Reece] Newman & wife [Mary A. Lockhart]
Alexander Porter Masengill	February 16th 1843	May 27th 1850	William Masengill [Sr.] & wife [Jane M. Nicholson]
Jeremiah Nicholson Masengill	March 14th 1845	Do	Do
Pharaoh Cobb Masengill	April 5th 1847	Do	Do
Susan Adaline Rankin	April 20th 1849	Do	William Rankin [Sr.] & wife [Susan Kimbrough]

---

[89] Birth date on gravestone, *Find A Grave*. Find A Grave. http://www.findagrave.com/cgi-bin/fg.cgi.

Samuel Houston Newman	June 3rd 1850	August 26th 1850	Aaron Newman & wife [Cassandra Branner]
Benjamine Harrison Newman	May 29th 1850	Do	Wm. M. [Milton] Newman & wife [Mahulda Henry]
Joseph Richard Bradshaw	August 15th 1850	February 9th 1851	Joseph C. Bradshaw & wife [Sarah Grizzle Blackburn]
Angeline Katherine Rankin	January 27th 1851	March 2nd 1851	Richard D. Rankin & wife [Mary Ann Carol Woods]
Rebecca Catharine Massengill	December 4th 1850	May 17th 1851	Wm. Massengill [Sr.] & wife [Jane M. Nicholson Massengill]

[Pages 212-213] No. 2

Name	Born	Baptized	Presented by whom
Hannah Rebecca Zirkle	June 17th 1848	September 8th 1851	Benjamin Zirkle & wife [Susannah Ruth "Susan" Pennywit]
Eleanor Louisa Zirkle	January 31st 1851	September 8th 1851	do
Christopher Houston Rankin	March 4th 1851	Do	Christopher Rankin & wife [Frances George Galbraith]
Elizabeth Harrison Rankin	[June 5th 1851][90]	Do	P. M. Rankin & wife [Louisa Jane Lockhart]
Martha Ann Rankin	November 18th 1847	Do	Josiah E. Rankin & wife [Mary Emma Gass Rankin]
Thomas Michael Harden Bradshaw	March 3rd 1852	June 20th 1852	Richard H. [Harden] Bradshaw & wife [Jane P. Rawlings]
Joseph Andrew Harrison Rankin	March 18th 1852	August 23rd 1852	James [Eaton] Rankin & wife [Julia Ann J. Newman]
Samuel Thomas Hood Newman	April 20th 1852	Do	William M. [Milton] Newman & wife [Huldah Henry] & wife [Mahulda Henry]
Henry Harrison Newman	November 8th 1851	Do	Joseph R. [Reece] Newman & wife [Mary A. Lockhart]
Almira Minerva Rankin	January 4th 1853	March 20th 1853	Richard D. Rankin & wife [Mary Ann Carol Woods]
Nancy Elizabeth Newman	June 29th 1853	September 11th 1853	Joseph R. [Reece] Newman & wife [Mary A. Lockhart]
Catharine Routh Rankin	February 13th 1853	October 16th 1853	Patrick M.[Patrick McGuire] Rankin & wife [Louisa Jane Lockhart]
Mary Emmons Rankin	March 29th 1853	April 9th 1854	Josiah E. Rankin & wife [Mary Emma Gass Rankin]
Catherine Cole Newman	December 18th 1853	April 9th 1854	John F. [Franklin] Newman & wife [Martha Matilda Gilbraith]
Barbary Elizabeth Zirkle	November 6th 1853	October 9th 1854	Benjamin Zirkle & wife [Susannah Ruth "Susan" Pennywit]
Joseph Alexander McMurry	[date not given]	Do	Polly Anne McMurry
William Henry Smith Newman	July 11th 1854	Do	William M. [Milton] Newman & wife [Huldah Henry] & wife [Mahulda Henry]

[90] *Tennessee, Jeffersom Co.. Bible Records*, WPA, "Patrick M. Rankin Bible Record of Mt. Horeb, TN" 1937, Historical Records Project #465-44-3-115, copy in McClung Collection, Knoxville, TN.

Joseph Thomas Franklin	March 11th 1854	Do	Rebecca Ann Franklin
Asa Luther Cline	April 15th 1853	Nov 15th 1854	George Cline & wife
Joseph Marshall Hood Rankin	October 6th 1854	February 19th 1855	Christopher Rankin & wife [Frances George Gilbraith]
Sarah J. [Jane] Alexander	October 19th 1844	May 21st 1854	Elias Alexander & wife [Jane Rankin]
Thomas T. [Theron] Alexander	October 8th 1850	Do	Do
Nancy E. [L.] Alexander	October 30th 1853	Do	Do
James Lafayette Rankin	July 27th 1854	September 3rd 1855	William Rankin & wife [Susan Kimbrough]
~~Emaline Rankin~~		Sept 11th 1855	

[Pages 214-215]   No. 2

Name	Born	Baptized	Presented by whom
Joseph Paluthiah Hood Bradshaw	November 16th 1854	October 28th 1855	Richard H. [Harden] Bradshaw & wife [Jane P. Rawlings]
Marjorah Emaline Rankin	May 11th 1855	Sept 16th 1855	Patrick M.[Patrick McGuire] Rankin & wife [Louisa Jane Lockhart]
[no name]	[no birthdate]	Sept 16th 1855	Aaron B. [Bogue] Rankin & wife [Marjary Copin Lockhart]
Samuel Doak Rankin	January 1st 1856	March 23rd 1856	Richard D. Rankin & wife [Mary Ann Carol Woods]
Archibald Blackburn Newman	November 17th 1855	March 23rd 1856	Joseph R. [Reece] Newman & wife [Mary A. Lockhart]
James Aaron Newman	December 31st 1855	May 4th 1856	John F. [Franklin] Newman & wife [Martha Matilda Gilbraith]
Sarah Margaret Lydia Bradshaw	April 29th 1856	July 6th 1856	Joseph C. Bradshaw & wife [Sarah Grizzle Blackburn]
Martha Jane Jolly	September 11th 1855	July 6th 1856	Charles [T.] Jolly & wife [Eliza J. Rankin]
Nancy Virgina Zirkle	April 28th 1856	July 20th 1856	Benjamin Zirkle & wife [Susannah Ruth "Susan" Pennywit]
Emma L. [Lillian] Alexander	May13 th 1856	August 30th 1856	Elias Alexander & wife [Jane Rankin]
Margaret Eleanor Franklin	[no date]	August 30th 1856	Rebecca Ann Franklin
Joseph Wilson Rankin	October 12th 1856	May 30th 1857	Josiah E. Rankin & wife [Mary Emma Gass]
David C. Gass	March 27th 1844	May 30th 1857	Andrew T. Gass & wife
William Daniel Gass	January 3rd 1850	May 30th 1857	Do
Frances Adaline Gass	April 17th 1855	May 30th 1857	Do
Richard Rankin Jolly	March 8th 1857	May 30th 1857	Charles T. Jolly & wife [Eliza J. Rankin]
Asahel Biddle Bradshaw	January 11th 1857	June 1st 1857	Richard H. [Harden] Bradshaw & wife [Jane P. Rawlings]
Nancy Iantha Isabella Newman	April 14th 1857	September 7th 1858	William M. [Milton] Newman & wife Mahulda [Henry] Newman

Susan Prudence Rankin	April 23rd 1857	September 7th 1858	Patrick M.[Patrick McGuire] Rankin & wife [Louisa Jane Lockhart]
Lydia Jane Newman	September 7th 1857	January 19th 1858	Joseph R. [Reece] Newman & wife [Mary A. Lockhart]
Mary Isabel Gass	October 22th 1857	January 19th 1858	Andrew T. Gass & wife
Rachel Isabell McMurry	March 2nd 1856	January 19th 1858	Samuel McMurray & wife [Mary Ann "Polly" Shadden]
Mark Alexander Newman	August 23rd 1857	January 19th 1858	John F. [Franklin] Newman & wife [Martha Matilda Gilbraith]
Charles W. Newman	October 16th 1857	January 19th 1858	Aaron Newman & wife
[no first name] Richards	[no date]	January 19th 1858	[no name]

[Pages 216-217]   No. 2

Name	Born	Baptized	Presented by whom
Henry D. [Darr] Newman	Feb 22nd 1853	Jan 24th 1858	[W.] Maddison Newman & wife [MaryAnn Nicholson]
Andrew J. [Johnson] Newman	November 3rd 1855	January 24th 1858	[W.] Maddison Newman & wife [Mary Ann Nicholson
Andrew Thomas Hood Bradshaw	January 26th 1858	April 24th 1858	Joseph C. Bradshaw & wife [Sarah Grizzle Blackburn]
Miranda Anjeronia Newman	September 21st 1857	April 26th 1858	Andrew P. Newman & wife [Sarah Melinda Nelson]
George W. Franklin	August 3rd 1854	April 26th 1858	Benjamin F. [Francis] Franklin & wife [Lucinda Harret Rankin]
Lucinda Ann [Lucy] Franklin	July 9th 1857	April 26th 1858	Benjamin F. [Francis] Franklin & wife & wife [Lucinda Harret]
Mary Josephine Newman	February 25th 1857	April 26th 1858	Samuel B. [Blair] Newman & wife [Nancy Elizabeth Rankin]
Andrew Nelson Rankin	July 19th 1856	June 20th 1858	Christopher Rankin & wife [Frances George Gilbraith]
Huldah Iantha Rankin	February 27th 1858	June 20th 1858	Christopher Rankin & wife [Frances George Gilbraith]
Mary Elizabeth Tiller	March 25th 1858	Sept 19th 1858	Sophia Emily Tiller
Benjamin Caswell Rankin	December 19th 1858	April 25th 1859	Patrick M.[Patrick McGuire] Rankin & wife [Louisa Jane Lockhart]
Emily Ann Zirkle	January 1st 1859	April 25th 1859	Benjamin Zirkle & wife [Susannah Ruth "Susan" Pennywitt]
Frances Cordelia Franklin	January 25th 1858	April 25th 1859	Campbell Franklin & wife
Mark Rufus Newman	Sept 1st 1858	April 25th 1859	Samuel B. Newman & wife [Nancy Elizabeth Rankin]
Boyd Robinson Newman	April 30th 1859	September 6th 1859	Joseph R. [Reece] Newman & wife [Mary A. Lockhart]
Huldah Estelle Alexander	April 11th 1859	September 6th 1859	Elias Alexander & wife [Jane Rankin]
Nancy Isabella Malcom	[no date]	September 6th 1859	[no name]

Thomas Harvy Smith McMurry	December 28th 1858	March 4th 1860	Samuel McMurry & wife [Mary Ann "Polly" Shadden]
Alice Athelia Newman	June 21st 1859	March 4th 1860	Andrew P. Newman & wife [Sarah Melinda Nelson]
Joseph Martin Newman	August 24th 1859	March 4th 1860	William M. [Milton] Newman & wife [Mahulda Henry]
Jennet Steele Rankin	March 21st 1860	April 28th 1860	Richard D. Rankin & wife [Mary Ann Carol Woods]
Elizabeth Jane Richards	October 25th 1858	April 29th 1860	John V. Richards & wife
Silas Martin Franklin	August 17th 1859	April 29th 1860	Campbell Franklin & wife
John Henry Cline	May 7th 1859	April 29th 1860	Erasmus H. [Harvey] Cline & wife [Juliet Emily Gass]
Sinea Frances Newman	September 16th 1859	June 3rd 1860	John F. [Franklin] Newman & wife [Martha Matilda Gilbraith]
Allis Mabell Richards	Dec 15th 1860	May 4th 1861	John V. Richards & wife

[Pages 218-219]   No. 2

Name	Born	Baptized	Presented by whom
John Edward Jolly	December 7th 1860	May 4th 1860 [1861]	Charles Jolly& wife [Eliza J. Rankin]
Ida Ella Newman	[no date]	May 6th 1861	John Mc Newman & wife [Mary Peck]
Cordelia Josephine Mathes	April 20th 1860	May 4th 1861	William A. Mathes & wife
Elizabeth Tymanda Bradshaw	July 4th 1860	May 4th 1861	Richard H. Bradshaw & wife [Jane P. Rawlings] [daughter of Richard Rawlings Bradshaw and Frances Berry Bradshaw]
Lee Converse Newman	September 11th 1861	January 5th 1862	Joseph R. Newman & wife [Mary A. Lockhart]
Cassander Elizabeth Ellen Newman	September 3rd 1861	January 5th 1862	Mary E. Newman
Luella May Newman	March 27th 1861	Do	Andrew C. [Carroll] Newman & wife [Catherine Emeline "Emily" Bradshaw]
Melville McElvain Rankin	January 5th 1861	Do	Josiah E. Rankin & wife [Mary Emma Gass Rankin]
Names of Rufus E. Carson's children			Transfered from New Market Church by order of that session
Susan C. Carson			
Nathaniel T. Carson			
Mary E. Carson			

Volume II (1866-1874)

[Title Page][91]

MOUNT HOREB PRESBYTERIAN CHURCH
JEFFERSON COUNTY, TENNESSEE
(In Dumplin Valley)

RECORD BOOK
1866-1873
Vol. 2

Blank Pages:
2 – 3, 26 -27, 38 – 51, 56 – 77, 128 – 235, 237 – 240

[p. 1]   (1)

Mount Horeb Church Record, January 1, 1866
Index Record Membership from page 4 to 50 inclusive.
Infant Membership from page 50 to 75 inclusive
Record of transactions of Session page 80th & onwards
Statistical Records pages 236 onward

[p. 2-3 blank]

[Session Minutes have been moved to the beginning of this section and the various rolls following the minutes. This makes them easier to search and better matches the order of the other volumes.]

[p. 56-77 blank]

[p. 78]   (21)

Mount Horeb, Tenn.
In January 4, 1866
Session was called together by Rev. Wm. H. Lyle, Moderator.
Present: Rev. Wm. H. Lyle, moderator, Elders: Wm. Rankin [Sr.], J. C. [John Calvin] Bradshaw, Chris Rankin, Elias Alexander, P. M. [Patrick McGuire] Rankin; Absent: Richard Bradshaw
The session was opened with singing and prayer by moderator. The following named persons presented themselves as candidates for admission to the privileges of the church having been baptized in infancy to wit:

---

[91] Page numbers in square brackets refer to pages in the original document. The numbers in the round brackets refer to the typed manuscript found in the McClung Historical Collection in Knoxville, Tennessee.

Benjamin [Francis] Franklin, Jr., William E. H. Mathes, Thomas T. Alexander, John W. M. Bradshaw, Samuel P. Rankin, Thomas M. H. Bradshaw, Joseph R. Bradshaw, Christopher H. Rankin, Nathaniel H. Franklin, Nathanield [sic] B. Mathes, John C. Bradshaw, Almira M. Rankin, Emma L. Alexander, Frances L. Rankin, Catharine R. "Kate" Franklin, Angaline C. Rankin, Mary E. Rankin, Sarah A. C. C. Rankin, Sarah E. Bradshaw, Margaret E. J. Newman, Susan A. Rankin, Rachel E. Mathes, James S. Fain & wife, N. J. Fain, Joseph A. H. Rankin, Sarah J. F. Rankin and at the same time Samuel T. L. [Thomas Luther] Rankin, Samuel N. Newman & Alfred Mooney who were baptized on the ground of their faith in Christ which were severally examined on the subject of their faith in Christ as their Savior and giving full satisfaction they were publicly received into the full communion of the church in all 29.

Session then adjourned.

P. M. Rankin, Clerk

(22)

Jan. 8, 1866

The session of Mount Horeb Church was called together by the Moderator Rev. Wm. H. Lyle. Present: Rev. Wm. H. Lyle, [p. 79] Moderator. Elders: Wm. Rankin, J. C. Bradshaw, Chris Rankin, Elias Alexander, P. M. Rankin. Absent: Richard Bradshaw

The session was opened with prayer by Moderator the following named persons who having been baptized in infancy were examined on the subject of experimental religion and were admitted to all the privileges of the church. Catharine R. [Ruth] Rankin, Sarah M. [Malinda] Rankin, William E. Rankin, Lydia E. Bradshaw, Eliza E. [Emaline] Coil, John T. Mathes, William P. M. [Porter Massengil] Bradshaw, Alexander P. [Porter] Rankin, who at the same time Florence D. Wisdom, Frances M. Lyle, Columbus H. Skein, James A. Bettis who were baptized upon their faith in Christ, 12 in all. Session adjourned.

P. M. Rankin,
clerk

By the same on Jan. 11th 1866.

Martha A. [Ann] Rankin, Margaret E. [Ellen] Rankin, Charlotte T. Rankin, James A. Newman, George Howard all having been baptized in infancy were examined and admitted to the full communion of the church also at the same time Margaret E. Malcomb, Mary J. Hall, Nancy C. Malcomb & George Collins who not having been baptized were examined as to their ability to exercise faith in Christ and thus were admitted publicly to the privileges of the church and were baptized 10 in all. The session then adjourned.

P. M. Rankin,
Clerk

Turn to page 81 to keep the connection.

(23)

Mount Horeb   July 30th 1865

The session of Mount Horeb Church being called together informally by the [blank], Present: Rev. [blank] Moderator. William Rankin, Elias Alexander, Christopher Rankin, Joseph C. Bradshaw, & P. M. Rankin, Elders. Absent Richard Bradshaw

The following minute was adopted whereas it is imminently desirable to have the stated means of grace established amongst us & where as the Pulpit of Mount Horeb Church is left vacant since Rev. Nathaniel Hood ceased preaching in it.

Therefore resolved that as it is understood that Rev. William H. Lyle will take charge of the church after the first of January next for one half of his time as S. S.

therefore resolved that the Rev. James A. Griffis of New Market be requested to preach for us every other Sabbath evening until the first of January 1866 and that the members of Mount Horeb Church & Congregation be called on to subscribe for his support. which resolution was decided in the affirmative.   P. M. Rankin, clerk

Mount Horeb Sept. 29, 1865

The session was called together by Rev. [blank], Present [blank] Moderator. William Rankin, Chris Rankin, Elias Alexander, J. C. Bradshaw, P. M. Rankin, Elders. Absent Richard Bradshaw

[p. 81]   (24)

The session was opened with prayer by moderator. Mr. John James Coil approved [appeared] before the session as a candidate for admission to full communion of the church, who having been baptized in infancy was examined respecting his acquaintance with experimental religion and the doctrines of the Presbyterian church and his readiness to submit himself to the discipline of the church and in examination being sustained by the session he was admitted publicly to all the privileges of the church.

The session then adjourned.   P. M. Rankin, clerk

Here to keep the connection turn back to page 78.

Mount Horeb January 27, 1866

The session was called together by Rev. Wm. H. Lyle, moderator at the instance of J. C. Bradshaw & P. M. Rankin. Present Rev. Wm. H. Lyle, moderator, Wm. Rankin, J. C. Bradshaw, Elias Alexander, P. M. Rankin, Elders, Absent Richard Bradshaw

Opened with prayer by moderator business what action ought this session to take in relation to members of the church who have participated in the late Rebellion or who have sympathized with the same & what course should this session take in relation to members (many of whom have) removed from the country without making application for letter of dismission as requested by the discipline of our church.

Which after much talking and discussion & nothing deffinite [sic] being determined the session adjourned over to Saturday 10th. (25) It being two weeks and Wm. Rankin [Sr.], Elias Alexander & P. M. Rankin was [sic] appointed a special committee to examine the records of this church and report at the adjourned meeting.

P. M. Rankin, clerk

[p. 82]   (26)
Mount Horeb, Tenn. Feb. 10, 1866
The session met pursuant to adjournment.

Present Rev. Wm. H. Lyle moderator, J. C. Bradshaw, Wm. Rankin, Elias Alexander, Chris Rankin, P. M. Rankin   Elders. Absent Richard Bradshaw

Opened with prayer by moderator

unfinished business of last meeting considered the committee appointed at last meeting. Report it appears from the records of this church that there are about twenty-one of the Recorded members of the church who have removed from the country without making application for letter of dismission. Your committee recommend that the names of all such be droped [sic] from the Records of this church which report after being discussed and amended was adopted and read as follows

whereas many of the members of Mount Horeb Church have removed from this part of the country without making application for letter of dismission therefore resolved by the session of Mount Horeb church that the names of all those members of the church who have so removed or who shall hereafter remove without applying for letters and who fail or neglect to make application for two entire years after their removal the clerk of the session be required to drop the names of all such persons from the records of the church

[on left margin of above paragraph, running bottom to top on the typed page is the word: **Repealed**]

Resolved further that the above resolution be read publicly from the pulpit to the church and be recorded on the minutes of this session.

The vote being taken by the moderator it was decided in the affirmative those voting for the resolutions were Wm. Rankin [Sr.], Elias Alexander, Chris Rankin & P. M. Rankin: Noes, J. C. Bradshaw. W. Madison Newman [p. 83.] (27) and his wife Mary A. [Ann Nicholson] Newman & sons, Patrick L. Newman & George W. Newman & also Enoch N. Bradshaw, having removed from the country leaving a request for letter of dismission and there being no charges against any or either of them their request was granted and the clerk of session was ordered to make out letters and forward to them accordingly.

At the same time the following Resolution in relation to the action of the General Assembly of the Presbytery of Union and also the views of the session in relation to the late Rebellion was adopted and ordered to be recorded and is in the words following to wit

Resolved by the session of Mount Horeb Church that we endorse the action of the General Assembly of the Presbyterian church in relation to the sin of Rebellion and also the action of Union Presbytery in endorsing the same in having aditional [sic] testimony in relation to the great sin of the Rebellion yet believing that many honest hearted Christians may have been led into the Rebellion by the force of surrounding circumstances and without due reflection or consideration,

Therefore resolved that we as a church session believe that under all the circumstances it [is] not necessary to require of any of the members of this church who may have participated in said Rebellion or who may have sympathized with the same any further proof that they have been led to see their error in this respect than what may be made manifest by such members by hereafter cheerfully and heartily cooperating with their brethren and Sisters harmonizing and building up the church together and in living in the faithful discharge of their duty as Christians in the future.

Order that the foregoing resolution be read by the moderator to the congregation from the pulpit on an early day. The vote being taken by Moderator those voting in the affirmative were William Rankin [Sr.], Christopher [p. 84]   (28)

Rankin, Elias Alexander & P. M. Rankin. Those voting in the negative were Joseph C. Bradshaw to which action Joseph C. Bradshaw entered his solemn protest and requested the same to be spread upon the record which is in the following records to wit

Mount Horeb Feb. 10, 1866

I this day enter my protest against the action of the session of Mount Horeb Church on the subject of the late Rebellion as contrary to the great law of love which is as ye would that men should do to you do ye even so to them for this is the law and the prophets. Matt. 7:12, and

I submit the following as Resolutions containing my views on that subject.

Resolved that we the session of Mount Horeb Church feel that the General Assembly was right in having their testimony against the sin of the Rebellion and that Union Presbytery was right in endorsing the action of the Assembly and in bearing additional testimony against the crime of Rebellion. Yet feeling as we do that many honest hearted Christians were led into the Rebellion from honest and pure motives; Therefore resolved that under all the circumstances we as a church session do not feel ourselves authorized from the word of God nor the confession of faith to debar any such members of the church from church privileges mearly [sic] on account of participating in or sympathizing with the Rebellion, feeling as we do that all such persons would be made welcome by the great head of the church. All of which is submitted Joseph C. Bradshaw.

A true copy   Joseph C. Bradshaw
A session then adjourned

                                   P. M. Rankin,
                                        clerk

Mount Horeb, Tenn. April 7, 1866   (29)
Session met on the call of moderator

Present Rev. Wm. H. Lyle, moderator, William Rankin, J. C. Bradshaw, Chris Rankin, Elias Alexander, P. M. Rankin, Elders, Absent Richard Bradshaw

Business to make out report to Presbytery and appoint delegate. Christopher Rankin was appointed to represent the church in Presbytery to meet on the 3d. Friday of the present inst. and Joseph C. Bradshaw appointed his alternate the Report being made out the session then adjourned.

                                   P. M. Rankin,
                                        Clerk

[Page 82] Examined and approved thus far except the action of the session relative to absent members The Presbytery requires of Mount Horeb Church session to conform to the decision of the Gen. Assembly on this subject which is that members removing from the bounds of the church without taking letters within the time specified by the book subject themselves to suspension. A session can suspend members for this offense, but cannot draft their names.

W. H. Lyle, moderator

Apr. 21, 1866

Mount Horeb, Tenn. June 2, 1866   (30)

[p. 86] Session met on call of moderator and was opened with prayer by moderator

Present Rev. Wm. H. Lyle moderator, C. Rankin, J. C. Bradshaw, E. Alexander, P. M. Rankin, Elders

Absent R. Bradshaw, Wm. Rankin

When Mrs. Mahala Sivels was received into the communion of the church on certificate from the Methodist church at Chapmans also Mrs. Adna J. Rankin & Miss Sarah L. Lyle on certificate from Oak Grove Congregation Cumberland Presbyterian Church, also letters of dismission and church standing were awarded to Mary Jane Titus formerly Rankin and Sarah Jane Blackburn formerly Rankin. It being reported that certain members of the church have connected themselves with the Methodist church not having applied for letters of dismission, Joseph C. Bradshaw was appointed a committee to confer with said members in order to learn the facts in the case and learn the wishes of said individuals when on motion session adjourned till Monday the 4th 8 o'clock A. M. closed with prayer by moderator

P. M. Rankin, clerk

[p. 87] Mount Horeb, Tenn. Monday June 4, 1866   (31)

Session met pursuant to Adjournment and was opened by prayer by moderator

Present Rev. Wm. H. Lyle, moderator, C. Rankin, E. Alexander, P. M. Rankin, Elder, Absent J. C. Bradshaw, Wm. Rankin, Richard Bradshaw

Minutes of last meeting was read and approved, the committee appointed at last meeting reported that he had conferred with Mrs. Sarah E. Zirkle and found the report that she had connected herself to another church to be true also that she was led to take this step under an erroneous impression which she would not have done if she had been rightly informed. She now makes application for a letter of dismission the report is accepted and a letter awarded.

Common fame having accused Mrs. Mary A. C. Newman one of the members of this church of disorderly and unchristian conduct and the session being satisfied that said reports are true the moderator Rev. Wm. H. Lyle and P. M. Rankin were appointed a committee to visit the accused in order to ascertain the facts in the case and learn the state of her mind in relation to the same, when a motion session adjourned to meet in the 17th instant after sermon closed with prayer, by C. Rankin   P. M. Rankin, clerk

Mount Horeb June 17, 1860

Session met pursuant to Adjournment and was opened by Prayer by the moderator (32) Present Rev. Wm. H. Lyle, moderator, E. Alexander, C. Rankin, Joseph C. Bradshaw, P. M. Rankin [p. 88] Absent: Wm. Rankin & Richard Bradshaw

Minutes of last meeting read and approved J. C. Bradshaw gave excuse of absence from last meeting approved the committee appointed at last meeting to visit Mrs. Mary A. C. Newman on the part of the session reported that they had discharged that duty and found the report existing in relation to her unchristian conduct to be true and that they found her deeply sensable [sic] of her wrong and honestly penitant [sic] for the same and desirous to be forgiven by the church and her membership continued

which Report was one motion received and then it was resolved on motion that she be continued as a member of the church.

The minutes were read and the question arrising [sic] as to the propriety of so amending them as to state offence which the accused has been guilty of the approval of the minuits [sic] was postponed till the next meeting of the session when on motion the session adjourned closed with prayer by Jos. C. Bradshaw.

P. M. Rankin, clerk

Mount Horeb September 2, 1866

Session met on call of the moderator and was opened with prayer by the same

Present Rev. W. H. Lyle, moderator, Elders Wm. Rankin J. C. Bradshaw, Elias Alexander, P. M. Rankin, Chris Rankin (33) Absent Richard Bradshaw

When J. C. Bradshaw was appointed to represent this church in Presbytery this fall and Wm. Rankin was appointed his alternate P. M. Rankin was appointed to attend the meeting of Synod from this church this fall and S. [Elias] Alexander his alternate. Aron[sic] B. [Aaron Bogue] Rankin having applied for letters of Dismission for himself & his [p. 89] wife, Marjory Rankin, his daughter Margaret E. [Ellen] Rankin & Son Thomas B. Rankin letters were thereupon awarded to them also John W. Richards haveing [sic] applied for a letter it was ordered.

Session then adjourned for public worship

P.M. Rankin, clerk

Mount Horeb February 16, 1867

Session met on call of the moderator

Present Rev. Wm. H. Lyle Moderator, Elders C. Rankin, J. C. Bradshaw, E. Alexander, P. M. Rankin, Absent Wm. Rankin [Sr.] & Richard Bradshaw

Business Minuits [sic] of the two last meetings of the session was read and approved. unfinished business

in accordince [sic] with the instructions of Presbytery the Minuts [sic] of the 10th February 1866 of this session relating to Members of this Church who have removed from the country without lefting [sic] letters was considered and replaced (See page 82)

Session then took into consideration the subject of Systematic benefficence [sic] when it was received that there be collections taken in this church annually for the benefit of Foreign Missions on the Second Sabbath [*sic*] of September every year and for Home Missions on the (34) fourth Sabbath in November every year and for Educational purposes on the fourth Sabbath of December every year when on Motion Session Adjourned to meet in two weeks on Saturday 2d day of March 1867 one o'clock. closed with prayer by C. Rankin

P. M. Rankin, clerk

[p.90] Mount Horeb Saturday 2 March 1867
Session met according to Adjournment, there not being a full session present Adjourned until Saturday 16th March 1867 at 1 o'clock P. M.

P. M. Rankin, clerk

Mount Horeb Saturday March 16th 1867
Session met according to Adjournment
Members present Rev. Wm. H. Lyle Moderator, Elders Wm. Rankin, J. C. Bradshaw, E. Alexander, P. M. Rankin, C. Rankin Absent Richard Bradshaw

Minuets [*sic*] of Previous Meeting Read & approved. It having come to our knowledge as a church session that John W. Bettis has connected himself with the Methodist church without asking for a letter of dismission from us therefore Resolved that his name be droped [sic] from the Roll those voting in the affirmative were Wm. Rankin [Sr.], C. Rankin & P. M. Rankin. those voting in the negative were J. C. Bradshaw, E. Alexander. Joseph C. Bradshaw was appointed to attend the meeting of Presbytery this spring at Washington Church & P. M. Rankin was appointed his alternate. when on motion Session Adjourned   (35)
colsed [sic] by Prayer

P. M. Rankin,
clerk

[p. 91] Mount Horeb April 28, 1867
Session met on call of the moderator and was opened by Prayer
Present Rev. Wm. H. Lyle Moderator, Elders Wm. Rankin, Jos. C. Bradshaw & P. M. Rankin, Absent C. Rankin, E. Alexander, R. Bradshaw

A conversation was had with the following persons on the subject of Experimental Religion with a view of their being admitted to the privileges of the Church to wit: Catharine Cole Newman, William T. Coil, Henry P. Coil, Alexander J. Coil, who giving satisfaction to the Session that they have experienced a change of heart they were publicly admitted into full membership in the Church
Session then Adjourned for Public worship

P. M. Rankin,
clerk

Examined and approved thus far.
Wm. Harrison, Mod

Mount Horeb May 12th 1867   (36)
Session met on call of Moderator opened by Prayer
Present Rev. W. H. Lyle Moderator, Elders, J. C. Bradshaw, C. Rankin, E.
Alexander, P. M. Rankin, Absent Wm. Rankin, R. Bradshaw
George A. Zirkle having applied for letter of dismission a letter was awarded him
when on motion Session Adjourned Prayer by C. Rankin.
                              P. M. Rankin clerk

[p.92] Mount Horeb June 2, 1867
Session met on call of the Moderator
Present Rev. Wm. H. Lyle Moderator, Elders C. Rankin, J. C. Bradshaw, P. M.
Rankin, Absent Wm. Rankin, E. Alexander, R. Bradshaw
George A. Mathes haveing [sic] Applied for a letter of dismission from the Church
it was granted when Session Adjourned for Public worship.
                              P. M. Rankin, clerk

Mount Horeb August 17, 1867
Session Met on call of the Moderator   (37)
Present Rev. Wm. H. Lyle Moderator, Elders E. Alexander, C. Rankin, J. C.
Bradshaw, P. M. Rankin, Absent Wm. Rankin, R. Bradshaw
Prayer by moderator. Christopher Rankin was appointed to Represent this Church
in Presbytery this fall at St. Paul's Church & P. M. Rankin was appointed to attend
Synod at Athens this fall in behalf of this Church it was agreed to have our Sacramental
Meeting this fall to embrace the 4th Sabbath of September and that the collection for
Foreign Missionary purposes be taken at that time by Subscription on three weeks time
in accordance with a resolution of this session of Feb. 16, 1867 when Session adjourned.
     Prayer by C. Rankin, Clerk

[p. 93] Mount Horeb August 25th 1867
Session met on call of the Moderator
Present Rev. Wm. H. Lyle Moderator, Elders J. C. Bradshaw, Wm. Rankin, C.
Rankin, E. Alexander, P. M. Rankin, Absent R. Bradshaw   (38)
Session constituted with Prayer by Moderator. Mrs. Susan Zirkle having [sic] made
application for letters of dismission for herself and two daughters Mary S. Zirkle &
Lydia J. [Jane] Zirkle it was ordered that letters be awarded them accordingly when
Session Adjourned
                              P. M. Rankin, Clerk

Mount Horeb, September 29th 1867
Session Met on call of Moderator, Present Rev. Wm. H. Lyle Moderator, Elders
C. Rankin, Jos. C. Bradshaw, P. M. Rankin, Absent R. Bradshaw, Wm. Rankin, E.
Alexander. Session opened by Prayer by the Moderator when Samuel Funk, Elizabeth

Funk and Isabella E. Newman haveing [sic] made application for letters of dismission from this Church letters were ordered to be given them   when on motion Session Adjourned for social Prayer meeting.

P. M. Rankin Clerk

[p. 94] Mount Horeb, Tenn. Oct. 13, 1867
Session met on call of the Moderator
Present Rev. Wm. H. Lyle Moderator, Elder C. Rankin, Jos. C. Bradshaw, E. Alexander, P. M. Rankin, Absent Richard Bradshaw, Wm. Rankin   (39)
Session constituted with Prayer by Moderator when Wm. N. [Milton] Newman & Mahulda [Henry] Newman his wife & also their daughter Margaret E. J. Newman haveing [sic] made application for letters of dismission from the church. letters were thereupon granted them when on motion Session Adjourned

P. M. Rankin, Clerk

Mount Horeb Tenn. Oct. 27th 1867
Session was called together by Moderator
Present Rev. Wm. H. Lyle Moderator, Elders Jos. C. Bradshaw, C. Rankin, E. Alexander, P. M. Rankin, Absent Wm. Rankin
When Mrs. Sarah Porter [Mathis] Lyle was received into the communion as by letter when Session Adjourned for Public worship.

P. M. Rankin Clerk

[p. 95] Mount Horeb Tennessee Nov. 10, 1867
Session met by appointment
Present Rev. Wm. H. Lyle Moderator, Elder Joseph C. Bradshaw, Christopher Rankin, Elias Alexander, P. M. Rankin, Absent Wm. Rankin   (40)
Session opened by Prayer by moderator when John R. Bradshaw, Susan C. Carson, Mary E. Carson, Nathaniel H. Carson, John A. Monroe, Joseph W. [Wilson] Rankin were examined on the subject of Experimental Religion and the Session being satisfied that they have each experienced a change of heart they were publicly admitted to full Communion in the Church. A communication was received from Richard Bradshaw notifying the Session that he had attached himself to another Church organization when his name was ordered to be droped [sic] from the Records of this Church. When Session Adjourned for Public worship.

P. M. Rankin Clerk

December 22, 1867
There was an Election held in Mount Horeb Church which took Place by previous arrangement of the Session and Presbytery for the purpose of Electing the Pastor which resulted in the unanimous election of Rev. Wm. H. Lyle as Pastor to labour as such in this church one half of his time.

P. M. Rankin Clerk

Mount Horeb, Tenn., January 12, 1868

At an informal meeting of Session immediately preceding Public Worship Mrs. Ellen Bowls was received as a member of this Church by certifficate [*sic*] from the Session of Newmarket Presbyterian Church.

P. M. Rankin, Clerk of Sessions [*sic*]

[p. 96] Mount Horeb, Tenn. February 29th 1868   (41)

Session Met on call of the Moderator, Present Rev. Wm. H. Lyle Moderator, Elders Jos. C. Bradshaw, E. Alexander, C. Rankin, P. M. Rankin, Absent Wm. Rankin

Session opened by Prayer by moderator. Minuets [*sic*] of previous Meetings of Session back to 29th August 1867 read and approved except the Minuet [*sic*] in relation to the election of Pastor of the 22d December 1867 was amended so as to show that the people of the church, decided by vote when the matter was brought before them by the Session and trustees, that they would go into the Pastoral relation after which the Election of a Pastor took place which resulted as stated in said Minuet [*sic*].

Elias Alexander was appointed to attend Presbytery this spring as delegate from this Church & P. M. Rankin his Alternate. It was moved and seconded that those of the Members of this church who have removed from this country years past without making application for letters of credence be suspended which was adopted the names of such are the following: David H. Bradshaw, Martha A. Newman, Wm. A. Bowers, Thomas C. Lyle, Joseph R. Newman, Thomas J. Newman, Sarah Newman, John J. Newman, Benjamin C. [Casper] Newman, Mary E. Newman, William H. [Henry Smith] Newman, Richard A. Newman, Martha E. Newman, Albert M. Newman, Martha Y. Newman.

Moved and seconded that the Clerk of this session when it shall certainly come to his knowledge that any of the members of this church have connected themselves with other Church organizations without (42) lifting letters of dismission from this Church he shall drop the names of all such from the Records of this church which was decided in the affirmative when on Motion. Session Adjourned by prayer.

P. M. Rankin Clerk

[p. 97] Mount Horeb April 25, 1868

A Meeting of the congregation was called for the purpose of making out and subscribing a call to Presbytery for the installation of Rev. Wm. H. Lyle as Pastor of Mount Horeb Church Rev. E. [Eli] H. Sawtell was called to the chair when the said call was read and when on motion the congregation delegated the Authority of subscribing the same to the Session as further action was had.   P. M. Rankin Clerk

Examined and approved thus far by action of Presbytery.

E. N. Sawtell, Mod.

Mount Horeb, Tennessee May 24, 1868

An informal Meeting of the Session & Trustees convened on call of the Moderator to consider matters pertaining to Installation expected to take place on the Second

Saturday of June 1868 when it was agreed the Friday preceding be observed as a day of fasting and prayer in view of the great responsibility then to be assumed by both Pastor and people also it was agreed that two or more deacons be then elected by the Members of this church in order that they may be ordained if convenient during the same meeting when the Meeting Adjourned for Public worship

P. M. Rankin, Clerk of Session

Mount Horeb August 22, 1868   (43)
Session met for the transaction of such business as might be brought before it all the Members of Session being present. constituted with Prayer by the Moderator when Wm. Rankin [Sr.] was appointed to attend the Meetings of Presbytery to represent the Church P. M. Rankin his alternate. Joseph C. Bradshaw was appointed to attend Synod and E. Alexander [p. 98] his alternate Session having learned that one of the individuals elected to the office of deacon recently declined to accept the position & that one of the others are still undecided. it was agreed to postpone the ordination of Deacons for the Present until such time as another Election can be held for the purpose of Electing one or more as the case may require in the place of the one or two refusing to serve session then adjourned for Public worship   P. M. Rankin, clerk

Mount Horeb Nov. 15th 1868
Session met on the call of the Moderator. Present Rev. Wm. H. Lyle Moderator, Elders J. C. Bradshaw, C. Rankin, E. Alexander, P. M. Rankin, Absent Wm. Rankin
Session Constituted with Prayer by Moderator Minuets [sic] of the two Previous Meetings read and approved the subject of Bennefficiened [sic] being brought up for consideration it was agreed to dispense with the rule primarily made by the session requiring an annual collection to be taken in this Church for the aid of home Missions and that no collection be had for the purpose in this church the present year. (44) Agreed that the (annual) collection for foreign Missionary purposes be taken up on the fifth Sabbath of Nov. 1868.
the unfinished business in relation to Deacons comeing [sic] up it was agreed on motion to hold an Election in (this) Church on the Second Sabbath of December next for the purpose of Electin [sic] one or two Deacons in the place of the one or two declining to serve as the case [p. 99] may be at that time. common fame haveing [sic] accused Thomas [John] J. Bradshaw & Cinderella C. Bradshaw of walking disorderly by committing a breach of the Seventh commandment the Session appointed Wm. Rankin a committee on the part of this session to visit the accused assertain the facts in the case   converse with the parties and learn the state of their minds in relation to the same and report to session at a Meeting to be held two weeks from this day when on Motion Session Adjourned   P. M. Rankin Clerk

Mount Horeb Tenn Nov. 29, 1868
Session Met according to Adjournment. Present Rev. Wm. H. Lyle Moderator, Elders: Wm. Rankin, E. Alexander, C. Rankin, P. M. Rankin, Absent: J. C. Bradshaw

Constituted with Prayer by Moderator. Wm. Rankin who was appointed a Committee at last Meeting of Session to visit Thomas J. Bradshaw and his wife Cinderella C. Bradshaw and report at the meeting of Session reported that he had discharged that duty and that the accused parties as above named acknowledged their guilt and professed Repentance for the same and expressed a hope of having obtained forgiveness of the (p. 45) great head of the Church. after hearing the above Report Session Adjourned to Meet the 12ᵗʰ of Dec. 1868.   P. M. Rankin, Clerk

Mount Horeb December 12ᵗʰ 1868
Session failed of a Meeting no corem [sic] being present
P. M. Rankin clerk

[p. 100] Mount Horeb Tenn., December 26ᵗʰ 1868
Session met by appointment
Present Rev. Wm. H. Lyle Moderator, Elders   C. Rankin, J. C. Bradshaw, E. Alexander, Wm. Rankin, P. M. Rankin
Constituted with Prayer by Moderator
The Election of Deacons which was to have takin [sic] place on the second Sabbath of the instant haveing [sic] been postponed by an informal Meeting of Session held on that day on account of annonimous [sic] letter recieved [sic] by the session in relation to the same, in relation to said annonimous [sic] letter it was agreed that it be read from the stand publicly together with an answer from the session to the same.
Wm. Rankin and J. C. Bradshaw was appointed a committee in the case of T. J. Bradshaw & C. C. Bradshaw to report a resolution to session who after conferring together reported the following
Resolved that Thomas J. Bradshaw & Cindrella [sic] C. Bradshaw having given satisfactory evidence of their Repentance and expressed a hope of forgiveness and reconciliation with the Great Head of the Church, they be and are hereby restored to their former standing and privileges in (46) the Church and that the above resolution be read publicly from the stand when on motion session adjourned.
P. M. Rankin, Clerk

Mount Horeb, Tenn. January 23, 1869
Session Met by appointment
Present Rev. Wm. H. Lyle Moderator, Elders Wm. Rankin, J. C. Bradshaw, C. Rankin, E. Alexander & P. M. Rankin.
[p. 101] Session constituted with Prayer by Moderator The Minuets [sic] of the three Previous Meetings were read and approved Session having received a communication from John F. Newman setting forth his objection to the ordination of S. E. [Samuel Edwin] Rankin to the office of Deacon in this Church and requesting that it be read publicly to the Church Session claiming the objective set forth to be altogether of A private nature and it appearing from the said communication that the writer had not taken the proper steps in order to bring about a reconciliation it was ordered that

the paper be returned to the writer and that he be informed of the reason Session could not comply with his request by making the matter public.

Session haveing [*sic*] received a paper signed by a goodly number of the Members of this Church setting forth their objections to the ordination of S. E. [Samuel Edwin] Rankin to the office of Deacon. Session appointed Rev. Wm. H. Lyle the Moderator and Wm. Rankin a committee to confer with S. E. Rankin and inform him that owing to the opposition on the part of many Members of this Church to his ordination Session consider that the peace and welfare of the [*sic*] would be best enhanced by his declineing [*sic*] to serve in said office if such a course should Meet his approbation Said committee to report as soon as practable [*sic*].

Session then on motion took a recess until after Public worship on tomorrow (47) Jany. 24th Session came to order when the Moderator and Wm. Rankin committee appointed yesterday to confer with S. E. Rankin Reported that they had done so and that he concured [*sic*] with the Session and thought it best under all the circumstances that Session proceed no farther with the matter which report was received and concured [*sic*] in it appearing to Session that there has been no Clerk to lead in the [p. 102] singing in the Church for several years past it was agreed to submit the question to the people of the church four weeks from today whether they wish to elect a Clerk or not and if they decide to elect a Clerk then the Election be held at once when on Motion Session Adjourned.

P. M. Rankin, Clerk

Mount Horeb Feb. 21, 1869

The question as to whether the Congregation desire to elect a Clerk or not was submitted to a vote also whether said Clerk be elected for four years or for life was also submitted to a vote of Church Members and both questions being decided in the affirmative the Election was then held by ballot and resulted in the election of Mark T. Rankin he haveing [*sic*] 47 votes out of 74 being a majority of the whole vote cast "he" was declared duly Elected Clerk

P. M. Rankin, Clerk of Session

Mount Horeb Tenn April 3d. 1869

Session Met on call of the Moderator

Present C. Rankin, J. C. Bradshaw, E. Alexander, P. M. Rankin

The clerk was directed to make out the usual Annual report to (48) Presbytery. C. Rankin was appointed to attend the meeting of Presbytery as the representative of this Church this spring the Moderator Rev. Wm. H. Lyle appearing took his seat when in application by William E. H. Mathes a letter of dismission was granted him when in motion Session Adjourned.

P. M. Rankin Clerk

[p. 103] Mount Horeb August 1869

Session Met on the Call of the Moderator

Present Rev. Wm. H. Lyle Moderator

Elders C. Rankin, Jos. C. Bradshae [sic], Elias Alexander, P. M. Rankin

Session constituted by Prayer by the Moderator when Elias Alexander was appointed to attend the fall session of Presbytery at Newmarket, Jefferson County as the Representative of the Church. P. M. Rankin was appointed to attend the Annual Meeting of the Synod of Tennessee this fall to be held at Maryville as the Representative of the Church when on Motion Session Adjourned

P. M. Rankin, Clerk

Mount Horeb March 15th 1870

Session met on call of the Moderator

Present Rev. Wm. H. Lyle Moderator, Elders Jos. C. Bradshaw, Chris Rankin, Elias Alexander, P. M. Rankin, Absent Wm. Rankin

Session was constituted with Prayer by Moderator when Miss Rachel (49) E. Mathes was granted a letter of Dismission she having made application for the same and the Clerk was directed to make out the letter accordingly there being no other business before the Session Adjourned for Public worship

P. M. Rankin Clerk

[p. 104] Mount Horeb March 26, 1870

Session met on the call of the Moderator

Present Rev. Wm. H. Lyle Moderator, Elders Jos. C. Bradshaw, Chris Rankin, Elias Alexander, P. M. Rankin, Absent Wm. Rankin

Session Constituted with Prayer by Moderator when P. M. Rankin was appointed to attend the spring Meeting of Presbytery at West Minster [sic] the collection for commissioners fund and Presbyteriall [sic] was to be taken on fourth Sabbath of April next Sacramental Meeting to embrace the second Sabbath of May.

Public rumor having [sic] accused John T. Mathes one of the Members of the Church of drunkenness and profanity and the Moderator haveing [sic] informed the Session that he had conversed with the said Mathes in relation to said Reports and that he confessed that in part they were true and further stated that he had come to the conclusion that he had been deceived in relation to his having experienced a change of heart and was not fit to receive Church privaliges [sic] he desired the session to drop his name from the list of Church Members & C. which after confering [sic] together the session decided that according to Book of Disciplin [sic] they are not authorized to comply with the request and the session appointed the Moderator and Joe C. Bradshaw a committee to visit the said Mathes and inform him of (50) the action of session and have an interview and conversation with him in relation to his case. C. Rankin and P. M. Rankin was appointed a committee to visit James [A.] Barbee one of the Members of a [sic] this Church who has long absented himself from the house of God and who Rumors has accused of immoral conduct when on motion session Adjourned.

[p. 105]   P. M. Rankin clerk

Mount Horeb May 8th 1870

Session met on call of the Moderator

Present Rev. Wm. H. Lyle Moderator, Elders C. Rankin, J. C. Bradshaw, Elias Alexander, P. M. Rankin, Absent Wm. Rankin

Session was constituted with Prayer by the Moderator when Mrs. Margaret Cordelia Franklin one of the Baptised members of the church was examined in the subject of experimental religion and the session being satisfied that she had experienced a change of heart she was admitted to full privaleges [sic] in the Church also the session conversed with Mrs. Sarah Emaly [sic] [Corbett] Franklin who gave satisfactory evidence that she had also been renewed by the holy Spirit and was trusting in the Lord Jesus Christ as her only Saviour. She was also received into the Church by the Session

Session then Adjourned for Public worship.

P. M. Rankin clerk

Mount Horeb June 4th 1870

Session was called together by the Moderator

Present Rev. Wm. H. Lyle Moderator, C. Rankin, J. C. Bradshaw, E. Alexander, P. M. Rankin, Absent Wm. Rankin

Session Constituted with Prayer by the Moderator when on application James A. Newman was awarded a letter of dismission from this Church in good standing and the clerk order [sic] to make out and forward the letter accordingly when session took a recess until tomorrow 4 o'clock P.M.   (51)

June 5th 4 o'clock P. M. Session came to order when the committee appointed March 26, 1870 to visit John T. Mathes and have some further conversation with him reported that they had discharged that duty and found him manifesting a disposition to withdraw from the church and insisting on his unfitness to receive church privileges and acknowledge that the charges made by rumor of drunkness [sic] and profanity were true in part and had no evidence of having repented of the [p. 106] same which report was received and a motion made and seconded that the said John T. Mathes be suspended from all the privaleges [sic] of this Church which motion was sustained and ordered that notice be given to the congregation of the action of session in this case from the stand by the Moderator   the committee appointed also on 26th March 1870 to visit James A. Barbee (one of the members of this Church who long absented himself from the house of God and neglected the Means of grace and who rumor accuses of drunkenness and profanity) reported that they had done so and found him evidently indisposed in relation to religious matters, not at all disposed to converse with the committee on the subject but acknowledged that his conduct at times was far from being what it should be but made no deffinite [sic] confession. Advised that the session strike off his name from the Church book but finally agreed that he would come to the approaching sacramental meeting, see the session, and have a conversation with them. the Report was rec'd and on motion further action was postponed for the present when on motion session adjourned.

P. M. Rankin Clerk

Mount Horeb Tenn June 19th 1870

Session Met on the call of the Moderator

Present Rev. W. H. Lyle Moderator Elder C. Rankin J. C. Bradshaw, E. Alexander, P. M. Rankin

Session was constituted with (52) Prayer by the Moderator when the Moderator brought before the session a notice from the Stated Clerk of Synod notifying session that Synod had passed a resolution at their last meeting requiring all Church Sessions within their bounds to report to Synod against their next meeting how much their several Churches have done during the last year towards the education of young men for the Ministry when it was agreed that the said notice be read to the congregation Publicly and a collection be [p. 107] taken up for the purpose aforenamed two weeks from to day [sic] Joseph C. Bradshaw was appointed to represent the Church at the meeting of Synod at New Market in July next. C. Rankin his alternate when on motion session adjourned to meet two weeks from today immediately after sermon in order to make out the Report alluded to July 3d. 1870 session met according Adjournment when the subject of making the required report was discussed and decided in the affirmative when session Adjourned

P. S. the amount Reported $14.45   P. M. Rankin, Clerk

Mount Horeb Aug. 28th 1870

Session met in Conjunction with the trustees by previous arrangement for the purpose of appointing a committee on the ? Million Memorial fund

Present Rev. Wm. H. Lyle Moderator, Elders C. Rankin, J. C. Bradshaw, E. Alexander, P. M. Rankin.

Trustees J. T. Rankin, P. D. Rankin, Jos. [or Jas.] Rankin, J. E. Rankin

opened by prayer by Moderator when John J. Coil, J. T. Rankin, John F. Newman, John C. Bradshaw & G. W. Newman were appointed on committee to secure and collect subscriptions in the bounds of Mount Horeb Church in aid of the above named fund

the session then appointed P. M. Rankin delegate to attend the meeting of Presbytery at Spring Place, Knox County, Tenn. in Sept. next. also C. Rankin (53) delegate to Synod to meet at Kingston, Roane County in Oct. next when on motion session Adjourned for public worship   P. M. Rankin clerk

Mount Horeb October 9, 1870

Session met on call of the Moderator

Present Rev. Wm. H. Lyle Moderator, C. Rankin, J. C. Bradshaw, E. Alexander & P. M. Rankin, Absent Wm. Rankin [p. 108] Session Constituted with Prayer by the Moderator.

Minuets [sic] of the meetings of Session since 20th January were read considered amended and approved unfinished business being called for the case of John T. Mathes which was voted upon by the session on the 4th day of June last recorded on page 105

when the clerk was directed to notify the said Mathes to come before the session on Saturday 22d instant in order to hear the decision of the Session in relation to the charges prepared by Public rumor against him of drunkenness and profanity when on motion session Adjourned to 22d instant 12 N closed with Prayer

P. M. Rankin Clerk

October 22 Session convened according to agreement Present as at the last meeting except E. Alexander who was absent Session not having certain information that the notice mentions in the minuets [sic] last above had been ? they adjourned over until after sermon three weeks from tomorrow (Nov. 14, 1870) closed with Prayer.

P. M. Rankin Clerk

Mount Horeb Tenn. Feb. 25th 1871

Session Met on call of Moderator. Present Rev. Wm. H. Lyle Moderator, Elders Joseph C. Bradshaw, Elias Alexander, P. M. Rankin   (54)

Session having heard of the Death of our esteemed Brother Wm. Rankin[92]

The following Minuet [sic] is unanimously adopted with humble submission to the dispensation of God's Holy Providence the session records the Death of one of its members Mr. Wm. Rankin who departed this life on Friday the 24th of February 1871 in the seventy fifth year of his age while we would thus submit to the will of God yet we feel that we have lost a safe and wise councilor

at the same time Joseph M. H. Rankin, James A. Newman, Martha J. Jolly, Sarah J. Carson and Jannet S. Rankin who all having been baptized in infancy came before the session and after being examined were admitted to church privleges [sic] when session took a recess until tomorrow morning 8½ o'clock A. M. 8½ o'clock [sic] Feb. 26th 1871

Session convened present as before when Andrew N. Rankin, James M. [Moore] McMurray, George M. Taylor, Asa B. [Asahel Biddle] Bradshaw, Andrew T. H. Bradshaw, George [W.] Franklin, Hellen Rankin, Lucinda Ann Franklin, Rachal [sic] Isabel McMurray, Benjamin Rankin, Inez Fain, James L. Rankin came before the session and were examined on experimental religion and giving satisfactory evidence of having experienced a change of heart and having been baptised in infancy were admitted to Church privleges [sic] also at the same time Isaac A. Franklin, Lewis A. M. Hazlewood, Belender [sic] V. Rankin,[93] Martha M. Rankin, and Thomas A. R. N. Williams were examined by the session and giving satisfactory evidence of their having been renewed by the Holy Spirit they were received into the church by Baptism also at the same time Milton Homer Gass was examined by the session and admitted to Church privleges [sic] he having been baptized in infancy his name to be transfered [sic] to Hopewell Church when session adjourned.

P. M. Rankin
clerk

---

[92] William Rankin, son of Thomas Rankin II and Jennet Bradshaw Rankin, born August 2, 1896.

[93] Probably Bellvada "Belle" Victoria Rankin b 1858, d 1934 Miami, Dade Co, FL m 1893 Orville Meigs Carson.

[p. 110] Mount Horeb Tenn April 8, 1871   (55)

Session Met on call of the Moderator. Present Rev. Wm. H. Lyle Moderator, Elias Alexander, P. M. Rankin, Absent C. Rankin, J. C. Bradshaw. Session constituted with Prayer by Moderator when P. M. Rankin was appointed to represent this Church in Presbytery to meet at Caladonia Church Knox County, Tenn. April 27, 1871 Joseph C. Bradshaw his alternate when in motion session adjourned closed with prayer.

P. M. Rankin Clerk

Mount Horeb Tenn, April 23, 1871

Session met on the call of the Moderator

Present Rev. Wm. H. Lyle Moderator, Elders Jos. C. Bradshaw, Chris Rankin, Elias Alexander, P. M. Rankin

Session was constituted with Prayer by the Moderator Minuets [sic] of the proceedings of session back to October 23, 1870 read their approval defered [sic] unfinished Business being called up the case of John T. Mathes which was considered by the session on the 4th day of June 1870 recorded on page 105 of these minuets [sic] was resumed when it appearing that session failed of a meeting which was appointed on the 17th day of November 1870 for finally disposing of the case and it now appearing certain that the notice refered [sic] to in the Minuets [sic] of the proceedings of session on 9th of October 1870 and subsequently on the 22d of the same Month had been received by the said Mathes in due time and it also appearing that he had been notified of the present meeting of session and failing to appear before the session as required by the said notice in order to hear the decision of the session in (56) relation to his case and that the sentence of suspension could be pronounced upon him in person it was resolved that the sentence of suspension so far as to the same being pronounced upon him or being made public as required by a previous act of this session [p. 111] be dispensed with

Frances Malinda Bales having made application for a letter of dismission from the Church it was awarded her and the clerk directed to make out and forward the letter accordingly when on motion session adjourned closed with prayer.

P. M. Rankin

Clerk

Records approved thus far

E. N. Sawtell Mod.

Mount Horeb Tenn August 13, 1871

Session met on call of Moderator

Present Rev. Wm. H. Lyle Moderator, Jos. C. Bradshaw, Chris Rankin, Elias Alexander, P. M. Rankin

Session was constituted with Prayer by the Moderator when Joseph N. Bradshaw was dismissed by letter on application through his father the Rev. Wm. H. Lyle having heretofore notified the Congregation that he intended to petition Presbytery at its next slated meeting do [*sic*] dissolve the Pastoral relation between him and this church. it was agreed to lay the matter before the Congregation two weeks from the day as to whether they are willing to join with the Pastor in the request and if so when it shall take affect [*sic*] and how they will make their wishes known to Presbytery when Session Adjourned for Public worship

P. M. Rankin

[p.112] Mount Horeb Aug. 27th 1871 (57)

Session met on call of the Moderator

Present Rev. W. H. Lyle Moderator, Elders C. Rankin, Jos. C. Bradshaw, E. Alexander, P. M. Rankin

Session was constituted with Prayer by the Moderator When P. M. Rankin was appointed to represent the Church in Presbytery at the next stated meeting at Dandridge 21st Sept. 1871 it was also arranged to take up a collection two weeks from this day for the purpose of paying some indebtedness of the Church the vote of the Congregation in relation to dissolving the Pastoral relation resulted in an agreement with the Pastor in the relation to Presbytery but differed at the time he wishing the disolution [*sic*] take place at the end of the present year and the congregation asking that it take affect [*sic*] the first of October the congregation also agreed to sign the petition on their part by their Elders

P. M. Rankin Clerk

Mount Horeb Oct. 15, 1871

Session met on the call of Moderator

Present Rev. Wm. H. Lyle Moderator, Elders C. Rankin, J. C. Bradshaw, Elias Alexander & P. M. Rankin

Session was opened with Prayer by the Moderator

when the following [p. 113] action was had Mark T. Rankin and his wife Nancy A. Rankin were dismissed by letter to join any Evangilical [*sic*] Church where their lot may be cast also Thomas W. Vance and Sarah A. Vance his wife were dismissed by letter to Hopewell Church, Dandridge, Tenn. P. M. Rankin was appointed to attend the fall meeting of Synod at Maryville on Ult. [*sic*] Dec. 26th 1871 when session adjourned for Public Worship

P. M. Rankin Clerk

Mount Horeb Jany.[*sic*] 7, 1872 (58)

Session came together by agreement and by request the Rev. Jas. A. Griffes acted as Moderator, Elders Present Jas. C. Bradshaw, Elias Alexander, C. Rankin, P. M. Rankin. Session was constituted with Prayer by the Moderator when it appearing that at an informal meeting of session in the 10th of December 1871 there was a letter of dismission awarded to Mrs. Barsheba W. Talbot the said informal act of the session as ratified when on motion session Adjourned.

P. M. Rankin Clerk

Mount Horeb March 17th 1872

Session held on [sic] informal meeting at which was present Joseph C. Bradshaw, C. Rankin & P. M. Rankin when letter of dismission was granted to Elizabeth C. Norton formerly Rankin also on April 28th 1872 by the same parties when letter of dismission was awarded to Mrs. Sarah Porter Lyle to join Hopewell Church at Dandridge.

Mount Horeb June 1st, 1872

Session came together by agreement when Joseph C. Bradshaw, E. [p. 114] Alexander, C. Rankin and P. M. Rankin were present when at the request of session Rev. E. N. Sawtell presided as Moderator and session was opened by Prayer by the same when the action of the two informal meetings of this session in granting letters of dismission to Elizabeth C. Norton formerly Rankin and also to Sarah Porter Lyleand considered and confirmed when session took recess until Sabbath evening when there being nothing more brought before the session for consultation session Adjourned with benediction.   P. M. Rankin, Clerk

Mount Horeb June 23d 1872   (59)

There was an informal meeting of Session at which E. Alexander, J. C. Bradshaw, C. Rankin and P. M. Rankin was present when Mrs. Ellen L. Snodgrass formerly Rankin was awarded a letter of dismission and on motion of E. Alexander leave was granted Rev. E. N. Sawtell to put before this church the Assemblys [sic] plans or system of finance and the clerk was directed to inform him of the action of session in regard to the matter.   P. M. Rankin Clerk

Mount Horeb Nov. 3, 1872

There was an informal meeting of the Session at which J. C. Bradshaw, Christopher Rankin & P. M. Rankin were present and letters of dismission were awarded to James S. Fain & N. J. Fain his wife to join Presbyterian Church at Dandridge.
                    P. M. Rankin Clerk

[p. 115] Mount Horeb, Tenn. Oct. 6, 1872

An informal Meeting of Session was held at which a letter of dismission was awarded to Daniel L. Bettis to join Hopewell Church.
                    P. M. Rankin Clerk

Mount Horeb, Tenn. Dec. 29th 1872

Session met and by request Rev. E. N. Sawtell acted as Moderator C. Rankin, J. C. Bradshaw, E. Alexander & P. M. Rankin being present Session was opened with Prayer by the Moderator when the informal Meeting of Session on Nov. 3, 1872 granting a letter of dismission to Jas. S. Fain & N. J. Fain his wife was confirmed also the meeting of Oct. 6, 1872 granting a letter of dismission to Daniel L. Bettis was ratified when Session adjourned with Benadiction [sic]
                    P. M. Rankin Clerk

Mount Horeb Tenn. Feb. 2d. 1873
An informal Meeting of session was had at which C. Rankin, J. C. Bradshaw & P. M. Rankin was present when a letter of dismission was (60) granted to Stephen R. Bradshaw.

P. M. Rankin Clerk

Mount Horeb April 12th, 1873
Session met by appointment Rev. T. A. [Isaac A.] Martin Moderator
Present C. Rankin, J. C. Bradshaw, Elias Alexander & P. M. Rankin
Session opened with Prayer by the Moderator when the proceding of an informal meeting of session of Feb. 3, 1873 at which Stephen R. [p. 116] Bradshaw was awarded a letter. a letter of dismission was considered and ratified and the Annual Report to Presbytery was made out and P. M. Rankin appointed to attend the meeting of Presbytery on the 24th of April 1873 to be held at New Prospect Church Knox County Tenn.

when Susan C. Carson one of the members of the Church who had fallen into a grievous sin by a violation of the seventh Commandment came before the session and acknowledged her sin and manifested deep sorrow and repentance for the same expressed a hope that she has obtained forgiveness and reconciliation with the Great Head of the Church and requested that she be allowed to remain in the Communion of the Church which requests the session granted the Moderator to give public notice of the action of session to the Congregation

when Session Adjourned closed with Prayer by Jos. C. Bradshaw.

P. M. Rankin Clerk

Approved to date New Prospect April 25th 1873
Geo. W. Lev Ven Mod.

Mount Horeb Aug. 2, 1873
Session convened by agreement Christopher Rankin was appointed to attend the Meeting of Presbytery at Washington Church, Knox County as delegate from the Church P. M. Rankin was appointed to attend the Meeting of Synod at Rogersville E. Alexander his alternate Session dispersed.

P. M. Rankin Clerk

[p. 117] Mount Horeb, Tenn. Sept. 27th 1873   (61)
Session met and was constituted with prayer by the Moderator Rev. T. A. Martin, Present C. Rankin, J. C. Bradshaw, E. Alexander and P. M. Rankin

the object of this meeting to consult together in relation to the election of some additional Elders when it was agreed to submit the question to the Church to be determined by ballot on the 12th day of Oct. 1873

it was also determined that there should be three additional Elders elected if the church decided to elect any at the present time it appearing that part of the session had awarded a letter of dismission to George W. Faigly the act was approved when session Adjourned closed with Prayer by C. Rankin.

P. M. Rankin,
Clerk

October 4, 1873 Pleasant J. Bettis was awarded a letter of dismission from the Church to join Hopewell Church

P. M. Rankin, Clerk

October 12th 1873 The Church voted by ballot on the Question as to Electing additional Elders which resulted in favor of Electing 41 votes for Electing to 14 in opposition therefore and the 26th of this month was fixed as the time.

[X's were drawn through this paragraph and "Disapproved" was written on the left margin beside this paragraph.]

P. M. Rankin Clerk

Oct. 26th 1873 the Election for Elders was held relating [resulting] in the Election of N. H. [Nathaniel Hood] Franklin on first ballot he receiving 68 votes out of 78 votes cast also in the Election of John G. Rankin he receiving 48 votes out of 78 cast when upon the 3d ballot T. C. [S. E.] Rankin rec'd 38 votes and out of 72 votes cast and was declared to be Elected. [X's were drawn through this paragraph and "Disapproved" was written on the left margin beside this paragraph.]

P. M. Rankin Clerk

[p. 118] Mount Horeb, Tenn. Nov. 22, 1873   (62)
Session convened on the call of the Moderator
Present C. Rankin J. C. Bradshaw, E. Alexander, P. M. Rankin
Session was constituted with Prayer by Rev. T. A. Martin Moderator
Business whether to proceed to the ordination of the newly Elected Elders or not. objections were offered to the ordination of T. E. [S. E.] Rankin on the ground that he is not aceptible [*sic*] to a considerable part of the congregation and that he is not certainly approved and that he is sustained by a majority of the whole church. when after much talk it seemed evident session would not come to any agreement
Session Adjourned.

P. M. Rankin Clerk

Afternoon of same day session convened again on call of the Moderator present as before session was constituted with prayer by the Moderator business same as in forenoon nothing definite being done Session adjourned closed by Prayer.

[X's were drawn through this paragraph.]

P. M. Rankin,
Clerk

Mount Horeb, Tenn. Nov. 23, 1873

Session met by agreement Present Rev. T. A. Martin Moderator C. Rankin, J. C. Bradshaw, E. Alexander, P. M. Rankin

Session was constituted with Prayer by the Moderator when William McMurry came before the Session and was examined on the subject of experimental Religion and giving full satisfaction that he had experienced a change of heart he was admitted to full communion in the Church having been baptised in Infancy

when session Adjourned for public worship.   P. M. Rankin Clerk

[p. 119] Mount Horeb, Tenn. December 21, 1878

Session met on call of the Moderator

Present Rev. T. A. Martin Moderator, Elders Christopher Rankin, Joseph C. Bradshaw, Elias Alexander, P. M. Rankin   (63)

when George T. McGee came before session and was examined on the subject of experimental religion and giving satisfactory evidence to session that he had been renewed in heart was admitted into full communion and fellowship in the Church as a Member of the same and was afterwards received publicly

when it was agreed that the Annual Collection of this Church for the Home Mission Cause be taken up at the time which was done during public services

when the unfinished business of the session of Nov. 22d. in relation to the ordination of the newly Elected Elders which had been postponed by the Moderator from that time until the present time came up for consideration when a motion was made by P. M. [Patrick McGuire] Rankin to postpone the Ordination of S. E. [Samuel Edwin] Rankin until such time as circumstances may justify decision in taking it up against which motion was seconded and on the vote being to [*sic*] was sustained by J. C. [Joseph Conway] Bradshaw and offered by C. [Christopher] Rankin and E.[Elias] Alexander when after conferring with the candidates for ordination the Moderator requested session to allow him two weeks further time in which to decide the matter in order that he might make an effort to reconcile alienated parties which was agreed to the whole session concurring when session dispersed for public worship.

[X's were drawn through this paragraph]

P. M. Rankin
Clerk

[p. 120] Mount Horeb, Tenn. Jan. 4, 1874

The Moderator of Sessions Rev. I. A. Martin proceeded to the ordination of S. E. [Samuel Edwin] Rankin & N. H. [Nathaniel Hood] Franklin as Elders in Mount Horeb Church assisted by Christopher Rankin and Elias Alexander session never having decided or determined the matter as to whether they should or should not be ordained.

[X's were drawn through this paragraph and "Disapproved" was written on the left margin beside this paragraph.]

P. M. Rankin,
Clerk of Session

Mount Horeb, Tenn. Jan. 10, 1874   (64)
An informal meeting of the session was held at which Christopher Rankin, Elias Alexander, P. M. Rankin, S. E. Rankin, N. H. Franklin was present when at his own request a letter of dismission was granted to P. M. Rankin by which the clerkship was left vacant when N. H. [Nathan Hood] Franklin was appointed clerk pro tem

N. H. Franklin,
Clerk Pro Tem

Mount Horeb, Tenn. Feb. 15, 1874
Session met on call of Moderator
Present Rev. I. A. Martin Moderator, C. Rankin, J. C. Bradshaw, E. Alexander, S. E. Rankin, N. H. Franklin Elders
Session was constituted by prayer by Moderator when letter of dismission was [p. 121] given to N. E. [Nancy Emily] Brown, John N. Bradshaw and John R. Bradshaw when Sessions agreed to meet on Feb. 28, 1874.

N. H. Franklin, Clerk Pro Tem

Mount Horeb, Tenn. Feb. 28, 1874
Session met according to adjournment and was constituted by prayer by Moderator
Present Rev. I. A. Martin Moderator
J. C. Bradshaw, C. Rankin, E. Alexander, N. H. Franklin Elders   (65)   N. H. [Nathaniel Hood] Franklin was elected stated clerk of session
On reading the minute, the session disapproved of that part of the records relating to the election and ordination of elders from Oct. 12, 1873 to Jan. 10, 1874 on the ground that it was not sessional business
Eliza E. Coile and Andrew J. Coile requested certificate of dismission from this church and a recommendation to other churches Their request was granted
having come within the Knowledge of the session that Henry O. Newman a member of this church has been guilty of profanity and Sabbath breaking Christopher Rankin and N. H. Franklin was appointed to visit him and report at the next meeting of session. The session adjourned to meet on March 15 before the public services Concluded with prayer.

N. H. Franklin Clerk

[p. 122] Mount Horeb, Tenn. March 15, 1874
Session met and was constituted by prayer
Present Rev. I. A. Martin Moderator, Christopher Rankin, S. E. Rankin, N. H. Franklin Elders
The following members requested certificates of dismission from this church and recommendations to other churches Joseph C. Bradshaw (an Elder), Catharine E. Newman, F. H. Bradshaw, W. A. [William A.] Mathes and Margaret Mathes also Luella M. [Coile] Newman and Emma C. Newman baptized non communing members Their request was granted

The committee appointed at the last meeting to visit H. O. Newman reported that they had discharged the duty assigned them and that he acknowledges the charges made against him and requested the session to drop his name from the roll as (66) he does not feel fit to remain in the church! When session excommunicated him on his own confession of guilt

Christopher Rankin was appointed to represent this session at the stated spring meeting of the Presbytery Session adjourned for public worship

N. H. Franklin
Clerk

Mount Horeb, Tenn. March 26, 1874

Session met and was constituted by prayer

Present Rev. I. A. Martin Moderator, C. Rankin, E. Alexander, S. E. Rankin, N. H. Franklin Elders

[p. 123] The minuts [sic] of last meeting was read and approved

The session made the following reports to the Presbytery.

Reciprocal reports of Mount Horeb Church

The church and session of Mount Horeb enjoyed one half of the ministerial services of Rev. Isaac A. Martin during the year 1873 for which they pledged him $196 of which $161.85 have been paid and satisfactory pledges given for the remainder and no further report that the Rev. I. A. Martin labored faithfuly [sic] and to the satisfaction of the church and congregation adjourned for public worship

N. H. Franklin
Clerk

Approved to date with exception that there were erasures after entry in the Book which present a very uncomely appearance

Mount Horeb, Tenn.

Isaac Emory, Moderator

Mch. 27th 1874

Mount Horeb, Tenn. Sept. 13, 1874

Session met and was constituted by prayer

Present Rev. I. A. Martin Mod. (67) Christopher Rankin, Elias Alexander, S. E. Rankin, N. H. Franklin Elders

When it appeared that at certain informal meetings of the Session held since the last regular meeting Hugh A. [Alexander] Newman and Lydia T. his wife also Darthula J. Riggs and William T. Bradshaw, [p. 124] Alexander M. Shadden & Joseph W. Shadden were dismissed and recommended to other churches. Whereupon it was resolved that the above proceedings of the informal meetings be approved and entered upon the minuts [sic]. [See next page]

The following members having joined other churches without applying for letters of dismission. It was resolved to drop their names from the roll of this church:

Thomas M. H. [Michael Harden] Bradshaw	John C. [Calvin] Bradshaw
William P. M. [Porter Massengil] Bradshaw]	Sarah E. Bradshaw
Nancy D. Bradshaw	Phebe [Phoebe Ann] Armentrout
Frances J. Bradshaw	J. P. [John Prigmore] Bradshaw
Harriet J. Bradshaw	J. 0. [James Oliver] Bettis
Thomas J. Bradshaw	Sarah Bradshaw
Rufus E. Carson	Asa B. Bradshaw
Harriet D. Carson	John J. Coile
William E. Coile	Mary E. Carson
Susan E. Carson	Sarah J. Carson
Nathaniel H. Carson	Jane R. Newman
Jane M. Massengill	Mary C. Newman
Gideon W. Newman	Catharine C. Newman
James A. Newman	Richard D. [Duffield] Rankin
Josiah E. Rankin	Mary M. Rankin
Louisa J. Rankin	John Rankin

(68)

Mary A. Rankin	John G. Rankin
Frances L. Rankin	Marjorah [sic] E. Rankin
Catharine R. Rankin	Hellen [sic] Rankin
Benj. C. Rankin	John F. Newman
Martha A. Rankin	

S. E. Rankin was appointed to represent this church in Presbytery in its regular fall meeting and N. H. [Nathaniel Hood] Franklin was appointed delegate to synod and Elias Alexander his alternate

[p. 125] Adjourned with prayer

N. H. Franklin,
Clerk

Indexed Record of Membership

from page 4 to 50 inclusive [p. 4-5] [94]

	Name of Members	When Rec'd	How Rec'd	When Bapt.	Dismis-sed	How Dismis-sed	Sus-pend ed	Re-stored	Remarks
X	Alexander, Elias	Apr. 9, 1854	By letter						
X	Alexander, Sarah J. [Jane]	Jan. 17, 1858	On exam.	Infancy	Nov. 7, 1880	By death			
X	Alexander, Jane	Oct. 12, 1842	"	"	May 5, 1867	"		Formerly Rankin	
X	Alexander, Thomas T.	June 4, 1866	"	"					
X	Ashmore, Davis	Jul. 16, 1854	By letter						
X	Ashmore, Polly	"	"						
X	Ashmore, Norrit	"	"						
X	Bradshaw, John W. M.	Jan. 4, 1866	On exam	Infancy	Feb. 15, 1874	By letter			
X	Bradshaw, Thomas M. H. [Michael Harden "Mike"]	Jan. 4, 1866	"	"	Sept. 13, 1874			Joined Southern Church	
X	Bradshaw, Joseph P. [Paluthiah Hood]	"	"	"	Aug. 13, 1871	By letter		Joined Southern Church	
X	Bradshaw, John C. [Calvin]	"	"	"	Sept. 13, 1874			Joined Southern Church	
X	Bradshaw, Sarah E.	"	"	"	"				
X	Bradshaw, Lydia T. [Timantha]	Jan. 8, 1866	"	"	March 28, 1874	By letter			
X	Bradshaw, William P. M..	"	"	"					
X	Alexander, Emma L.	Jan. 4, 1866	"	"					
X	Armentrout, Phebe A.	July 11, 1859	certificate		Sept. 13, 1874	Joined Cumber-lains		Wife of John [Prigmore] Rankin	
	B								
X	Bradshaw, Richard	Nov. 20, 1841	Organiza-tion of church		Nov. 10, 1867	By notice in writing that he had attached himself to another organization on account of the Assembly holding, on the subject of the sin of the Rebellion and also the action of this church Session on the same.			

---

[94] The column of Xs was in the original for some unknown reason. It apparently meant something to the Clerk of Session but was never explained in writing.

X	Bradshaw, Lydia [Prigmore]	"	"			Oct. 20, 185_ [Nov. 27, 1853][95]	By death			
X	Bradshaw, Joseph C.	"				Mar. 15, 1874	By letter			
X	Bradshaw, Sarah C. [Grizzle "Sally" Blackburn]	"				Nov. 6, 1860	By death	Wife of Joseph C. Bradshaw		
X	Bradshaw, Richard H. [Harden]	"				Jan. 1 [7], 1863	By death			
X	Bradshaw, Jane [P. Rawlings]	"				Feb. 14, 1863	By death			
X	Bradshaw, Thomas R. [Rankin]	"				April 3, 1859	Minister			
X	Bradshaw, Margaret [Blackburn]	"				May 28, 1847	By death	Wife of Rev. T. R. [Thomas Rankin] Bradshaw		
X	Bradshaw, Elizabeth W. [Rawlings]	"				Jan. 14, 1860		Wife of John P. Bradshaw		
X	Bradshaw, John P. [Prigmore]	"				Sept. 13, 1874			Joined Southern Ch.	
X	Bradshaw, Richard R. [Rawlings]	May 26, 1850	On exam	Infancy		Feb. 2, 1872	By letter			
X	Bradshaw, Stephen R.	Nov. 27, 1851	"	"		Sept. 13, 1874			Joined Southern Ch.	
X	Bradshaw, Nancy D. [Dorthulia]	Apr. 9, 1854	"	"						

[Page 6-7]

	Name of Members	When Rec'd	How Rec'd	When Bapt.	Dis-missed	How Dismissed	Suspended	Remark
X	Bradshaw, Frances J. [Jane]	Oct. 8, 1854	On Exam	Infancy	Sept 13, 1874	Joined Southern Church		formerly Miss Berry
X	Bradshaw, Orlena C. [Eglentine Clementine]	Jan. 16, 1858	"	"	Apr. 7, 1863	By death	daughter of Rev. T. R. [Thomas Rankin] Bradshaw	
X	Bradshaw, Edward A. [Alexander]	"	"	"	Oct. 12, 1865 [1863]	"		
X	Bradshaw, William M. [Minnis]	"	"	"	March 21, 1884	"		
X	Bradshaw, Harriet J.	Jan. 17, 1858	"	"	Sept, 13, 1874	Joined Southern church		
X	Bradshaw, David H.	"	"	"	Feb. 29, 1868	Suspended for long absence without letter.		

[95] The date was impossible to read in the Minutes. Find-A-Grave had a photo of the headstone with November 27, 1853 as the death date, Memorial # 10675288,<http://www.findagrave.com/cgi>.

X	Bradshaw, Thomas J. [John]	Jan. 18, 1858	"	"	Sept, 13, 1874	Joined Southern church	
X	Barbee, David	Oct. 16, 1842	"	Adult	Oct. 27, 1850	Suspended	
X	Barbee, James A.	Jan. 18, 1858	"	"	Dec. 10, 1870	Joined Baptist Church at Dandridge.	
X	Bettis, John W.	Oct. 13, 1842	"	"	Mar. 16, 1867	Informally	He connected himself to Methodist
X	Bettis, Isabella [Henderson Lyle]	Organization	"	"	April 26. 1872	By death	From Hopewell Church
X	Bettis, Mary E. [Elizabeth]	"	"	"	May 16, 1847	By letter	Now Mary Coil
X	Bettis, Sarah M.	Oct. 14, 1842	"	"	"		Now Sarah Coil
X	Bowls, Eunice	Apr. 16, 1842	By letter	"	Jan. 2, 1848	"	
X	Bettis, James O. [Oliver]	Jan. 8, 1866	Examination	Adult	Sept. 13, 1874		Joined Cumberlain's
X	Bradshaw, Sarah	Oct. 2, 1864	Certificate	"	"	Joined Southern Church	From Baptist Church. Chattanooga
X	Bradshaw, Martha A. [Ann]	Apr. 9, 1854	Examination	Infancy	Feb. 29, 1868	Suspended	Leaving country without letter. Wife of R. [Joseph Reece] Newman
X	Bradshaw, Margaret		"	"	Jan. 19, 1867	By death	Wife of Richard Bradshaw
X	Bettis, Pleasant J.	Jan. 22, 1858	"	Adult	Oct. 4, 1873	By letter	
X	Bowers, William A.	"	"	"	Feb. 29, 1868	Suspended for leaving country without letter, two years	
X	Bradshaw, John R.	Nov. 10, 1867	Exam	In infancy	Feb. 15, 1874	By letter	Son of Rev. T. R. Bradshaw
X	Bowles, Ellen	Jan. 12, 1868	Certificate	"	April 23, 1873	By letter	Formerly Ellen Richards
X	Bradshaw, Asa B. [Asahel Biddle]	Feb. 26, 1811	Examination	"	Sept. 13, 1874		Joined Southern Church
X	Bradshaw, Andrew T. H. [Thomas Hood]	"	"	"	Mar. 15, 1874	By letter	
	Bettis, Daniel L. [Lyle]	Jan. 20, 1858	"	"	Oct. 6, 1872	By letter	

Pages [8-9]

	Name of Members	When Rec'd	How Rec'd	When Bapt.	Dismissed	How Dismissed	Suspended	Remarks
X	Cox, James	Oct. 16, 1842	Examination	Adult	Oct. 1, 1848	By Letter		
X	Cox, Rachel	"	"	"	"	"		
X	Cokenhour, James	Jan. 16, 1858	"	"				

	Name	When Rec'd	How Rec'd	When Bapt.	Dismissed	How Dismissed	Suspended	Remarks
X	Cokenhour, Mary A.	"	"	"				
X	Cline, Mary E.	Jan. 19, 1858	"	Infancy				Now Franklin
	Cline, Joseph H.	Jan. 20, 1858	"	"				
X	Cline, Mary A. [Ann Sina Newman]	"	"	"	By Death			
X	Carson, Rufus E.	June 5, 1861	On Cert.		Sept. 13, 1874			Joined Cumberland
X	Carson, Harriet D.	"	"		"			"
X	Collins, George	Jan. 11, 1866	Exam.	Adult	April 21, 1867	By Letter		
X	Coil, Eliza E.	"	"	Infancy	Feb. 28, 1874	By Letter		
X	Cline, Erasmus H. [Harvey]	July 17, 1859	Certificate		Sept. 12, 1875			
X	Cline, Juliet E.	July 17, 1859	"		"			
X	Coil, John James	Sept. 29, 1865	Examination	Infancy	Sept. 13, 1874			Joined Cumberland
X	Coil, William T.	Apr. 28, 1867	"	"	"			Joined Cumberland
X	Coil, Andrew J.	Apr. 28, 1867	"	"	Feb. 28, 1874	By Letter		
X	Coil, Henry P.	Apr. 28, 1867	"	"	Apr. 20, 1873	By Letter		
X	Carson, Susan C.	Nov. 10, 1867	"	"	Sept. 13, 1874			Joined Cumberlains
X	Carson, Mary E.	"	"	"	"			"
X	Carson, Nathaniel H.	"	"	"	"			"
X	Carson, Sarah Jane	Feb. 26, 1871	"	"	"			"

[Pages 10-11]

	Name of Members	When Rec'd	How Rec'd	When Bapt.	Dismissed	How Dismissed	Suspended	Remarks
X	Darr, James H.	Aug 22, 1852	Examination	Adult	Jan. 18	By Letter		
X	Darr, Nancy J.	Sept. 8, 1851	"	Infancy	"	"		Formerly Bradshaw
X	Eaton, Robert P.	May 17, 1851	"	"	Mar. 6, 1859	"		
X	Eaton, Elenor C.	"	"	"	"	"		
X	Easterly, Moses	Nov 20, 1842	"	"	June 11, 1844	"		
X	Easterly, Mary B.	"	Certificate		"	"		

[Pages 12-13]

	Name of Members	When Rec'd	How Rec'd	When Bapt.	Dismissed	How Dismissed	Suspended	Restored	Remark
X	Franklin, Benjamin F.	Nov. 20, 1841	On exam.						
X	Franklin, Lucinda H.	"	"						
X	Franklin, John H.	"	"						
	Franklin, Ann	Aug. 26, 1849	On exam.	Infancy	July 27, 1861	By death			
X	Funk, Samuel	Aug. 30, 1856	On certif.		Sept, 1864	"			
X	Funk, Elizabeth	"	"		Sept. 29, 1867	By letter			
X	Franklin, Laura A.	Jan. 23, 1858	On exam.	Adult	"	"			
X	Franklin, Thomas P.	Jan. 18, 1858	"	Infancy	Dec. 30, 1870	By death			
X	Franklin, Samuel H.	Jan. 20, 1858	"	Adult					
X	Franklin, Campbell	Jan. 21, 1858	"	"		By letter			
X	Franklin, Elizabeth	Nov. 8, 1842	By Letter		June 22, 1843	By death			
X	Franklin, Rebecca A.	Oct. 13, 1842	Examination	Infancy	Sept.17, 1861	"			Formerly McCuistion
X	Franklin, Benjamin, Jr.	Jan. 4, 1866	"	"					Joined Cumberlains, Formerly Jacob [?]
X	Franklin, Nathan H.	"	"	"					
X	Franklin, Catherine R.	"	"	"					Wife of C. H. Rankin
X	Fain, James S.	"	"	"					
X	Fain, N. J.	"	"	"	Nov. 5, 1872	By letter			
X	Franklin, Margaret C. [McMurray]	May 8, 1870	"	"	"	"			Wife of Benjamin Franklin, Jr.
X	Franklin, Sarah E. [Corbett]	"	"	Adult					Wife of Thomas P. Franklin
X	Franklin, Isaac Anderson	Feb. 26, 1871	Exam.	Adult					
X	Franklin, George	"	"	Infancy					
X	Franklin, Lucinda Ann	"	"	"					
X	Faigley, George W.	"	"	"	Sept 14, 1873	By letter			
X	Fain, Inez	"	"	"					

[Page 14-15, 17]

	Name of Members	When Rec'd	How Rec'd	When baptized	When dis.	How Dismissed	Suspended	Remarks
	Gass, Emily W.	Sept. 8, 1851	Exam-Ination	Infancy	Mar. 31, 1873	Dropped from records		
	Gass. Adaline	Sept. 26, 1852	Certifi-cate	Adult	July 1862 Aug. 18, 1870	By death[96]		
	Gass, Andrew T.	May 30, 1857	Exam-ination	Infancy	Nov. 6, 1871		Suspen-ded	Left country. Man of Color
	Gass, David C.	Feb. 21, 1858	"	Adult	Nov. 6, 1871	By death - Killed suddenly by wagon running over him		
X	Hannah of colour	Aug. 26, 1849	"	"				
X	Hall, Mary Jane	Jan. 11, 1866	"	"				
X	Howard, George	Jan. 11, 1866	"	Infancy				
X	Hazelwood, Lewis A. M.	Feb. 26, 1871	"	Adult			Joined Cumberlains	
X	Jacobs, Thomas	May 26, 1850	Letter	"				
X	Jacobs, Elizabeth	May 26, 1850	"	"	Feb. 14, 1865	By Death		
X	Jolly, Charles T.	May 17, 1851	"	Infancy	April 20, 1873	Drop-ped		Joined Cumberlains, Talbot Sta.
X	Jolly, Margaret A.	Jan. 16, 1858	"	"	Apr. 20, 1873	"		"
X	Jolly, Mary E.	"		"	Apr. 20, 1873			"
X	Jolly, John	May 17, 1851	"	"	Apr. 20, 1873			"
X	Jolly, Martha Jane	Feb. 26, 1871	Exam-ination	"				
X	Kelly, Mary A. E.	May 26 1850	Exam-ination	"	July 12, 1853[97]	By Death		

[Page 18-19]

	Name of Members	When Rec'd	How Rec'd	When Bapt.	Dis-missed	How Dis.	Suspended	Remarks
X	Lyle, L. William [or William Harris Lyle]	Apr. 9, 1854	Exam-ination	Infancy	1864			Minister
X	Lyle, Nancy C.	Jan. 24, 1858	"	Adult	Mar. 31, 1873	Dropped from records	Now Nancy C. Moore	

[96] Adaline Gass was taken off the roll when she died. However, there seems to be two dates, July 1862 and Aug. 18, 1870. Are these death dates or when removed from roll?

[97] Death date of 1853 should be 1858 per Find-a-Grave.

X	Lyle, Thomas C.	Jan. 22, 1858	"	"	Feb. 29, 1868		Susp-ended	Long absence from county, not writing letter
X	Lyle, Frances M.	Jan 8 1866	Certifi-cate	Infancy	Apr. 23, 1871	By letter		Now Bales
X	Lyle, Sarah Porter	Oct. 27, 1867	"	"	Apr. 28, 1872	By letter		Wife of Rev. Wm. H. [Harris] Lyle
	M							
	McCuistion, Joseph	Nov. 20, 1842	Transfer		Dec. 24, 1862	By death		Transferred from Hopewell at the organization of the church
	McCuistion, Rachael	"	"		June 12, 1868	By death		Organ. of church
	McCuistion, James	"	"		Aug. 26, 1850	By letter		"
	McCuistion, Mary J. [Jane]	Nov 10, 1863 [98]	Exami-nation	Adult	Jan. 30, 1871	By death		Now Ashmore wife of [J. M,] from Hopewell at organ.
	Massengill, Jane M.	Nov. 20, 1852	Transfer-red	"				
	Massengill, William [Sr.]	May 26, 1850	Exam-ination	"	Sept. 13, 1874	Joined Southern church		From Hopewell at organ.
	Malcom, Margaret Y.	Nov. 18, 1858	"	Infancy	June 17, 1852	By death		[It appears these dates were not transcribed correctly from the original book.]
	McMurry, Mary Ann	May 10, 1862	Certifi-cate	"		By death		
	Malcom Joseph A.	April 9, 1854	"		Mar. 7, 1855	By death		
	Malcom, Mary W.	"	"					
	Mountcastle, Cordelia F.	May 30, 1857	Exam-ination	Adult	Feb. 29, 1868	Dismissed		Joined another church without letter
	McMurry, Samuel	Jan. 17 1858	"	Infancy	1864	By Death		Died at Galatin, Tenn. in U.S. Army

[Page 20-21]

	Name of Members	When Rec'd	How Rec'd	When Bapt.	Dis-missed	How Dismis-sed	Sus-pended	Remarks
	Meadows, Albert M.	Jan. 18, 1858	Exam.	Adult				
X	Meadows, Daniel	"	"	"	Sept. 13, 1874	By letter		
X	Mathes, William A.	June 30, 1860	Certifi-cate	Infancy	Mar. 15, 1874	"		
X	Mathes, Margaret	"	"	"	"	"		
X	Mathes, George A.	June 3, 1860	"	"	June 2, 1867	"		

---

[98] Error. Date on another roll said Nov. 5, 1843.

X	Mathes, William E. H.	Jan. 4, 1866	Exam- ination	"	Apr. 3, 1869	"		
X	Mathes, Nathaniel B.	"	"	"	Sept. 12, 1875	"		
X	Mathes, Rachael E.	"	"	"	Mar. 15, 1870	"		
X	Mathes, John T.	Jan. 8, 1866	"	"	June 5, 1870	Suspen- ded		
	Malcomb, Margaret E.	Jan. 11, 1866	"	Adult				
	Malcomb, Nancy E.	"	"	"				
X	Mooney, Alfred	Jan. 4, 1866	"	"	Oct. 28, 1866	By Letter	Gone to Liberia. Man of colour	
	Monroe, John Asa	Nov. 10, 1867	Exam- ination	Adult				
X	McMurray, Jas. M. [Moore]	Feb. 26, 1871	"	Infancy				
X	McMurray, Rachel T.	"	"	"				
X	McMurry, William	Nov. 23, 1873	"	"				
X	McGee, George S. [Samuel]	Dec. 21, 1873	"	"				

[Page 22-23]

	Name of Members	When Rec'd	How Rec'd	When Bapt.	Dis- missed	How Dismissed	Remarks
X	Newman, James	Nov. 20, 1842	Transfer- red		Feb. 29, 1868	Dismissed. Joined another church. Transferred from Hopewell Church	
X	Newman, Isabella	"	"		"	Dismissed. Joined another church.	
X	Newman, Joseph. R.	"	"		Feb. 29, 1868	Suspended for leaving country, not getting letter	
X	Newman, Mary A. [Nicholson]	"	"		Feb. 10, 1866	By letter	Wife of [W.] Madison
X	Newman, John, Sen.	"	"		Oct. 8, 1865	By death	Transferred from Newmarket [sic]
X	Newman, Sophriah E.	"	"		June 12, 1868	By letter	Now Mrs. Tiller
X	Newman, Ellinor	"	"		Dec. 25, 1864	By death	Wife of G. W. [George W.] Newman
X	Newman, Blair	"	"		Feb. 29, 1868	Dismissed	Joined Mossy Creek
X	Newman, Margaret	"	"		Feb. 29, 1868	"	"
X	Newman, Catharine	"	"				
X	Newman, Thomas J.	"	"		Feb. 29, 1868	Suspended	Left country. No letter.
	Newman, Margaret	"	"		Aug. 19, 1857	By death	Wife of T. J. Newman

X	Name						
	Newman, John, Jr.	"	"		Mar. 23, 1864	By death	Joined at organization
X	Newman, Jane R.	"	"		Sept. 13, 1874		Joined Cumberlains
X	Newman, William M. [Milton]	"	"		Oct. 13, 1867	By letter	
	Newman, Mahulda "Huldah"	"	"		"	"	
X	Newman, Catherine E.	"	"		Mar. 15, 1874		Now McSpadden.
X	Newman, Mary C.	"	"		Sept. 13, 1874		Joined Cumberlains
	Newman, Mary A.	"	"				
	Newman, Aron [Aaron]	"	"		Feb. 15, 1870	By Death	Son of Jonathan
X	Newman, Samuel B. [Blair]	Oct. 14, 1842	Examination	Infancy			
	Newman, Andrew C.[Carroll]	"	"	"	Feb. 25, 1864	By Letter	
	Newman, Charles [Coffman]	Oct. 19, 1842	"	"	1861	Ministry	
	Newman, Mary A. [Lockhart]	Oct. 21, 1848	"	Adult	Sept. 1863	By death	Wife of J. R. [Joseph Reece] Newman
	Newman, Lydia J. [Lidea Jane]	Nov. 17, 1850	"	Infancy	Oct. 5, 1857	" [Oct. 28, 1857][99]	Daughter of Col. J. [James] Newman
X	Newman, James H.	"	"	"	Apr. 1851	By letter	Transferred to Newmarket
	Newman, Sarah	Nov. 20, 1853	"	"	Feb. 29, 1868	Suspended	Left no letter. Daughter of J. T. Newman
X	Newman, John F. [Franklin]	Apr. 9, 1854	"	"	Sept. 13, 1874		Joined Cumberlains
	Newman, Martha M.	"	"	"		By death	Wife of John F. Newman
X	Newman, David G. [George]	Oct. 8, 1854	Examination	Infancy			
X	Newman, Gideon W.	Jan. 16, 1858	"	"	Sept. 13, 1874		Joined Cumberlains
X	Newman, Isabella E.	Jan. 17, 1858	"	"	Sept. 29, 1867	By Letter	
X	Newman John J. [Joseph]	Jan. 18, 1858	"	"	Feb. 29, 1868	Suspended	Left country, no letter
X	Newman, Mary A. C.	"	"	"	Sept. 13, 1874		Joined Cumberlains
	Newman, Jonathan A.	"	"	Infancy	Oct. 3, 1864	By Death	Son of Elder John ["Black Jack"] Newman
	Newman, [W.] Madison	Jan. 24, 1858	"	"	Feb. 16, 1866	By Letter	

[Page 24-25]

---

[99] *Find A Grave*, http://www.findagrave.com/cgi-bin/fg.cgi.

	Name of Members	When Rec'd	How Rec'd	When Bapt.	Dis-missed	How Dismissed	Remarks
X	Newman, Benj. C.	Jan. 24, 1858	Exam-ination	Infant	Feb. 29, 1868	Suspended	Left country Son of Aron Newman
X	Newman, Mary E.	"	"	Adult	Feb. 29, 1868		Left country Daughter of T. J. Newman
X	Newman, William H.	"	"	"	Feb. 29, 1868		Left country
X	Newman, Thomas	Mar. 21, 1858	"	Infancy	Feb. 29, 1868		Joined at Mossy Creek
X	Newman, Martha J.	Sept. 18, 1858	"	Adult	Feb. 29, 1868	Suspended	Left country
X	Newman, Nancy J. [Jane]	"	"	Infancy	Oct. 15, 1871	By letter	Now wife Mark T. [Thomas] Rankin
X	Newman, Margaret L.	Jan. 18, 1858	"	Adult	1862	By death	Daughter of Aron or Blair[100]
	Newman, Margaret J.	Jan. 19, 1858	"	"			
	Newman, George W. Jr.	"	"	Infancy	Feb. 10, 1866	By letter	Son of Nathan Newman
X	Newman, George W. Senr.	Jan. 20, 1858	"	"	Apr. 9, 1867	By death	
X	Newman, Hugh A.	"	"	"	Mar. 28, 1874	"	
	Newman, Silas J. A. [John Anderson]	"	"	"		"	During the war
	Newman, Richard A.	"	"	Adult	Feb 29, 1868	Suspended	Left country Son of T. J. Newman
X	Newman, Henry O.	"	"	"	Mar. 15, 1874	Excommuni-cated	Son of Blair
	Newman, Patrick L.	"	"	Infancy	Feb. 10, 1866	By letter	
	Newman, William F.	"	"	"	1863	By death	
	Newman, John W.	"	"	Adult			
	Newman, Martha E.	Jan. 21, 1858	"	"	Feb. 29, 1868	Suspended	Left country Now wife of C. Johnson
X	Newman, Matilda E.	"	"	Infancy			
	Newman, George W.	Nov. 20, 1858	"	"	Feb. 29, 1868	Suspended	Left country
X	Newman, Aron, Jr.	Nov. 20, 1842	Trans-ferred	Adult			
	Newman, Samuel H. [Houston]	Jan 4, 1866	Exam-ination	"	July 25, 1861	By death	[Son of Aaron Newman & Cassandra Branner]
X	Newman, Margaret E. J.	"	"	Infancy			

[100] Margaret L. Newman or Margaret J. Newman might be daughter of Blair Newman who is the son of Aaron Newman, Sr. Not clear on typed chart. Impossible to match columns on second page with names on first page.

	Name of Members	When Rec'd	How Rec'd	When Bapt.	Dismissed	How Dismissed	Remarks
X	Newman, James A.	Jan 11, 1866	"	"	Oct. 15, 1867	By letter	
	Newman, Alexander A.	Apr 17, 1842	"	"	June 4, 1870	By letter	Son of Wm. M. Newman
X	Newman, Catherine Cole	Apr 23, 1867	Examination	Infancy	Sept. 13, 1874	Joined Cumberlanins	Daughter of John F. [Franklin] Newman
X	Newman, James A. [Aaron]	Feb. 26, 1871	"	"	"	"	Son of John F. [Franklin] Newman

[Page 26-27 Blank] [Page 28-29]

	Name of Members	When Rec'd	How Rec'd	When Bapt.	Dismissed	How Dismissed	Remarks
X	Patton, John	May 6, 1855	Certificate			By death	
X	Patton, Edith	May 6, 1855	"		Aug. 1867	By death	
X	Rankin, William [Sr.]	Nov. 20, 1841	Transferred	Infancy	Feb. 25, 1871	By death	Chosen elder at organization of church
	Rankin, Jane	"	"	"	Jan 17, 1846	"	Wife of Richard Rankin
X	Rankin, Richard D.	"	"	"	Sept. 13, 1874		Joined Southern Church
X	Rankin, Mary A. C.	"	"	"			
X	Rankin, James	"	"	Adult			
X	Rankin, Josiah E.	"	"	Infancy	Sept. 13, 1874		Joined Cumberlains
X	Rankin, Christopher	"	"	"			
X	Rankin, Frances	"	"	Adult			
	Rankin, Lucinda	"	"	Infancy	June 14, 1846	By death	
	Rankin, Thomas Jr.	Apr. 17, 1842	Excommunication	"	Aug. 13, 1849	By death	
X	Rankin, Mary M.	"	"	"	Sept. 13, 1874		Wife of J. E. Rankin
X	Rankin, P. M. [Patrick McGuire]	"	"	"	Jan. 10, 1874	By letter	
X	Rankin, Louisa J.	"	"	Adult	Sept. 13, 1874		
X	Rankin, Susan	Oct. 9, 1842	"	"			Baptist church, Well Spring
X	Rankin, Julia	Aug. 4, 1850	Certificate	"			
X	Rankin, Eliza [J.]	Nov. 18, 1850	Examination	Infancy	June 14, 1872	By death	Wife of C. T. [Charles T.] Jolly
X	Rankin, James T.	Sept. 7, 1851	"	"			
X	Rankin, Nancy E. [Elizabeth Rankin]	Sept. 5, 1854	"	"			Wife of S. B. [Samuel Blair] Newman

	Name of Members	When Rec'd	How Rec'd	When Bapt.	Dismissed	How Dismissed	Suspended	Remarks
X	Rankin, Mary E. [Emily Rankin]	"	"	"				Wife of D. G. [David George] Newman
X	Rankin, Elizabeth C.	Oct. 8, 1854	"	"				Wife of John M. Rankin

[Page 30-31]

	Name of Members	When Rec'd	How Rec'd	When Bapt.	Dismissed	How Dismissed	Suspended	Remarks
X	Rankin, Nancy E. [Emily]	Sept. 12, 1855	Examination	Infancy	Feb. 15, 1874	By letter		Wife of B. F. [Dr. Benjamin Franklin] Brown
X	Rankin, Aron B. [Aaron Bogue]	July 6, 1856	Certificate	"	Sept. 2, 1866	By letter		
X	Rankin, Marjory [Copin]	"	"	Adult	Sept. 2, 1866			
	Rankin, Mary Jane	Aug. 31, 1856	Examination	Infancy	June 2, 1866	By letter		Now Mary Jane Titus
	Rankin, Alexander J. [James]	May 26, 1857	"	"				
	Rimmer, Delila	May 3, 1857	"	"	Dec. 28, 1857	By death		
X	Rankin, Samuel E.	Jan. 16, 1857[8]	"	"				
X	Rankin, Sarah J. [Jane]	Jan. 17, 1858	"	"	June 2, 1866	By letter		Wife of Wm. E. [Emmons] Blackburn
X	Rankin, Mary A. [Ann]	"	"	"	Sept 13, 1874			Joined Cumberlains. Wife of G. W. [Gideon] Newman
X	Rankin, John M. [McCampbell]	"	"	"	April 15, 1871	By death		
X	Rankin, John	"	"	"	Sept 13, 1874			Joined Cumberlains
X	Rankin, John C. [Calvin]	"	"	"	Oct. 23, 1870	By letter		
X	Rankin, Ellen L. [Leander]	"	"	"	June 23, 1872	"		
X	Rankin, Isabella	"	"	"	Dec. 7, 1874	"		
X	Rankin, Mark T.	"	"	"	Oct. 15, 1871	"		
X	Rankin, John F.	"	"	"				
	Rankin, William, Jr.	Jan. 18, 1858	"	"	May 29, 1862	By death		Son of William Rankin [Sr.]
X	Rankin, John G. [Gass]	"	"	"	Sept. 13, 1874			Joined Cumberlains [Son of Josiah Emmons Rankin]
X	Rankin, Margaret E.	"	"	"	Sept. 2, 1866	By letter		
X	Rankin, Elizabeth C. [Clendenin]	Jan. 19, 1858	Examination	Infancy	Mar. 17, 1872	"		Daughter of R. D. [Richard Duffield] Rankin
	Rankin, William T. [Thomas]	Jan. 20, 1858	"	"	Oct. 7, 1865	By death		Son of Josiah E. [Emmons] Rankin
X	Rankin, Martha Jane	Jan. 21, 1858	"	"				

X	Name	When Rec'd	How Rec'd	When Bapt.	Dismissed	How Dismissed	Suspended	Remarks
X	Rankin, Sarah A.	Jan. 23, 1858	"	"		By death		
	Rimmer, Alexandrer	Jan. 24, 1858`	"	Infancy				
	Rankin, Harriett M	Sept. 4, 1859	"	"	June 11, 1862	By death		
X	Rankin,Samuel D. [Doak]	Jan. 6, 1866	"	"				
X	Rankin, Christopher H. [Houston]	"	"	"				
X	Rankin, Samuel T. L. [Thomas Luther]	"	"	Adult				
	Rankin, Sarah J. F.	"	"	"				
X	Rankin, Almira M. [Minerva]	"	"	Infancy	Sept 13, 1874			Joined Southern Church
X	Rankin, Frances L. [Leanna]	"	"	"	Dec. 25, 1870	By letter		
X	Rankin, Angaline C. [Catherine]	"	"	"	Nov. 4, 1874	By letter		
X	Rankin, Mary Emmaus [Emmons]	"	"	"				
X	Rankin, Sarah A. C. C. [Amanda Caroline Campbell]	"	"	"				
X	Rankin, Susan A.	"	"	"				Wife of J. T. Rankin

[Page 32-33]

X	Name of Members	When Rec'd	How Rec'd	When Bapt.	Dismissed	How Dismissed	Suspended	Remarks
X	Rankin, Catherine R.	Jan. 8, 1866	Examination	Infancy	Sept. 13, 1874			Joined Cumberlains
X	Rankin, Sarah M.	"	"	"	Apr 18, 1866	By Letter		
X	Rankin, William E.	"	"	"				
X	Rankin, Alexander P. [Porter]	"	"	"				
X	Rankin, M. A.	Jan. 11, 1866	"	"	Sept. 13, 1874			
	Rankin, Thomas B.	"	"	"	Sept. 2, 1866	By Letter		
X	Rankin, Margaret E.	"	"	"	Sept. 10, 1874			Joined Cumberlains
X	Rankin, Charlotte T.	"	"	"				
	Rankin, Andw J.	Jan. 2, 1866	Certificate	"				
X	Richards, John V.	Jan. 24, 1856	Examination	"	Sept. 2, 1866	By Letter		
X	Rankin, Elizabeth	Apr. 14, 1867	"	Adult				Wife of W. E. Rankin

X	Rankin, Joseph W. [Wilson]	Nov. 10, 1867	"	Infancy				
X	Rankin, Joseph M. H.	Feb. 26, 1871	"	"				
X	Rankin, Andrew N. [Nelson]	"	"	"				
X	Rankin, Jennet Steel	"	"	"				
X	Rankin, Hellen	"	"	"	Sept. 13, 1874			Joined Cumberlains
X	Rankin, Benj. C. [Caswell]	"	"	Adult	"		"	
X	Rankin, Belvada V. ["Belle" Victoria]	"	"	"	Sept. 13, 1874	By Letter		
X	Rankin, Martha M.	"	"	"				
X	Rankin, James. L. [Lafayette]	"	"	Infancy				

[Page 34-35]

	Name of Members	When Rec'd	How Rec'd	When Bapt.	Dis-missed	How Dismissed	Sus-pended	Remark
X	Shadden, Joseph W.	Jan. 21, 1858	Examina-tion	Adult				
X	Shadden, Rachel L.	"	"	"				
	Shadden, Sonorub E.	Jan 24, 1858	"	Infancy				
	Shadden, Thomas C.	"	"	Adult	Sept. 13, 1874	By letter		
X	Shadden, Alexander M. [Malcolm]	Sept. 23, 1860	Certifi-cate					
	Skein, Columbus H.	Jan 11, 1866	Exam-ina-tion	"				
X	Sibils,Mahula	June 2, 1866	Certifi-cate	"	Sept. 13, 1874	By letter		
	Thomas, Florence	Sept. 7, 1851	Exam-ination	Adult				
X	Talbott, John	Jan. 24, 1858	"	"	Feb. 29, 1868	Dismissed		Joined at Mossy Creek
X	Talbott, Bersheba W.	July 20, 1857	Certifi-cate		Dec. 10, 1871	By letter	"	
X	Vina of colour	Aug. 26, 1848	Exam-ination	Adult	Sept. 1869	By death		
X	Vance, Thomas W.	Oct. 14, 1842	"	"	Oct. 15, 1871	By letter		
X	Vance, George G.	May 26, 1850	"	"	Oct. 9, 1870	"		
X	Vance, Sarah A.	Jan 24, 1858	"	"	Oct. 15, 1871	By letter		Wife of T. W. Vance

[Page 36-37]

	Name of Members	When Rec'd	How Rec'd	When Bapt.	Dis- missed	How Dismis- sed	Sus- pended	Remarks
X	Wright, George	Aug. 25, 1850	Certifi- cate		Oct. 21, 1851	By death		
X	Williams, Thos. A.	Feb. 26, 1871	Examina- tion	Adult	Aug. 26, 1867	By letter		[Transcription error for dismissed date. It appears that he joined Hebron Church on April 1st 1876.]
X	Zirkle, Susan	Aug. 14, 1856	Certifi- cate		June 4, 1866	By letter		Joined Methodist before hand
X	Zirkle, Sarah C.	Jan.16, 1858	Examina- tion	Infancy	Aug. 25, 1867	By letter		
X	Zirkle, Lydia J. [Jane]	Jan. 17, 1858	"	"	"	"		
X	Zirkle, Mary L.	Jan. 22, 1858	"	"	May 12, 1867	"		
	Zirkle, George A.	"	"	"				

[Page 38-51 Blank]

[Page 52-53]

Baptismal Records

Names of Children	When Born	When Baptized	By Whom Pres.
Edmond S. Rankin	Sept. 3, 1862	Oct. 14, 1862	By John Mc Newman & wife [Mary Peck]
Hellen [sic]Rankin	Aug. 15, 1860	Sept. 13, 1863	By P. M. [Patrick McGuire] Rankin & wife [Louisa Jane Lockhart]
Effie Lillen Rankin	Dec. 10, 1862	Sept. 13, 1863	"
Ida Elizabeth Rankin	Sept. 4, 1864	July 30, 1865	By Mark T. Rankin & wife [Nancy Jane Newman]
Leonidas Smith Rankin	Aug. 26, 1861	"	By John Mc. Rankin & wife [Elizabeth Catherine Rankin]
Willis [William] Melvin Rankin	July 22, 1864	"	"
John McNitt Alexander	Sept. 19, 1861	"	By Elias Alexander & wife [Jane Rankin]
Samuel R Alexander	June 13, 1864	"	"
David [C.] Jolly	Feb. 4, 1866	June 3, 1866	By Charles T. Jolly & wife [Eliza J. Rankin]
James Lamar Lyle	Dec. 1, 1865	"	By Rev. Wm. H. Lyle & wife [Sara Porter Mathis]
Emma Carrol Newman	June 5, 1863	Oct. 7, 1864	By Mrs. Catharine E. Newman
Harry Smith Bradshaw	June 17, 1863	Oct. 7, 1866	By A. B. [Aaron Bogue] Rankin & wife [Marjary Copin Lockhart]
Oliver Smith Rankin	July 23, 1860	Aug. 19, 1866	By A. B. Rankin & wife
March 31, 1867 Reported 3 during the last year			
Susan Minnie Newman	Feb. 24, 1867	Oct. 27, 1867	By Gideon W. Newman & wife [Mary Ann Rankin]
John Cockenour	May 1, 1867	"	By David Cockenour & wife
Jim Evert Fain	Apr. 4, 1866	Apr. 26, 1868	By James L. Fain & wife
Willie Ann Rankin	" [Apr 7, 1867][101]	"	By John G. [Gass] Rankin & wife [Adiadne Jane "Adna" Lyle]
William Alexander Lyle	Apr. 16, 1868	Aug. 21, 1868	By Rev. W. H. Lyle & wife [Willie Ruth Harris]
Blank [probably Orlando Porter Rankin]	[Oct 29, 1867][102]	Aug. 21, 1868	By Wm. E. [Erskine] Rankin & wife [Nancy Elizabeth "Lizzie" Newman]
Emily A. [Augusta] Newman	Aug. 16, 1860 [Aug 26, 1860 ?]	Aug. 21, 1868	By Samuel Blair Newman & wife [Nancy Elizabeth Rankin]
John G. [Grant] Newman	Oct. 16, 1862	Aug. 21, 1868	"
Francis J. Newman	Apr. 7, 1865	Aug. 21, 1868	"
Charlotte [Eglantine "Lottie"] Newman	Mar. 8, 1867	Aug. 21, 1868	"
April 3, 1869 Report 8 during last year			
Roger Amanda Rankin	Nov. 1, 1867	May 9, 1869	By S.E. Rankin & wife
Charlie Elton Coil	June 11, 1869	May 9, 1869	By John J. [James] Coil & wife [Martha Ann Rankin]

[101] *Tennessee, Jefferson Co. Bible Records*, Historical Records Project #465-44-3-115, p. 342, WPA, 1937, John G. Rankin Bible, Mt. Horeb, Jefferson Co., TN, McClung Library, Knoxville, TN.
[102] David H. Templin & Cherel Bolin Henderson, *Stories in Stone, Vol. I*, (1986, Knoxville, TN).

William T. A. Carson	Aug. 5, 1867	Aug. 21, 1868	By Rufus [E.] Carson & wife
Jonathan Alva Newman	Oct. 5, 1868	May 9, 1869	By Gideon W. Newman & wife [Mary Ann Rankin]
Frederic J. Newman	Apr. 11, 1869	Oct. 26, 1869	By John T. Newman & wife

April 24, 1870   Reported 4 for last year

William P. Rankin	Oct. 23, 1867	May 9, 1867	By Mark T. Rankin & wife [Nancy Jane Newman]
Emily Leaner [Leannah] Rankin	Jan. 24, 1868	May 9, 1869	By John F. Rankin & wife [Martha Jane "Mattie" Williams]

[Page 54-55]

Names of Children	When Born	When Baptized	By Whom Pres.
Thomas Tappan Cockenhour	June 6, 1870	Oct. 23, 1870	David Cockenhour & wife
Ulysses Luther Franklin	Mar. 1, 1864	"	Mary A. [Elizabeth Cline] Franklin
Alice May Franklin ["Allie"]	April 6, 1866	"	"
George Melvin Franklin	May 2, 1868	"	"
Tantha Eseltine Biddle	Jan. 7, 1866	"	Dr. Harry Biddle & wife Dr. Biddle is a member of Westminster Church
Acanthus ? Biddle	Jan. 27, 1868	"	"
Samuel Wilson Sylvanus Biddle	Apr. 1, 1870	"	"
Lura Jane Lyle	Aug. 20, 1870	"	Mr. H. Lyle & wife [Harriet Louisa Mathis]
Charles H. Fain	July 2, 1869	June 11, 1871	James S. Fain & wife
Martha Galbraith Newman	June 21, 1871	Nov. 19, 1871	John F. Newman & wife [Mary Jane Corbett]
Ida Clemintine Carson	Oct. 2, 1870	"	Rufus E. Carson & wife
Cuma Desaree Rankin	April 5, 1871	"	Alexander P. [Porter] Rankin & wife [Mary Ann McGhee]
Ira Marshall Coil	July 18, 1870	"	John J. Coil & wife [Martha Ann Rankin]
Henry Main[e] Rankin	Sept. 1, 1869	Apr. 13, 1873	William E. Rankin & wife [Nancy Elizabeth "Lizzie" Newman]
Mary Jane Josephine Rankin	Nov. 3, 1870	"	"
Nora Judson Rankin	Aug. 17, 1872	"	"
Bedford P. Rankin	July 8, 1872	May 26, 1873	Mrs Isabella Randle, his mother
William Edward Bradshaw	Nov. 17, 1870	"	John C. Bradshaw & wife [Frances Leannah Rankin]
Charles Clinton [Cleton] Bradshaw	June 24, 1872	"	"
Martha Frances Miller	Dec. 9, 1869	"	" Adopted child
Charles Walter Franklin	Nov. 16, 1872	"	Benj.[Francis] Franklin [Jr.] & wife [Margaret Cordelia McMurray]
George Elbert Rankin	March 3, 1870	"	John G. [Fain] Rankin & wife [Martha Jane "Mattie" Williams]
Gordon Bennett Rankin	May 21, 1872	"	"
Ida Jane Franklin	[no date]	"	Thos. P. Franklin & wife [Sarah Emily Corbett]

Mary Emily McFee [McGhee]	Sept. 20, 1869	Mar. 29, 1874	G. S. McFee [George Samuel McGhee] & wife [Susan Adeline Rankin][103]
James Calvin McFee [James Calloway McGhee]	July 19, 1811 [1871]	"	"
Menta Jane McFee [Mintie Jane McGhee, daughter of George Samuel McGhee]	Jan. 4, 1873	"	A. P. [Alexander Porter] Rankin & wife [Mary Ann McGhee]
Ban Barzilia Rankin [son of Alexander Porter Rankin][104]	Nov. 1, 1873	"	James [Moore] McMurry & wife [Almyra Minerva Rankin]

[Page 210- 211]

Names of Children	When Born	When Baptized	By Whom Pres.
Martha Ann Rankin	Dec. 17, 1846	Sept. 16, 1849	By Patrick M. Rankin & wife [Louisa Jane Lockhart]
Harriett Malinda Rankin	"	"	"
Patrick Thomas Rankin	July 22, 1849	"	"
John William Massengill Bradshaw	Jan. 4, 1850	May 27, 1850	By Richard H. [Harden] Bradshaw & wife [Jane P. Rawlings]
Oliver Hood Newman	Apr. 12, 1850	"	By Joseph R. [Reece] Newman & wife [Mary A. Lockhart]
Alexander Porter Masengill	Feb. 16, 1843	"	By William Masengill [Sr.] & wife [Jane M. Nicholson]
Jeremiah Nicholson Masengill	Mar. 14, 1845	"	"
Pharaoh Cobb Masengill	Apr. 5, 1847	"	"
Susan Adaline Rankin	Apr. 20, 1849	"	By William Rankin [Sr.] & wife [Susan Kimbrough]
Samuel Houston Newman	June 3, 1850	Aug. 26, 1850	By Aaron Newman & wife [Cassandra Branner]
Benjamin Harrison Newman	May 29, 1850	Feb. 9, 1851	By Wm. M. [Milton] Newman & wife [Mahulda Henry]
Joseph Richard Bradshaw	Aug. 15, 1850	Mar 2, 1851	By Joseph C Bradshaw & wife [Sarah Grizzle Blackburn]
Angeline Catherine Rankin	Jan. 27, 1850	"	By Richard D. Rankin & wife [Mary Ann Carol Woods]
Rebecca Catherine Massengill	Dec. 4, 1850	May 17, 1851	By Wm. Massengill [Sr.] & wife Jane M. Nicholson Massengill
Hannah Rebecca Zirkle	Je.17, 1848	S. 4, 1851	By Benjamin Zirkle & wife [Susannah Ruth Pennywitt]
Eleanor Louisa Zirkle	Ja. 31, 1851	"	"

[103] George Samuel McGhee and Susan Adeline Rankin had nine children. Their three oldest children were Mary Emily, James Calvin, and Menta/Mintie Jane. Alexander Porter Rankin was Menta's uncle, brother of her mother Susan Adeline Rankin McGhee. (Reva Rankin Hammer, "Ancestry of the Rankin Families of Jefferson Co. Tennessee, Thomas Rankin 1764-1821," Salt Lake City, Utah, 1962, Bible records copied from families in Jefferson Co., TN.)

[104] Ban/Bani Barzilla Rankin wss the daughter of Alexander Porter Rankin and Mary Ann McGhee. Bani was a second cousin once removed of Almyra Minerva Rankin McMurray. (Reva Rankin Hammer, "Ancestry of the Rankin Families of Jefferson Co., Tennessee," 1962)

[Page 212-213]

Names of Children	When Born	When Baptized	By Whom Pres.
Christopher Houston Rankin	Mr. 4, 1851	S. 4, 1851	By Christopher Rankin & wife [Frances George Gilbrearh]
Elizabeth Harrison Rankin	[Jun 5, 1851]	"	By P. M. Rankin & wife [Louisa Jane Lockhart]
Martha Ann Rankin	N. 14, 1847	"	By Josiah E. [Emmons] Rankin & wife [Mary Emma Gass]
Thomas Michael Harden Bradshaw	Mr. 3, 1852	Je. 20, 1852	By Richard H. [Harden] Bradshaw & wife [Jane P. Rawlings]
Joseph Andrew Harrison Rankin	Mr. 14, 1852	Ag. 23, 1852	By James [Eaton] Rankin & wife [Julia Ann J. Newman]
Samuel Thomas Hood Newman	Ap. 20, 1852	"	By Wm. M. [Milton] Newman & wife [Mahulda Henry]
Henry Harrison Newman	Nov. 8, 1851	"	By Joseph R Newman & wife [Mary A. Lockhart]
Almira Minerva Rankin	Jan 4, 1853	Mar. 20, 1853	By Richard D. Rankin & wife [Mary Ann Carol Woods]
Nancy Elizabeth Newman	June 29, 1853	Sept. 11, 1853	By Joseph R. Newman & wife [Mary A. Lockhart]
Catharine Routh Rankin	Feb. 13, 1853	Oct. 16, 1853	By Patrick M. Rankin & wife [Louisa Jane Lockhart]
Mary Emmons Rankin	Mar. 29, 1853	Apr. 9, 1854	By Josiah E. [Emmons] Rankin & wife [Mary Emma Gass]
Catherine Cole Newman	Dec. 14, 1853	Apr. 9, 1854	By John F. Newman & wife [Martha Matilda Gilbraith]
Barbary Elizabeth Zirkle	Nov. 6, 1853	Oct. 9, 1854	By Benjamin Zirkle & wife [Susan Pennywitt]
Joseph Alexander McMurry	[no date given]	"	By Polly Ann McMurry
William Henry Smith Newman	July 11, 1854	"	By William M. Newman & wife [Mahulda Henry]
Joseph Thomas Franklin	Mar. 11, 1854	"	By Rebecca Ann Franklin
Asa Luther Cline	Apr. 15, 1853	Nov. 13, 1854	By George Cline & wife
Joseph Marshal Hood Rankin	Oct. 6, 1854	Feb. 19, 1855	By Christopher Rankin & wife [Frances George Gilbreath]
Sarah J. [Jane] Alexander	Oct. 19, 1844	May 21, 1854	By Elias Alexander & wife [Jane Rankin]
Thomas T. [Theron] Alexander	Oct. 8, 1850	"	"
Nancy E. Alexander	Oct. 30, 1853	"	"
James Lafayette Rankin	July 27, 1854	Sept. 3, 1855	By William Rankin [1796-1871] & wife [Susan Kimbrough]

[Page 214-215]

Names of Children	When Born	When Baptized	By Whom Pres.
Joseph Palathiah Hood Bradshaw	N. 16, 1854	Oct. 25, 1855	By Richard H. Bradshaw & wife [Jane P. Rawlings]
Marjorah Emaline [Marjorie Emmaline] Rankin	May 11, 1855	Sept. 16, 1855	By Patrick M Rankin & wife [Louisa Jane Lockhart]
Samuel Doak Rankin	Jan. 1, 1856	Mar. 23, 1856	By Aaron B. [Bogue] Rankin & wife [Marjary Copin Lockhart]
Archibald Blackburn Newman	Nov. 17, 1855	"	By Joseph R. Newman & wife [Mary A. Lockhart]

James Aaron Newman	Dec. 31, 1855	May 4, 1856	By John F. Newman & wife[Martha Matilda Gilbraith]
Sarah Margaret Lydia Bradshaw	Ap. 29, 1856	July 6, 1856	By Joseph C. Bradshaw & wife [Sarah Grizzle Blackburn]
Martha Jane Jolly	Sept. 11, 1855	"	By Charles [T.] Jolly & wife [Eliza J. Rankin]
Nancy Virginia Zirkle	April 24, 1856	July 20, 1856	By Benjamin Zirkle & wife [Susannah Ruth "Susan" Pennywitt]
Emma L. [Lillian] Alexander	May 13, 1856	Aug.30, 1856	By Elias Alexander & wife [Jane Rankin 1831-1867]
Margaret Eleanor Franklin		"	By Rebecca Ann Franklin
Joseph Nelson [Wilson] Rankin	Oct. 12, 1856	May 30, 1857	By Josiah E. [Emmons] Rankin & wife [Mary Emma Gass]
David C. Gass	March 27, 1848	"	By Andrew T. Gass & wife
William Daniel Gass	Jan. 3, 1850	"	"
Frances Adaline Gass	Ap. 17, 1855	"	"
Richard Rankin Jolly	Mar 8, 1857	"	By Charles T. Jolly & wife [Eliza J. Rankin]
Asahel Biddle Bradshaw	Jan. 11, 1857	June 1, 1857	By Richard H. Bradshaw & wife [Jane Rawlings]
Nancy Iantha Isabella Newman	Apr. 14, 1857	Sept. 7, 1857	By William M. [Milton] Newman & wife [Mahulda Henry]
Susan Prudence Rankin	Apr. 23, 1857	"	By Patrick M. Rankin & wife
Lydia Jane Newman	Sept. 7, 1857	Jan. 19, 1858	By Joseph R. Newman & wife [Mary A. Lockhart]
Mary Isabel Gass	Oct. 22, 1857	"	By Andrew T. Gass & wife
Rachael Isabell McMurry	Mar. 2, 1856	"	By Samuel McMurry & wife [Mary Ann "Polly" Shadden]
Mark Alexander Newman	Aug 23, 1857	"	By John F. Newman & wife [Martha Matilda Gilbraith]
Charles W. Newman	Oct. 16, 1857	"	By Aaron Newman & wife

[Page 216- 217]

Names of Children	When Born	When Baptized	By Whom Pres.
Henry D. [Darr] Newman	Feb. 22, 1853	Jan. 24, 1858	[W.] Maddison Newman & wife [Mary Ann Nicholson]
Andrew J. Newman	Nov. 3 1855	"	"
Andrew Thomas Hood Bradshaw	Jan. 26, 1858	Apr. 24, 1858	By Joseph C. Bradshaw & wife [Sarah G. Blackburn]
Miranda A. [Anjeronia]Newman	Sept. 21, 1857	Apr. 26, 1858	By Andrew P. Newman & wife [Sarah Melinda Nelson]
George W. Franklin	Aug. 3, 1854	"	By Benjamin F Franklin & wife [Lucinda Harriet Rankin]
Lucinda Ann Franklin	July 9, 1857	"	"
Mary Josephine Newman	Feb. 25, 1857	"	By Samuel B. Newman & wife [Nancy Elizabeth Rankin]
Andrew Nelson Rankin	July 19, 1856	June 20, 1858	By Christopher Rankin & wife [Frances George Gilbraith]
Mary Elizabeth Tiller	March 25, 1858	Sept. 19, 1858	By Sophia Emily Tiller
Hulda Iantha Rankin	Feb. 27, 1858	Je. 20, 1858	By Christopher Rankin & wife [Frances George Gilbraith]
Benjamin Caswell Rankin	Dec. 19, 1858	Apr. 25, 1859	By Patrick M. Rankin & wife

Emily Ann Zirkle	Jan. 1, 1859	"	By Benjamin Zirkle & wife [Susan Pennywitt]
Frances Cordelia Franklin	Jan. 25, 1858	"	Campbell Franklin & wife
Mark Rufus Newman	Sept. 1, 1858	"	Samuel B. Newman & wife [Nancy Elizabeth Rankin]
Boyd Robinson Newman	April 30, 1859	Sept. 6, 1859	By Joseph R. Newman & wife [Mary A. Lockhart]
Huldah Estelle Alexander	April 11, 1859	"	By Elias Alexander & wife [Jane Rankin]
Nancy Isabella Malcom		"	[blank]
Thomas Harvy Smith McMurry	Dec. 24, 1858	March 4, 1860	By Samuel McMurry & wife [Mary Ann "Polly" Shadden]
Alice Athelia Newman	June 21, 1859	"	By Andrew [P.] Newman & wife[Sarah Melinda Nelson]
Joseph Martin Newman	Aug. 24, 1859	"	By William M. [Milton] Newman & wife [Mahulda Henry]
Gennet [sic] [Jennet] Steele Rankin	Mar. 21, 1860	April 24, 1860	By Richard D. Rankin & wife [Mary Ann Carol Woods]
Elizabeth Jane Richards	Oct. 25, 1858	April 29, 1860	By John V. Richards & wife
Silas Martin Franklin	Aug. 17, 1859	"	By Campbell Franklin & wife
John Henry Cline	May 7, 1859	"	By Erasmus H. Cline & wife [Juliet Emily Gass]
Sinea Frances Newman	Sept. 16, 1859	June 3, 1860	By John F. Newman & wife [Martha Matilda Gilbraith]
Allis Mabell Richards	Dec. 15, 1860	May 4, 1861	By John V. Richards & wife

[Page 218]

Names of Children	When Born	When Baptized	By Whom Pres.
John Edwin [Edward] Jolly [105]	Dec. 7, 1860	May 4, 1860 [1861]	By Charles [T.] Jolly & wife [Eliza J. Rankin]
Ida Ella Newman	[no date]	May 6, 1861	By John Newman & wife
Cordelia Josephine Mathes	Apr. 20, 1860	May 4, 1861	By William A. Bradshaw & wife
Elizabeth Tymanda Bradshaw	July 4, 1861	"	Richard H. Bradshaw & wife [Jane Rawlings]
Lee Converse Newman	Sept. 11, 1861	Jan. 5, 1862	By Joseph R. Newman & wife [Mary A. Lockhart]
Cassander Elizabeth Ellen Newman	Sept. 3, 1861	"	By Mary E. Newman
Luella May Newman	March 27, 1861	"	By Andrew C. [Carroll] Newman
Melville McElvin Rankin	Jan. 5, 1861	"	By Josiah E Rankin & wife [Mary Emma Gass]
The names of the children of Rufus E. Carsons transferred from New Market church by order of that session: Susan C. Carson, Nathaniel T. Carson, Mary E. Carson			

---

[105] Mount Horeb Session Minutes, Vol. I, pp. 218-9, has Edward Jolly.

[p. 236]   (69)

Statistics of Mount Horeb Church

April 7, 1866	The Session Report Communicants	208
	Adult Baptisms during the year	8
	Infant Baptisms during the year	5
	Additions to church "	52
March 31, 1867	Session Report Communicants	200
	Additions by certificate during the year	3
	Dismissions	10
	Infant Baptisms "	3
April 15th 1868	Session Report Communicants	176
	Infant Baptism	3
	Dismissions	24
	Additions	1
April 15, 1869	Session Report Communicants	169
	Dismissions	7
	Infant Baptisms	8
April 24th 1870	Session Reports Communicants	171
	Dismissions	3
	Infant	8
	Infant Baptisms	4
April 11th, 1871	Session Reported Communicant	186
	Adult Baptisms	8
	Infant Baptisms	8

(70)

April 22, 1872	Session Reported Communicant	174
	Infant Baptized	6
	Non residents for five years	16
April 20, 1873	Session Reported Communicants	163
	Infant Baptism	3

Volume III (1874-1923)

May 30, 1874 – April 11, 1923.

[Page 1]

Index

The book is divided into seven parts[106]

[Page 3]
Mount Horeb, E. Tenn.[107]
May 30 1874
We the undersigned being, or desiring to become members of the Presbyterian Church and believing that it will be for the glory of God and for the good of our common unity, to have a Presbyterian church organized at or near Mount Horeb, Jefferson County, Tennessee, and desiring said church to be in connection with Holston Presbytery and Synod of Nashville of the Presbyterian Church in the United States, do hereby petition the proper authority of said Holston Presbytery to aid us, at as early a day as practicable in effecting said organization according to the dates and usages of said Presbytery.

---

[106] The page numbers for this original Volume III are in square brackets, usually on the left side of the page but sometimes imbedded in the text.
[107] Mount Horeb in East Tennessee.

Jos. C. Bradshaw	John W. [William Massengill] Bradshaw
Andrew [Thomas Hood] Bradshaw	Nancy A. Franklin
Catherine E. Newman	Thomas J. [John] Bradshaw
John P. [Prigmore] Bradshaw	Cinderella C. [Caldwell] Bradshaw
Sarah J. (Bowers) Bradshaw	John C.[Calvin] Bradshaw
Florence O. [Obalma] Wisdom	[Frances] Leanna [Rankin] Bradshaw
William P. [Porter Massengil] Bradshaw	Jane Massengill
Mary L. [Louise Lyle] Bradshaw	Lydia [Praytor] Franklin
F. J. [Francis] Bradshaw	Susan Zirkle
R. D. [Richard Duffield] Rankin	Mary A. Zirkle
Nancy D. [Dorthulia] Bradshaw	James Newman
Hannah J. Bradshaw	Rebecca McGhee
Sarah E. Bradshaw	S. [Samuel] R. McGhee
Michael H. Bradshaw	Hugh A. [Alexander] Newman
	Pinlanda Newman
	Joseph R. [Richard] Bradshaw

[Page 4]

The Commission of Holston Presbytery consisting of Rev. Misters William Harrison, A. [W.] Wilson, A. C. Snoddy and Elais S. N. Fain met the above petitioners at Mount Horeb on Saturday 30 May 1874 and proceeded to the organization of the church by the election of the following officers, viz.

Elders	Deacons
R. D. [Richard Duffield] Rankin	Hugh A. [Alexander] Newman
James Newman	William P. [Porter] Bradshaw
John P. [Prigmore] Bradshaw	
J. [Joseph] C. Bradshaw	
John W. [William Massengill] Bradshaw	

Joseph C. Bradshaw, being a Ruling Elder in the Presbyterian Church, signified his acceptance of the office. James Newman, John W. Bradshaw, and John P. Bradshaw, having accepted the call to the office of Ruling Elder; also William P. Bradshaw accepted the office of Deacon, being regularly set apart and Rev. A. C. Snoddy proposed the questions and Rev. A. W. Wilson offered the organization prayer – Rev. William Harrison conducting the service.

John P. Bradshaw,
Clerk of Session

June 14, 1874

R. D. [Richard Duffield] Rankin having accepted the office of Ruling Elder was regularly ordained by the Rev. John M. Daniel presiding.

John P. Bradshaw,
Clerk.

Sept 6th 1874
Session met and was opened with prayer by Rev. John Daniel the moderator. Elders present J. C. Bradshaw, R. D. Rankin, James Newman, John W. Bradshaw & J. P. Bradshaw. Joseph C. Bradshaw was appointed delegate & R. D. Rankin alternate to attend the Presbytery of Holston to convene at Rutledge Sept 24th, 1874.
John P. Bradshaw, Clerk of Session

[Page 5] Sept 7th 1874
Note. The church contributed five dollars to Evangelistic fund.
John P. Bradshaw, Clerk

Sept 16th 1874 Mount Horeb
Session met and was opened with prayer by Rev. John Daniel the Moderator. Elders present J. C. Bradshaw, R. D. Rankin, J. W. Bradshaw & J. P. Bradshaw. Richard D. Rankin was appointed delegate. Joseph C. Bradshaw alternate to the Synod of Nashville to convene at Bristol Tennessee October 21st 7½ o'clock, P. M.

Also Joseph C. Bradshaw was appointed permanently to provide wine for communion, and for the time being James Newman the bread. Session closed with prayer.
John P. Bradshaw,
Clerk of Session

Note the church contributed for Synodical expense three dollars.
John P. Bradshaw, Clerk

March 30th 1875 Mount Horeb
Session met (having no moderator) was organized with prayer by Joseph C. Bradshaw. Elders present Richard D. Rankin, James Newman, Joseph C. Bradshaw and John P. Bradshaw being present. John P. Bradshaw and John W. Bradshaw his alternate was appointed to attend the Presbytery of Holston to convene at Morristown Wednesday April 14th at 1 o'clock A.M. Session closed with prayer.
John P. Bradshaw,
Clerk of Session

Approved thus far
April 17, 1875
A. M. Doak, Moderator

Note
August 15 Mount Horeb
The church contributed $5.85 cents for miscellanous or church purposes.
John P. Bradshaw, Clerk.

[Page 6]

Minutes of Session

Aug 15, 1875, Mount Horeb

Session met and was opened with prayer by Rev. A. C. Snoddy the moderator. Elders present J. C. Bradshaw, R. D. Rankin, John W. Bradshaw, James Newman & John P. Bradshaw. John W. Bradshaw was appointed to attend the presbytery of Holston to convene at Strawberry Plains September 9th, 1875.

John P. Bradshaw, Clerk of Session

Sep 19th Mount Horeb

Session met and was opened with prayer by Rev. A. C. Snoddy the moderator. Elders present R. D. Rankin, Joseph C. Bradshaw & John P. Bradshaw. R. D. Rankin & J. C. Bradshaw, alternate to attend the Synod of Nashville to convene at Pulaski on the 13th of October 1875.

John P. Bradshaw,
Clerk of Session

A.D. 1876, March 19th Mount Horeb

Session met and & opened with prayer by Rev. Wm Cameron Moderator. Elders present Richard D. Rankin, Joseph C. Bradshaw, and John P. Bradshaw.

R. D. Rankin was appointed delegate with John P. Bradshaw alternate .to attend the Presbytery of Holston to convene at Dandridge on Wednesday, April 5th, 7 P.M., A. D. 1876.

John P. Bradshaw
Clerk of Session

Examined and approved as far as written with the exception; viz.

On page 6 it would have been better to say by Rev. A. C. Snoddy who was requested to act as Moderator.

Apr. 8, 1876

S. B. Campbell, Moderator Pres. Holston

[Page 7]

1876   Minutes of Session

Sept 17th   Mount Horeb

Session met and was opened with prayer by Rev. A. C. Snoddy, the moderator, Elders present R. D. Rankin, James Newman, Joseph C. Bradshaw, and John P. Bradshaw On motion John P. Bradshaw with R. D. Rankin alternate was appointed to attend the Synod of Nashville to convene at Shelbyville on Thursday the 28th of Sept 1876 at 7½ P.M.

John P. Bradshaw,
Clerk of Session

1877 April 15   Mount Horeb

Session met and was opened with prayer by Rev. A. C. Snoddy, the moderator, Elders present Richard D. Rankin, Joseph C. Bradshaw and John P. Bradshaw. On motion Joseph C. Bradshaw, with John P. Bradshaw alternate, was appointed to attend the Presbytery of Holston to convene at Jonesborough on Wednesday April 25th 7 P.M. A. D. 1877

John P. Bradshaw, Clerk of Session

Examined approved
Jonesboro Apr. 26 '77
John R. King, Moderator, Holston Pres.

1877 Sept 1st   Mount Horeb

Session met and was opened with prayer by J. C. Bradshaw. Elders present R. D. Rankin, J. C. Bradshaw & J. P. Bradshaw by request of Elders J. Albert Wallace acting as moderator on motion R. D. Rankin with J. C. Bradshaw was appointed to attend the Presbytery of Holston to convene at Mount Carmel, Lee county Va. On Wednesday Sept. 19th 1877 at 7 ½ P.M

Session also at the same time on motion appointed J. C. Bradshaw, with R. D. Rankin alternate, to attend the Synod of Nashville to convene at Cleveland, Tennessee October 18th 1877 at 7½ P.M.

John P. Bradshaw, Clerk of Session

[Page 8] 1878 March 17   Minutes of Session

Mount Horeb Session met and was opened with prayer by J. Albert Wallace the Moderator. Elders present J. Newman, R. D. Rankin, J. C. Bradshaw & J. P. Bradshaw On motion R. D. Rankin with J. C. Bradshaw alternate was appointed to attend the Presbytery of Holston to convene at Mount Horeb Wednesday April 10th 1878 at 11 o'clock A.M.

John P. Bradshaw, Clerk of Session

Examined and approved thus far.
Apr. 13, 1878 Mount Horeb Ch. Geo. A. Caldwell, Mod. Holston Presb.

1878 August 18   Mount Horeb

Session met and was opened with prayer by J. A. Wallace Moderator. Elders present James Newman, R. D. Rankin, J. C. Bradshaw & J. P. Bradshaw. On motion J. C. Bradshaw with R. D. Rankin was appointed to attend the Presbytery of Holston to convene atLeesburg Tenn. Sept. 10th at 11 o'clock A.M.

Also on motion the Session Recommended to the church the propriety of electing additional Elders in the church and appointed the third Sabbath of Sept. next as the day of Election.

John P. Bradshaw, Clerk of Session

1878 Sept. 15th
Mount Horeb Session met and was opened with prayer by J. Albert Wallace Moderator of session. Elders present James Newman, R. D. Rankin, J. C. Bradshaw & J. P. Bradshaw On motion Joseph C. Bradshaw with R. D. Rankin alternate was appointed to attend the Synod of Nashville to convene at Morristown on Thursday the 10 of October at 7½ P.M.   John P. Bradshaw, Clerk of Session

[Page 9] 1878 Oct. 30th Minutes of Session
Session of Mount Horeb met opened with prayer by Rev. J. Albert Wallace Moderator. Elders present James Newman, R. D. Rankin, J. C. Bradshaw, I. A. L. [Isaac Anderson Loag] Wilson, G. A. [George Adam] Zirkle & J. P. Bradshaw. On motion Mary A. C. Rankin was received into the church on letter from Hebron Church.
John P. Bradshaw, Clerk of Session

1879 March 16 Mount Horeb
Session met, constituted with prayer by the Moderator J. Albert Wallace. Elders present R. D. Rankin, I. A. L. Wilson, G. A. Zirkle, J. C. Bradshaw & J. P. Bradshaw. On motion G. A. Zirkle with I. A. L. Wilson was appointed to attend the Presbytery of Holston to convene at Pisgah Church Newport at 7 ½ P.M. April 2nd A. D. 1879.
John P. Bradshaw, Clerk of Session

Examined & approved at Pisgah Apr. 5th 1879.
J. C. [Chalmers] Cowan Mod., Holston Pres

1879 June 15 Mount Horeb
Session met, constituted with prayer by the Moderator J. Albert Wallace. Elders present R. D. Rankin, I. A. L. Wilson, G. A. Zirkle, J. C. Bradshaw & J. P. Bradshaw. On presents of the letter of Belle [Isabelle Tittsworth] Bradshaw from the Baptist Church and Also the letter of Wm. E. [Erskine] Rankin and Elizabeth [Nancy Elizabeth "Lizzie" Newman] his wife Hebron Church, for admittance into this Church, on motion. They were unanimously and cordially Received.
John P. Bradshaw, Clerk of Session

[Page 10]   Minutes of Session
1879 Aug 17th   Mount Horeb
Session met and was opened with prayer by J. Albert Wallace the Moderator of session. Members present James Newman, R. D. Rankin, J. C. Bradshaw, I. A. L. Wilson, G. A. Zirkle & John P. Bradshaw. Session then appointed I. A. L. Wilson with R. D. Rankin alternate was appointed to attend the meeting of Holston Presbytery to convene at Mossy Creek September 25th 11 o'clock in the morning 1879.
Session Also appointed G. A. Zirkle with J. P. Bradshaw Alternate to attend the meeting of the Synod of Nashville to convene at Columbia Tennessee on the 22nd of October 1879.   John P. Bradshaw, Clerk of Session

1880 March 7th

Mount Horeb Session met and organized by requesting Rev. E. McNair to Moderate. Elders present R. D. Rankin, I. A. L. Wilson, G. A. Zirkle, J. C. Bradshaw & J. P. Bradshaw. John P. [Pennywitt] Zirkle was presented for admission to the communion in the Church and was unanimously and cordially received.

John P. Bradshaw, Clerk of Session

[1880] April 4

Mount Horeb Session met by request by Rev. E. McNair acting as Moderator. Elders present R. D. Rankin, J. C. Bradshaw, I. A. L. Wilson, G. A. Zirkle, & John P. Bradshaw. Prayer being offered by Moderator. John P. Bradshaw with G. A. Zirkle alternate was appointed to attend the Holston Presbytery to convene at Rogersville on the 21st day of April at 7½ P.M. 1880.

John P. Bradshaw,
Clerk of Session

Examined & approved in Presby at Rogersville.
April 21, 1880,
A. W. Wilson, Mod.

[Page 11] 1880 August 1 Minutes of Session Mount Horeb Church

Mount Horeb Session met there being no moderator present. Prayer was offered by I. A. L. Wilson. Elders present Joseph C. Bradshaw, I. A. L. Wilson, George A. Zirkle & John P. Bradshaw. On motion George A. Zirkle, with I.A. L. Wilson, was appointed to attend the meeting of presbytery to convene at New Providence Thursday August 19th at 11 o'clock P.M. [A.M.] 1880.

John P. Bradshaw,
Clerk of Session

Session of Mount Horeb Church met was opened with prayer by Elder I. A. L. Wilson. Present Joseph C. Bradshaw, R. D. Rankin, Geo. A. Zirkle, I. A. L. Wilson, John P. Bradshaw. Session granted letters of dismissal to the following persons, viz. Elder George A. Zirkle & his wife Florence O. Zirkle, Elder I. A. L. Wilson and A. C. [Angeline Catherine Rankin] Wilson together with their Baptized children, also Elder John P. Bradshaw and his wife Sary J. Bradshaw. Session closed with prayer by Elder Joseph C. Bradshaw. Oct. 10th 1880.

Joseph C. Bradshaw
Clerk of Session

1881 February 6

Session of Mount Horeb Church Met. was Opened with prayer by Rev. L. F. Smith the Moderator. Present R. D. Rankin, J. C. Bradshaw On motion the Session granted a letter of dismission to Mrs. Lydia J. [Zirkle] Bell. Closed with prayer.

Joseph C. Bradshaw, Clerk of Session

June 5th 1881

Session of Mount Horeb Church Met. was Opened with prayer by Rev. L. F. Smith the Moderator. Present R. D. Rankin, J. C. Bradshaw on Motion Mrs. Fannie J. Newman was received by letter from the Mossy Creek Presbyterian Church into the full communion of this church, also her Baptized children.

Joseph C. Bradshaw, Clerk of Session

[Page 12] Oct 3, 1881 Minutes of Session Mount Horeb

Session Met and was duly organized with Prayer by the Moderator Rev. John Daniel who by request of the Session acted as Moderator. Elders Present R. D. Rankin, Joseph C. Bradshaw. on motion Mr. John P. Bradshaw and his wife Sarah J. Bradshaw was received by letter from the Cumberland Presbyterian Church tehes[?] as Members in good and regular standing to the full Communion of the Church. Session was closed with Prayer by the Moderator.

Joseph C. Bradshaw, Clerk of Session

March 5th 1882

Session met and was duly organized with Prayer by the Moderator Rev. John Daniel who by request of the Session acted as Moderator. Elders Present R. D. Rankin, and Joseph C. Bradshaw. on motion Joseph C. Bradshaw with R. D. Rankin his Alternate was appointed to attend the meeting of Presbytery to convene at Morristown on the 29th day of March 7½ P. M.

Joseph C. Bradshaw,
Clerk of Session

Examined and approved in Presbytery at Morristown Tenn. Apl 6th 1882. See copt [sic]

1st Not in Presbytery since 1880.

2nd In the minutes of Oct. 15th 1880 and Feby 6th 1881- members are dismissed without stating to what church.

3rd No record of closed with prayer in the minutes of Aug. 1st 1880 – Jany 5th 1881 - & Mar. 5th 1882.

4th No mention of the appointment of Delegates to Presbytery & Synod in past.

5th No reports of diligence required from Delegates to Presbytery & Synod.

6th No Statistical Reports to Presbytery records

P. S. Anderson, Moderator

[Page 13] Nov. 28, '82 Minutes of Session Mount Horeb Presbyterian Church

Session Met and was duly organized with Prayer by the Moderator Rev. M. W. Millard. Elders Present R. D. Rankin, Joseph C. Bradshaw. on motion R. D. Rankin with J. C. Bradshaw his Alternate was appointed to attend the Meeting of the Synod of Nashville to convene at Rogersville on the 22nd of November 1882.

Joseph C. Bradshaw, Clerk of Session

March 4th 1883
Session Met and was duly organized with Prayer by the Moderator Rev. M. W. Millard. Elders Present R. D. Rankin, Joseph C. Bradshaw. on Motion R. D. Rankin principle with Joseph C. Bradshaw his Alternate was appointed to attend the Meeting of the Presbytery of Holston to Convene in Mossy Creek Church on the 18 day of April 1883. Closed with Prayer.

Joseph C. Bradshaw, Clerk of Session

Examined & approved by trustee of Holston Modr.
Mossy Creek. J. Albert Wallace.

May 6th 1883
Session Met, and was duly organized with Prayer by the Moderator Rev. M. W. Millard. Elders Present R. D. Rankin & Joseph C. Bradshaw. on Motion Allice Casandar Hinkle was received on Examination as a member into the full Communion of the Church. The Session closed with Prayer.

Joseph C. Bradshaw,
Clerk of Session

December 2nd 1883
At an informal Meeting of Mount. Horeb Church Session. Elders Present R. D. Rankin & J. C. Bradshaw it was agreed to give to Mr. Joseph W. Shadden a letter of Dismission at his own request to the Hebron Church all of which is herewith submitted

Joseph C. Bradshaw
Clerk of Session

[Page 14] June 1st 1884 Minutes of the Session of Mount Horeb Church
Session met and was duly organized with Prayer by the Moderator Rev. John Daniel who by request of the Session acted as Moderator. Elders present R. D. Rankin, and J. C. Bradshaw. on motion Margaret Elizabeth Hinkle was received on Examination into the full Communion of the Church. Also George A. Zirkle and his wife Florence O. Zirkle were received by letter from the Dandridge Church together with their Baptized children. Closed with Prayer by Moderator.

Joseph C. Bradshaw,

Clerk of Session

July 6th 1884
Session met and was duly organized with Prayer by the Moderator Rev. John [M.] Daniel. Elders present R. D. Rankin, and J. C. Bradshaw. on motion Miss Josephine Rankin was received on Examination into the full Communion of the Church. Closed with Prayer by the Moderator.

Joseph C. Bradshaw,
Clerk of Session

Aug. 3rd 1884

Session met and was duly organized with Prayer by the Moderator Rev. John Daniel who by request of the Session acted as Moderator. Elders present R. D. Rankin, and J. C. Bradshaw on motion Mrs. Mary A. [Lockhart] Newman was received on Examination into the full Communion of the Church. Closed with Prayer by Moderator.
Joseph C. Bradshaw, Clerk of Session

Examined and approved by Holston Presby, Jonesboro, Tenn.
April 1885   J. D. Tadlock, Mod.

August 2nd 1885

Session met and was duly organized with Prayer by the Moderator Rev. John Daniel. Elders Present R. D. Rankin, Joseph C. Bradshaw. on Motion R. D. Rankin was appointed principle with J. C. Bradshaw his Alternate to attend the Meeting of the Presbytery of Holston to convene at Newport the 19th of August 1885. Adjourned with Prayer by the Moderator.   Joseph C. Bradshaw, Clerk of Session

[Page 15] November 22, 1885 Minutes of Session of Mount Horeb Church

Session Met and was duly organized with Prayer by the Moderator Rev. John Daniel. Elders present R. D. Rankin, and J. C. Bradshaw. On motion the following named persons were received in to the full Communion of the Church. To wit, Fannie Miller, Jinnie C. Newman, Louisa J. Cannon, Sallie Bradshaw, Oakley D. Bradshaw, William E. [Edward] Bradshaw, Frank A. [Adam] Newman, Charley C. [Charles Cleton] Bradshaw, Bob C. Bradshaw, Frank A. [Ashley] Bradshaw, Catherine J. Franklin, Sue Ella Newman, Arley M. [Arlen Weihl] Bradshaw, James C. Bradshaw. Closed with Prayer by the Moderator.   Joseph C. Bradshaw, Clerk of Session

April 4th 1886

At an informal meeting of the Session of Mount Horeb Church R. D. Rankin, was appointed to attend the Meeting of Holston Presbytery to convene Mount Horeb April 17th 1886 by order of Session.   Joseph C. Bradshaw, Clerk of Session

Examined and Approved as far as written. Mount Horeb April 17, 1886
Rev. J. S. Anderson, Mod.

April 18th 1886

Session met and was duly organized with Prayer by the Moderator Rev. William H. Smith who by the request of the Session acted as Moderator. Elders present R. D. Rankin, and J. C. Bradshaw. On motion Hannah M. Hinkle & Lula C. [Cassander] Rankin were received on examination to the full communion of the church. Also Letters of dismission were granted at their own request to Lula M. Newmannow Coil, also to Emma C. [Carroll] Newman now Rankin. Closed with Prayer by the Moderator.
Joseph C. Bradshaw, Clerk of Session

August 1st 1886

Session met, and was duly organized with Prayer by the Moderator Rev. C. J. Ralston who by request acted as Moderator. Elders Present R. D. Rankin & J. C. Bradshaw on motion J. C. Bradshaw was appointed to attend the Meeting of Holston Presbytery to convene in Jonesville August the 12, 1886. Adjourned with Prayer by the Moderator.   Joseph C. Bradshaw, Clerk of Session

[Page 16] Oct. 3, 1886 Minutes of the Session of Mount Horeb Church

Session Met, and was duly organized with Prayer by the Moderator Rev. C. J. Ralston. Elders Present R. D. Rankin & J. C. Bradshaw on Motion Mrs. Mary A. [Lockhart] Newman was granted a letter of dismission from this Church to join the Lebanon Cumberland Church. Also Elder R. D. Rankin was appointed to attend the Meeting of the Synod of Nashville to convene at Bristol October 7th 1886. Session Closed with Prayer by the Moderator.   Joseph C. Bradshaw, Clerk of Session

April 5th 1887

Session Met, and was duly organized with Prayer by the Moderator Rev. C. J. Ralston Elders Present R. D. Rankin & J. C. Bradshaw. The Sessional reports to Presbytery were named and Elder R. D. Rankin principle & J. C. Bradshaw his Alternate was appointed to attend the Meeting of Holston Presbytery to Convene at Rogersville April the 8th, 1887 7:30 P.M. Closed with Prayer.
                    Joseph C. Bradshaw, Clerk of Session

May 1st 1887

Session met, and was duly organized with Prayer by the Moderator Rev. C. J. Ralston Elders Present R. D. Rankin & J. C. Bradshaw. The following named persons were received on examination into the Communion of the Church, George [W.] McMurry, James C. Barbee, Mary F. Barbee, Ernest N. [Neal] Bradshaw, Clide P. [Park] Bradshaw & Henry Darr. Also George A. [Arthur] Newman was received by letter. Also Session decided to elect three additional Elders and it was so Publicly announced to the Congregation and Saturday before the first Sabbath of June was the time set for the Election. Closed with Prayer.   Joseph C. Bradshaw, Clerk of Session

June 4th 1887

The congregation of Mount Horeb Church assembled at the usual place of worship. The Rev. C. J. Ralston delivered an address on the dutyes [sic] of Pastors, Elders and Deacons after which the Congregation according to previous announcement went into the Election of Elders which resulted as follows: to viz. George A. Zirkle, Andrew T. [Thomas Hood] Bradshaw & William P. [Porter Massengil] Bradshaw. Mr. George A. Zirkle being an ordained Elder and expressing his willingness to serve the church in that capacity was duly installed on Sabbath morning by Rev. C. J. Ralston and declared in the face of the Congregation a ruling Elder in Mount Horeb Church.
                    Joseph C. Bradshaw, Clerk of Session

[Page 17] June 5th 1887 Minutes of the Session of Mount Horeb Church

Session met, and was duly organized with Prayer by the Moderator Rev. C. J. Ralston Elders Present R. D. Rankin & J. C. Bradshaw. Henry Lyle Bradshaw was received on examination to the full Communion of the Church. Also, Mr. Thomas Newman , an Elder from the Mossy [Creek] Presbyterian Church together with his wife Jennie H. [McGhee] Newman was received by letter from the Mossy Creek Presbyterian Church. Closed with Prayer.   Joseph C. Bradshaw, Clerk of Session

September 4th 1887

Session met, and was duly organized with Prayer by the Moderator Rev. C. J. Ralston Elders Present R. D. Rankin, G. A. Zirkle & J. C. Bradshaw. According to a previous announcement A. T. [Andrew Thomas Hood] Bradshaw and William P. [Porter Massengil] Bradshaw who were Elected to the office or ruling Elder June 4th and having signified their willingness to serve the Church in that Capacity was regularly ordained and installed into the office of Ruling Elder in Mount Horeb Church. Also G. A. Zirkle was appointed principal with A. T. Bradshaw his Alternate to attend the meeting of Presbytery to Convene in New Bethel Church September 22nd 1887 at 11 Ocl [sic] A. M. Closed with Prayer.   Joseph C. Bradshaw, Clerk of Session

Oct 2, 1887 Mount Horeb, Tenn.

Session met and was organized with prayer by Rev. John Daniel, Rev. J. C. Ralston Moderator. Elders present J. C. Bradshaw, R. D. Rankin, W. P. Bradshaw, A. T. Bradshaw & G. A. Zirkle.

Resignation of J. C. Bradshaw as Clerk of Session was presented before session and accepted. By resolution a vote of thanks was tendered J. C. Bradshaw for his service as Clerk. G. A. Zirkle was chosen to the Clerkship. Representative A. T. Bradshaw reported his attendance at Presbytery. Recess till after service was then taken.

[Page 18] Minutes of Mount Horeb Church

Session being continued after service W. P. Bradshaw as appointed to represent Mount Horeb Church in Synod of Nashville& meet at Mount Pleasant Oct. 27, 1887. Session adjourned with prayer.   G. A. Zirkle, Clerk

Nov. 6, 1887 Mount Horeb, Tenn.

Session organized with prayer by Mod. Rev. C. J. Ralston. Elders present J. C. Bradshaw, W. P. Bradshaw, A. T. Bradshaw & G. A. Zirkle. Minutes of last meeting approved. The Clerk was required to make an assignment on the record that Michael H. Bradshaw had left the bounds of Mount Horeb Church & had connected himself on profession with Westminster Church, Presbytery of Union, U.S.A. Presbyterian Church, North.

Election of two Deacons having been ordained and legally announced G. A. [George Arthur] Newman & J. P. [John Pennywitt] Zirkle were chosen, and their installation announced for Dec. 4, 1887. Session closed with prayer.
          G. A. Zirkle, Clerk

December 4, 1887

[These minutes had lines drawn through them.]

~~Session convened without Moderator Rev. C. J. Ralston not being present. Business before session was to appoint commissioners to Called meeting of Presbytery to meet at Morristown December 20, 1887 2 o'clock P.M.~~

~~G. A. Zirkle & W. P. Bradshaw were appointed principal & Alt. R. D. Rankin, J. C. Bradshaw, A. T. Bradshaw, W. P. Bradshaw — Elders being present. On transaction of this business Session adjourned.~~

~~G. A. Zirkle,~~

~~Clerk~~

[Page 19] Minutes of Mount Horeb Church

Dec. 4, 1887 Mount Horeb

Session duly organized with prayer by moderator, Rev. C. J. Ralston. Elders present, R. D. Rankin, J. C. Bradshaw, W. P. Bradshaw, A. T. Bradshaw and G. A. Zirkle. G. A. [George Arthur] Newman having signified his willingness to accept the office of Deacon in Mount Horeb Church was duly installed. No other business being before session adjourned with prayer.

G. A. Zirkle,

Clerk

Dec 11, 1887 Mount Horeb

Session met without moderator for the purpose of appointing delegate to Called meeting of Presbytery to First at Morristown, Tenn. Dec 20, 1887, 2 o'clock P.M. Elders present, R. D. Rankin, J. C. Bradshaw, W. P. Bradshaw, A. T. Bradshaw, G. A. Zirkle.

G. A. Zirkle prin. & W. P. Bradshaw Alt. were appointed.

G. A. Zirkle,

Clerk

January 15, 1888 Mount Horeb, Tenn.

Session met with moderator not present. Elders present Jos. C. Bradshaw, W. P. Bradshaw, A. T. Bradshaw & G. A. Zirkle. On Sept. 4, 1887 the session ordered prayer meeting to be held each Sabbath not occupied by preaching: this order does not appear in the record of that meeting. At this meeting of this day a motion to rescind that motion is carried, J. C. Bradshaw putting motion, two members voting for the motion to rescind and one not voting.

A motion was then made and passed to hold prayer meeting on such [Page 20] Sabbaths as may not be occupied by service in Mount Horeb Church or in the Lebanon Cumberland Presbyterian Church, two voting for and one against the motion.

Meeting Closed

G. A. Zirkle,

Clerk of Session

March 17, 1888 Mount Horeb, Tenn.

Session was opened with prayer by the Moderator, Rev. J. B. Converse, Evangelist for Holston Presbytery. Elders present, R. D. Rankin, J. C. Bradshaw, A. T.. Bradshaw, W. P. Bradshaw & G. A. Zirkle.

Minutes of Sessions from last approved by Presbytery to the present time were read and approved. Joseph C. Bradshaw, delegate to Presbytery at Jonesville, August 1886 was required to show cause of nonattendance. Cause-physical disability which was sustained. R. D. Rankin was required to show cause of nonattendance at Synod, Bristol Oct. 1886. Cause-physical disability-sustained. R. D. Rankin was required to show cause for nonattendance at Presbytery, April 1887. Cause-Disability-sustained. W. P. Bradshaw delegate to called meeting of Presbytery at Morristown December 1887 reported his diligence.

Session was required to show cause of absence of Sessional records at presbytery at Rogersville Aprl. 1887. Inability of Delegate to attend & take them. G. A. Zirkle Principal & A. T. Bradshaw Alt. were appointed to attend Presbytery at Bristol May 1st 1888. A collection was ordered to be taken on Sabbath March 18, 1888 [Page 21] for incidental expenses. Motion to adjourn until after service was carried.

After service session called to order by the Moderator and as no other business was brought before it, it was closed with prayer.

George A. Zirkle,
Clerk of Session

March 18, 1888 Mount Horeb, Tenn.

Session was opened with prayer by the Moderator, Rev. J. B. Converse, Evangelist of Holston Presbytery. Elders present R. D. Rankin, Joseph C. Bradshaw, A. T. Bradshaw, W. P. Bradshaw, G. A. Zirkle.

Martha ["Mattie"] L. L. Cannon on profession of her faith in our Lord Jesus Christ after examination was admitted into the full communion of Mount Horeb Church the ordinance of Baptism having been duly administered.

On motion a Committee consisting of one elder & one deacon was appointed to confer with Rev. John Daniel as to the possibility of his serving Mount Horeb Church as Stated supply once per month until other arrangements might be necessary. G. A. Zirkle, elder, and John C. [Calvin] Bradshaw, deacon, were appointed. The Session having no other business closed with prayer.

Geo. A. Zirkle, Clerk of Session

[Page 22]

Narrative of the Session of Mount Horeb Church
for the year ending April 1st 1888

This church has not, since its organization entered into the Pastoral Relation, but has from year to year been served by a Stated Supply. For the year ending April 1st 1888, we were able to secure the services of Rev. C. J. Ralston one Sabbath per month for seven months, his connection with us being severed at the end of the calendar year. He was faithful in the discharge of his duties while with us, unless perhaps it be in the matter of Pastoral work. But when his wide fields, and the exacting nature of his special work are considered we are not disposed to lay much stress on that failure. The Elders and deacons of Mount Horeb Church have also been unaccountably faithful to their change, though some opportunities have been permitted to pass without improvement. It may not be out of place to mention in this connection that three Elders and one Deacon have been added to the session within the year and that the outlook is hopeful, the young brothern [sic] being deeply interested in this inheritance of God's work in the land. It is hoped that they will be the means of improving the attendance of the membership on the services of the sanctuary, which is now good, very few habitually remaining away, and they perhaps with excuses. The year has marked no special outpouring of the Holy Ghost, nor has it been barren of results, eight having been added to the communion of the church on profession.

The chief evidence that we have advanced in grace lies in the fact that interest is [Page 23] manifested in a greater degree in the Sabbath School work. This branch of work has not been permitted to fall behind but it is a matter of regret that we have no information leading us to the conclusion that all duties are so well performed, and even in this, some of its most important parts are neglected. No systematic catechetical nor Bible instruction is practiced within Sabbath School independent of lesson sheets or family, nor is family worship general in the church.

We have no complaint to make of Sabbath observance. It is very generally recognized as God's day. The Mosaic practice of Tithing is not in vogue with us, nor indeed do we find a thorough discharge of duty in that respect according to any plan, neither has there been a united effort made to relieve the destitute. This duty has been left to the charity of such individuals have so felt disposed to act.

Drunkenness is unknown amongst us, nor do we find any gross forms of sin prevailing.

Geo. A. Zirkle, Clerk of Session

Statistical Report of Mount Horeb Church
for the year ending April 1st 1888

Shows that there are five Ruling Elders, two Deacon and fifty-four communicating private members, aggregating sixty-one members. On examination there have been added eight members and by letter two. There have also been three baptisms, adult, and three infant. The Church also reports sixty scholars in the Sabbath school and twelve teachers. A number of these are members of other churches. (over)

[Page 24] Funds as collected by the Church are as follows:

Sustentation [sic]	$0.37
Evangelistic	5.92
Invalid	1.43
Foreign Missions	4.66
Education	2.44
Publication	.00

Tuskaloosa [Tuskagee?] Institute (colored)   .00
Presbyterial   2.00
Pastor's Salary, actually paid (for 7 mo.)   64.40
    Congregational   4.89
Miscellaneous   .00
Geo. A. Zirkle, Clerk of Session
Sabbath School Report Shows:

There are on Roll	Teachers	12
"	Pupils	61
With an average attendance of Teachers		8
"	Pupils	40
And new pupils admitted		8
The contributions amounting to		$15.40

The school is under nominal control of the Session. The Pastor and Elders are attentive so far as preaching and attendance are concerned. The Elders are also employed as teachers in the school.

The Confession of Faith, Catechism, and forms of government are not taught. The Children's Friend only is taken. The young people do not memorize the scripture nor have we any books of instruction other than the Bible and the lesson leaf issued by our church authority.

We have to report no special religious interest during the year, and no collections other than for our own expenses. [Page 25] Our young people are frustrated [?] in their attendance on the preaching of the Word. There are no colored people within our bounds.
Geo. A. Zirkle, Clerk of Session

Bristol May 3, 1888
Examined & approved except
1. The Records not before Presbytery last year.
2. On p. 14 two meetings were held without a moderator.
3. No quarterly reports from deacons.
4. The treasurer's book has not been examined.
M. P. Jarnagin
Moderator of Holston Presbytery

[Page 26] Minutes of Mount Horeb Church
April 1st 1888 Mount Horeb, Tenn.
Session was opened with prayer, Rev. John Daniels, moderation by request. Elders present R. D. Rankin, Joseph C. Bradshaw & Geo. A. Zirkle. The committee appointed to confer with Rev. Jno. Daniels reported that Mr. Daniels would serve the church as stated supply one Sabbath per month beginning April 1st.1888, and to continue till circumstances might indicate otherwise. A motion to adjourn till 3 o'clock P.M. to meet at the house of R. D. Rankin carried.

3 P.M. The Session was called to order by the moderator and proceeded to make out Sessional Reports to Presbytery, which business being performed session closed with prayer.   George A. Zirkle, Clerk of Session

April 29, 1888 Mount Horeb Tenn.
Session was opened with prayer. Rev. John Daniels moderating by request. Elders present R. D. Rankin, Jos. C. Bradshaw, A. T. Bradshaw & G. A. Zirkle. The business before the Session was the approval of the Sabbath School Report which having been done the Session closed with prayer.
Geo. A. Zirkle, Clerk of Session

[Page 27] Minutes of Mount Horeb Church
May 6th 1888 Mount Horeb, Tenn.
Session was opened with prayer. Rev. John Daniels moderating by request. Elders present, R. D. Rankin, Joseph C. Bradshaw, W. P. Bradshaw, A. T. Bradshaw & G. A. Zirkle. Minutes of April 1st & April 29th were read and approved. A motion was carried to not attend the call for a two weeks prayer meeting before and during the missionary conference at London, England. The delegate to the Presbytery at Bristol was required to make a report, which was approved and, and his diligence was commended. Session closed with prayer.
G. A. Zirkle, Clerk of Session

May 27, 1888 Mount Horeb Tenn.
Session met at Jos. C. Bradshaw's and was opened with prayer. Jos. C. Bradshaw moderating. Elders present, J. C. Bradshaw, A. T. Bradshaw, W. P. Bradshaw, G. A. Zirkle. It having been found that the Records of Mount Horeb Church are defective, resolutions as follows were adopted: Whereas the records of Mount Horeb Church do not show the election of Jno. P. Bradshaw & Jno. C. [Calvin] Bradshaw as trustees of Mount Horeb Church Property, therefore, Resolved 1st that the election of the above named persons as Trustees is hereby affirmed and ordered to be reconciled.
Resolved 2nd: That the Session recommended that the church hold an election on June 3rd for the purpose of electing Trustees of said Church property.
Session Closed with prayer.
Geo. A. Zirkle, Clerk of Session

[Page 28] Minutes of Mount Horeb Church
June 3, 1888 Mount Horeb, Tenn.
Session was opened with prayer. Rev. John Daniels moderating by request. Elders present, J, C. Bradshaw, A. T. Bradshaw, W. P. Bradshaw & G. A. Zirkle. Minutes of meeting of May 2nd were approved as far as resolutions. 2nd. Motion to reconsider Res. 2nd was carried. Motion to postpone indefinitely the election of trustees was carried. Session closed with prayer.
Geo. A. Zirkle, Clerk of Session

July 1, 1888 Mount Horeb, Tenn.

Session opened with prayer. Rev. Jno. Daniels moderating by request. Elders present R. D. Rankin, J. C. Bradshaw, A. T. Bradshaw, W. P. Bradshaw & G. A. Zirkle. Minutes of meeting of June 3 were read and approved. Session Closed with prayer.

G. A. Zirkle, Clerk of Session

Aug. 5, 1888 Mount Horeb, Tenn.

Session opened with prayer. Rev. John. Daniels moderating by request. Elders present J. C. Bradshaw, A. T. Bradshaw, R. D. Rankin & G. A. Zirkle. At this meeting it was agreed to hold a Sacramental meeting on the first Sabbath of October, and on Saturday preceding to elect Trustees of Mount Horeb Church Property. Session Closed with prayer.

G. A. Zirkle, Clerk of Session

[Page 29] Minutes of Mount Horeb Church

Sept. 2, 1888 Mount Horeb, Tenn.

Session opened with prayer. Rev. John Daniels moderating by request. Elders present J. C. Bradshaw, A. T. Bradshaw, W. A. Bradshaw, R. D. Rankin & G. A. Zirkle.

W. P. Bradshaw Principal & A. T. Bradshaw Alt. were appointed to attend meeting of Presbytery at New Providence, Sept. 20, '88. Session closed with prayer.

G. A. Zirkle, Clerk of Session

Sept 29, 1888 Mount Horeb, Tenn.

Session opened with prayer. Rev. J. B. Converse, Evangelist of Holston Presbytery moderating. Rev. Jno. Daniels being present. Elders present J. C. Bradshaw, W. P. Bradshaw & R. D. Rankin. (The time of Sacrament & Election of Trustees having been changed to make Rev. J. B. Converse's ministrations available at that time.) Election of Trustees was proceeded with & resulted as follows: T. J. [Thomas John] Bradshaw, W. E. [William Erskine] Rankin, G. A. [George Arthur] Newman & J. P. [John Pennywitt] Zirkle.

Session Closed with prayer.

G. A. Zirkle, Clerk of Session

Sept. 30, 1888 Mount Horeb, Tenn.

Session opened with prayer. Rev. J. B. Converse moderating. Rev. Jno. Daniels was present. Elders present R. D. Rankin, J. C. Bradshaw, W. P. Bradshaw, & G. A. Zirkle. Mr. W. A. McMurray of Hebron Church & Mrs. Kate C. [Catherine Cole Newman] McMurray of Lebanon Church were received by letter into the communion of Mount Horeb Church.

W. P. Bradshaw Principal with G. A. Zirkle Alt. was appointed to attend Synod at Clarksville Oct 17, 1888. Session Closed with prayer.

G. A. Zirkle,
Clerk of Session

[Page 30]

Nov. 10, 1888 Mount Horeb, Tenn.

Report of Board of Trustees of Mount Horeb Church Property

The board met this day for the purpose of Reorganization, and was called to order by the Chairman, R. D. Rankin, Mr. R. D. Rankin having resigned the Office of Chairman. Thos. J. Bradshaw was chosen to the Chair, and Geo. A. [George Arthur] Newman to the secretaryship.

There being no other business to transact the Board adjourned. Sine Die.[*sic*]

Geo. A. Newman, Sec.

The above Report with Names appended by the Secretary of the Board of Trustees.

Names of Board

T. J. [Thomas John] Bradshaw
J. P. [John Prigmore] Bradshaw
J. C. [Joseph C.] Bradshaw
R. D. [Richard Duffield] Rankin
W. E. [William Erskine] Rankin
J. P. [John Pennywitt] Zirkle
Geo. A. [George Arthur] Newman, Sec.

G. A. Zirkle,
Clerk of Session

Oct. 21st 1888 Mount Horeb

Session opened with Prayer. Rev. John. [M.] Daniels moderating by request. Elders present Jos. C. Bradshaw, R. D. Rankin, A. T. Bradshaw, W. P. Bradshaw, & G. A. Zirkle. Minutes July 1st, Aug. 5th, Sept 2nd, Sept. 29th, Sept. 30th were read and approved.

Session closed with prayer.

G. A. Zirkle, Clerk of Session
Per. A. T. Bradshaw

[Page 31]

Nov. 4th, 1888 Mount Horeb, Tenn.

Session opened with prayer.

Rev. John. Daniels moderating by request. Elders present Jos. C. Bradshaw, R. D. Rankin, W. P. Bradshaw, A. T. Bradshaw, and G. A. Zirkle.

W. P. Bradshaw gave his excuse for not attending Presbytery which was accepted. A. T. [Andrew Thomas Hood] Bradshaw also was excused because of ill health. W. P. Bradshaw Principal and G. A. Zirkle alt. was excused from attendance on Synod. Session Closed with prayer.

G. A. Zirkle, Clerk of Session
Per. A. T. Bradshaw

Jan. 6th, 1889 Mount Horeb, Tenn.

Session opened with prayer. Rev. John. Daniels moderating by request. Elders present Jos. C. Bradshaw, G. A. Zirkle, W. P. Bradshaw, and A. T. Bradshaw. Minutes of meetings Oct. 21st and Nov. 4, 1888 were approved.

A request was received from G. A. Zirkle for letters of dismission for himself and Family, request was granted and letters ordered on motions of session.

A. T. Bradshaw was elected clerk.

Session Closed with prayer.

A. T. Bradshaw,
Clerk of Session

Feb. 3[d] 1889 Mount Horeb, Tenn.

Session opened with prayer. Rev. John. Daniels moderating by request. Elders present Jos. C. Bradshaw, R. D. Rankin, W. P. Bradshaw & A. T. Bradshaw. Jos. C. Bradshaw Principal, W. P. Bradshaw alt. were appointed to attend Presbytery at Johnson City April 11, 1889.

A.T. Bradshaw,
Clerk of Session

[Page 32]

Approved as far as written except that the Record shows no settlement with the treasurer nor any collection. The reports are not copied. The delegates have not reported their attendance.

Geo. F. Robertson,
Moderator Holston Presbytery
Johnson City, Tenn., April 13, 1889

June 16, 1889 Mount Horeb, Tenn.

Session Was opened with Prayer. Rev. John Daniels moderating by request. Elders present Jos. C. Bradshaw, R. D. Rankin and A. T. Bradshaw. Jos. C. Bradshaw delegate to Presbytery at Johnson City made his report, which was approved by the Session.

Session Closed with prayer.

A.T. Bradshaw,
Clerk of Session

Aug. 18th 1889 Mount Horeb, Tenn.

Session was opened with Prayer. Rev. John Daniels moderating by request. Elders present R. D. Rankin, Jos. C. Bradshaw, W. P. Bradshaw and A. T. Bradshaw. R. D. Rankin delegate and W. P. Bradshaw alt. were appointed delegates to Presbytery to meet at Mossy Creek Sep. 5th 1889.

Session Closed with prayer.

A.T. Bradshaw,
Clerk of Session

[Page 33] Oct. 20th 1889 Mount Horeb, Tenn.

Session was opened with Prayer. Rev. John Daniels moderating by request. Elders present Jos. C. Bradshaw, W. P. Bradshaw and A. T. Bradshaw. Rev. James B. Converse being present as Visiting Bro. Florence A Peck and Lila [Lelia] M. Peck came before Session and after being examined as to their faith in Jesus Christ were admitted into the Communion of the Mount Horeb Church. Session then took recess until after Service it being our Communion Season. After Service Session was called to order by the moderator. Session resolved to administer the Sacrament of the Lord's Supper to Elder. R. D. Rankin who was confined at home on account of the infirmities of old age. Session Closed with prayer.

A. T. Bradshaw, Clerk of Session

March. 29th 1890 Mount Horeb, Tenn.,

Session was opened with Prayer. Rev. James Haynes Evangelist elect Moderating by request. Elders present R. D. Rankin, Jos. C. Bradshaw, W. P. Bradshaw and A. T. Bradshaw. Minutes of meetings of Jun. 16th, Aug 18th, Oct. 20th 1889 were read and approved. Session filled blank reports to Presbytery. Mrs. Fannie J. A. Newman requesting letter of dismission to Mossy Creek Church. Clerk was ordered to prepare and forward the same. Session Closed with prayer.

A. T. Bradshaw, Clerk of Session

[Page 34] March. 30th 1890 Mount Horeb Tenn.

Session was opened with Prayer. Rev. James Haynes Evangelist elect moderating by request. Elders present Jos. C. Bradshaw, R. D. Rankin, W. P. Bradshaw and A. T. Bradshaw. The following Persons came before Session and after being examined as to their faith in Jesus Christ were admitted into the Communion of the Church—Samuel F. [Franklin] McMurray, Mack [Calvin] Franklin, Milton F. Newman, Howard M. Peck, John M. [McCampbell] Mcmurry, B. [Benjamin] Wallace Mcmurry, James F. Peck, Ella Porter Peck, Flora M. [May] Bradshaw, Lizzie Cate Newman.

Jos. C. Bradshaw Principal, W. P. Bradshaw Alt. were appointed delegates to Presbytery to meet at White Pine April 3rd 1890. The Report of the Deacons were received and approved. Amt. collected Sustentation $2.89, Foreign Missions $6.97, Education .40cts, Tuscaloosa Institute $1.00, Pastors Salary $40.00, Congregational. 60cts., Miscellaneous $1.40 cts.

Minits [sic] of the meeting were read and approved.

Session Closed with prayer.

A. T. Bradshaw, Clerk of Session

Approved as far as written
White Pine, Tenn.
April. 4th 1890
J. Chalmers Cowan,
Mod. Holston Pres.

[Page 35] May 18th 1890 Mount Horeb Tenn.

Session was opened with Prayer. Rev. John Daniels moderating by request. Elders present Jos. C. Bradshaw, W. P. Bradshaw and A. T. Bradshaw. Jos. C. Bradshaw Delegate to Presbytery at White Pine April 3rd 1890 reported his diligence in his attendance. Report was received by the Session. minits [sic] of the meeting were then read and affirmed. Session Closed with prayer.

A. T. Bradshaw,
Clerk of Session

April. 12th 1891 Mount Horeb Tenn.

Session was opened with Prayer. Rev. W. C. Broady of the Presbyterian Church North Moderating by invitation. Elders present Jos. C. Bradshaw, W. P. Bradshaw and A. T. Bradshaw. Miss Mary S. Zirkle Collins for letter of dismission to the Cumberland Presbyterian Church at Mount Horeb, Tenn. The Clerk was ordered to prepare and forward the same. On motion A. T. Bradshaw Principal, W. P. Bradshaw alt. were appointed to attend Presbytery at Rogersville, Tenn. April 22th 1891. Session heard Report of Deacons which was Sustained. Amt. Contributed by the Church, Evangelistic $1.40, Invalid fund $1.50, Foreign Missions Ladies Society $20. 75, Childrens mission Band $10.00, Church Collections $3.17, Total $33.92. Publication 1.00 (over) [Page 36] American Bible Society $1.94, Presbyterial $2.48, Pastors paid Salary for 8 mo. Preaching $43.75, Congregational $5.00.

Minits [sic] of the meeting were read and approved.

Session Closed with prayer.

A. T. Bradshaw,
Clerk of Session

Examined and approved as far as written with the exception that the minute is too brief and Sec. 58 of Manual not complied with.

Rogersville, Tenn.

Apr. 24, 1891

J. Albert Wallace, Moderator

[Page 37] May 25th 1891 Mount Horeb, Tenn.,

Session was opened with Prayer. Elder Jos. C. Bradshaw was Elected Moderator. A Request was read from G. A. [George Arthur] Newman calling for a letter of Dismission to the Presbyterian Church at Harriman, Tenn. Request was granted and the Clerk was ordered to Prepare and forward the letter.

A. T. Bradshaw reported his diligence in attending meeting of Presbytery at Rogersville May 22nd 1891 which was approved by the Session.

Elders present Jos. C. Bradshaw, W. P. Bradshaw and A. T. Bradshaw. Minits [sic] of the Meeting were read and approved. Session Closed with prayer.

A.T. Bradshaw,
Clerk of Session

[Page 38] Sep. 13, 1891
Mount Horeb
Session met and was opened with Prayer. Elder Jos. C. Bradshaw was chosen Moderator. Elders present Jos. C. Bradshaw, W. P. Bradshaw and A. T. Bradshaw. On motion W. P. Bradshaw Principal and A. T. Bradshaw alt. were appointed delegates to attend the meeting of Presbytery at Rutledge Sept. 17th 1891. Session adjourned and was Closed with Prayer.

A. T. Bradshaw
Clerk of Session

Oct. 11, 1891
Mount Horeb
Session met and was opened with Prayer. Rev. James B. Converse moderating by request. Elders present Jos. C. Bradshaw, W. P. Bradshaw and A. T. Bradshaw. On motion Jos. C. Bradshaw Principal and A. T. Bradshaw alt. were appointed delegates to attend the meeting of Synod to be held at Columbia Tenn. Oct 13th 1891.

Whereas Reports concerning the conduct of Nienia Cannon have reached the ears of the Session. Therefore the Session appointed Jos. C. Bradshaw to visit her and confer with her and report to the Session on Saturday before the 2nd Sabbath of Nov. 1891.

Minits [sic] of the meeting were read and approved. Session adjourned and was closed with prayer.

A. T. Bradshaw
Clerk of Session

[Page 39] Sep. 11, 1891
Mount Horeb Tenn.
Session met and was opened with Prayer. Rev. James B. Converse moderating by request. Elders present Jos. C. Bradshaw, W. P. Bradshaw and A. T. Bradshaw.

Jos. C. Bradshaw made his report as to his Conference with Miss Nienia Cannon which was approved by the Session.

Whereas Miss Nienia Cannon a young girl without the advantages of early parental training in Conference with Jos. C. Bradshaw expressed herself guilty of Violation of the Seventh Commandment expressed her penitence for the Same has resolve to lead a new life. Submitted her call to the Session without Process. The Session resolved to take up the case judicially the Court was charged and the Moderator led in Prayer After full conference the court resolved that she be Privately admonished and that she be Suspended from the Sacrament of the Church for six mo.

Session resolved that the decision of the Session be read to the Congregation by the moderator. The Session then appointed Rev. James B. Converse and Jos. C. Bradshaw a committee to admonish her.

Session closed with prayer.

A. T. Bradshaw,
Clerk of Session

[Page 40] March 13th, 1892
Mount Horeb, Tenn.

Session met and was opened with Prayer. Rev. James B. Converse moderating by request. Elders present Jos. C. Bradshaw, W. P. Bradshaw and A. T. Bradshaw. Session took recess until after public Service. after recess Minits [sic] of the Meetings of session of Sep. 15th and Nov. 7th 1891 were read and approved.

W. P. Bradshaw delegate to Presbytery which met at Rutledge, Tenn. Sep. 17th 1891 made his report which was approved by the Session. On motion A. T. Bradshaw Principal and W. P. Bradshaw alt. were appointed delegates to attend the meeting of Presbytery at Bristol April 6th 1892. Jos. C. Bradshaw gave reasons for his nonattendance at the meeting of Synod in Columbia Tenn. Oct 13th 1891 which were sustained by the Session. Rev. James B. Converse and Jos. C. Bradshaw the committee appointed to give the admonition to Miss Nienia Cannon mad [sic] their report which was approved and the Committee was discharged. [Page 41] on motion of Session.

The Statistical report to Presbytery and Sessional report on Sabbath Schools were referred to Clerk of Session to fill out. Session then proceeded to answer the questions in the Narrative. After which they were read and approved.

Rev. James B. Converse was requested to read the Narrative to the Congregation. Minutes of the meeting were then read and approved.

Session closed with prayer.

A. T. Bradshaw,
Clerk of Session

[Page 42] May 8th, 1892 Mount Horeb, Tenn.

Session met and was opened with Prayer. Rev. James B. Converse moderating by request. Elders present Jos. C. Bradshaw and A. T. Bradshaw. Misses Lula and [Ethel] May McMurry appeared before the Session and after giving Satisfactory evidence of their faith in Christ Jesus were received into the Communion of the Church.

Session closed with prayer.

A. T. Bradshaw,
Clerk of Session

Sep. 18th 1892
Mount Horeb, Tenn.

Session met and was opened with Prayer. Rev. James B. Converse moderating by request. Elders present Jos. C. Bradshaw, W. P. Bradshaw and A. T. Bradshaw. The Session was asked to give letters of dismission to F. A. [Frank Adam] Newman and W. E. [William Edward] Bradshaw on motion the letters were granted and the Clerk was ordered to prepare and forward the same. Minits [sic] of the meeting were then read and approved.

Session closed with prayer.

A.T. Bradshaw,
Clerk of Session

[Page 43] Jan. 8th 1893
Mount Horeb, Tenn.

Session met and was opened with Prayer. Rev. James B. Converse moderating by request. Elders present Jos. C. Bradshaw, W. P. Bradshaw and A. T. Bradshaw. A request was heard from Mr. F. A. [Frank Ashley] Bradshaw calling for a letter of dismission to the Presbyterian Church at Harriman, Tenn. The letter was granted and the Clerk was ordered to prepare and forward the same.

Session closed with prayer.

A.T. Bradshaw,
Clerk of Session

[Page 44] April 23rd 1893
Mount Horeb, Tenn.

Session met and was opened with Prayer. Jos. C. Bradshaw was chosen moderator. Elders present Jos. C. Bradshaw, W. P. Bradshaw and A. T. Bradshaw. On motion of session the Minits [sic] of the meetings of Session on May 8th 1892 and Jan. 8th 1893 were read and approved.

A.T. Bradshaw principal and W. P. Bradshaw alt. were appointed delegates to attend the meeting of Presbytery at Johnson's City [sic] April 26th 1893. On motion the statistical Report to Presbytery and the Sessional report on Sabbath Schools were referred to the Clerk of Session to fill out. Session then proceeded to answer the questions in the Narrative after which they were read and approved.

Session Closed with Prayer.

A.T. Bradshaw,
Clerk of Session

[Page 45] April 25th 1893
Mount Horeb, Tenn.

Statistical Report to Presbytery at Johnson's City April 26th 1893

To amt Contributed for

"	Sustentation	.40 cts
"	Foreign Mission	$7.55
"	Education	2.40
"	Colored Evan. Fund	.73
"	Church Erections	.20
"	Presbyterial	2.00
"	Salary	68.95
"	Congregational	53.79

A. T. Bradshaw,
Clerk of Session

[Page 46] May 15th 1893
Mount Horeb, Tenn.

Session met and was opened with prayer. Rev. James B. Converse moderating by request. Elders present Jos. C. Bradshaw, W. P. Bradshaw and A. T. Bradshaw.

A.T. Bradshaw princ. and W. P. Bradshaw alt. delegates elect to Presbytery which met at Johnson's City [sic] April 26th 1893 gave reasons for their nonattendance which were sustained. Minits [sic] were read and approved. Session Closed with Prayer.

A. T. Bradshaw, Clerk of Session

[Page 47] Sep. 12th 1893
Mount Horeb, Tenn.

Session met and was opened with prayer. Rev. James B. Converse moderating by request. Elders present Jos. C. Bradshaw, W. P. Bradshaw and A. T. Bradshaw.

On motion of Session W. P. Bradshaw Principal and A.T. Bradshaw alt. were appointed delegates to attend the meeting of Synod at Cleveland Tenn. Oct. 15th 1893.

Minits [sic] were read and approved. Session Closed with Prayer.

A. T. Bradshaw, Clerk of Session

[Page 48] Sep. 14th 1893
Mount Horeb, Tenn.

Session was convened at the Close of Sermon 10-50 ock [sic] A. M. Rev. J. H. Morrison Moderating. The following appeared before Session. Porter [A.] Barbee, Edward Barbee, Malinda Newman, William [F.] Miller and after giving Satisfactory evidence as to their faith in Christ were received in to the Communion of the Church.

Session Closed with Public Service.

A. T. Bradshaw, Clerk of Session

Sep. 14th 1893 Mount Horeb, Tenn.

Session was called together at the Close of Sermon 7 ock [sic] P. M. Rev. J. H. Morrison Moderating by request. Elders present W. P. Bradshaw, A. T. Bradshaw. Rev. J. Carroll of the C. P. Church [Cumberland Presbyterian Church] being present by invitation. The following Persons came before Session Ola [Ann] Mcmurry, Lucy (Moore) Newman, Mattie Lee Newman and after giving evidence as to their faith in Christ were received into the Communion of the Church.

Session Closed with Public Service.

A. T. Bradshaw, Clerk of Session

[Page 49] Sep. 15th 1893 Mount Horeb, Tenn.

Session met after public Worship. Rev. James B. Converse Moderating. Present W. P. Bradshaw Elder. Rev. J. H. Morrison and Rev. J. J. Carroll as Corresponding member.

John H. Miller and Emma his wife were received into the Communion of the Church on profession of faith in Christ. Session Closed with the Benediction.

A. T. Bradshaw, Clerk of Session

Sep. 16th 1893 Mount Horeb, Tenn.

Session met at the Close of Service. Rev. James B. Converse Moderating. Rev. J. H. Morrison and Rev. J. J. Carroll present as Corresponding members. Elders present W. P. Bradshaw and A. T. Bradshaw.

Emma Cate ["Katie"] Bradshaw and Alice L. [Lavinia] Rankin came before the Session and after giving good evidence as to their faith in Christ were received into the Communion of the Church. Session Closed with the Benediction.

A. T. Bradshaw

[Page 50] April 8th 1894 Mount Horeb, Tenn.

Session met and was opened with Prayer. Rev. James B. Converse moderating. Elders present Jos. C. Bradshaw, W. P. Bradshaw and A. T. Bradshaw. Minits [sic] of the meetings of Session of Sep. 14th – 15 – 16 - 1893 were read and approved. Sessional report on Sabbath School was filled out. Narrative of the Session was taken up and the questions answered. Statistical Report was made out and read and approved.

Res -- 1st

Whereas the following persons have been out of our Bounds for a long period of time we do instruct the Clerk to place their Names on the retired list. John W. [William Massengill] Bradshaw, Sarah E. [Elizabeth] Bradshaw and Isabel B. [Belle Tittsworth] Bradshaw.

Res –2nd

That Whereas H. S. [Harvey Smith] Bradshaw is now a licensed Minister in the Presbyterian Church. The Clerk is instructed to drop his name from the roll.[108]

A. T. Bradshaw Prin., W. P. Bradshaw alt. were Chosen delegates to Presbytery to meet at Morristown Tenn. Wed. 18th April 1894.

Session Closed with Prayer.   A. T. Bradshaw, Clerk of Session

[Page 51]

Statistical Report to Presbytery
to meet at Morristown April 18th 1894

On Settlement with Church Treasurer we have contributed the following

Sustentation	$1.00
Evangelistic	28.66
Foreign Missions	4.81
Education	1.69
Publications	.50
Col. Evangelistic	.93
Church Erection	.61
Presbyterial	2.00
Pastors Salary Paid	66.70
Congregational	20.00

A. T. Bradshaw, Clerk of Session

---

[108] An ordained minister is a member of Presbytery and no longer a member of an individual church.

Approved as far as written, except
1. Sessions not opened and closed with prayer.
2. The minute in regard to licentiate H. S. Bradshaw is not approved.
Wm. M. Grayvill
Moderator Holston Presbytery
Morristown Tenn. Apr 20, 1894

[Page 52]
In the fall of 1893, the stated supply of the church requested the Presbytery of Holston to appoint two elders to act with him in considering the care of a member upon which the elders felt incompetent to act on account on near relationship. The Presbytery appointed a commission consisting of Rev. Misters [J. G.] McFerrin, Richardson & [James B.] Converse & elders Jarnagin & Fair. This commission, at the request of the elders, considered the case of Mr. Thomas J. [John] Bradshaw,[109] and after due & repeated citations suspended him indefinitely from the Communion of the church for contumacy.[110] The commission reported its action to the Presbytery in the spring of 1894, and it was approved. Application has been made to the Stated Clerk of Presbytery for an official copy of the action of Presbytery, but it has not been furnished and therefore this unofficial note of the action of Presbytery is here recorded.
James B. Converse, Stated Supply

[Page 53] July 8th 1894
Mount Horeb, Tenn.
Session met at the Church and was opened with Prayer. Rev. James B. Converse moderating by request. Elders present Jos. C. Bradshaw, W. P. Bradshaw and Rev. T. R. [Thomas Rankin] Bradshaw by invitation. Mrs. Jerusha Furgesson was received into the Communion of the Church by letter from The Leesburg Church, Washington Co. Tenn. Session Closed with Prayer.
A. T. Bradshaw,
Clerk of Session

[Page 54] March 30th 1895
Mount Horeb, Tenn.
Session met and was opened with Prayer. Rev. A. S. Doak of Mossy Creek Tenn. Moderating by request. Elders present Jos. C. Bradshaw, W. P. Bradshaw and A. T. Bradshaw.
The Narrative & Statistical Reports to Presbytery were made out and approved. The Report on Sabbath Schools was referred to the Superintendent of School to fill out.

---

[109] Thomas John is a brother of William Porter Massengil Bradshaw, a member of Session. Joseph C. Bradshaw, member of session, and Rev. Thomas R. Bradshaw are his uncles.
[110] Insubordinate, stubborn resistance to authority, willful contempt of court (*Webster's Seventh New Collegiate Dictionary*, G. & C. Merriam Company, Publishers, Springfield, Massachusetts, U.S.A, 1965.)

W. P. Bradshaw as principal and Jos. C. Bradshaw alt. were elected delegates to attend the meeting of Presbytery at Rogersville, Tenn. April 1895.

Prof. F. [Frank] M. Killgore and wife Mrs. Kate M. [Roddy] Killgore presented their Letters from Presbyterian Church at Limestone, Ala. The Session received them into the Communion of The Church and ordered the Clerk to enroll their Names.

Session adjourned and was Closed with Prayer.

A. T. Bradshaw,
Clerk of Session

[Page 55] April 19th 1896
Mount Horeb, Tenn.

The Session met and was opened with Prayer. Elders present Jos. C. Bradshaw, W. P. Bradshaw and A. T. Bradshaw. Jos. C. Bradshaw was elected moderator. The Blank reports to `Presbytery were made out and approved

W. P. Bradshaw as Princ. and A. T. Bradshaw Alt. were appointed delegates to attend the meeting of Presbytery at Leesburg Tenn. on April 22nd 1896. Session was Closed with Prayer.

A. T. Bradshaw,
Clerk of Session

Approved as far as written except that
1. Records not at Presbytery since 1894.
2. Reports not to Presbytery not recorded.
Leesburg, Tenn.
Apr. 22, 1896   Frank McCutchan, Moderator

[Page 56] Aug. 2nd 1896
Mount Horeb, Tenn.

The Session met at the Church and was opened with Prayer. Rev. W. H. Smith Moderating by request. Elders present Jos. C. Bradshaw and A. T. Bradshaw.

W. P. Bradshaw as Principal and A. T. Bradshaw Alt. were appointed delegates to Presbytery to be held at Russellville Tenn. Aug. 20th 1896.

Session Closed with Prayer.

A. T. Bradshaw, Clerk of Session

[Page 57] April 3rd 1897
Mount Horeb Tenn.

The Session met and was opened with Prayer. The Rev. W. H. Smith moderating by request. Elders present Jos. C. Bradshaw, W. P. Bradshaw and A. T. Bradshaw. Reports to Presbytery for the year ending April 1st 1897 were filled out and approved. W. P. Bradshaw was appointed to represent the Church at the meeting of Presbytery to be held at Mossy Creek Tenn. April 14th 1897.

Statistical report. Pastors Salary Paid $40.15, Congregational $7.00. There was nothing contributed for other causes. Minit [sic] of the meeting of the Session on Aug. 2nd 1896 were read and approved. Our delegate to Presbytery was instructed to ask permission of Presbytery to employ the Rev. W. H. Smith for one year for one fourth of his time.

Minit of the meeting was read and approved. Session was Closed with Prayer.

A. T. Bradshaw, Clerk of Session

Ex'd & Apr'd in Pres. of Holston at Mossy Creek. Apr. 16th 1897.

J. G. McFerrin – Moderator

[Page 58] April 3th 1898
Mount Horeb, Tenn.
Session of Mount Horeb Church met and was opened with Prayer. Rev. W. H. Smith Moderating by request. Elders present W. P. Bradshaw and A. T. Bradshaw. The Session appointed A. T. Bradshaw Principal and W. P. Bradshaw Alt. to represent the Church at the meeting of Presbytery to be held at Morristown Tenn. April 27th 1898. The Reports to Presbytery were filled out and approved and Read to the Congregation.

Statistical Report

Pastors Salery [sic] Paid $52.20
Sabbath School expenses $4.75
Foreign Missions $5.04
There was nothing Contributed to the other Causes of the Church.
Session Closed with Prayer.   A.T. Bradshaw, Clerk of Session

[Page 59] June 5th 1898
Mount Horeb, Tenn.
The Session of The Mount Horeb Church met and was opened with Prayer. Rev. W. H. Smith Moderating by request. Elders present W. P. Bradshaw and A. T. Bradshaw. A letter of dismission was granted to A. B. [Asahel Biddle] Bradshaw to The Presbyterian Church Fifth Avenue Knoxville Tenn. The Session Closed with Prayer.

A. T. Bradshaw, Clerk of Session

Mount Horeb, Tenn.
Sep. 4th 1898
Session met and was opened with Prayer. Rev. W. H. Smith Moderating by request. Elders present W. P. Bradshaw and A. T. Bradshaw. It was decided to hold a sacramental meeting on the 1st Sunday in Sep. W. P. Bradshaw Principal and A. T. Bradshaw Alt. were appointed delegates to attend the meeting of Presbytery at Tarwell Sep 22d 1898. Mr. Frank A. [Ashley] Bradshaw was received into the Church on examination. The Session Closed with Prayer.

A. T. Bradshaw, Clerk of Session

[Page 60] Oct 6th 1898
Mount Horeb, Tenn.
Session met and was opened with Prayer.
Rev. W. H. Smith Moderating by request. Elders present W. P. Bradshaw and A. T. Bradshaw.
A request was presented asking for letters of dismission for Prof. F. [Frank] M. Killgore and wife [Kate M. Roddy Killgore] The request was granted and the Clerk was ordered to prepare and forward the Same. Session Closed with Prayer.

A. T. Bradshaw, Clerk of Session

Nov 6th 1898
Mount Horeb, Tenn.
Session met and was opened with Prayer.
Rev. W. H. Smith Moderating by request. Elders present W. P. Bradshaw.
A request was presented asking for letters of dismission for A. T. [Andrew Thomas Hood] Bradshaw & wife [Isabelle "Belle" Tittsworth]. The request was granted. The Clerk was ordered to prepare the letters. Thay [sic] was dismissed to join the Presbyterian Church Fifth Avenue Knoxville Tenn.
Session Closed with Prayer.

W. P. Bradshaw, Clerk of Session

[Page 61]
Session met at the call of the Moderator at the house of Wm. P. Bradshaw. Members present. W. H. Smith Moderator, & W. P. Bradshaw. Opened with prayer. The blanks for Presbytery being in hand, were filled out, approved, & ordered to be spread as record for future reference, & also to be read before the congregation, & is as follows.

Statistical

Elders 1, Communicants added on Examination 1, Total number of Communicants 47, Baptized non communicants 3, Officers & Teachers in Sabbath School 9, Shollars [sic] in S. S. & Bible classes ___, Funds Collected for Foreign Missions, $6.00, For Presbyterial 4.00, For Congregational 5.10 cts, Pastor Salary paid 40.95 cts.

Narrative

The attendance upon the service of the sanctuary by some of the members very good, & other members of the church attend but seldom. -- Family worship is poorly observed. -- The observance of the Lords Day by some members good, By others not so good. -- The Training of Children in the scriptures and Catechism is greatly neglected. -- The acts of benevolence are few & far between. -- The church has paid its Minister something near the amount promised. – There is but very little life & [?] among the most of the members of our church. We have but little or no worldly conformity among any of our members. – We are not engaged in any evangelistic work, & have hard work to live, & keep our heads above water. There being no other business before the session it was closed with prayer.

W. P. Bradshaw, Clerk of Session

[Page 62] July 2, 1899, Mount. Horeb, Tenn.

Session met and was opened with Prayer.

Rev. W. H. Smith Moderating by request. Elders present W. P. Bradshaw.

Mr. John M. Lyle, Miss Luella May Lyle & Mack Lyle Presented for letters from the Methodist church at Chestnut Grove Tenn.

The Session received them into the communion of the Church & ordered the Clerk to inroll [sic] their names. Session adjourned & was Closed with Prayer.

W. P. Bradshaw, Clerk of Session

[Page 63] Apr. 8th /00 Mount Horeb, Tenn.

Session met at the church and was opened with Prayer.

Elders present W. P. Bradshaw & Wm. McMurry. W. P. Bradshaw was appointed moderator. The blank reports to Presbytery were made out and approved.

Session adjourned & was Closed with Prayer.

W. P. Bradshaw, Clerk of Session

Rev. W. H. Smith Minister

The blank reports to presbytery were ready & ordered to be spread upon the book as a record, for future reference and are as follows.

Statistical Report

Elders 2, Deacons 0,

Communicant added on examination none, on certificate Three, Total No. of communicants 50,

No adult or infant Baptized. Baptized non communicants 3.

Officers & Teaching in Sabbath School, & Bible Classes 8, Schollars [sic] in S. S. & Bible Classes 32.

Funds Contributed, For Foreign Missions 4.00, For Presbyterial 4.00,

Pastors Salary actually paid 46.05.

Congregational 36.00,

Po. Office of the Pastor, Morristown,

Po. office of Clerk of Session, Mount Horeb.

Sabbath School

No of Officers & Teachers, 8, No. of Schollars [sic] 32. Total 38.

Current expenses, 4.00, For other objects, 32.00 Total 36.00.

Our School is under the supervision & control of the session, While its Officers, Teachers, [Page 64] & Schollars [sic] all almost without exception attend the public worship. The standards of the Church are not taught especially in the school. Neither do the Schollars [sic] memorize the Scriptures & the Catechism. Our literature is the Richmond Publications. We have had four additions to the Church from the Sunday School by Profession. We have no teachers meetings. George R. Zirkle is our Superintendent P. Office Mount Horeb.

Narrative

The attendance upon the services of the sanctuary, by some of the members of the church is very good. While other members attend but seldom. Family worship is better attended too than formally. The observance of the Lord's Day by some of the members good, by others not so good, & by none, I would say, as it should be kept.

The training of children in the scriptures, & catechisms, in the families is greatly neglected. The acts of benevolence is almost a blank.

The church has paid its minister something near the amount promised.

There is more life among the members of our church of both young & old, than formally.

We have but little, or no worldly conformity among any of our members.

We are not engaged in any evangelical work.

By order of the Session. W. H. Smith, Moderator

Wm. P. Bradshaw, Clk. of Ses.

[Page 65] May 6, 1900

Session met at the call of the Moderator. Opened with prayer. Members present W. H. Smith, Moderator, Wm. P. Bradshaw & Wm. N. [William Newton] McMurry. Four persons appeared before the Session as candidates for admission into the church. Namely Charles W. [Walter] McMurry, Ephraim Cawood Bradshaw, Martha Matilda "Tilda" McMurry, & Carry May Corbit [sic]. After an examination of their experimental religion & their faith & trust in Christ, they were received into full communion & recommend to the care & fellowship of the church. There being no other business before the session it was closed with prayer. By order of the Session

W. H. Smith, Mod., Wm. P. Bradshaw, Clk. of Sess.

Sep. 6, 1900 Mount Horb [sic]Tenn

Session met & was opened with prayer. Rev. W. H. Smith moderating by request. Elders present W. N. Mcmurry [sic] & W. P. Bradshaw. A request was presented asking for letter of dismission for Mrs. Sallie Tittstworth [sic] the request was granted the clerk was orderd [sic] to prepair [sic] the letter. There beeing [sic] no other buisiness [sic] the Session closed with prayer.

W. H. Smith Mod.

W. P. Bradshaw, Clerk of Session

[Page 66] April 6th 1901

Session met at the house of Frank A. [Ashley] Bradshaw. Constituted with prayer. Members present W. H. Smith moderator, Wm. P. Bradshaw & William McMurry. The blank reports to presbytery being present were filled up & approved and ordered spread upon the minutes as record for future references. W. P. Bradshaw was appointed as principal delegate to Presbytery to meet at Rutledge May 1st 1901 & Wm. N. McMurry [sic] his alternate. There being no other business before the session it was closed with prayer.

The following are the reports to Presbytery.

Statistical Report

Elders 2,

Added on examination 4 or Certificate 0.

Total number of Communicants 31.

Adult Baptisms 1. Infant Baptisms 1. Baptized non Communicants 3.

Officers & Teachers in Sabbath Schools & Bible Classes 10. Schollars [sic] in Sabbath School & Bible Classes 57.

Fund Contributed. Foreign Missions 2.82 cts. For Local Missions 3.52 cts. For Presbyterial 4.00. Pastor's Salary Actually Paid 64.75. Congregational 2.00.

Sabbath School

No. of Teachers & officers 10. Scholars 57. Total 67.

Average No. of Teachers ___ of scholars 34. Schollars [sic] admitted to the communion 4. Current expenses 14.78 cts. Funds Contributed for other causes 30.77. Total 45.55cts.

Our school is under the Supervision & Control of the Session. While its Officers, Teachers & Scholars generally attend & take some interest in the services of the day. The Schollars [sic] all attend public worship. The school takes the Richmond Pub. Literature. [Page 67] The Scholars do not memorize the Scripture or Shorter Catechism. There has been no special religious interest in the School during the last year.

Mr. George A. Zirkle is our Superintendent.

Narrative

The attendance upon the services of the sanctuary, by all members reported, is very good. Most of the heads of the families of our church have Family worship. The observance of the Holy Sabbath by most of the members, is tolerably good, & yet not what it should be. The training of children in the home & Sabbath School in the Scriptures is greatly neglected, & in the Catechisms of the church, almost entirely neglected. In regard to benevolence the church has been doing but little. Some improvement in that line.

We have settled all accounts with our Minister for the year ending Apr. the 1, 1901.

We think the church has made some improvement in spirituality. We think there is but little, or no worldly conformity among the great majority of the members, if among any.

We are not engaged in any Evangelical work as a church.

By order of the Session.

W. P. Bradshaw, Clk. of Session

[Page 68] Nov 1, 1901 Mount Horeb Tenn.

Session met & was opened with prayer. Rev. W. H. Smith moderating. Elders present W. N. McMurry & W. P. Bradshaw. Miss Laura C. Zirkle was received in to the church by profession in faith in Christ there being no other business before the Session it closed with prayer.

W. H. Smith Mod.

W. P. Bradshaw, Clerk of Session

Nov 30, 1901

Mount Horeb Tenn.

Session met was Constituted with prayer. Rev. W. H. Smith moderating. Elders present W. N. McMurry & W. P. Bradshaw. The Session granted letters of dismission to Mrs. C. C. [Cinderella Caldwell] Bradshaw & sons Bob, & Clyde P. [Clide Park] Bradshaw at their own request to the Presbyterian church Thomisville, [sic] Ga. There being no other business before the Session it was closed with prayer.

W. H. Smith Mod.

W. P. Bradshaw, Clerk of Session

April 4, 1902

Session met at the house of William P. Bradshaw was constituted with prayer. The blank reports to presbytery being present was [sic] filled up, & approved & ordered spread as record for future references & is as follows.

Statistical Report

Elders 2, Added on examination 1 or Certificate 1.

Whole number of Communicants 30. [Page 69]

Adult Baptisms 1. Baptized non Communicants 3.

Officers & Teachers in Sabbath Schools & Bible Classes 9.—

Schollars [sic] in Sabbath School & Bible Classes 50.

Fund Contributed

For Foreign Missions $18.45, -- For Local Home Missions 5.27 –

For Ministerial Relief 1.57 -- For Education 4.00 –

For Presbyterial 4.00 –

Pastor's Salary Actually Paid 68.40 -- Congregational 7.29

Sabbath School Report

Whole Number of Teachers 9. Whole Number of Scholars 50.   Average Number of Teachers 9. & scholars 24. Total 33.

The amount Contributed by the School. The School is under the Supervision of the Elders, who attend the school & Teachers & Scholars all attend public worship. The Scholars do not as a matter of Study memorize the Scriptures or Shorter catechism. The School uses nothing but the Bible, The Quarterly & Lesson leaf. We have had no special interest of religion in the School during the last year

Mr. George A. Zirkle is our Superintendent.

The Narrative of the Session

The attendance upon the services of the sanctuary, by all members of the church & others Tolerably good. The observance of Family worship we think tolerably good. The observance of the Lord's day, by the members of the church is tolerably well observed, still room for improvement. The Training of children & youth in the homes & Sabbath School in the Scriptures, & Catechisms is greatly [Page 70] Neglected by all. The benevolence of our people is only tolerable. Our Minister has received in full promptly all that is promised him. There has been no special Religion interest in our church during the past year. Worldly Conformity, as we understand it, has but little hold upon our people.

We are not, as a church, engaged in any evangelical work outside of our own congregation.

There was no Elder who could represent the church at the coming Presbytery.

There being no other business before the Session, it was closed with prayer.

Wm. P. Bradshaw, Clk. of Session

[Page 71] July 6, 1902
Mount Horeb Tenn.

Session met & was opened with prayer. Rev. W. H. Smith moderating. Elders present W. N. Mcmurry & W. P. Bradshaw.

Mr. J. M. [James Moore] Mcmurry, Almira M. [Minerva Rankin] Mcmurry, Ann Bell Mcmurry, John M. [McCampbell] Mcmurry, Benj. W. [Wallace] Mcmurry, Elda May McMurry, George [W.] Franklin, Sallie A. [Ann Bell] Franklin, Mc. C. [Mac Calvin] Franklin, G. A. Zirkle, F. O. Zirkle & G. A. Rankin presented there [sic] letters.

The Session received them into the Communion of the Church & ordered the Clerk to inrole [sic] there names. There being no other business the Session closed with prayer.

W. P. Bradshaw, Clerk of Session

Aug. 3, 1902 Mount Horeb Tenn.

Session met & was organized with prayer. Rev. W. H. Smith moderating by request. Elders present W. N. Mcmurry & W. P. Bradshaw. Mr. Samuel D. [Duffield] Mcmurry [Sr.] & Love J. [Jane Seahorn] Mcmurry Presented there letters. The Session received them into the full communion of church & ordered the Clerk to inrole [sic] there names there being no other business the Session was closed with prayer.

W. P. Bradshaw, Clerk of Session

[Page 72 Blank]
[Page 73] Aug 3, 1902, Mount Horeb, Tenn.

At an informal meeting held in May 1902 between Representative of members of Hebron and members of Mossy Creek Presbyterian Churches on the one part and the Session of Mount Horeb Church on the other part. It was agreed as follows: That these be represented members of Hebron and Mossy Creek should unite with Mount Horeb Church and that when they did so unite with Mount Horeb Church that the Session of

Mount Horeb Church should resign so that the entire congregation might have an opportunity to elect an entire Board of Officers including both Elders and Deacons.

On July 6, 1902 This agreement was ratified by part of the contending members of the Hebron and Mossy Creek Churches uniting with Mount Horeb Church (see Minutes of July 6) and by the remaining members so uniting on August 3rd (see minutes of Aug. 3)

The Elders of Mount Horeb Church then resigned as per agreement and there being no Descent an Election of Elders and Deacons which had been previously announced was proceeded with, and resulted, with and resulted as follows: Elders M. C. [Mac Calvin] Franklin, S. D. [Samuel Duffield] McMurray [Sr.], W. P. [William Porter Massengil] Bradshaw, and G. A. [George Adam] Zirkle; Deacons Geo. [W.] Franklin, W. N. [William Newton] McMurray, and J. M. [James Moore] McMurray. Of this number W. P. Bradshaw and G. A. Zirkle had previously been ordained Elders and J. M. McMurray Deacon. All these brethren having signified their acceptance of the offices to which they had been chosen. M. C. Franklin and [Page 74] S. D. McMurray, and Geo. Franklin and W. N. McMurray were ordained, and all were installed in the respective offices to which they had been chosen, entire harmony prevailing.

The newly ordained and installed Session was then convened, prayer by G. A. Zirkle, Rev. W. H. Smith moderating. Elders present W. P. Bradshaw, M. C. Franklin, S. D. McMurray and G. A. Zirkle was chosen Clerk of Session. Motion to adjourn prevailed and Session closed with prayer.

G. A. Zirkle, Clerk of Session

Sept. 5, 1902 Mount Horeb, Tenn
The Session was convened with prayer by the Moderator, Rev. W. H. Smith. Elders present W. P. Bradshaw, M. C. Franklin, and G. A. Zirkle. Minutes of Aug. 3 and Record of action of Mount Horeb Church were read and approved. M. C. Franklin Principal and G. A. Zirkle Alternate were appointed to attend the meeting of Presbytery to be held at New Providence Church Sept. 10, 7:30 P.M.

It was moved and ordered that a revised and corrected register of the communicants and baptized non communicants of Mount Horeb Church be made and that a Committee be appointed to make said revisions. W. P. Bradshaw & G. A. Zirkle were appointed to this committee. The minutes of Sessional meeting of Sept 21, 1902 [Page 75] Were also read and approved. Session closed with prayer which was made the opening prayer of regular church service.

G. A. Zirkle, Clerk of Session

Sept. 21, 1902 Mount Horeb, Tenn.
Session met and was opened with prayer. W. P. Bradshaw moderator. Elders present W. P. Bradshaw, M. C. Franklin, and G. A. Zirkle. It was moved and approved that three additional Trustees be chosen for Mount Horeb Church property such election to be held Oct. 5, 1902. Session closed with prayer.

G. A. Zirkle, Clerk of Session

Oct. 5, 1902 Mount Horeb, Tenn.

Session was opened with prayer by the Moderator, Rev. W. H. Smith. Elders present M. C. Franklin, W. P. Bradshaw and G. A. Zirkle. Minutes of Meetings of Sept. 7 & Sept. 21 were read and approved. The Committee on revision of the Register of Mount Horeb Church reported the revised Register completed. The Report was accepted and ordered to be placed on record (See p. 147)

Geo. Franklin, G. A. Zirkle and W. P. Bradshaw were chosen Trustees of Mount Horeb Church property. The Delegates to presbytery at New Providence having failed to attend no Report of said meeting was made. Session was closed with prayer.

G. A. Zirkle,
Clerk of Session

[Page 76] Dec. 7, 1902 Mount Horeb, Tenn.

The Session was convened with prayer by the Moderator, Rev. W. H. Smith. Minutes of Meeting of Oct. 5 was read and approved. The Session accepted the obligation for Mount Horeb Church to pay Ten Dollars ($10.00) to the support of Sustentation work in the bounds of Holston Presbytery for the year 1903. The payment to be made quarterly $2.50 each in January, April, July and October.

Session was closed with prayer.

G. A. Zirkle, Clerk of Session

[Written on margin by Dec. 7, 1902 minutes.] Elders present Bradshaw, Franklin & Zirkle

Jan. 4, 1903 Mount Horeb, Tenn

Session opened with prayer by the Moderator, Rev. W. H. Smith. The Report of the Board of Deacons for the Quarter ending Dec. 31, 1902 was received and approved. A subscription for the Continued ministerial services of Rev. W. H. Smith as Stated Supply to Mount Horeb Church was presented by the Board of Deacons and accepted by Brother Smith. Session adjourned with prayer which was made the opening prayer of the regular church Service.

G. A. Zirkle, Clerk of Session

[Written on margin by Jan. 4, 1903 minutes.] Elders present Bradshaw, Franklin & Zirkle

[Page 77] Feb. 1, 1903 Mount Horeb, Tenn

The Session was opened with prayer by the Moderator, Rev. W. H. Smith. Elders present W. P. Bradshaw, M. C. Franklin & G. A. Zirkle. Minutes of meeting of Dec. 7, 1902 and Jan. 4, 1903 were read and approved. Letters of Dismissal from the Justin, Texas Cumberland Presbyterian Church were presented by Mr. F. A. & Mrs. Sue [Owen] Newman, and They were received into the communion and fellowship of Mount Horeb Church. Session adjourned with opening prayer which was made the opening prayer of the regular church service.

G. A. Zirkle, Clerk of Session

April. 4, 1903 Mount Horeb, Tenn
Session was opened with prayer. Rev. W. H. Smith moderating. Elders present M. C. Franklin, G. A. Zirkle. Geo. Franklin, Secretary Treasurer of the Board of Deacons was also present. The minutes of meeting of Session on Feb. 1 were read and approved. The report of the Board of Deacons was read and approved for the quarter ending March 31, 1903. G. A. Zirkle Principal and M. C. Franklin Alternate were appointed to represent Mount Horeb Church in Presbytery at Morristown, Tenn. 11 o'clock A. M. April 15, 1903. The Statistical Report. The Sabbath School Report and the Narrative of the Session of Mount Horeb Church were made, approved and ordered to be read before the congregation of the Church, and are as follows:

[Page 78]

Annual Statistical Report of Mount Horeb Church
to Presbytery of Holston for the year ending March 31, 1903.

Shows 4 Elders, & 3 Deacons,

0 Communicants added on Examination, 19 Communicants added on Certificate. Total of Communicants 44.

No adult Baptisms, no Infant Baptisms, 8 Baptised non communicants,

10 Officers and Teachers in Sabbath Schools & Bible classes and 58 scholars in Sabbath School & Bible Class.

Funds Contributed to

Foreign Missions	$9.80	Publication	1.50
Assembly's Home Missions	1.80	Bible Cause	2.00
Local Home Missions	4.16	Presbyterial	4.00
Colored Evangelization	.60	Pastor's Salary actually Paid	66.50
Ministerial Relief	1.86	Congregational	107.58
Education	.00	Miscellaneous	6.00
			$204.63

Post Office of Pastor, Morristown, Tenn.
"   "   of Clerk of Session, Mount Horeb, Tenn.,
Dated April 4, 1903 G. A. Zirkle, Clerk of Session

[Page 79]

Annual Report on the Sabbath School of Mount Horeb Church
to the Presbytery of Holston of the year ending March 31, 1903.

Sabbath School Membership

No. of Schools	1
" " Officers and Teachers	10
" " Scholars	58
Total	68

Average Attendance

Officers and Teachers	8
Scholars	26
Total	34

Scholars admitted to Communion 0
Contributions

To Current Expense	$20.66
" Foreign Missions	0.00
" Home Mission	0.00
" S. S. Miss. of Gen. Assembly	0.00
" Other Causes	86.92
Total	107.58

The School is not controlled by the Session, but the members of the Session attend and take part in the School. The pupils attend the Church Service. We note no specific religious interest during the year. We have no separate Departments, nor separate class rooms, nor have we a Library. The International Lesson is used and our own publications entirely, but we do not use The Graded Supplemental Lessons. Part of the pupils memorise the Scriptures and Catechism & part study the confession of Faith, Gospel Hymns No's 1-6 are used. Each pupil is not supplied with Bible in class. We have no maps, charts, chalkboard, nor Teachers' meetings, nor do we contribute to the Assembly's Causes, But we have a plan [Page 80] of giving, viz.: 1 collection per month for Monroe Harding Orphanage, 1 per yr, for Soul Winners Society, 1 for Thornwell Orphanage, and the remaining Sabbaths for various purposes. The school engages in no special exercises; and has not been represented at Institutes but at conventions.

Superintendent, Geo. A. Zirkle, P. O. Address Mount Horeb, Tenn.

Geo. A. Zirkle, Clerk of Session

Narration of Session of Mount Horeb Church to Holston Presbytery
for the year ending March 31, 1903.

Attendance on Services of the Sanctuary by Members and others is fairly good. Family worship is not fully observed. The Lord's Day is well observed. The training of children in the scripture and catechism at home is not well attended to. The worship of God with gifts is much improved. The church has paid its minister its full promise and offers evidences of spiritual life and growth.

Worldly conformity is unknown amongst us. We are not engaged in any outside evangelistic work.

Geo. A. Zirkle, Clerk of Session

Session was closed with prayer. The entire minutes outstanding approved.

Geo. A. Zirkle, Clerk of Session

[Page 81]

Approved in Presbytery at Morristown, Tenn. April 17, 1903. Except. The book was not before Presbytery since 1897.

J. M. Clark, Moderator

[Page 82] July 12, 1903 Mount Horeb, Tenn

Session met and was constituted with prayer. Elder W. P. Bradshaw moderating. Elders present, W. P. Bradshaw, M. C. Franklin & G. A. Zirkle. The church being deprived of preaching service by the illness of Rev. W. H. Smith. It was ordered that a prayer Service be offered to the Church on the first and third Sabbaths of each month till arrangements could be made to supply the pulpit. This prayer service to be held immediately after the closing of the Sabbath school. Session closed with prayer.

G. A. Zirkle, Clerk of Session

August 16, 1903 Mount Horeb, Tenn

Session was opened with prayer. W. P. Bradshaw moderating. Elders present, W. P. Bradshaw, M. C. Franklin & G. A. Zirkle. Also deacons Geo. Franklin, J. M. McMurray, W. N. [William Newton] McMurray.

Minutes of meeting of July 12 were read and approved. G. A. Zirkle Principal and M. C. Franklin Alternate were appointed delegates to Presbytery to meet at New Bethel, Sep. 2, 1903.

After consultation amongst Elders & Deacons it was agreed to ask for the Ministerial services of Rev. F. L. Leeper for one Sabbath per month till the close of this Presbyterial year. Session closed with prayer.

G. A. Zirkle, Clerk of Session

[Page 83] Oct 25, 1903 Mount Horeb, Tenn

Session was opened with prayer. Rev. F. L. Leeper moderating. Elders present, W. P. Bradshaw & G. A. Zirkle. The question whether a protacted meeting should be held at Mount Horeb Church at some time during the winter was discussed and continued for further consideration. Inquiry was made into the system of giving in practice in Church and the Envelope system was suggested. This was also left for further consideration. Delegates failed to attend Presbytery at New Bethel Sept. 2, 1903, hence made no report. Session closed with prayer.

G. A. Zirkle, Clerk of Session

March 27, 1904 Mount Horeb, Tenn

Session met and was opened with prayer. Rev. F. L. Leeper moderating. Elders present, W. P. Bradshaw, M. C. Franklin & G. A. Zirkle, also Deacons Geo. Franklin, J. M. McMurray, W. N. McMurray. Minutes of meeting of Oct. 25, 1903 read and approved. Letter of dismission was granted to S. F. [Samuel Franklin] McMurry to unite with the 3rd Presb'ian Church Knoxville. G. A. Zirkle & M. C. [Mac Calvin] Franklin were appointed delegates to Presbytery at Bristol Apl 19, 1904. The Session asks Pres. for the services of Rev. F. L. Leeper for the current year. The Board of Deacons exhibited Book and made Report which was approved. Sessional Report on Sabbath Schools. Statistical Report to Presbytery and Narrative of the Session were approved and the latter two ordered to be engrossed on Sessional Record. Adjourned with prayer.

G. A. Zirkle, Clerk

[Page 84]

Statistical Report to Presbytery
Annual Report of Mount Horeb Church to the
Presbytery of Holston for the year ending March 31, 1904.

Elders   4
Deacons   3
Communicants added on exam   0
   "   "   on certif. 0
Total of Communicants   43
Adult Baptisms   0
Infant   "   0
Baptized Non communicants   8
Officers & Teachers in Sabbath Schools & Bible Classes   8
Scholars in Sabbath Schools and Bible Classes   42

Funds Contributed to
Foreign Missions $ 3.04
Assembly's Home Missions   1.06
Local Home Missions   6.50
Colored Evangelization   1.00
Ministerial Relief   0.00
Education   0.00
Publication   0.00
Bible Cause   0.00
Presbyterial   4.00
Pastor's Salary actually Paid   76.00
Congregational   0.00
Miscellaneous   0.00
Post Office of Pastor, Jefferson City
Post Office of Clerk of Session, Mount Horeb
Dated March 27, 1904
                    G. A. Zirkle, Clerk of Session

[Page 85]

Narrative of the Session
of Mount Horeb Church for the year ending March 31, 1904.
to Presbytery of Holston

1. Attendance in church services is Good.

2. Family worship is only partially attended to.

3. Sabbath observance is good amongst church members.

4. The training of children and youth in the Scriptures and Catechisms is not well attended to.

5. The church is fairly faithful in worshiping God with their substance. There is yet room for increase.

6. The Church has fully paid, and promptly paid its minister.

7. We can only note only a steady growth in grace.

8. Worldly conformity does not prevail amongst us.

9. We are not engaged in any outside evangelistic work as a Church.

G. A. Zirkle, Clerk

[Page 86]

Sessional Report on the Sabbath Schools

Report on the Sabbath School at Mount Horeb Church

to the Presbytery of Holston for the year ending March 31, 1904

No. of Schools	1
Officers and Teachers	8
Number of Scholars	34
Total	42
Average attendance of Officers and Teachers	6
& Scholars	23
Total	29
Scholars admitted to Communion	0
Current Expense	$10.25
S. S. Missions of Gen. Assembly	1.60
Other Causes	23.00
Total	35.00

1. The School is controlled by the Session.

2. Session attends and takes part in school.

3. The pupils attend Public Worship.

4. There has been no special religious interest in the school during the year.

5. We do not have the Six departments.

6. We have no separate class rooms.

7. We have no Library.

8. We use the International Lesson.

9. We use our own Literature.

10. But not the Graded supplemental lessons.

11. Some memorizing the Bible, none the Hymns.

12. The Confession of Faith, Church Govt. and Catechisms are studied to some extent.

13. Gospel Hymns Nos. 1-6 are used.

14. Bible in class are not in General use.

15. We have neither maps, charts, nor chalkboard.

16. We have no teachers' meetings.

17. The School contributes to the Assembly's S. S. Work.

[Page 87] 18. We have a definite plan of regular contributing – Current Expenses twice per month, Monroe Harding Orphanage once per month, Soul Winners Society - - once per month.

19. We have no special exercises for Foreign Missions in May nor for Home Missions in September.

20. We do not observe Sabbath school day in October.

21. The school has had representation at S. S. Conventions.

Superintendent W. P. Bradshaw, Post Office Mount Horeb, Tenn.

G. A. Zirkle, Clerk of Session

Approved so far as written

April 21, 1904 __?__ steed, Moderator

[Page 88] July 24, 1904 Mount Horeb, Tenn

Session was opened with prayer by the moderator, Rev. F. L. Leeper. Elders present, W. P. Bradshaw, S. D. McMurray & G. A. Zirkle. Delegate to Presbytery at Bristol. M. C. Franklin, not being present, no report of diligences was made. It was intended that there should be a meeting of the session each month. It was ordered that a prayer meeting be established under the direct care and conduct of the members of the session, and that the meetings be held on such Sabbath evenings as may not be occupied by preaching service. The elders to conduct for one month each in rotation and to use the Sabbath School lessons as topics. G. A. [George Adam] Zirkle was appointed to serve for first month. Session adjourned with prayer by Elder McMurray.

G. A. Zirkle, Clerk

Aug. 28, '04 Mount Horeb, Tenn

Session met at call of moderator, Rev. F. L. Leeper, and was opened with prayer. Elders Bradshaw, Franklin & McMurray were present. W. P. Bradshaw was appointed Delegate to Presbytery at Johnson City with S. D. McMurray as alternate. W. P. Bradshaw was also appointed to conduct Prayer meeting for month of Sept. Session adjourned with prayer   G. A. Zirkle, Clerk

[Page 89] Oct. 23, 1904 Mount Horeb, Tenn

Session met and was opened with prayer by the moderator, Rev. F. L. Leeper. Elders present, W. P. Bradshaw, S. D. McMurray, M. C. Franklin & G. A. Zirkle. M. C. Franklin, Delegate to spring Presbytery at Bristol reported his diligence. W. P. Bradshaw, Delegate to Fall Presbytery at Johnson City reported failure to attend and was excused.

Elder McMurray reported fair attendance on prayer meeting for October. Elder Franklin was appointed to conduct prayer meeting for November. Session closed with closing prayer of a burial Service held immediately after the business of the Session was transacted.

G. A. Zirkle, Clerk

Nov. 27, 1904 Mount Horeb, Tenn

Session met on the call of moderator, Rev. F. L. Leeper, and was opened prayer. Elders Bradshaw, ~~Franklin~~, McMurray & Zirkle were present. Minutes of meeting of August 28 & Oct. 23 were read and approved.

A Letter of Dismission was granted to Mrs. Alice Rankin Garberto unite with the Central Presbyterian Church, Knoxville, Tenn. or any other Evangelical Church with which God may order her lot. Elder G. A. Zirkle was appointed to conduct the Prayer meeting for the month of December. Session adjourned with prayer.

G. A. Zirkle,
Clerk of Session

[Page 90] Dec. 25, 1904 Mount Horeb, Tenn

Session met on call of moderator, Rev. F. L. Leeper, and was opened prayer. Elders Bradshaw, Franklin, McMurray & Zirkle were present. Minutes of meeting of Nov 27 were read and approved. Elder Zirkle reported no prayer meeting held in December owing to inclement weather and potential service held in a neighboring Church.

After some discussion a motion to suspend all night services at Mount Horeb Church during the months of January & February 1905 was carried. Session closed with the closing prayer of preaching services.

G. A. Zirkle,
Clerk of Session

Jan. 22, 1905 Mount Horeb, Tenn

Session met and was opened with prayer by the moderator, Rev. F. L. Leeper. Elders McMurray, Bradshaw, Franklin & Zirkle were present. Minutes of meeting of December 25, 1904 were read and approved. Motion to adjourn carried and Session closed with the closing prayer of preaching service.

G. A. Zirkle,
Clerk of Session

[Page 91] Feb. 26, 1905 Mount Horeb, Tenn.

Session opened with prayer by the moderator, Rev. F. L. Leeper. Elders Bradshaw, McMurray, Franklin & Zirkle were present. Minutes of meeting of January 22, 1904 were read and approved. Deacon W. N. McMurray was invited to sit with the Session to take action in reference to the death of Brother George [W.] Franklin, a Deacon in Mount Horeb Church. Resolutions of respect were adopted and ordered to be written on the pages of the Church Record devoted to that purpose.

Session adjourned with prayer.

G. A. Zirkle,
Clerk of Session

For Memorial of George Franklin See page 92.

[Page 92]

George Franklin

The following action was taken by the board of Officers of Mount Horeb Presbyterian Church February 26, 1905

George Franklin was born near Dandridge, Jefferson County, Tenn. August 3, 1854, and died at his home in Mount Horeb in said County February 20, 1905, leaving a wife, a son and a bereaved Church to mourn his loss

Resolved.

1. That in the death of our brother and fellow worker, George Franklin. This church has lost a devoted member, a very efficient deacon and Treasurer, and efficient and faithful Sabbath school teacher. The community has lost a large-hearted and public spirited citizen and trusted public servant; his family has lost a faithful, pure and trusted husband and father.

2. That while we bow in humble submission to the will of him who doeth all things well and nurse in our hearts the sure hope that he has entered into the Joy of our Lord, we yet sincerely mourn his loss as a great misfortune to the Church and we will cherish his memory and endeavor to imitate his many virtues.

3. That a page of the records of this Church be set apart to his memory and that these [Page 93] resolutions be recorded thereon.

4. That a copy of this action be sent to the family, also to the *Christian Observer* and to the *Herald* and *Presbyter*, requesting said papers to publish same.

F. L. Leeper, Chairman of Meeting
George Zirkle, Clerk

Approved
Rogersville Apr. 26, 1905
J. T. Brown, Mod.

[Page 94] Mch. 26, 1905
Mount Horeb, Tenn.

Session came to order as a continuation of the preaching service, Rev. F. L. Leeper moderating. Elders Bradshaw, Franklin, McMurray and Zirkle were present. Minutes of meeting of Feb. 26 were read and approved. Geo. A. Zirkle, principal and S. D. McMurray, alternate were appointed delegates to attend meeting of Presbytery of Holston at Mossy Creek Church Jefferson City, Tenn. April 18 1905. The report of the Board of Deacons was received and approved.

Full Sessional reports to Presbytery for the year ending March 31, 1905 were made and approved entire. Session adjourned with prayer.

G. A. Zirkle,
Clerk of Session

[Page 95]

Statistical Report to Presbytery
Annual Report of Mount Horeb Church to the Presbytery of Holston
for the year ending March 31, 1905

Elders	4
Deacons	2
Communicants added on exam	0
" " on certif.	0
Total of Communicants	41
Adult Baptisms	8
Infant "	0
Baptized Non communicants	8
Officers & Teachers in S S & Bible Classes	10
Scholars in S S and Bible Classes	49

Funds Contributed to

Foreign Missions	$11.35
Assembly's Home Missions	.00
Local Home Missions	6.90
Colored Evangelization	1.00
Ministerial Relief	2.27
Education	.87
Publication	.00
Bible Cause	.08
Presbyterial	4.00
Pastor's Salary actually Paid	120.00
Congregational	.00
Miscellaneous	.00

Post Office of Pastor, Jefferson City,
Post Office of Clerk of Session, Mount Horeb
Dated March 26, 1905,

G. A. Zirkle, Clerk of Session

[Page 96]

Narrative of the Session
Of Mount Horeb Church to Presbytery of Holston
for the year ending March 31, 1905.

1. Church attendance is Regular.
2. Family worship is partially.
3. Sabbath observance is good.
4. Training in Scriptures and Catechisms, poor.

5. Contributions to the Lord's Work, fairly good.
6. Minister is fully paid.
7. No special but normal growth in spiritual life.
8. Worldly conformity does not prevail.
9. We are not engaged in any outside evangelistic work.

G. A. Zirkle, Clerk of Session

[Page 97]

Sessional Report on the Sabbath Schools

Report on the Sabbath School at Mount Horeb Church to the Presbytery of Holston for the year ending March 31, 1905

Sabbath School Membership

No. of Schools	1
Officers and Teachers	10
Number of Scholars	49
Total	59

Average attendance

of Officers and Teachers	7
Scholars	21
Total	28
Admitted to Communion	0

Contributions

Current Expense	$9.00
Foreign Mission	2.00
Other Causes	21.78
Total	32.82

1. The School is controlled by the Session.
2. Session attends and takes part in school.
3. Pupils attend Public Worship.
4. No special religious interest during the year.
5. We have Primary, Intermediate & Senior Classes.
6. We have no separate class rooms.
7. We have no Library.
8. We use the International Lessons.
9. Our own Publications entirely.
10. We do not use the Graded supplement.
11. Do not memorize Bible, Hymns nor Catechism.
12. Do not study Confessions nor form of Govt.
13. We use Gospel Hymns Nos. 1-6.
14. There is not a Bible to each Pupil.
15. No maps, charts, nor chalkboard.

16. No teachers' meetings.

17. We are not regular contributors to any of the Assembly's causes.

[Page 98]   Sessional Report on Sabbath School continued

18. Contribute every Sabbath – Current Expenses, Monroe Harding Orphanage, Emergency and Miscellaneous.

19. We have no special exercises for Foreign Missions.

20. Observe no Sabbath school day.

21. Have been represented at Sabbath School Conventions.

Superintendent Name: S. D. [Samuel Duffield] McMurray

Post Office Address, Jefferson City

Signed: G. A. Zirkle,

Clerk of Session

There are no Reports on Women's & Young People's Societies. We have no such Organizations.

G. A. Zirkle,

Clerk of Session

Approved Apr. 20, 1905

Jefferson City

A. H. Doak, Mod.

[Page 99] May 23, '05 Mount Horeb, Tenn.

Session opened with prayer by the moderator, Rev. F. L. Leeper. Elders Mr. McMurray, Bradshaw, Franklin & Zirkle were present. A letter was read from Monroe Harding Memorial Orphanage asking for a contribution of Nine dollars to assist in lifting a mortgage which rests on the institution. The letter was ordered to be read to the church, and a committee of three was appointed to try to raise the said amount. Com. Mrs. J. M. [James Moore] McMurray [Almyra M. Rankin McMurray], Mrs. Geo. [W.] Franklin [Sallie Ann Bell Franklin], with G. A. Zirkle, Chairman.

G. A. Zirkle, delegate to Presbytery at Jeff. City Tenn. reported his diligence. Session adjourned with prayer at close of preaching and sacramental service.

G. A. Zirkle,

Clerk of Session

June 25, '05 Mount Horeb, Tenn.

Session opened with prayer by the moderator, Rev. F. L. Leeper. Elders Mr. McMurray, Bradshaw & Zirkle were present. Minutes of May 23 were read and approved. The Committee appointed to raise money to assist in paying mortgage on Monroe Harding Orphanage reported the duty preformed, and was ordered to pay to Darlean McKay Lewson [?]. The Com. was discharged. Session closed with prayer.

G. A. Zirkle,

Clerk of Session

[Page 100] July 23, 1905
Mount Horeb, Tenn.
Session was called order and prayer offered by the Moderator, Rev. F. L. Leeper. Elders Franklin, McMurray, Bradshaw & Zirkle were present. Minutes of June 25 were read and approved. A letter of dismission to Hebron Presbyterian Church, Presbytery of Union, was granted Mrs. Ethel May Cokenour at her own request. Letters of dismission were also granted to Elder S. D. [Samuel Duffield] McMurray [Sr.] & his wife Mrs. Sara J. [Love Seahorn] McMurray at their own request to join whatever evangelical church to which God may direct them. These latter letters to be issued at call. Motion to adjourn prevailed and Session closed with prayer.

G. A. Zirkle,
Clerk of Session

Aug. 27, '05 Mount Horeb, Tenn.
Session was called to order and prayer offered by the Mod., Rev. F. L. Leeper. Elders McMurray, Bradshaw, Franklin, & Zirkle were present. Minutes of July 23 were read and approved. A brief of the minutes of this meeting were read and approved. Motion to adjourn carried. Session closed with prayer.

G. A. Zirkle,
Clerk of Session

[Page 101] Oct. 22, 1905 Mount Horeb, Tenn.
Session was called to order and prayer offered by the Moderator, Rev. F. L. Leeper. Elders Franklin, Bradshaw & Zirkle were present. Miss Annie Rose Rankin came before the session, professed her faith in Christ and was received into the full communion and fellowship of Mount Horeb Church.

By order of this session the scheme of Ministerial relief by means of any endowment fund was placed before the church and commended to their consideration. The Clerk was authorized to issue a certificate of membership to Mrs. Jennie [H. McGhee] Newman on case of her request on removal to other bounds. Session closed with prayer.

G. A. Zirkle, Clerk

Dec. 24, 1905
Mount Horeb, Tenn.
Session was called to order and prayer offered by the Moderator, Rev. F. L. Leeper. Elders Bradshaw, Franklin & Zirkle being present. Minutes of Oct. 22, 1905 were read and approved. The Assembly's Home & School at Fredericksburg, Va. was recommended to the Christian liberality of the Church. Mrs. [Misters] D. P. Bradshaw and W. N. [William Newton] McMurray were appointed a committee to repair the stove and windows of the Church. Session adjourned with prayer.

G. A. Zirkle,
Clerk

[Page 102] Jan. 28, 1906 Mount Horeb, Tenn.

Session was called to order and opened with prayer by the Moderator, Rev. F. L. Leeper. Elders Bradshaw, Franklin & Zirkle were present. Minutes of Dec. 24, 1905 were read and approved. Committee on stove and window repairs reported the work done and the cost discharged and were released. M. C. Franklin & Jno. McMurray were appointed a Comm. to superintend the repairing of the Church roof.

Letter of dismission was granted to Mrs. Florence A. Peck Newman.

Session Closed with prayer.

G. A. Zirkle, Clerk

Mch. 25, 1906 Mount Horeb, Tenn.

Session was called to order and opened with prayer by the Moderator, Rev. F. L. Leeper. Elders Bradshaw, Franklin & Zirkle were present. Minutes of meeting of Jan. 28, '06 were read and approved. Mrs. Effie Belle Blackburn Franklin presented her application with letter of dismission from Hopewell Presbyterian Church of Dandridge, Tenn. and was received into the full communion and fellowship of Mount Horeb Church.

G. A. Zirkle with W. P. Bradshaw and M. C. Franklin as alts. Was appointed to represent the Church in Presbytery at Rogersville, Tenn. Apl. 25, '06.

Session Closed with prayer.

G. A. Zirkle,
Clerk of Session

[Page 103] April 22, 1906 Mount Horeb, Tenn.

Session was opened with prayer, Rev. F. L. Leeper Moderating. Elders Bradshaw, Franklin & Zirkle were present. Minutes of meeting of Mch. 25 were read and approved. A date for a congregational meeting was made for the purpose of electing an additional deacon. Rev. F. L. Leeper should continue to serve Mount Horeb Church as Stated Supply for the current year. Full Sessional Reports to Presbytery were made and approved together with this minutes.

G. A. Zirkle, Clerk of Session

Sessional Report on the Sabbath School of Mount Horeb Church
to the Presbytery of Holston for the year ending March 31. 1906.

Schools	1	
Officers & Teachers	10	
Scholars	49	
Total	59	
Average Officers & Teachers	8	
Scholars Average	26	
Total	34	
Contributions	Current Ex.	$9.75
	Other causes	15.00
	Total	$24.75

1. Session controls and attends School.
2. Scholars attend Public Worship.
3. Church Standards are partially Taught.
4. Scriptures & catechism are memorized to a limited extent.
5. Our Church Publications are used entirely.
6. We note no special religious[sic] in the school during the year.
7. We do not have teachers' meetings.
[Page 104] S. S. Report cont'd.
Superintendent Name G. A. Zirkle
Post Office Address, Jefferson City, R. D. #4, Tenn.
G. A. Zirkle, Clerk of Session

Narrative of the Session of Mount Horeb Church
for the year ending March 31, 1906 to Presbytery of Holston.

1. Attendance in Divine Service is good.
2. Family worship is very limited.
3. The Sabbath is well observed.
4. The training of the young at home & school in the scriptures is fairly well observed.
5. The Church members are faithful in worshiping God with their substance.
6. The Church has paid its minister promply [sic] & in full.
7. We note no special witness, but the church shows healthy life. It responds when called.
8. Worldly conformity does not prevail.
9. Our church is engaged only in the causes as directed by the Assembly.
G. A. Zirkle, Clerk of Session
Jefferson City, Tenn., R. D. #4

Statistical Report to Presbytery
Annual Report of Mount Horeb Church to the Presbytery of Holston
for the year ending March 31, 1906.

Elders	3
Deacons	2
Communicants added on exam	7
"　　　" on certificate	1
Total of Communicants	39

[Page 105]

Adult Baptisms	0
Infant　"	0
Baptized Non communicants	8
Officers & Teachers in Sabbath Schools & Bible Classes	10
Scholars in Sabbath Schools and Bible Classes	34

Funds Contributed to

Foreign Missions	$ 5.41
Assembly's Home Missions	2.70
Local Home Missions	5.02
Colored Evangelization	.00
Ministerial Relief (Invalid)	7.61
Education	10.51
Publication	0.60
Bible Cause	0.00
Presbyterial	4.00
Pastor's Salary actually Paid	104.90
Congregations	1.65
Miscellaneous	0.00

Post Office of Pastor, Jefferson City, Tenn.
 "   "   " Clerk of Session, " " " R. D. #4
Dated Apl. 22, 1906

G. A. Zirkle,
Clerk of Session

For approval of foregoing by Presbytery at Rogersville Apr 26, 1906
See page 93.

[Page 106] June 24, 1906
Mount Horeb, Tenn.

Session was constituted with prayer by the Moderator, Rev. F. L. Leeper. Elders Bradshaw, Franklin & Zirkle being present. Delegates failed to attend Session of Presbytery at Rogersville & made no report.

Session closed with prayer.

G. A. Zirkle,
Clerk of Session

July 22, 1906 Mount Horeb, Tenn.

Session was opened with prayer by the Moderator, Rev. F. L. Leeper. Elders Bradshaw, Franklin & Zirkle were present. Minutes of meeting of June 26, '06 were read and approved. The ordination and installation of John McMurray who was elected to the office of Deacon on May 27, 1906 was ordered for July 5, 1906 at 3 o'clock P.M. service. The fourth Sabbath of September was agreed upon as the beginning of a protracted service at Mount Horeb Church.

Session Closed with prayer.

G. A. Zirkle,
Clerk of Session

July 5, 1906
Mount Horeb, Tenn.
Session was called to order and opened with prayer by the Moderator, Rev. F. L. Leeper. Elders Bradshaw, Franklin & Zirkle were present. After a sermon appropriate to the occasion the Moderator proposed the prescribed questions to deacon elect Mr. John M. McMurray and to the congregation which being answered in the affirmative the service proceeded to set apart to his office the deacon by laying on of hands and by prayer. G. A. Zirkle & Mc C. Franklin were appointed principal and alternate to attend Presbytery at Cold [Page 107] Spring Aug. 29, 1906.
Session Closed with prayer.

G. A. Zirkle

Aug. 26, 1906 Mount Horeb, Tenn.
Session was opened with prayer by the Moderator, Rev. F. L. Leeper. Elders Bradshaw, Franklin & Zirkle were present. Minutes of meeting of June 24 & July 22 were read and approved. The protracted service appointed for Sept. 23 was postponed till the fourth Sabbath of October. Delegate to Presbytery did not attend, hence made no report.
Session Closed with prayer.

G. A. Zirkle,
Clerk

Sept. 23, 1906 Mount Horeb, Tenn.
Session was called to order and opened with prayer by the Moderator, Rev. F. L. Leeper. Elders Bradshaw, Franklin & Zirkle were present. Minutes of meeting of July 5 and Aug. 26 were read and approved. The holding of a protracted service appointed for Sept. 26 and postponed to Oct. the 4th Sabbath was postponed till such time so Rev. J. M. Clark could assist. The appointment in Oct. interfering with the meeting of Synod by including that date.
Session Closed with prayer.

G. A. Zirkle, Clerk

Dec. 23, 1906 Mount Horeb, Tenn.
Session was called to order and opened with prayer by the Moderator, Rev. F. L. Leeper. Elders Bradshaw, Franklin & Zirkle were present. ~~Minutes of meeting of Sept. 23, '06 were read and approved.~~
A letter dismissing Mrs. Lillie Neal Bradshaw, at her own request from the New Market Presbyterian [Page 108] Church to the Mount Horeb Church was received and she is heartily commended to the Christian fellowship of Mount Horeb Church. The protracted service was held in the latter part of Nov. and early part of Dec.
Session Closed with prayer.

G. A. Zirkle,
Clerk of Session

Mch. 24, 1907 Mount Horeb, Tenn.

Session was opened with prayer by the Moderator, Rev. F. L. Leeper. Elders Bradshaw, Franklin & Zirkle were present. Also the Board of Deacons James M. & John M. McMurry made partial report. Minutes of meeting of September 23 and Dec. 23, 1906. 26 were read and approved. The Board of Deacons were directed to file full report with Clerk of Session. Presbyterial Reports were filled out and approved and G. A. Zirkle principal and W. P. Bradshaw alternate were appointed delegates to meeting of Presbytery at Bertha King Church Apl. 24, 1907. These minutes were also approved.

Session Closed with prayer.   G. A. Zirkle, Clerk of session

[Page 109]

Sessional Report on the Sabbath School of Mount Horeb Church
to the Presbytery of Holston for the year ending March 31. 1907.

No. of schools 1, Officers & Teachers 10, Scholars 34, Total 44.

Average Attendance. Officers & Teachers 8, Scholars 17,   Total 25

Contributions   Current Ex. $8.52

Other causes   13.13

Total $21.65

1. School is controlled by Session.
2. Session takes part in the School work.
3. Pupils attend Public Worship.
4. No special religious interest during the year.
5. School has not seven departments.
6. Has not separate classrooms.
7. Has no library.
8. Uses the International Lessons.
9. Uses our own publications exclusively.
10. Does not use the Graded supplemental lessons.
11. Does not memorize the Bible.
12. Pupils do not study our standards.
13. School uses Gospel Hymns 1-6.
14. The Bible is not used in class.
15. Have no maps, charts, nor blackboards.
16 Have no teachers' meeting.
17. Does not contribute to Assembly's Causes.
18. Contributes to current expense & incidentals three Sabbaths & to Monroe Harding one Sabbath each month.
19. Have no special exercises March nor May.
20. Do not observe Sabbath School Day in October.
21. Has been represented in Sunday School conventions.

Supt. W. P. Bradshaw,   Jeff. City

Stated Supply. F. L. Leeper,"   "

G. A. Zirkle, Clerk of Session, Jeff. City

[Page 110]

Narrative of the Session of Mount Horeb Church
for the year ending March 31, 1907

1. Attendance on the service of the sanctuary by members is good.
2. Family worship is loosely observed.
3. The Church members observe the Sabbath well.
4. There is no home training in Bible and catechisms.
5. Members are reasonably faithful in worship God with their substance.
6. The Church pays its minister promptly and in full.
7. There has been no special evidence of spiritual life and growth.
8. Worldly conformity does not prevail.
9. The church is not energized in any outside evangelistic work.

F. L. Leeper, S. S., Jefferson City, Tenn
        G. A. Zirkle, Clerk of Session, Jefferson City, Tenn

Session has no report on young people's Societies from the fact that she has no societies for the young.
        G. A. Zirkle, Clerk of Session

[Page 111]

Statistical Report to Presbytery of Holston of Mount Horeb Church
for the year ending March 31, 1907

Elders	3
Deacons	3
Communicants added on exam	0
Communicants added on certificate	1
Total of Communicants	48
Adult Baptisms	0
Infant "	0
Baptized Non communicants	0
Officers & Teachers in Sabbath Schools & Bible Classes	10
Scholars in Sabbath Schools and Bible Classes	34

Funds Contributed to

Foreign Missions	$ 2.75
Assembly's Home Missions	1.82
Local Home Missions	3.00
Colored Evangelization	.75
Ministerial Relief (individual)	1.00
Education	2.70
Publication	0.00
Bible Cause	0.00

Presbyterial	4.00
Pastor's Salary actually Paid	98.40
Congregations	0.00
Miscellaneous	0.00

Pastor's name F. L. Leeper
Post Office of Pastor, Jeff. City
G. A. Zirkle, Clerk of Session, Jeff. City, Tenn.

Approved thus far at Bertha King Mem. Church
April 26, 1907
Lawrence Rolfe Mod.

[Page 112] April. 28, 1907 Mount Horeb, Tenn.
Session was called to order and opened with prayer by the Moderator, Rev. F. L. Leeper. Elders Bradshaw, Franklin & Zirkle were present. Rev. Mr. Leeper made report of Presbyterial meeting at Bertha King Church, neither of the delegates having attended. Miss Susie Kate Lyle came before the session and on profession of her faith was received into the communion of the church. Session Closed with prayer.
G. A. Zirkle, Clerk
Aug. 25, 1907 Mount Horeb, Tenn.
Session was called to order and was opened with prayer by the Moderator, Rev. F. L. Leeper. Elders Franklin, Bradshaw and Zirkle being present. Elder Franklin principal and elder Bradshaw alternate were appointed delegates to Presbyterial meeting at Newport Wednesday, Sept. 4, 1907. Session adjourned with prayer.
G. A. Zirkle, Clerk of Session

Jan. 26, 1908 Mount Horeb, Tenn.
Session was called to order and was opened with prayer by the Moderator, Rev. F. L. Leeper. Elders Bradshaw, Franklin and Zirkle being present. Minutes of meetings of April 28 and August 25, 1907 were read and approved. Elder Franklin, principal and Elder Bradshaw, alternate having attended Presbytery at Newport no report was made. Session adjourned with prayer.
G. A. Zirkle, Clerk of Session

[Page 113] Mar. 22, 1908 Mount Horeb, Tenn.
Session was called to order and opened with prayer by the Moderator, Rev. F. L. Leeper. Elders Franklin and Zirkle being present. Minutes of meetings of July 26 were read and approved. G. A. Zirkle principal and M. C. Franklin, alternate were appointed to attend Presbytery at Bristol, April 15, 1908. G. A. Zirkle, Clerk, was authorized to make up Reports when they should arrive. Session adjourned with prayer.
G. A. Zirkle, Clerk

April 12, 1908 Mount Horeb, Tenn.

Session was opened with prayer by the Moderator, Elder W. P. Bradshaw with elders Franklin and Zirkle present. The Deacons made a report which was approved. The Reports to Presbytery were completed and approved. Minutes of meeting of March 22, '08 together with minutes of this day were read and approved.

Session closed with prayer. G. A. Zirkle, Clerk

Sessional Report on the Sabbath School of Mount Horeb Church
to Presbytery of Holston for the year ending March 31. 1908.

Officers & Teachers 7, Scholars 34, Total 41

Average Officers & Teachers 5, Scholars 14, Total 19

Scholars admitted to Communion 1

Contributions to Current expense $7.68
"   "   Other causes   1.92
                Total   9.60

1. The Session controls and attends School.
2. "   "   attends & takes part in the School.
3. The pupils attend public worship.
4. No special religious interest in the school.
5. No primary, cradle Roll, Beginners course, junior, inter. course, senior nor Teachers' course.

[Page 114] **Sabbath School report** Continued

6. No separate classrooms.
7. No Library
8. We use International Lessons.
9. We use our own Literature alone.
10. We do not use the Assembly's Supplemental Lessons.
11. Pupils do not memorize the Bible, hymns or catechism.
12. They do not study the Confession of Faith nor form of Government.
13. School uses Gospel Hymns 1-6.
14. Pupils are not supplied with Bibles.
15. We have no maps, charts, nor blackboards.
16 We have no teachers' meeting.
17. Pupils do not contribute to Assembly's Causes.
18. Pupils contribute each Sabbath for miscellaneous purposes.
19. We have no special exercises for Foreign Mission in May nor Home Missions in March.
20. We do not observe Sabbath School Day in October.
21. The School has been represented at S. S. conventions.

Superintendent   W. P. Bradshaw
Stated Supply.   F. L. Leeper
Signed: Clerk of Session G. A. Zirkle, , P. O. Jefferson City

Narrative of the Session of Mount Horeb Church
for the year ending March 31, 1908, to Holston Presbytery

1. Church attendance by members is fairly good.
2. Family worship is poorly observed.
3. Sabbath is well observed by members.
4. Scriptural and Catechetical home training and in Sabbath School are neglected.
5. Members are fairly faithful in worshiping God with their substance.
[Page 115]   **Narration of Session** Continued
6. The Church has paid promptly.
7. There has been no special religious evidence in the church.
8. Worldly conformity does not prevail.
9. The church is not engaged in any outside evangelistic work.

Stated Supply F. L. Leeper
          Clerk of Session G. A. ZirkleP.O. Jefferson City, Tenn.

Statistical Report of Mount Horeb Church to Presbytery of Holston
for year ending March 31, 1908.

		Funds Contributed	
Elders	3		
Deacons	2	Foreign Missions	$ .00
Communicants added on exam	1	Assembly's Home Missions	1.00
" " on certificate	0	Local Home Missions	2.12
Total of Communicants	33	Colored Evangelization	.80
Adult Baptisms	0	Ministerial Relief	2.30
Infant "	0	Education	3.00
Baptized Non communicants	0	Publication & S. S. Missions	.00
Officers & Teachers in Sabbath		Bible Cause	.00
School & Bible Classes	7	Presbyterial	4.00
Scholars in Sabbath Schools	Pastor's Salary actually paid		5.45
and Bible Classes	34	Congregational	.00
		Miscellaneous	.00

Name of Stated Supply   F. L. Leeper
Post Office   Jefferson City, Tenn.
Dated April 12, 1908
          G. A. Zirkle, Clerk of Session

Approved at Windsor Ave. Apr. 15, 1908
E. C. Bingham, Moderator

[Page 116] Jan. 24, 1909 Mount Horeb, Tenn.
Session was opened with prayer by the Moderator F. L Leeper. Elders Bradshaw,
Franklin & Zirkle being present. At her own request Mrs. Kate McMurry was dismissed

by letter to join the M. E. Church near Kingston, Tenn. and W. N. McMurry, Ola A. [Ann] McMurray, Charles [Walter] McMurray, Matilda [Martha Matilda "Tilda"] McMurray requested that their names be dropped from the roll of Mount Horeb Church they having joined the M. E. Church on profession. The request was granted. Session closed with prayer.

G. A. Zirkle, Clerk of Session

Mch. 28, 1909 Mount Horeb, Tenn.

Session was opened with prayer by the Moderator F. L Leeper. Elders Bradshaw, Franklin & Zirkle present. Minutes of meeting of Jan. 24 were read and approved. G. A. Zirkle Principal & M. C. Franklin Alternate were appointed to attend meeting of Presbytery at Westminster, Mch. 31, 1909.

Session resolved to meet on the 4th Sabbath of each month hereafter. Report of Deacons was received and approved. Sessional Reports to Presbytery were completed and together with this minute approved. Closed with prayer.

G. A. Zirkle, Clerk of Session

[Page 117]

Narration of the Session of Mount Horeb Church
for the year ending Mch 31, 1909, Presbytery of Holston.

1. Attendance in church Service & Sabbath School is medium, on prayer meeting very poor.

2. About one fourth of the families observe family worship.

3. The Lord's Day is well observed.

4. However training in the Scriptures and Catechism is poorly attended to.

5. Sabbath School training is the same is unsatisfactory.

6. The people give of their substance fairly well.

7. The Church has paid its Stated Supply promptly & fully.

8. There has been no special manifestation of the Holy Spirit during the year.

9. Worldly conformity does not have much hold.

10. No Evangelistic work is done outside.

11. No special effort is made by Session or pastor to secure recruits for the Ministry.

Stated Supply F. L. Leeper, Jefferson City
G. A. Zirkle, Jefferson City, Tenn.

Sessional Report to Presbytery on Systematic Benevolence
To the Presbytery of Holston from Mount Horeb Church
for year ending March 31, 1909.

To Foreign Missions	$ 8.68
Assembly's Home Missions	2.00
Local Home Missions	1.00
Colored Evangelization	.60
Ministerial Relief	.00

[Page 118]
Systematic Benevolence Continued

To Ministerial Education	.00
S. S. Missions & Education	.00
Assembly's Home & School (Fredericksburg)	.00
Bible Cause	.00
Schools & Colleges, Assembly's & Tyand.[?] Coll.	.00
Total	12.28

Collections are taken at Public Worship

By or of Session
F. L. Leeper S. S., Jeff. City

G. A. Zirkle,
Clerk, Jeff. City

Statistical Report
Annual Report of the Mount Horeb Church to the Presbytery of Holston
for the year ending with Mch. 31, 1909.

Elders	3	Funds contributed	
Deacons	2	Foreign Missions	$8.68
Communicants added on exam	0	Asembly's Home "	2.00
" " on certif.	0	Local " "	1.00
" Total	33	Colored Evangeliz.	.60
Adult Baptisms	0	Ministerial	.00
Infant "	0	Education	1.37
Officers & Teachers in S. S.	8	S.S. Extension & Publications	.00
Scholars in S. S.& Bible Classes	34	Bible Cause	.00
Baptized non Communicants	0	Ass. Home & School	.00
Pastor paid	84.12		
Congregational & Pres. Tax	6.18		
Miscellaneous	.00		

F. L. Leeper S. S., Jeff. City
Dated Mch. 28, 1909

G. A. Zirkle,
Clerk of Session,
Jefferson City, Tenn.

[Page 119]

Sessional Report on the Sabbath School Form
Mount Horeb Church to Presbytery of Holston
for the year ending March 31. 1909.

Supt. W. P. Bradshaw, Jeff. City, Tenn.
Stated Supply F. L. Leeper, Jeff. City, Tenn.

Officers & Teachers	6
Pupils	34
Total	40
Average Officers & Teachers	3½
Average Scholars	14
Total	17½
Current Expenses of School (Paid)	$8.88

1. School is not under control of Session.
2. S. S. does not take part in School but entire Session attends & takes part.
3. All the pupils attend public worship.
4. No special religious interest and no special effort to reach non-professors.
5. 15 Church members enrolled in School.
6. Cradle Roll-no, Beginners-no, Primary-yes, junior-yes, Intermediate-yes, Senior-yes, Organized Adult-no, Home-no, Missionary-no
7. One classroom only in use.
8. We have no Library
9. We use the Publications of the Presbr. Church alone.
10. We do not use Supplemental Lessons.
11. Pupils do not memorize the Bible, Hymns nor Catechism.
12. Adults do not study Confession Faith nor Government.
13. Gospel Hymns 1-6 are used.
14. Very few Bibles are used in the School.
15. We use no maps, charts, nor boards.
16. We have no teachers' meeting or Officers' meetings.
17. We observe no Mission or Rally Days.
18. Have no Teachers' Training Classes.
19. We have no Mission Com. or Study Class.
20. We have no Missionary Exercises.
21. School contributes nothing to Assembly Causes.
23. General purpose collection is taken each Sabbath.
24. School had no representation at Institutes.
25. School was open all the year.
20. We do not observe Sabbath School Day in October.

Signed: G. A. Zirkle,
Clerk of Session, Jeff. City

[Page 120] Approved except session does not meet "at least quarterly."
S. R. Crockett Mod.

April 23, 1909 Mount Horeb, Tenn.
Session was opened with prayer by the Moderator F. L Leeper. Elders Bradshaw, Franklin & Zirkle being present, also the Board of Deacons. The letter of Dismission from Hopewell Presbyterian Church of Mrs. Edna E. Blackburn McMurray was received and she is affectionately commended to the Christian love & fellowship of this church. The question of ministerial supply was discussed and postponed to await further development. Session closed with prayer.
Approved May 23, 09   G. A. Zirkle, Clerk

May 23, '09 Mount Horeb, Tenn.
Session was opened with prayer. Rev. G. .J. McFerrain moderating; Elders Bradshaw, Franklin & Zirkle present. Minutes meeting of April 25 [sic] were read and approved. G. A. Zirkle delegate to Presbytery at Morristown reported his attendance. It was agreed that Rev. F. L Leeper should preach in an evening service at 3 P.M. and monthly thereafter at that hour till a regular supply could be secured. Mr. & Mrs. E. C. [Ephraim Cawood] Bradshaw [Lillie Neal Bradshaw] presented their infant daughter for baptism at the open service. [probably Lucille Henry Bradshaw] Session closed with prayer at the close of service.
Approved Aug. 8, '09   G. A. Zirkle, Clerk of Session

[Page 121] July 18, 1909 Mount Horeb, Tenn.
Session was opened with prayer. W. P. Bradshaw moderating, all the elders being present. After much discussion of the question of union with the Presbyterian Church U.S.A., it was agreed that the Clerk of the Session should be authorized to issue letters of dismission to all persons desiring thus and he was ordered to make a public statement to that effect. Session closed with prayer peace and harmony prevailing.
Approved Aug. 8, '09   G. A. Zirkle, Clerk of Session

Aug. 8, 1909 Mount Horeb, Tenn.
Session met and was opened with prayer. M. C. Franklin moderating; Elders Bradshaw & Zirkle also present. Minutes of meeting of May 23 and July 18 were read and approved as was also this minute. Session closed with prayer.
G. A. Zirkle, Clerk of Session

Mch. 20, 1910 Mount Horeb, Tenn.
Session was opened with prayer. W. P. Bradshaw moderator. Elders Franklin & Zirkle present. A request for letters of dismission to Hebron Church by J. M. McMurry, Alvira [Almyra] McMurry, Anne Belle McMurry, John McMurry, Elda McMurry, Ben McMurry & Eva [Elizabeth Blackburn] McMurry was granted. Session closed with prayer.   G. A. Zirkle, Clerk of Session

Apr. 24, 1910
Mount Horeb, Tenn.
Session opened with prayer by moderator Bradshaw, he and Zirkle present. Minutes of meeting of Mch. 20 was read and approved. No report from Deacons was had further than informal report Feb. 27, 1910. G. A. Zirkle principal W. P. Bradshaw Alt. were appointed to attend Pres. at New Providence May 4th 1910. This minute and Sessional Reports were approved. Session closed with prayer.

G. A. Zirkle,
Clerk of Session

[Page 122]

Narration of the Session of Mount Horeb Church
for the year ending March 31, 1910, to Presbytery of Holston.

1. Attendance on Service is poor.
2. 10 per cent attend to family worship.
3. Ordinary observance of Sabbath.
4. Home training in the Scriptures neglected.
5. Sabbath School training is poor.
6. The church is not faithful in contributing.
7. Mount Horeb Church has no pastor.
8. There has been no special manifestation of the Holy Spirit.
9. Worldly conformity is limited.
10. No Evangelistic work has been undertaken.
11. Nothing has been done to recruit the Ministry.

The Sabbath evening prayer meeting carried on by the two senior elders alone of the church has been well attended by the young people of the community. They have given excellent attention to the service acquainted themselves well in every way.

G. A. Zirkle,
Clerk of Session

Sessional Report on Systematic Benevolence

Mount Horeb Church for the year ending March 31, 1910
to Presbytery of Holston

This Church has contributed to the Presbyterial Home Mission Fund alone; Subscriptions and Collections all paid in full. $37.24

Failure to secure Pastoral Service and service disruptions in the church have paralyzed every effort.

G. A. Zirkle,
Jefferson City, Tenn.

[Page 123]

Statistical Report
Annual Report of Mount Horeb Church to the Presbytery of Holston
for the year ending with March 31, 1910.

Elders 3,   Deacons 0

Communicants added on examination 0

"   " on certificate   0

Total communicants   28

Adult Baptisms 0, Infant Baptism   1

Officers & Teachers in S. S.   6

Scholars in S. S.& Bible Classes   19

Contributed

Foreign Missions   .00   Assembly's Home 0.00

Local Home Mission,   Presbyterial   37.24

Colored Evangelization   0.00

Ministerial Relief .00, Ministrial Education 0.00

Schools & Colleges   0.00

S.S. Extension & Publications   0.00

Bible Cause   0.00

Assembly's Home & School Fredricksburg, Va .00

Orphan Homes   0.00

Presbyterial Tax   2.00

Miscellaneous   0.00

G. A. Zirkle, Clerk of Session,
Jefferson City, Tenn.

Dated & Approved Apr. 24, 1910

Sessional Report on Sabbath School Form
of Mount Horeb Church to Presbytery of Holston
for the year ending March 31. 1910.

Supt. W. P. Bradshaw, P. O. address Jefferson City, T.

No. Pastor

No. on roll Officers & Teachers   6

Pupils   19

Total   25

Total Contributions $29.26

Current Expenses of School (Paid) $24.91

Cash on hand $ 4.35

Ques.

1. School is not under control of Session.

2. Have no pastor. Sessional attendance partial.

3. All pupils attend worship.

4. No special religious interest during year.

5. Have intermediate and senior classes only.

[Page 124]   Ques.   Continued from page 123

6. Have no separate classrooms.

7. Have no Library.

8. Use our own Literature and Bible.

9. Use no Graded Lessons.

10. Memorize no Bible, Hymns nor Catechism.

11. Do not study Confession of Faith nor Government.

12. Use Gospel Hymns 1-6.

13. To a limited extent.

14. Use no maps, charts, nor blackboards.

15. Have no teachers meetings.

16. Have no Teacher Training Class.

17. Do not observe any Mission Days.

18. Have no Miss. Com. Dept.

19. Have no Missionary Exercises.

20. Contribute to none of Gen. Assembly's causes.

21. We have weekly free will offering.

22. School was open all the year.

23. Was represented in one Convention.

G. A. Zirkle, Clerk of Session
Jefferson City, Tennessee

Approved as far as written.

April 6, 1910

J. D. Fancitle Moderator

Feb. 26, 1911 Mount Horeb, Tenn.

Session met and was organized with prayer. W. P. Bradshaw moderating by request Elders present M. C. Franklin & W. P. Bradshaw. A letter of dismission for J. P. [John Pennywitt] Zirkle & Wife the request was granted the clerk was ordered to prepair [sic] the letter. Thay[sic] was dismissed to join any Evangelical church of God there being no other [Page 125] business the Session was closed with prayer.

W. P. Bradshaw, Clerk of Session

June 4, 1911 Mount Horeb, Tenn.

Session met and was moderated by Rev. L. F. Smith. Elders present W. P. Bradshaw & M. C. Franklin. A request was presented asking letter of dismission for Mrs. Ella Potter Peck Hayworth the request was granted in usial [sic] form. Elder W. P. Bradshaw moved that M. C. Franklin be acting Clerk of Session. No opposition, was elected until other was elected Elders in Mount Horeb Church.

Moved to adjourn & closed by prayer.   M. C. Franklin, Clerk

Sept. 3, 1911 Mount Horeb, Tenn.

Session met and was moderated by Rev. L. F. Smith: Elders present Bradshaw & Franklin. A request was presented asking letter of dismission for Mrs. F. O. [Florence Obalma] Zirkle the request was granted in usual way: Also receiving Miss Ella Mae Cutts into the Church in full fellowship of Session & Members.

Moved to adjourn & closed by prayer by Moderator Rev. L. F. Smith.

M. C. Franklin, Clerk

Oct 29, 1911 Mount Horeb, Tenn.

Session met and was moderated by Rev. L. F. Smith: Elders pres. Bradshaw & Franklin. A request was presented asking letters of dismission for Miss Christina Bradshaw & Mrs. Sue [Owen] Newman the request was granted in the usual way:

There being no other business Session was closed by prayer.

M. C. Franklin, Clerk of Session

Continued to Page 170. [See below]

[Membership, Baptism and other charts moved to end of Minutes.]

[Pages 152 to 169 blank]

[Page 170] March 17, 1912 Mount Horeb

Session was opened by Prayer by Rev. Duncan, Moderator Elders W. P. Bradshaw & M. C. Franklin, Present. J. J. [Jonathan James] Rankin & Mrs. Mable [Garber] Rankin requested to become Members of this Church was Examined by Session & received into the Church in full fellowship. Closed by Prayer.

M. C. Franklin, Clerk of Session

Annual Narrative of Christian of Life and Work.
The Mount Horeb Church of Union Presbytery of Tenn.
Congregational Services
1. What is the Membership of your church?   40
   What is the net gain during past year?   15
2. How many united with your church on examination during yr?   3
3. How many preaching services do you usually hold on the Lord Day? 2
   What is the average attendance?   30
4. How many Communion Service have you during the yr?   1
5. To what extent are the children & the youth of the Congregation present at preaching Ser.? Most all
6. Have you a weekly prayer Meeting? one organized
Sabbath School
10. Is the Shorter Catechism Regularly taught?   No
11. Are the Westminster Leman [*sic*]Helps used?   2 yes

12. Are teaching meeting held?   No
13. Has the school a library?   No
14. How many adult Bible classes have you?   1
18. What is the total Membership of your school?   40
30. Are Christian parents faithful in presenting their children for Baptism? Yes
[Page 171]

31. How many persons baptized in infancy were received during the year into the full communion of the church?   Two
41. Are the financial obligation of the congregation met?   Yes
42. Are the Temporalities managed by the Elders or Deacons?   by Both

This is about all questions that I can answer under existing conditions.
This Apr 5, 1911

M. C. Franklin, Clerk of Ses

Mount Horeb Church Congregational Meeting June 2, 1911

Called to order by Rev. McFerren Acting as Chairman of the meeting.

Mr. D. M. Coile Elder, Mr. Fisher Elder from Morristown & Mr. McFerren representing Holston Presbytery.

Mr. D. M. Coile as representing Holston presbytery & Committee present Moved that old Mount Horeb Church property, members, Elders, Deacons (if any), building and real estate all be transferred to the Presbyterian Church of the U.S.A.

The question was discussed briefly and to the point by the two Committees & Others.

The Union Presbytery Committees Present gave their acceptance to the aforesaid Motion (over) [Page 172] Mr. Fisher Elder from Holston Presbytery second what was done & gave an encouraging talk for this move.

W. P. Bradshaw Elder made a united talk & urged all members & people to unite & work for their Master.

This bringing us up to question which was called to a rising vote which carried for Union & was declared so. Moved & Second to adjourn and closed by Prayer

M. C. Franklin,
Secy Meeting

March 30, 1912

Mount Horeb Congregational Meeting called to Order by Rev. L. F. Smith and opened by Song & prayer.

A report of the Chairman of the Committee appointed to draft resolutions for the congregational meeting of Mount Horeb Church.

Mov'd. & Sec to elect or appoint a building committee to consider & see what can be done and how much money can be raised among the people for the repair of the Church. They was [sic] appointed and names as following: M. C. Franklin, J. R. [Joseph

R. "Joe"] Lyle, W. P. Bradshaw, O. P. [Orlando Porter] Rankin, A. J. Rankin, Mrs. B. F. Brown [Nancy Emily Rankin 1841-1927], Mrs. Sallie [Bell] Franklin.

Next in Order to elect more Officers to the Church.

Nominations Opened; there being none; The Session gave forth the following Names J. R. [Joseph R.] Lyle & B. C. [Benjamin Caswell] Rankin Elders; M. C. Stoner & George M. [Mack] Lyle Deacons: then being no other nominations proceeded to election, elected by ballot all members voting. [Page 173] Also Ordination & Installation was in order next, as there was not much time to wait; Therefore the aforesaid Brethren were inducted into the power & Spirit of the Offices. Also the Members of the Church voted that the Elders & Deacons shall be Trustees of the property of the church.

This closing the congregational meeting. Moved and Sec to adjourn. Was closed by Prayer of Dr. Duncan

M. C. Franklin, Cl.

March 30, 1912

Session was called together & opened by Prayer Dr. C. A. Duncan Moderating. Elders Present W. P. Bradshaw & M. C. Franklin, the following names were received into the church by letters J. R. [Joseph R.] Lyle & Mrs. Luella M. [May Bettis] Lyle a recess was taken until evening. Session and the following names were received by letter Harry [Lee] Lyle and George M. [Mack] Lyle, also a recess of the Session was taken until next day Service was past. There being no further business the Session was closed by Prayer.

M. C. Franklin,
Clerk of Session

[Page 174] 1912 August 11

Session was called to order and opened by prayer Rev. L. F. Smith acting moderator Elder present B. C. Rankin, J. [Joseph] R. Lyle, W. P. Bradshaw and M. C. Franklin. The following name was received by letter Mrs. W. F. Cutts (M. A. Cutts written above name). And the action of Session was receiving Mrs. Cutts in full fellowship & communion of the church. There being no other business Session was closed by prayer.

M. C. Franklin, Clerk

Sept 21 [year missing]

Session met and was called to order by Rev. L. F. Smith. Opened by Prayer and proceeded to it business. The business being to elect an Elder. O. P. [Orlando Porter] Rankin being the only nominee: the Election was next. In the motion by Elder J. R. [Joseph R.] Lyle to Instruct the Clerk of Session to cast the vote of the members present was second & carried. the vote cast was fifteen & therefore O. P. Rankin was declared elected. The installed was set to take place immediately after the morning Sermon the following day. Session was closed by the benediction of the Service.

M. C. Franklin Clerk

1912 Sept 22

Session was called to order after the morning service for the purpose of installing O. P. [Orlando Porter] Rankin elder which was followed in the regular form. Brother O. P. Rankin was received by all members and elder in full fellowship and love of all present. Also appointing one elder to go to Presbytery & Synod which met in Forest Hill & Maryville Tenn. Elder O. P. Rankin was appointed to go as Principal & J. R. [Joseph R.] Lyle as alternate. Closed by Prayer.

M. C. Franklin Clerk

[Page 175]   March 23, 1913

Session was called to order and opened by prayer M. C. Franklin Moderator. Elder present J. R. Lyle, B. C. Rankin, W. P. Bradshaw and M. C. Franklin.

First was the reading and approving of the previous meetings of the Sessions since the Transfer of the Church. There being some few errors: was corrected and approved by all present.

Next was yearly reports to be made out and approved which was done and sent to the Stated Clerk. There being no further business Session voted to adjourn and closed by Prayer.

M. C. Franklin

Thus far examined and approved by the Presbytery of Union.
Samuel T. Wilson, Moderator
Westminster
April 9, 1913

Over

[Page 176] Nov. 9, 1913

Session was called to order and opened by prayer. Rev. Penland Moderator. Elder present M. C. Franklin, J. R. Lyle, O. P. Rankin, B. C. Rankin, and W. P. Bradshaw.

The business of the call was the receiving of members into the church.

Those received was Ralph Miller and Lizzie Lyle Miller which was received on confession and baptized the same day. Then they were received into the church in full fellowship. Also, we had a revival meeting in our church for most two weeks, conducted by Rev. Bob Houston & Rev. Penland they did us good service and we all enjoyed their stay with us, we had thirteen professions two reclaimed and two united with our church.

They had communion service on Wednesday night which was very enjoyable to all and on that night there was a collection taken for Home Mission. Almost ten dollar was collected we also made up thirty dollars for Rev. Houston & Rev. Penland.

This did not express by no means how much we did enjoy having them with us in our church and in our Homes.

There being no further business moved & second to adjourn and closed by Prayer.

M. C. Franklin

[Page 177] Apr 5, 1914

Session was called to order and opened by prayer: M. C. Franklin acting as Moderator. Elders present B. C. Rankin, J. R. Lyle, and W. P. Bradshaw.

The business was first in order was the reports to Presbytery which was read and filled out and approved also appointing delegate to Presbytery.

Mr. B. C. [Benjamin Caswell] Rankin, Principal, M. C. Franklin alternate. There being no further business session was closed with Prayer.

All previous meeting was read and approved.

M. C. Franklin,
Clerk of Session

Thus far examined and approved
by the Presbytery of Union.
A. J. Coile, Stated Clerk
April 15, 1914

Minutes of Mount Horeb Church May 1, 1914-15

May 10, 1914

Session was called to order and opened by prayer. Rev. Edgar Vance acting as Moderator. Elders present M. C. Franklin, W. P. Bradshaw, J. R. Lyle and O. P. Rankin and B. C. Rankin. The business was accepting Edgar Vance as Pastor for the following year.

There being no further business the Session was closed by Prayer.

M. C. Franklin,
Clerk

[Page 178] Nov. 22, 1914

Session was called to order and opened by prayer. Also a congregational meeting was call for the purpose of electing another Deacon.

M. M. [Milton Mack] Newman was nominated and elected; Session remained open until night service in which M. M. Newman was ordained as Deacon of the Church.

There being no further business the Session was closed by the Benediction.

M. C. Franklin,
Clerk

↑ Who moderating? [written above session meeting]

↑ Margin notes beside above minute: It appears that this call and the election occurred on same day. If so, irregular. 10 days should intervene.

H. J. Wilson

Jan. 31, 1915

Session called to gather and properly opened for the purpose of accepting Rev. Edgar Vance resignation as pastor of Mount Horeb Church.

Elders pre't. M. C. Franklin, J. R. Lyle. Mr. B. C. Rankin and W. P. Bradshaw. All Present voted accepting the Resignation (with regrets)

Also Letter of dismission was granted upon request to Jennie E. Newman, Mrs. M. A. Cutts which was granted by Session and forward to same.

There being nothing to do: Session closed by Prayer.

M. C. Franklin, Clerk

↑ Margin note by above minute: O.K. [initials] H.J.W. [Wilson]

[Page 179] March 28, 1915

Session called to order and opened by Prayer of W. P. Bradshaw.

Elders pres. M. C. Franklin, W. P. Bradshaw, J. R. Lyle and B. C. Rankin.

A request for Letter of dismission was granted to Geo. M. [George Mack] Lyle and wife Ella M. Cutt[s] Lyle

Next was electing delegates to Presbytery at New Providence Church Maryville.

Elder W. P. Bradshaw Principal, M. C. Franklin Alternate: Also all report of Church & Sabbath School was approved by Session.

All meetings of previous Sessions was read and approved.

This completed the work of Session. Elder J. R. Lyle moved to adjourn: and Sec. by W. P. Bradshaw. And closed by Prayer.

M. C. Franklin, Clerk

↑ Margin note by above minute: O.K. H.J.W.

Thus far examined and approved by the Presbytery of Union.
April 14, 1915
John B. Creswell – Mod.

[Baptism Charts on pages 180-183 moved to end of Minutes with other Baptismal Records.]

[Page 186] Apr 1, 1915

Session called to order and opened by Prayer Elders present M. C. Franklin, W. P. Bradshaw, J. R. Lyle and B. C. Rankin.

The call of the Session was for the acceptance of Rev. C. E. Hoffmeister. As pastor for the coming year. He being accept as same. Session was close by Moderator and Prayer.

M. C. Franklin
Clerk

Nov 3, 1915

Session called to order and opened by Prayer Rev. C. E. Hoffmeister Moderating. Elders present M. C. Franklin, W. P. Bradshaw, J. R. Lyle and B. C. Rankin.

The business of this call was to grant Letters of dismission to Miss Jennie Newman & Miss Laura Hinkle which was done in regular form and approved.

There being no farther [sic] business.

Session close by Prayer.

M. C. Franklin,
Clerk

1916, Jan

Session called to order and opened by Prayer: M. C. Franklin acting as Moderator. Elders present M. C. Franklin, W. P. Bradshaw, J. R. Lyle and B. C. Rankin.

The call was to grant a Letter of dismission to Mrs. Lucy Newman Hendrix. Which was done in regular form and approved by all of the Session.

Closed by Prayer.

M. C. Franklin,
Clerk

[Page 187]

Apr 9, 1916

Session meet and opened by Prayer. W. P. Bradshaw acting as Moderator. Elders present M. C. Franklin, B. C. Rankin and W. P. Bradshaw.

The Minutes of all of the Session meeting was read and approved. The Reports of the Church and Sabbath School was read and approved by same.

Elder B. C. Rankin was elected Principal and M. C. Franklin as alternate to Presbytery which was held at Knoxville Kirkwood (?) Church. There being no farther business adjourned & closed by prayer.

M. C. Franklin,
Clerk

Approved by Presb. Apr. 1916
W. J. Shelton, Mod.

[Page 188]

March 18, 1917

Session meet Opened by Prayer. Rev. Penland, acting as Moderator. Elders present W. P. Bradshaw, B. C. Rankin, J. R. Lyle and M. C. Franklin.

The meeting was to grant letters of dismission to Elder O. P. Rankin [Orlando Porter Rankin] , Dr. B. F. [Benjamin Franklin] Brown and wife Mrs. Brown [Nancy Emily Rankin 1841-1927]. Which was done in the regular form and approved by others of Session. Closed by prayer.

M. C. Franklin, Clk.

Apr 1917

Session meet. Opened by Prayer. Clerk of Session acting as Moderator. Elders present W. P. Bradshaw, B. C. Rankin, J. R. Lyle and M. C. Franklin.

The meeting was to grant letter of dismission to Miss Jennie [E.] Newman. Which was granted in regular order. There being no other business Session was closed with prayer.   M. C. Franklin, Clk.

March 24, 1918

Session meet Opened by Prayer. Rev. W. C. Broady acting as Moderator. Elders pres. M. C. Franklin, J. R. Lyle, B. C. Rankin, and, W. P. Bradshaw.

The Session meeting was to make out the Church & Sabbath School report which was done and approved also all previous Session calls and records was read and approved by Session at this meeting and also arranged with Rev. W. C. Broady to Preach with or for us for the next year. This closed the meeting. Closed by prayer.
M. C. Franklin, Clk.

[Page 189] Oct 1918

Session meet Opened by Prayer. Rev. W. C. Broady acting as Moderator. Elders pres. W. P. Bradshaw, B. C. Rankin, J. R. Lyle and M. C. Franklin.

The meeting was for the purpose of church work and also approving a Communion Day and about arranging services for same. That being all Session closed by Prayer.
M. C. Franklin, Clk.

1919 Mar 23

Session meet Opened by Prayer. Elders pres. W. P. Bradshaw, B. C. Rankin, J. R. Lyle and M. C. Franklin. The meeting of session was to consider the New Era Movement and to make up Church budget and Benevolences which was acted upon and approved. Also election of Delegate to Presbytery which resulted in election of M. C. Franklin Prin, alt B. C. Rankin. Closed by Prayer.
M. C. Franklin, Clk.

Approved by Presbytery
White Pine, April 9, 1919
George L. Hamilton

Over

[Page 190] Apr 6, 1919

Session meet Opened by Prayer. Elder W. P. Bradshaw acting as Moderator. Elders present M. C. Franklin and J. R. Lyle & W. P. Bradshaw.

The meeting of Session was to make out the Church & Sabbath School report which was done and approved. Also all Sessional meeting on record was read and approved by Session. Closed by prayer.
M. C. Franklin, Clk.

Approved by Presbytery
White Pine
Aug 1919   George L. Hamilton

May 1919
Session meet Opened by Prayer.
Elders present, W. P. Bradshaw, J. R. Lyle, B. C. Rankin, and M. C. Franklin.
The Session meet in conference as to when to have Sacramental Service and also to get report of our Deacons work. The day or Sabbath for Service and report were read and Service announced. This closed the business meeting
Closed by prayer of Moderator Rev. W. C. Broady.

M. C. Franklin,
Clk.

[Page 191] 1919 May 25
Session meet Opened by Prayer.
Elders present, W. P. Bradshaw, J. R. Lyle, B. C. Rankin, and M. C. Franklin.
The meeting of Session was to receive Mr. G. M. [George Mack] Lyle and Mrs. G. M. Lyle [Ella Mae Cutts] into the Church which was done in regular form.
They were members of the Presbyterian Church of Greenville Tenn. formerly; were dismissed by Letter to the Mount Horeb Presbyterian Church of Pres. Union. They were gladly received by Session and Church into full membership of Same.
Rev. W. C. Broady acting as Moderator of Session.

M. C. Franklin,
Clk.

Sept [no day or year given]
Session meet Opened by Prayer. Rev. W. C. Broady Moderator. Elders pres. W. P. Bradshaw B. C. Rankin, J. R. Lyle and M. C. Franklin.
The meeting was to receive new members into the church and at this meeting Two presented themselves Mrs. Cora Brotherton Franklin and Miss Grace Brotherton After an examination by Session as to their Belief & Faith in Christ they were received into the church in full Fellowship and Communion. Closed by Prayer.

M. C. Franklin,
Clk.

[Page 192] 1919 Oct 12
Session meet Opened by Prayer. Rev. W. C. Broady Moderator. Elders pres. W. P. Bradshaw, J. R. Lyle, B. C. Rankin and M. C. Franklin.
At this meeting of Session Mrs. Minnie Newman was received into the church by letter from the Fifth Presbyterian Church of Knoxville Tenn.
This Closing the business: Session Closed by Prayer.

M. C. Franklin,
Clk.

1920 Jan 25
Session Opened by Prayer. Rev. W. C. Broady Moderator. Elders pres. M. C. Franklin, B. C. Rankin, W. P. Bradshaw and J. R. Lyle

Session at this time received two members on confession. Martin [Master ?] Paul Rankin and Fredric George Franklin into the Church. This meeting was closed by Prayer.

M. C. Franklin, Clk.

1920 Mar 28
Session Opened by Prayer. Rev. W. C. Broady acting as Moderator. Elders pres. J. R. Lyle, W. P. Bradshaw, B. C. Rankin and M. C. Franklin.

The business of Session was to make out all of the Church's report which was done in legal form and approved. Also an Order was made to adopt the New Era budget for the year 1920 and 1921 ending next March 31, 1921.

[Page 193]

Annual report of the Mount Horeb Church
to the Presbytery of Union from Apr 1 A.D. 1919 to March 31 A.D. 1920

Officers: Elders 4, Deacons 2

Communicants: Examinations 4, Certificate 2, Suspended 2, Total 35

Baptism: Confession 2, Infants 0

Sabbath School Membership 40

Funds Contributed

Home Mission	$90.00
Foreign "	50.
Education	56.
Sabbath School work	5.
Church Erection	0.
Retired and Sustentation	14.
Freedman	6.
Temperance	2.
General Assembly	5.25
Congregational	4.
Miscellaneous	9.

The Session at this time voted to employ Rev. W. C. Broady for the half of his time or twice a month by the help of the Board to the Amount of Two Hundred dollars.

All Sessional meetings was read and approved by Session and all reports approved. March 3, 1920

M. C. Franklin Clk.

Approved by Presbytery April 14, 1920
E. W. Hall, Mod.

[Page 194]
Beginning of year 1920 & 1921
1920 Apr 4

Session Opened by Prayer. Rev. W. C. Broady Moderator. Elders present W. P. Bradshaw, J. R. Lyle, B. C. Rankin, M. C. Franklin. The business of the Session was to hear report of Deacon on the Every Member canvas and their success. The canvas was made by the Deacons and their report was not complete. Also the Session ordered the Rev. W. C. Broady continue his work with Mount Horeb Church as in the past years.

Closed by Prayer.

M. C. Franklin, Clk.

1920 June 27

Session Opened by Prayer. Rev. W. C. Broady Moderator. Elders pres. J. R. Lyle, B. C. Rankin, W. P. Bradshaw and M. C. Franklin. The business of this meeting was receiving member at which Mrs. M. A. Cutts name was presented by letter to same and was accepted by vote of same. This closed all of the business.

Closed by Prayer.   M. C. Franklin, Clk.

1921 Mar 27

Opened by Prayer. Rev. W. C. Broady Moderator. Elders present W. P. Bradshaw, B. C. Rankin, J. R. Lyle and M. C. Franklin.

Session met and filled out the Church & School report in full and approved same. Also records and appointed Delegate to Presbytery M. C. Franklin & B. C. Rankin. This bring close of the years business

Session closed by Prayer.

M. C. Franklin

[Page 195] May 3, 1921
Session Opened by Prayer.

Rev. W. C. Broady Mod. Elders present W. P. Bradshaw, J. R. Lyle, B. C. Rankin, M. C. Franklin.

The business of the Session was the report of Deacon as to their Ever [sic] Member canvass [sic], which was made and reported complete. Also accepting Rev. W. C. Broady as Pastor for the coming year. Closed by Prayer.

M. C. Franklin, Clk.

1921 June 19

Session met at the call of the Mod. Pres Rev. W. C. Broady, Mod. and Elders B. C. Rankin, W. P. Bradshaw and J. R. Lyle. Absent Elder M. C. Franklin. Upon regret letters of dismission were granted to Mrs. Elizabeth Rankin, Miss Annie Rose Rankin to unite with Fifth Ave. Pres. Ch. Vis. of Knox. Adjourned. Closed with Prayer.

W. C. Broady Mod. & Clerk
M. C. Franklin

1921 Sep 12
Session meet at the call of the Moderator. Pres. Rev. W. C. Broady Mod. Elders pres. W. P. Bradshaw, J. R. Lyle and M. C. Franklin and B. C. Rankin. Present business of the Session was to Elect Delegate to Presbytery W. P. Bradshaw alt. and J. R. `Lyle to the church which was done. [extremly difficult to read] This being all of the business closed by Prayer.   M. C. F. [Mac Calvin Franklin], Clk.

[Page 196] 1921 & 1922
Nov 27, 1921
Mount Horeb Congregational Meeting called to order by Rev. W. C. Broady and opened by Song & Prayer. The purpose of this meeting was to elect additional Elders & Deacons which was carried out and resulted in the Election of G. M. [George Mack] Lyle as Elder and J. [John] R. Garber as Deacon. Also in this meeting are Election of Trustees for the Cementery [sic] nearby was held. The result of this was Electing B. W. [Benjamin Wallace] McMurry, Q. D. [Quince David] Brotherton, Jno Coukour, [sic] M. C. Stoner and M. C. Franklin and act so long as were useful in this capacity. This closing the business for the meeting was closed with Song & Prayer.   M. C. Franklin, Clk.

Feb 10, 1922
Session called to meet at Elder B. C. Rankin home. Rev. W. C. Broady Mod. Meet and opened by prayer. The Order of business was in regard to completing the years work and finances of the Church. This Sessional meeting was continued for call of Moderator or continuance until Feb 23 1922 and at this Time the business was completed and full report of Deacons was made Satisfactory to all. This closing the business of the meeting was closed by Prayer.
                    M. C. Franklin, Ck.

[Page 197] This should be placed before the Congregational Meeting
Nov 10, 1921
Session meet at the call of the Moderator in connection with church service.
Present Rev. W. C. Broady Mod. and Elders B. C. Rankin, J. R. Lyle and M. C. Franklin. Absent W. P. Bradshaw. The Session called the Congregation to meet Nov 19 for the purpose of Electing additional Officers.
                    W. C. Broady Mod.
                    M. C. Franklin, Ck.

Apr 1922
Session meet and opened by prayer. Rev. W. C. Broady acting as Moderator. Elder-pres. W. P. Bradshaw, B. C. Rankin, J. R. Lyle, G. M. Lyle and M. C. Franklin.
The business before the Session was to make all report which was done in regular form and approved. Also adopted a budget for the Church and all of it working forces of Four Hundred dollar or more for the coming year.
    (over)

[Page 198]
Annual report of Mount Horeb Church to the Presbytery of Union
from Apr 1 A.D. 1921 to March 31 A.D. 1922

Officers	Elders		5
"	Deacons		3
Communicants		Examination	2
"		Certificate	1
"		Restored	2
"		Dismissed	2
		Total	38

Sabbath School Membership   38

Funds Contributed

Home Missions	$75.00
Foreign "	55.00
Education	15.00
Sabbath School Work	8.00
Church Erection	5.00
Relief & Sustentation	12.00
Freeman	8.00
Temperance	2.00
General Assembly	5.60
Congregational Expenses	$500.00

The Session at this meeting voted to Employ Rev. W. C. Broady for the half of his time or Twice a month by the help of the Board.

All posted meeting of the Sessions was read and approved by Session. Also all report was approved by said meeting

This closing the years work the session adjourned and closed by Prayer.
M. C. Franklin Clk., W. C. Broady Mod.

Examined and approved in Presbytery April 12, 1922.
Horace Cady Wilson, Moderator
[Pages 199-200 were torn out of the book]

[Page 201] May 14 1922
Session met and opened by prayer. Rev. W. C. Broady Moderator. Elder present J. R. Lyle, G. M. Lyle, B. C. Rankin and M. C. Franklin. Absent W. P. Bradshaw.

The order of business was arrange the date of the Communion Service which was announced two weeks hence, May 28, 1922. With morning and evening Services. This closing the order of business was closed by Prayer.
W. C. Broady, Mod., M. C. Franklin, Clk.

May 28 1922

Session met in connection with the Communion Service. Elders present J. R. Lyle, G. M. Lyle, B. C. Rankin and M. C. Franklin, W. C. Bradshaw. Rev. W. C. Broady Mod.

Miss Lucile H. Bradshaw was received into the Church on her confession of faith in Christ. And received into the Church having been baptized in infancy. Session adjourned with closing of the Service.

W. C. Broady, Mod.
M. C. Franklin Clk.

Oct. 8, 1922

Session met and opened by prayer. Rev. W. C. Broady Moderator. Elder present J. R. Lyle, G. M. Lyle, and M. C. Franklin.

Elder B. C. Rankin absent on account of sickness. And W. P. Bradshaw absent on account of change of resident [sic]. The purpose of the meeting was to arrange time to have our Fall Communion Service. All voted to have the service Oct 22, 1922. And also G. M. Lyle at this meeting was elected principal delegate [Page 202] to Synod Oct 10th, 11th, and 12, at Maryville. Which was to convene at Maryville. Also M. C. Franklin as his alternate.

Session was close by prayer.

W. C. Broady, Mod.
M. C. Franklin, Clk.

Nov 12, 1922

Session met and opened by prayer. Rev. W. C. Broady Mod. Elders present J. R. Lyle, G. M. Lyle and M. C. Franklin. Elders absent B. C. Rankin and W. P. Bradshaw. At this meeting the Session voted to assume or pay a part of the Home Mission Board indebtedness. The amount paid by the Church was $10.00.

Closed by prayer.

W. C. Broady, Mod.
M. C. Franklin Clk.

March 25 1923

The Session of Mount Horeb Church met at the call of the Mod. At the home of Elder B. C. Rankin at 3 P.M. and was opened with prayer by Elder J. R. Lyle. Elders present B. C. Rankin, J. R. Lyle, G. M. Lyle and Rev. W. C. Broady Mod. Absent Elders M. C. Franklin and W. P. Bradshaw.

The Deacons M. C. Stoner, M. M. [Milton Mack] Newman, J. R. Garber were present.

And reported that the salary of the Pastor had been paid up Feb 1st and that there were good subscriptions for the balance and that seventy five ($75.00) was on hand for Benevolence. They reported also that they had made the canvas of the congregation for the coming year and that Four hundred and fifty eight ($458.00) had been subscribed for [Page 203] Pastor Salary and Benevolences.

The Session, the Deacons concerning invited the minister Rev. W. C. Broady to continue his services for another year. And pledged him on behalf of the Congregation the same Salary as for the past year viz. $350.00, and decided to ask the Board of Home Missions for a grant of the same amount as received this year toward the support of the minister, viz. $250.00.

The Sunday School reported that it consisted of
Officers and Teachers 8, and Scholars 30   Total 38
That there had been contributed by the school $53.03
Expenses for the school $46.67
"   for Home Missions   3.00
"   for Foreign "   2.00
And for Sunday School Mission Work   2.00

The Ladies Aid and Missionary Society reported that it consists of 11 members and that they have contributed about twenty-five dollars $25.00 for our own Church and to Missions as follows, viz.

Home Mission	$12.00
Foreign "	10.00
Freedmens Work	2.00
Contingent Fund	1.00

The Session made out its annual report to the Presbytery of Union as follows, viz.
We consist of Elders   5
                Deacons   3
Received on Examination   1
Total Membership   39
Sunday School enrollment   38

The Church including this Ladies Society and S. School   [Page 204]   and individuals have contributed for Benevolence as follows:

Home Missions	66.00
Foreign Missions	42.00
Education	73.00
Sabbath School Work	5.00
Church Erection	4.00
Ministerial Relief & Sust.	6.00
Freedman	4.00
Temperance	1.00
General Assembly Fund	6.08
Congregational Expenses	$500.00

M. C. Franklin was elected principal delegate to the Spring meeting of Union Presbytery to convene in the Erin Church, Bearden Tenn. April 10, 7:00 P.M. and Geo M. Lyle his alternate upon motion the session adjourned. Closing with prayer. W. C. Broady moderator & Clerk protem.

M. C. Franklin
Clk.

Apr 8, 1923

Session met and opened by prayer of Rev. W. C. Broady Moderator. Elders present J. R. Lyle, G. M. Lyle and M. C. Franklin. Absent Elders B. C. Rankin and W. P. Bradshaw.

First in order was the reading and approving of all the minutes of the past year and also that it was voted by the Session that all Rail Road fare of Delegates to and from Presbytery be paid out of the Church general fund now and here after. This minute was approved. Session adjourned. Closed by prayer.

W. C. Broady, Mod.
M. C. Franklin, Clk.

Examined and approved in Presbytery at Erin Ch.
Bearden Tenn. April 11, 1923

Isaac C. Menler [?], Moderator

[Pages 205 to 207 blank]

[Editors Note: Charts were moved so they are grouped together for ease of use in this published book. Page numbers in the original books are kept in brackets but will be out of sequence with the original minute pages. All pages are accounted for, just rearranged for convenience.]

[Pages 126 -127]

Register of Elders

When Ordained	Name	Dismissed or ceased to act	Died
30 May 1874	James Newman		Sept 29th 1879
30 May 1874	John P. [Prigmore] Bradshaw	Oct 10th 1880	
30 May 1874	John W. [John William Massengill] Bradshaw	Ceased to act and left our bounds Aug 15th 1875	
Being an Elder	Joseph C. Bradshaw		July 4th 1897
June 14th 1874	Richard D. [Duffield] Rankin		Oct 21 1890
Oct 19th 1878	George A. [Adam]Zirkle	Oct 10th 1880	
Being an Elder	I. A. L. [Isaac Anderson Loag] Wilson	Oct 10th 1880	
Reinstalled June 5	Geo. A. [Adam] Zirkle	Jan. 6th 1889	
Sept 4, 1884	A. T. [Andrew Thomas Hood] Bradshaw	Nov 6, 1898	

Sept 4, 1884	Wm. P. [Porter Massengil] Bradshaw	Resigned July 6, 1902	
Jly 1-1899	W. N. [William Newton] McMurry	Resigned July 6, 1902	
July 6, 1902			
"	Mc. C. [Mac Calvin] Franklin		
"	S. D. [Samuel Duffied] McMurry [Sr.]	Dismissed	
Reinstated July 6, 1902			
"	W. P. [William Porter Massengil] Bradshaw		
"	G. A. [George Adam] Zirkle		Sept 25 1910
March 30, 1912	J. [Joseph] R. Lyle, Reinstalled		
Ordained & installed Sept 22, 1912	B. C. [Benjamin Caswell] Rankin	·	
"	O. P. [Orlando Porter] Rankin, ordained & installed	Dismissed	
[elected Nov 27, 1921]	G. M. [George Mack] Lyle		

[Page 128 to 131 blank]

[Pages 132-133]

Register of Deacons

When Ordained	Name	Dismissed or ceased to act	Died	Ordained as Elder
May 30th 1874	William P. Bradshaw	Ceased to act		Being elected Elder May 27th 1887
Oct. 31st 1874	George A. Zirkle	Ceased to act		Being elected Elder Oct 20th 1878
Oct. 31st 1874	John F. [Franklin] Bradshaw	May 14th by letter to Presbyterian Church at Cisco, Texas		
Dec. 4, 1888 [1887]	Geo. A. Newman	Dismissed to Morristown May 24 1891		
July 6 1902	Geo. [W.] Franklin		Feb 5, 1905	
"	W. N. [William Newton] McMurray	Dismissed to Haigrue [?] Tenn		
Reinstalled	J. M. [James Moore] McMurray McMurray]	Dismissed to Hebron Church		
Ordained Installed March 30 1912	George M. Lyle	Dismissed to Greenville, Tenn.		
"	M. C. Stoner			
Nov 22, 1914	M. M. [Milton Mack] Newman			
[Elected Nov, 27, 1921]	Jno [John R.] Garber			

[Pages 134 to 137 Blank]

[Pages 138-139]

Register of Communicants

No. of Communicant	Name	Date of Admission	How received	No. of Deaths and Dismissions	Dismissions When and Whither	Died When	Remarks
1	Joseph C. Bradshaw	May 30th 1874	Organization	1		July 4th 1897	
2	Andrew T. H. [Thomas Hood] Bradshaw	"	"		Nov. 6, 1897		
3	Catherine E. Newman	"	"				
4	John P. Bradshaw	"	"	1	Oct 10th 1880 to Texas		
5	Sarah J. (Bowers) Bradshaw	"	"	1	"		
6	Florence O. Wisdom	"	"	1	Now Zirkle "		
7	William P. Bradshaw	"	"	1	Oct 10th 1880 to Texas		
8	Mary L. [Lyle] Bradshaw	"	"	1			
9	Francis J. Bradshaw	"	"	1		Oct 3rd 1892	Aged 90 years 6 mo
10	Richard D. Bradshaw	"	"	1		Oct 21st 1890	Aged 90 years 3 mo, 17 days
11	Nancy D. [Dorthulia] Bradshaw	"	"	1	Died	March 7 1898	
12	Harriet J. Bradshaw	"	"	1		April 15th 1883	Aged 40 years 7 days
13	Sarah E. Bradshaw	"	"		Retired list April 8th 1894		
14	Michael H. Bradshaw	"	"	1	Left in irregular manner to join Westminster Church, Union Presbytery		
15	John W. [William Massengill] Bradshaw	"	"		Retired list April 8th 1894		
16	Nancy Ann Franklin	"	"	1		Oct 30th 1892	Aged 75 years 5 mo
17	Thomas J. [John] Bradshaw	"	"	1	Suspended	April 20th 1894	
18	Cindrilla C. [Cinderella Caldwell] Bradshaw	"	"		Dismissed by letter	November 1901	
19	John C. Bradshaw	"	"	1	May 14 1895 To Presbyterian Church at Cisco Texas		
20	Lea Anne Bradshaw	"	"	1	"		

No.	Name	Date of Admission	How received	No.	Deaths and Dismissions	Dismissions	Died When	Remarks
21	Jane Massengill	"	"	1			February 26th 1887	Aged 78 years 1 month 22 days
22	Lydia P. [Praytor] Franklin	"	"	1			Nov 26th 1890	Aged 57 years 10 mo
23	Susan Zirkle	"	"	1			Jan 5th 1890	Aged 71, 11 mo 4 days
24	Mary S. Zirkle	"	"	1	April 14th 1891 to Cumberland Church Mount Horeb, Tenn.			
25	James Newman	"	"	1	Sept 29th 1879			Aged 81 years 27 days
26	Rebecca McGhee	"	"	1			March 5th 1880	Aged 77 years 7 mo 22 d (?)
27	Samuel R. McGhee	"	"	1			1889	
28	Hugh A. Newman	"	"					
29	Lydia T. [Timantha "Tim"] Newman	"	"	1			April 30th 1896	
30	Asahel B. [Biddle] Bradshaw		"		Retired List April 8th 1894, Dismissed to Presbyterian C Knoxville			
31	Daniel Meadows	Oct 31st 1874	By letter	1		deceased		
32	George A. Zirkle	"	"	1	Oct 10th 1880 to Texas			
33	Luella M. Newman	"	"	1	April 18th 1896 Hopewell Church			
34	Joseph W. Shadden	Jan 3rd 1875	"	1	Sep 2nd 1883 to Hebron Church			
35	Harvey S. [Smith] Bradshaw	Jan 15th 1875	On examination		Entered the Ministry and dropped from roll Ap 8th 1894			
36	Elizabeth T. Bradshaw	"	"	1			Oct 9 1887	Aged 27 yrs 3 mo 5 da
37	Joseph R. [Richard] Bradshaw	May 30th 1874	By organization	1			June 3rd 1875	Aged 24 y 8 m 19 days

[Pages 140-141]

No. of Communicant	Name	Date of Admission	How received	No. of Deaths and Dismissions	Dismissions When and Whither	Died When	Remarks
38	Emma Carrol Newman	May 7th 1876	On Examination	1	April 18th to Lebanon Ev Church		
39	Laura Angeline Hinkle	May 7th 1876	On Examination				
40	Lydia J. [Jane Zirkle] Bell	Sept 1st 1877	By letter from Mossy Creek	1	Feb 6th 1881 to the Morristown Church		
41	Mag E. J. Lyle	April 13th 1878	As by letter	1			
42	I. A. L. [Isaac Anderson Loag] Wilson	"	by letter	1	Oct 10th 1880 to Texas		

43	A. C. [Angeline Catherine Rankin] Wil[l]son	"	by letter			Oct 10th 1880 to Texes		
44	Mary Ann Carrol Rankin	October 20th 1878	by letter from Hebron	1			Nov 16th 1886	Aged 70 years 23 days
45	Belle T. [Tittsworth] Bradshaw	June 15th 1879	by letter from New Market			Dismissed Nov 6th /98		
46	William E. [Erskine] Rankin	June 19th 1879	by letter from Hebron	1			died	
47	Elizabeth Rankin	June 15th 1879	by letter from Hebron					
48	John P. [Pennywitt] Zirkle	March 7th 1880	Examination			Dismissed Feb 26th 1911		
49	Fannie J. Newman	June 5th 1881	by letter	1		March 25th 1890 to Mossy Creek		
50	John P. Bradshaw	Oct 3rd 1881	by letter	1			Died March 15 1896	Aged 85 years 9 mo
51	Sarah J. Bradshaw	"	"	1			Died Jan 4th 1896	
52	Miranna J. Rankin	Nov 5 1882	Examination			Retired List p. 208		
53	Alice C. Hinkle (Zirkle)	May 6 1883	On examination					
54	Margaret E. Hinkle	June 1st 1884	Examination					
55	George A. Zirkle	June 1st 1884	by letter	1		Jan 6th 1889 to Mossy Creek		
56	Florence O. Zirkle	"	"	1		"		
57	Mary A. [Lockhart] Newman	August 8th 1884	On examination	1		Oct 3rd 1886 to Lebanon Church		
58	Josaehene Rankin [sic]	"	"	1		July 10th 1892 to Knoxville Tenn		
59	Fannie M. Miller	November 22nd 1885	On examination	1		May 14th 1895 to the Presbyterian Church at Cisco Texas		
60	Jinnie M. Newman	"	"			Retired List p. 205		
61	Louisa J. Cannon	"	"			"		
62	Sallie Bradshaw	"	"	1		Sep 6 1900 dismissed by letter		
63	Oakley D. Bradshaw	"	"	1		July 10 1892 to Texas		
64	William E. [Edward] Bradshaw	"	"	1		Sep 18 1892 to Texas		
65	Frank A. Newman	"	"	1		Sep 18 1892 to Texas		
66	Charley C. [Charles Cleton] Bradshaw	"	"			Retired List p. 208		
67	Bob E. [Lea] Bradshaw	"	"			Dismissed by letter	Nov 1901	

68	Frank A. [Ashley] Bradshaw	"	"	1	Jan 9 1893 to Harriman, Tenn.		
69	Catherine J. Fra[nklin]	"	"	1		Jan. 1st 1887	Aged 22 years 7 mo 21 d
70	Sue Ella Newman	"	"	1	Sep 3rd 1894 to Sronron [?]TX		
71	Arley W. Bradshaw	"	"		Retired List p. 208		
72	James C. [Crawford] Bradshaw	"	"	1	May 14th 1895 to Presbyterian Church at Cisco, Texas		
73	Hannah M. Hinkle	April 18th 1886	On examination	1	March 7th to the Presbyterian Church Mossy Creek		
74	Lula C. Rankin	"	"	1	To Mossy Creek Church		
75	James C. Barbee	May 1st 1887	Examination		Retired List p. 208		
76	Mary G. Barbee	"	"		"		

Pages 142-143

No. of Communicant	Name	Date of Admission	How received	No. of Deaths and Dismissions	Dismissed How and When
77	George [W.] McMurry	May 1st 1887	On examination	1	Feb 16th to Presbyterian Church at Hebron at Hebron, Tenn.
78	Earnest N. Bradshaw	"	"	1	May 14th 1895 to Presbyterian Church at Cisco. Texas
79	Clide M. [Park] Bradshaw	"	"		Dismissed by letter to Thornisville [sic], Ga
80	Henry Darr	"	"	1	Dec 11th to Cumberland Presbyterian Church, Mount Horeb, Tenn.
81	George A. [Arthur] Newman	"	By letter		May 24th 1891 Dismissed to Presbyterian Church at Morristown
82	Henry Lyle Bradshaw	June 5th 1887	On examination		Retired List p. 208
83	Thomas Newman	"	By letter		" Oct. 19, 1902
84	Jennie H. [McGhee] Newman	"	"		"
85	Martha L. L. Cannon	March 18, 1888	On examination		"
86	W. N. [William Newtom] McMurray	Sept. 30, 1888	By letter		
87 [no 88,89]	Kate C. [Catherine Cole "Cate" Newman] McMurray	"	"		
90	Florence A. Peck	Oct. 20th 1889	On examination		
91	Lelia M. Peck	"	"	1	Sep. 15th 1896 to Presbyterian Church at Hebron, Tenn.
92	Samuel F. [Samuel Franklin "Frank"] McMurry	March 30th 1890	On examination		
93	Mack C. Franklin	"	"	1	Oct. 20th 1895 to Presbyterian Church at Hebron Tenn.

94	Milton M. [Milton Mack] Newman	"	"		Retired List p. 208
95	Howard M. Peck	"	"		"
96	Benjamin ["Ben"] W. [Wallace] McMurry	"	"	1	Feb 16th 1896 to Presbyterian Church at Hebron Tenn
97	John M. McMurry	"	"	1	"
98	James F. Peck	"	"		Retired List p. 208
99	Ella Porter Peck	"	"		
100	Flora M. [May] Bradshaw	"	"	1	May 14th 1895 to Presbyterian Church at Cisco, Texas
101	Lizzie K. Newman	"	"		deceased
102	Ethel May McMurry	May 8th 1892	"		
103	Lula Belle McMurry	"	"		Died [?]
104	Porter A. Barbee	Sep. 14th 1893	On Examination		Dismissed by letter
105	Malinda J. Newman	"	"		Retired List p. 208
106	William F. Miller	"	"		Retired List p. 208
107	Samuel Edward Barbee	"	"		
108	Ola A. [Ann] McMurry	"	"		
109	Lucy M. [Moore] Newman	"	"		
110	Mattie Lea Newman	"	"		
111	John H. Miller	Sp. 15th 1893	On Examination		Retired List p. 208
112	Emma Miller	"	"		"
113	Emma Cate Bradshaw	Sep. 16th 1893	On Examination	1	May 14th 1895 to Presbyterian Church at Cisco, Texas
114	Alice L. [Lavinia] Rankin	"	"		
115	Jerusha Ferguson	July 8th 1894	By letter		From Leesburg Church, Leesburg Tenn.
116	Nellie A. Alexander	Sep 15th 1893	On examination		Retired List p. 208

[Pages 144-145]

No. of Communicant	Name	Date of Admission	How received	Dismissed How and When
117	F. [Frank] M. Killgore	March 31st 1895	By letter	Oct 10th 1898 Dismissed to Newport Church Tenn.
118	Cate M. Killgore	"	"	Dismissed "
119	Frank A. Bradshaw	Sep. 4th 1898	On Examination	
120	John M. Lyle	July 2-1899	By letter	

121	Louella May Lyle	"	"	
122	Mack Lyle`	"	"	
123	Charles W. [Walter] McMurray	May 6th 1900	By Profession	
124	Ephraim Cawood Bradshaw	"	"	
125	Martha Matilda McMurry	"	"	
126	Carry May Corbet	"	" Baptised	Dismissed
127	Laura C. [Crenora] Zirkle	Sept 1-1901	By Profession	
128	G. A. Zirkle	July 6-1902	By Letter	
129	F. O. Zirkle [Florence Obalma Wisdom]	"	"	
130	J. M. [James Moore] McMurry	"	"	
131	Almira M. [Minerva Rankin] McMurry	"	"	
132	Ann Bell [Anne Belle] McMurry	"	"	
133	John M. McMurray	"	"	
134	Benj. W. McMurry	"	"	
135	Elda May McMurry	"	"	
136	George [W.] Franklin	"	"	
137	Sallie A. [Ann] (Bell) Franklin	"	"	
138	Mc. C. Franklin	"	"	
139	J. A. Rankin	"	"	
`140	Samuel D. [Duffield] McMurry	August 3 1902	By letter	
141	Love J. [Jane Seahorn] McMurry	"	"	

For Revised Register See Page 146
Also see Minutes of Sep. 7 & Oct. 5, 1902 p.p. 74 & 75

[Pages 146-147]

Revised Member Register

taken from page 138. Oct. 5, 1902

Name	Admitted	How	Dismissed How and When
1 Catherine E. Newman	May 30th 1874	Organization	Died March 3, 1914
2 W. P. Bradshaw	"	"	
3 Mary L [Louise Lyle]. Bradshaw	"	"	
4 Laura A. Hinkle	May 7, 1876	Profession	Dismissed to Lebanon Cum. Church
5 Mag E. J. Lyle	Apl. 13, 1878	Letter	Died June 28, 1907
6 Elizabeth Rankin	June 15, 1879	Letter	Deceased
7 John P. Zirkle	Mch 7, 1880	Profession	Dismissed Feb 26, 1911
8 Alice C. Zirkle	May 6, '83	"	"
9 Margaret E. Hinkle	June 1, '84	"	Died July 24, 1909
10 W. N. [William Newton] McMurray	Sept 30, '88	Letter	Name dropped from Roll, See Minute page 116
11 Kate M. McMurray	"	"	Dismissed to Methodist Church Jany. 24, 1909
12 Ella Porter Peck	Mch. 30, '90	Profession	Dismissed June 4, 1911
13 Ethel May McMurray	May 8, '92	"	Dismissed to Hebron Church July 23, 1903
14 Ola A. McMurray	Sept. 14, '93	"	Name dropped. See Minute page 116
15 Lucy M. [Moore] Newman Hendrix	"	"	Dismissed Dec 1915
16 Mattie Lee Newman	"	"	
17 Alice L. Garber	Sept. 16, '90	"	Dismissed to Central Presbn. Church, Knoxville Nov. 27, '04
18 Jerusha Ferguson	July 8 '94	Letter	Died April 10, 1926
19 John M. Lyle	July 2 '99	"	Died Feb. 1911
[no 20] 21 Luella May Lyle Cannon	"	"	
22 Mc. Lyle	"	"	Retired
23 Charles W. McMurray	May 6 1900	Profession	Name dropped. See page 116 minutes
24 Ephraim Cawood Bradshaw	"	"	
25 Martha Matilda McMurray	"	"	
26 Laura C. Zirkle Leeper	Sept. 1, '01	"	Joined the Baptist Church
27 G. A. Zirkle	July 6, '02	Letter	Died Sept. 25, 1910 at 6:40 P.M.
28 F. O. Zirkle	"	"	Dismissed Sept. 3, 1911
29 J. M. [James Moore] McMurray	"	"	Dismissed Mch. 20, 1910
30 Almira M. McMurray	"	"	"
31 Anna B.[Belle] McMurray	"	"	"
32 John M. McMurray	"	"	"
33 Ben W. [Benjamin Wallace] McMurray	"	"	"
34 Elda May McMurray	"	"	"
35 George [W.] Franklin	"	"	Fell in sleep Feb. 20, 1902
36 Sallie A. [Ann Bell] Franklin	"	"	

[Pages 148-149]

Name	Admitted	How	Dismissed How and When
37 Mc [Mack] B. Franklin	July 6, 1902	Letter	
38 J. A. Rankin	"	"	

39 Samuel D. [Duffield] McMurray	Aug. 3, 1902	"	Dismissed July 23, 1905
40 Love J. [Jane Seahorn] McMurray	"	"	"
41 Florence A. Peck	Oct. 20, 1889	Profession	Dismissed January 28, 1906
42 Hugh A. Newman	May 30, 1874	Organization	Deceased
43 Frank A. [Ashley] Bradshaw	Sept. 4, 1898	Profession	Under care of Holston Presby. Ordained May 1905
Error page 147. No. 20 is omitted			
43 Frank A. Newman	Febr. 1 1903	Letter	
44 Sue [Owen] Newman	"	"	Dismissed Oct. 29, 1911
45 Samuel F. McMurray	Mch. 30, 1890	Profession	Dismissal Mch. 27, 1904 to 3rd Presbyterian Ch Knoxville
46 Anne Rose Rankin	Oct. 22, 1905	"	
47 Effie Belle Blackburn Franklin	Mch. 25, 1906	Letter	
48 Lillian Neal ["Lillie"] Bradshaw	Dec. 23, 1902	"	
49 Susie Kate Lyle Garber	Apl. 24, 1908	Profession	
50 Mrs. Eva E. Blackburn McMurray	Ap. 25, 1909	Letter	Dismissed Mch. 20, 1910
Ada & Lulla Rankin	June 4 1911	Organization	Lulla Rankin dismissed by letter May 10, 1914
Dr. B. F. [Benjamin Franklin] Brown	June 4 1911	"	Dismissed by letter
Mrs. B. F. Brown	June 4 1911	"	"
Mr. O. P. Rankin [Orlando Porter Rankin]	June 4 1911	"	"
Mrs. O. P. Rankin [M. Lavinia Riggs]	June 4 1911	"	Died
Miss Christina Bradshaw	June 4 1911	"	Dismissed Oct. 29, 1911
Miss Fairy Webb	July 30, 1911	"	Deceased 1921
M. C. Stoner	July 30, 1911	"	
Grace Bradshaw Stoner	July 30, 1911	"	
B. C. [Benjamin Caswell] Rankin	July 30, 1911	Letter	
Emma E. [Carroll] Rankin	July 30, 1911	"	
Hubert Rankin	July 30, 1911	"	Retired List
Ruby Rankin	July 30, 1911	"	
Mrs. Mary Ann Newman	July 30, 1911	"	Deceased Nov. 1923
Miss Ella Mae Cutts	Sept. 3, 1911	Profession	Dismissed March 28, 1915
Mr. John James Rankin	March 17, 1912	"	
Mrs. Mable Rankin	March 17, 1912	"	
Joe R. Lyle	March 30, 1912	Letter	
Mrs. Lulla M. [Bettis] Lyle	March 30, 1912	"	
Harry L. Lyle	March 30, 1912	"	
George M. [Mack] Lyle	March 30, 1912	"	Dismissed March 28, 1915
Mrs. W. T. Cutts	Aug. 11, 1912	"	Dismissed on request
M. M. [Milton Mack] Newman	Nov. 5, 1913	Profession	

Pages 150-151

Name	Admitted	How	Dismissed How and When
Ralph Miller	Nov. 9, 1913	Confession	
Lizzie Lyle Miller	Nov. 9, 1913	"	
E. C. Bradshaw	"	"	
M. M. Newman [Milton Mack]			
Mr. Geo M. Lyle		Letter	
Mrs. Geo M. Lyle [Ella Mae Cutts]		Letter	
Miss Grace Brotherton		Confession	

Mrs. Cora Brotherton Franklin		"	
Mrs. Minna Bradshaw Newman		Letter	
Fredrie G. [Frederick George "Fred"] Franklin	Jan 25, 1920	Confession	
Paul Rankin	Jan 25, 1920	"	
Mrs. W. T. Cutts	1921	Letter	
Mrs. Cora Brotherton Franklin			
Miss Grace Brotherton			
Jno [R] Garber		Letter	
Mrs. E. E. Bradshaw	Feb 28 /22	Letter	
Miss Mildred Nora Rankin	Mar 12 /22	Confession	
Miss Lucille H. [Henry] Bradshaw	Mar 12 /22	"	
Marguerite Stoner	Oct. 1923		Dismissed Mar. 28, 1926
O. D. [Quincy David] Botherton	Oct 1923		
G. L. [George Lee] Brotherton	Feb 24, 1924		
Mrs. G. L. Brotherton [Julia]	Feb 24, 1924		

[Page 180]

Register of Baptisms

When Baptized	Name of person	Name of parent	When born
May 31st 1874	Bob E. [Lea] Bradshaw	T. J. [Thomas John] & C. C. [Cinderella Caldwell] Bradshaw	Aug. 23rd 1868
" " "	Frank A. Bradshaw	" " "	June 21st 1870
" " "	Oakley D. Bradshaw	" " "	Aug. 28th 1871
" " "	Sally Bradshaw	" " "	Nov. 14th 1872
" " "	Arley Weihl Bradshaw	W. P. [Wm. Porter Massengil] & M. L. [Mary Louise Lyle] Bradshaw	Sep 1st 1872
May 7th 1876	Henry Lyle Bradshaw	W. P. [Wm. Porter Massengil] & M. L. [Mary Louise Lyle] Bradshaw	Dec 10th 1875
" " "	James Crawford Bradshaw	J. C. [John Calvin] & Leanna Bradshaw	Apr. 28th 1874
" " "	Earnest Neil Bradshaw	" " "	Feb. 23rd 1876
" " "	Clide Park Bradshaw	T. J. [Thomas John] & C. C. [Cinderella Caldwell] Bradshaw	Dec 20th 1875
" " "	Laura A. Hinkle (adult)		
March 17th 1878	~~David Rankin Willson~~	~~Logan & Augative Willson~~	Oct 30th 1877
Sept 1st 1877	Luther Lee Bell	J. H. [James Houston]& L. J. [Lydia Jane "Lidie" Zirkle] Bell	Dec 20th 1874
Sept 1st 1877	George Alexander Bell	" " "	April 10th 1877
Sept 1st 1877	George Paul Zirkle	George A. & F. O. Zirkle	Nov 27th 1876
" " "	Virginia Elizabeth	G. A. & F. O. Zirkle	" " 1876
May 19th 1872	Audley Rhea Willson	I. A. L [Isaac Anderson Loag] & A. C. [Angeline Catherine Rankin] Wil[l]son	July 28th 1871
May 14th 1873	Amner Viola Willson	" " "	July 14th 1873
June 4th 1876	Ann Elisabeth Willson	" " "	Nov 9th 1875
Mar 17th 1878	David Rankin Willson	" " "	Oct 30th 1877
Oct 20th 1878	Frank Adam Newman	L. T. [Lydia Timantha "Tim" Bradshaw] & Hugh A. [Alexander] Newman	Dec 6th 1867

" " "	Sue Ella Newman	" " "	Sept 12th 1870
" " "	Jinnie Belle Newman	" " "	Feb 10th 1872
" " "	Nancy Hulda Newmqn (dead)	" " "	March 25th 1873
" " "	Lizzie Kate Newman	" " "	Aug 13th 1874
" " "	Harnet Jantha Newman	" " "	Mar 9th 1876
" " "	David Pearl Newman (dead)	" " "	May 29th 1877
" " "	Milton Mack Newman	" " "	Sept 29th 1878
Mrch 20, 1879	Robert Earl	F. O. & G. A. Zirkle	Dec 30th 1878
" " "	Flora May	F. L. [Frances Leannah Rankin] & J. C. [John Calvin] Bradshaw	[no birth date]`
May 2nd 1880	James Kendle	I. A. L [Isaac Anderson Loag] & A. C. [Angeline Catherine Rankin] Wilson	Dec 14th 1879
August 25th 1880	Braxton Benjamin	G. A. & F. O. Zirkle	June 9 1880
June 5th 1881	Corine McGhee	John E. Newman	June 5, 1881 [*sic.*]
	Nellie Josephine	Fannie J. Newman	
	William McAdo		
	Eva Moore		
Nov 5th 1882	Miranna J. Rankin	Adult	
May 6, 1883	Allice C. [Cassandra] Hinkle	Adult	
June 1st 1884	Miss Margaret E. Hinkle	Adult	

[Page 181]

When Baptized	Name of person	Name of parent	When born
June 1st 1884	Emma Kate Bradshaw	John C. Bradshaw & wife [Frances Leanah Rankin]	March 7th 1881
"	Ralph Rankin	John C. Bradshaw & wife [Frances] Leanna Bradshaw	May 31st 1883
June 1st 1884	Lucy Moore	Hugh A. & L. T. Newman	Feb 1st 1880
"	Mattie Lee	"	Sept 2nd 1881
July 6th 1884	Emmerson Bunyan Rankin	Andrew & Miranna [Almira Jeanette "Miranna" Parrott] Rankin	
"	Lee Wilson Rankin	"	
June 6th 1884	Jonathan James Rankin	William [Erskine "Will"] & Elizabeth [Nancy "Lizzie" Newman] Rankin	
"	Isac Buel Rankin	"	
"	Lula Cassander Rankin	"	
"	Alice Lavinia Rankin	"	
Aug 3rd 1884	Itha Pirla Newman	Hood & Mary A. [Lockhart] Newman	March 18. 1881
Nov 22nd 1885	Ephriam C. [Cawood] Bradshaw	William & Mary Bradshaw	Oct 9th 1884
"	Catherine J. Franklin	Adult	
"	Louisa J. Cannon	Adult	
April 18, 1886	Hannah M. Hinkle	Adult	
May 1st 1887	James C. Barbee	Adult	
"	Mary F. Barbee	Adult	
Nov 6, 1887	Annie Lee Newman	G. A. & T. E. Newman [George Arthur & Elizabeth Tymanda]	
"	Samuel Harvey Newman	"	

Mar 18, 1888	Laura Crenora Zirkle	John P. [Pennywitt] & Alice C. [Cassandra] Zirkle	Oct 29, 1886
"	Martha L. L. Cannon	Adult	
Dec 13th 1890	Martha M. [Matilda "Tilda"] McMurry	William [Newton] & Cate McMurry	
"	Mary Elgin Bradshaw	John & Leanoh Bradshaw	
Nov 12th 1892	Joseph [Newton] McMurry	W. N. [William Newton] & Cate McMurry	
Sep 14th 1893	Edward Barbee	Adult	
"	Malinda Newman	Adult	
"	William Miller	Adult	
"	Porter [A.] Barbee	Adult	
Sep 15th 1893	Emma Miller	Adult	
"	Esa Miller	John [H.] & Emma Miller	
"	McCloud (?)	"	
Sep 17th 1893	Anna Rose Rankin	William [Erskine] and Elizabeth Rankin	
Aug 2nd 1896	Anna Earnestine Killgore	Frank and Cate (Roddy) Killgore	
"	Catharine Carroll Killgore	"	

[Page 182-183]

When Baptized	Name of person	Name of parent	When born	Baptized by	Where
Nov 29, 1900	Alphie Helors	F. A. [Frank Ashley] & E. H. [Edna] Bradshaw	[no date]		
May 23, 1909	Henry Lucile [or Lucille Henry?]	E. C. [Ephraim Cawood] & L. M. [N.] [Lillie Neal] Bradshaw	Sept. 23, 1908		
July 30, 1911	Mary Emma	M. C. & Grace Stoner	March 11, 1911	Rev. L. F. Smith	Mt Horeb
Marh 17, 1912	Mrs. Mable [Garber] Rankin			Rev. C. A. Duncan	"
"	Paul Lester Rankin	J. J. [Jonathan James] & Mable Rankin		"	"
"	Nora Mildred Rankin	"		"	"
Nov 9, 1913	Ralph Miller			Rev. Reland	"
"	Lizzie Lyle Miller			Rev. A. N. Penland	"
July 9, 1916	Marguerite Stoner	M. C. & Grace Stoner		"	"
Feb 18, 1917	Robt Lyle Miller	Ralph & Lizzie Miller		"	"
March 18, 1917	Hal D. [Dean] Franklin Hal Dean Franklin	M. C. & Effie Franklin	May 19, 1915	"	"
Apr 1917	[Cawood] Lyle Bradshaw	E. C. [Ephraim Cawood] & L. N. [Lillie Neal] Bradshaw		"	"
Oct 1923	Q. D. [Quince David] Brotherton	R. P. [Richard] & Lillie [Lillian Kidwell] Brotherton		Rev. W. C. Broady	"
Feb 24, 1924	G. L. [George Lee] Brotherton	R. P. & Lillie Botherton		"	"

[Pages 184-185 blank]

[Pages 208-209]

Retired List

The following action was had by the Session at its regular meeting **April 6, 1901.**

Whereas the following named persons having absented themselves from the church for several years, without charge of immorality of any kind brought against them.

Therefore be it resolved that their names be transferred to the retired list which is as follows.

Louisa J. Cannon
Charley C. [Charles Cleton] Bradshaw
James C. Barbee
Mary G. Barbee
Jennie M. Newman
Henry Lyle Bradshaw
Thomas Newman   Died Oct. 19, 1902
Jennie H. Newman   Dismissed Apr 1917
Mattie [Martha] L. L. Cannon
William F. Miller
Samuel Edward Barbee
James H. Miller
Nellie Alexander   Deceased
Emma Miller
~~Porter A. Barbee~~
Miranna J. [Almira Jeannette] Rankin Transferred Oct 5, 1902, Died Jan. 31, 1917
Arley W. [Arlen Weihl] Bradshaw   Transferred Oct 5, 1902
Milton M. [Milton Mack] Newman   Transferred Oct 5, 1902
Howard M. Peck   Transferred Oct 5, 1902
James H. Peck   Transferred Oct 5, 1902
Malinda J. Newman   Transferred Oct 5, 1902

[Pages 210 thru 219 blank]

[Page 220 - 221]

Register of Marriages

Date of Marriage	Name of male	Name of female
Dec 8th 1874	Thomas M. H. [Michael Harden] Bradshaw	Sarah Malinda Rankin
Feb 13th 1878	Andrew T. [Thomas Hood] Bradshaw	Belle [Isabelle] Titsworth
Jan 26th 1876	G. A. [George Adam] Zirkle	F. O. [Florence Obalma] Wisdom
March 21st 1882	Isaac [A.] Coil	Luella M. ["Lula" May] Newman
March 15th 1880	Elias Alexander	Harriet J. [Jane] Bradshaw

[Pages 222 thru 229 blank]

[Page 230 - 231]

Register of Deaths

Date of Death	Name	Remarks
June 3rd 1875	Joseph R. [Richard] Bradshaw son of J. C. [Joseph C.]	Had completed study of medicine attended the Lectures and died aged 24y 8m 19 days
Sept 29, 1879	James Newman	Aged 81years & 27 days
Mar 5, 1880	Rebecca McGhee	Aged 77 years 7 [m] & 5 days
April 15th 1883	Harriet [Jane Bradshaw] Alexander	Aged 40 years and 7 days
Nov 16, 1886	Mary A. C. [Ann Carol Woods] Rankin	Aged 70 years and 23 days
Jan 14, 1887	Catherine J. Franklin	Aged 22 years 7 mo 21 days
Feb 16, 1887	Jane Massingille	Aged 78 years 1 mo 22 days
Oct 9, 1887	J. Elizabeth T. [Tymanda Bradshaw] Newman	Aged 27 years 3 mo 5 days
Jan 5, 1890	Susan Zirkle	Aged 71 years 11 mo 4 days
Oct 21st 1890	Richard D. Rankin	Aged 90 years 3 mo 17 days
Nov 26th 1890	Lidia Rankin	Aged 57 years 10 mo
Jl [?] 30 1890	Nancy A. Franklin	Aged 75 years 5 mo
Oct 3rd 1892	Fannie J. Bradshaw	Aged 59 years 6 mo
Jan 4th 1896	Sarah J. [Bowers] Bradshaw	[wife of John P. Bradshaw]
March 15th 1896	John P. Bradshaw	Aged 85 years 9 mo
April 30th 1896	Lydia T. [Timantha "Tim" Bradshaw] Newman	Aged 51 years 4 mo
July 4th 1897	Joseph [C.] Bradshaw	Aged 85 y 11 mo
Oct 19, '02	Thomas Newman	

[Page 232 blank]

[Pages 233 thru 238 missing]

[Page 239]
[List of Special Collections at Back of Session Book]

Special Collections

Church Collection for the year 1896

		$ cts
Nov. 1st	For Thornwell Orphanage	7.00

Church collection for the year 1897

Nov 7th	For Foreign Missions	5.04

Church collection for the year 1898

Oct 1st-2nd	For Foreign Missions	6.00

Church collection for the year 1900

June 3	For sufferors in India	6.47
July 1	For Foreign Missions	2.42
Mar 17	Collection of local home missions	3.52

For the year 1901

May 1	Collection for Foreign Missions	10.05
Jul 1	For Invalid Fund	1.57
Aug 4	Col for Local Home Missions	2.57
Oct 6	Col for Education	4.00
Nov 1	Col for Foreign Missions	8.40

For the year 1902

Mar 2	Col for Local Home Missions	2.70
April 6	Col for Presbyterial Tax	4.00

1902

Aug 4	To Col for foreign missions	3.21
July 6	To Col for Invalid Fund	1.86

[Page 240 blank, end of book]

Chapter 5

Sunday School Records

Overview

The Sunday School Roll Books give the names of the students, as well as the teachers. The lessons studied were various books of the Bible. They did not have graded materials so it was up to the teacher to make it understandable for that age group. There were no blackboards or workbooks. All classes were in the one room of the church, each having their corner or area.

Roll Book (1884-1888)

Mount Horeb Sabbath School
The Improved Record and Roll-Book For
Sunday Schools, Primary Classes, Etc.
American Sunday School Union
1122 Chestnut Street, Philadelphia,
copyright, 1877

Mount Horeb 1884

Class #1 Taught by R. D. Rankin	Class #2 Taught by A. T. [Thomas Hood] Bradshaw	Class #3 Taught by Jos. C. Bradshaw
W. P. Bradshaw G. A. [George Arthur] Newman I. A. [Isaac Anderson] Coile Bradley Bettis	Miss Carrol Newman Mrs. Lizzie T. Newman Mrs. Hannah Hinkle Mrs. Alice C. [Cassandra Zirkle] Hinkle Mrs. Bettie Zirkle Mrs. Maggie Hinkle Florence Zirkle Mrs. Lee Bradshaw Mrs. Sallie [Ann Bell] Franklin Miss Laura Hinkle Mrs. Emma Massongal Miss Kate Mcguire Mrs. Lula Coile	J. P. [John Pennywitt] Zirkle H. S. Bradshaw S. R. [Samuel Richard] Alexander R. S. Bradshaw John M. [McNitt] Alexander
Class #4 Taught by G. A. Zirkle	Class #5 Taught by Mrs. Almira McMurray	Class #6 Taught by John C. Bradshaw Sallie Bradshaw Annabelle McMurray
Frank [Ashley] Bradshaw Ersey Alexander Oakley Bradshaw Eddie [William Edward] Bradshaw Rufus Cotter Bob [Lea] Bradshaw Frank [Adam] Newman	Arlen [Weihl] Bradshaw Jimmie [James Crawford] Bradshaw Sam McMurray Charley Bradshaw John Lyon William Collier Harvey Barbey Rankin Monroe	Fannie Miller Sue E. Newman Susie Biddle Annie Holdman Jinnie Newman Jacie Patton Mintie Barbee Florence Lowe Kate Collier Nancie Corbet

Class #7 Taught by Mrs. Belle Bradshaw	Class #8 Taught by Mrs. Mary Bradshaw	
Clide [Park] Bradshaw Henry L. Bradshaw George [W.] McMurray Earnest Bradshaw Luther [Lee] Belle Henry Darr Bob Cotter	John McMurray Katie Bradshaw Flora [May] Bradshaw Virginia [Elizabeth] Zirkle Jimmie Barbee George [A.] Bell Fanny Love Kate Newman Kate Patton Paul Zirkle Milton Newman Sammie Collier Bob Zirkle Mary Massongill Thom Massongoll Jimmie Barbee	

Mount Horeb 1885

Class #1 Taught by R. D. Rankin	Class #2 Taught by A. T. Bradshaw	Class #3 Taught by Jos. C. Bradshaw
W. P. Bradshaw S. R. [Samuel Richard] Alexander G. A. Newman I. A. [Isaac Anderson] Coile John P. Zirkle Bradley Bettis John M. [McNitt] Alexander Ebert Bettis George [W.] Franklin W. A. [William A.] Mathis Rev. T. R. [Thomas Rankin] Bradshaw	Mrs. Hannah Hinkle Miss Kate Mcguire Miss Maggie Hinkle Mrs. Lula [Luella May] Coile Mrs. Lizz T. Newman Miss Alice C. Zirkle Miss Sallie Bradshaw Mrs. Almira McMurray Miss Kate Franklin Miss Ella Newman Miss Mollie McMurray Mrs. Lee A. Bradshaw	Frank [Adam] Newman Frank A. Bradshaw W. E. [Walter Erskine] Alexander Sam [Samuel Richard] Alexander

Class #4 Taught by John C. Bradshaw	Class #5 Taught by H. S. Bradshaw	Class #6 Taught by Mrs. Sallie Franklin
Sallie Bradshaw Ann Belle McMurray Fannie Miller Nancy Corbet Susie Biddle Jinnie Newman Miss Sue Newman Ella Alexander Jacie Patton Florence Lowe	Ruffus Cotter O. J. Bradshaw Eddie Bradshaw Bob Bradshaw	Sam McMurray Jimmie [James Crawford] Bradshaw A. W. [Arlen Weihl "Arley"] Bradshaw Charlie [Charles Cleton] Bradshaw Jhan [John] Lyon Kate Franklin

Class #7	Class #8	
Taught by Mrs. Belle Bradshaw	Taught by Mrs. Mary Bradshaw	
George [W.] McMurray	John McMurray	
Henry Darr	Julia Smith	
Clide [Park] Bradshaw	~~Fanny Love~~	
Bob Cotter	Mary Massongall	
Henry L. Bradshaw	Thomas Massongall	
Earnest [N.] Bradshaw	Flora Bradshaw	
Fannie Love	Katie Bradshaw	
Lou Cannon	Olly Patton	
~~Bennie Mathis~~	Willie Denton	
~~Harvey Mathis~~	`Josie Bradly	
	B. Wallace McMurray	

Mount Horeb 1886

Class #1	Class #2	Class #3
Taught by R. D. Rankin	Taught by G. A. Newman	Taught by Jos. C. Bradshaw
T. R. [Thomas Rankin] Bradshaw	Miss Maggie Hinkle	~~J. H. Zirkle~~
John P. Bradshaw	Mrs. Hannah Hinkle	S. R. [Samuel Richard] Alexander
John C. Bradshaw	Miss Sallie Bradshaw	F. A. [Frank Ashley] Bradshaw
W. A. [William] Mathis	Mrs. Almira McMurray	W. E. [Walter Erskine] Alexander
William Barbee	~~Mrs. Lula Coile~~	F. A. [Frank Adam] Newman
A. T. Rankin	Miss Ella Newman	Bradley Bettis
	Miss Kate Franklin	H. S. Bradshaw
	D. M. Coile	George Zirkle
	Mrs. Mike Denton	

Class #4	Class #5	Class #6
Taught by George [W.] Franklin	Taught by I. A. Coile	Taught by Mrs. Sallie [Ann Bell] Franklin
Sallie Bradshaw	Eddie Bradshaw	
Annbelle McMurray	Bob E. [Lea] Bradshaw	A. W. [Arley Weihl] Bradshaw
~~Susie Biddle~~	Rufus Cotter	Sam McMurray
Fannie Miller	Oakley Bradshaw	Charlie Bradshaw
Sue Newman	Harvey Barbee	Jimmie Bradshaw
Florence Lowe	Rankin Monrowe	John Lyon
Belle Mathis	J. A. Love	
Annie Haldman	John Love	

Class #7	Class #8	Class #9
Taught by Mrs. Belle Bradshaw	Taught by Mrs. Mary Bradshaw	Taught by ~~Mrs. Leanna Bradshaw~~
Flora Bradshaw	~~John Smith~~	Hanna Hinkle
Mrs. Emma Masingill	Dave Newman	Katie Bradshaw
Kate Newman	John McMurray	Nellie [A] Alexander
Mrs. Sarah Bradshaw	[Benjamin] Wallace McMurray	Ralph Bradshaw
Susie Biddle	~~Milton Newman~~	Estella Coile
Jinnie Newman	Mack [Calvin] Franklin	Cora Bettis
Katie Barbie	Ollie Patton	Ore Denton
Mrs. George Zirkle	Thomas Massengill	Mary Barbee
Virginia Zirkle		Julia S. Miller
Lula Cannon		
Jinnie Newman		

Class #10	Class #11	Class #12
Taught by J. P. Zirkle	Taught by Mrs. Emma Massingill	Taught by M. McMurray
Henry Darr	Lou Cannon	Luther Love
Henry L. Bradshaw	Mintie Barbee	Walter Love
Earnest Bradshaw	Jennie Barbee	Hubert Hendricks
George [W.] McMurray	Fannie Love	Milton Newman
Clide [Park] Bradshaw	Lizzie Datsan	William "Willie" Barbee
Bob Cotter	Mary Massingill	Eddie Barbee
Harvey Mathis		Porter Barbee
Paul Zirkle	(Class broken up)	William Barbee, Senior
Bob Zirkle		Jimmie Barbee

Class #13		
Taught by George Zirkle		
Paul Zirkle		
Henry Bradshaw		
Clide [Park] Bradshaw		

Mount Horeb 1887

Class #1	Class #2	Class #3
Taught by R. D. Rankin	Taught by G. A. Newman	Taught by Jos. C. Bradshaw
T. R. Bradshaw	Miss Maggie Hinkle	S. R. [Samuel Richard]
John P. [Prigmore] Bradshaw	Mrs. Almira [Minerva Rankin]"	Alexander
W. P. Bradshaw	McMurray	W. E. [Walter Erskine]
John C. Calvin] Bradshaw	Mrs. Lula [Newman] Coile	Alexander
W. A. Mathes	Miss Ella Newman	F. A. [Frank Adam] Newman
A. T. [Andrew Thomas Hood]	D. M.(W.?) Coile	George Zirkle
Bradshaw	Mrs. McMurray	R. B. Bettis
J. F. McCready		

Class #4	Class #5	Class #6
Taught by George [W.] Franklin	Taught by I. A. Coile	Taught by Mrs. Sallie Franklin
Sallie Bradshaw		
Annie McMurray	Eddie Bradshaw	A. W. [Arley Weihl] Bradshaw
Fannie Miller	Bob E. [Lea] Bradshaw	Sam McMurray
Sue [Ella] Newman	Rufus Cotter	Charlie Bradshaw
		Jimmie Bradshaw
		John Lyon

Class #7	Class #8	Class #9
Taught by Mrs. Belle Bradshaw	Taught by J. P. Zirkle	Taught by George Zirkle
Flora [May] Bradshaw		Paul Zirkle
Kate Newman	Henry Darr	Henry [Lyle] Bradshaw
Mrs. Sarah [Malinda Rankin]	Earnest [N.] Bradshaw	Clide [Park] Bradshaw
Bradshaw	George McMury	
Susie Biddle	Bob Zirkle	
Jinnie Newman	Bob Cotter	
Virginia Zirkle		
Lou Cannon		

Class #10	Class #11	
Taught by Mrs. Mary Bradshaw	Taught by-Miss-Hanna Hinkle	
John Smith		
John McMurray	Nellie [A.] Alexander	
[Benjamin] Wallace McMurray	Estella Coile	
Ollie Patton		
Willie Denten	Cora Bettis (moved in March)	
Milton [Mack] Newman	Brox Zirkle	
David Newman	Louis Zirkle	

Mount Horeb 1887 [1888]

Class #1 Adult	Class #2 Adult	Class #3 Adult
Taught by T. R. Bradshaw	Taught by Jos. C. Bradshaw	Taught by Geo. Franklin
Mrs. Almira McMurray		
J. M. [James Moore] McMurray	Sam [Samuel Richard] Alexander	Sallie Bradshaw
Maggie Hinkle	W. E. [Walter Erskine] Alexander	Annie McMurray
L. M. Coile	J. P. Zirkle	Fannie Miller
B. F. Stoner	Frank [Adam] Newman	Sue Newman
N. D. Bettis	J. F. McCready	
Mrs. Alice Zirkle	Frank [Ashley] Bradshaw	
Annie Holman	H. S. Bradshaw	
Pam Carden		
Class #4 Adult	Class #5 Adult	Class #8 Adult
Taught by R. C. Rankin	Taught by Sallie [Ann Bell]	Taught by George Zirkle
	Franklin	Mrs. Sallie Bradshaw
John P. Bradshaw		Mrs. Horace Zirkle
John C. Bradshaw	Arlie [Weihl] Bradshaw	Mrs. Lee Bradshaw
John H. Alexander	Sam McMurray	Mrs. Emma Massingill
H. A. Newman [Hugh Alexander]	James Bradshaw	Mrs. B. F. Stoner
	John Line [Lyon]	Mollie Newman
		Mary Newman
		Laura Hinkle
Class #7 Intermediate	Class #8 Adult	Class #13 Intermediate
Taught by Miss Belle Bradshaw	Taught by D. M. Coile	Taught by G. A. Newman
Mary Massengill	Rufus Cotter	Paul Zirkle
Jinnie Newman	Robert Bradshaw	Henry [Lyle] Bradshaw
Susie Biddle	Eddie Bradshaw	Clyde [Park] Bradshaw
Effie Huff	Mc. Franklin	
Lou Cannon	Q. D. [Quince David] Bradshaw	
Virginia Zirkle	W. R. Edger	
Cate Newman	S. R. Hinkle	
Emma Miller		
Class #10 Intermediate	Class #11 Primary	Class #12 Primary
Taught by G. P. Bradshaw	Taught by Mrs. Mary Bradshaw	Taught by-Miss-Hannah Hinkle
	Oliver Patton	Estella Coile
Henry Darr	Willie Denton	Emma C. Bradshaw
Bob Zirkle	Mack [Calvin] Franklin	Nellie [A.] Alexander
Earnest Bradshaw	Josie Bradley	Vinie Cannon
George McMury	Sam Lee Newman	Brax Zirkle
	Thomas Massengill	Ora Denton
	John McMurray	Louis Zirkle
	Wallace McMurray	Mattie [Lee] Newman
	Dave Newman	Lucy Newman
	Milton [M.] Newman	Ralph Bradshaw

]The following information was written in the back of the Sunday School Record book. It was written in pencil and some of it was very light and hard to read.]

For the Record of any Facts of Special Interest
in the Sunday School during the year.

April 20th 1884

Deligates [*sic*] elected to the S. S. Convention R. D. [Richard Duffield] Rankin, I. A. [Isaac Anderson] Coile , H. S. [Harvey Smith[Bradshaw. Deligates went to the Co. S. S. Convention R. D. Rankin, I. A. Coile. Deligate [sic] elected to the State Convention to be held at Greenville. D. M. Coile. Went to the Convention June 22. Motion made and carried to supply the school with catechisms. Delegates elected to the S. S. Convention to be held at New Market May first and second 1885. A. T. Bradshaw & Zirkle (?), J. P. [John Pennywitt] Zirkle and wife—deligate [sic] went to the Convention. A. T. [Andrew Thomas Hood] Bradshaw & wife Delegate Elected to S. S. Convention be held at Mossy Creek Oct ___ '86.

D. M. Coile & wife.

May 2, 1886

Deligates elected to the S. S. Convention to be held at Wesley's Chapel. Rev. T. R. [Thomas Rankin] Bradshaw, I. A. [Isaac Anderson] Coile, D. M. Coile, Mrs. Belle Bradshaw, G. A. [George Arthur] Newman, H. S. Bradshaw, -- Deligates [sic] went to the convention D. M. Coile, Rev. J. R. Bradshaw. Deligates [sic] elected to the state convention Rev. T. R. Bradshaw & D. M. Coile July 25. Moved and seconded to suspend. The constitution & by laws and to elect an assistant Supt. Motion to elect by acclamation carried.

D. M. Coile elected assistant supt.

Aug. 1

Article 3rd of constitution & by-laws was read by I. A. [Isaac Anderson] Coile. Motion to amend. Article third of con.-- & by-laws. Carried. Motion to appoint a committee of three to amend the constitution & by-laws. Carried.

Committee appointed: John C. Bradshaw, George Franklin, and I. A. Coile. Report of committee, adopted.

Mount Horeb Oct. 17, 1886. Deligates [sic] elected to attend the convention which will be held in this church Oct. 21 and 22, 1886

Secretary's Record (1922-1923)

Myer's Paramount, No. 1
Space for Fifteen Classes
1913
Published by
Meyer & Brother
77 W. Washington Street
Chicago, ILL.

March 26, 1922 to March 25, 1923
Mount Horeb Sunday School

of Mount Horeb, Tennessee
Grace Brotherton Secretary

Annual Report of attendance and offering

For the year beginning March 26, 1922 and ending March 25, 1923

Enrollment at the beginning of the year 38
Number in Cradle Roll Dept.   12
New classes organized during the year   1
Total contributions for the year $55.57
Total expenditure for the year $46.67

On March 26, 1922 attendance 30 and March 18, 1923, 16 pupils
and average of 20.7 each Sunday, with five Sundays without any school.
Total attendance for the year 1080.

Total contributions $52.03,
an average of 4.7 cents per each present

Last year total attendance 1356 with an average of 26.
Only one Sunday missed during year.
Total contributions $61.72 and average of 4½ cents each.

John Garber J. R. Garber, Supt.
M. C. Franklin Assist. Supt.
Grace Brotherton, Sec.

Mount Horeb 1922-1923

`Class #1	Class #2	Class #3
Mrs. M. C. [Mac Calvin] Franklin [Effie Belle Blackburn], teacher	Mrs. J. R. [Joseph R.] Lyle [Luella M. Bettis] , teacher	Mrs. Sallie [Ann Bell] Franklin, teacher
Frances [M.] Lyle	Fred Franklin	Mrs. G. M. Lyle [Ella Mae Cutts]
Hal Dean Franklin	Lucille Bradshaw	
Isaac Hinkle	Marguerite Stoner	Mrs. John [R.} Garber
Lyle Bradshaw	Mildred Rankin	Mrs. M. M. [Milton Mack] Newman
Robert [Lyle] Miller		Mrs. J. J. [Jonathan James] Rankin [Mable Garber]
Charlotte Stoner		Mrs. Ralph Miller
		Mrs. Ema Bradshaw
		Mrs. Cutts
Class #4	Class #5	
Mrs. G. L. [George Lee] Brotherton [Julia] , teacher	J. R. Lyle, teacher	
	M. C. Franklin	
Elda McMurray	B. C. [Benjamin Casswell] Rankin	
Ruby Rankin	W. P. Bradshaw	
Grace Brotherton	John Garber	
Paul Rankin	Ralph Miller	
Richmond Bartley	H. L. [Harry Lee] Lyle	
Quince [David] Brotherton	G. M. [George Mack] Lyle	
George Brotherton	E. C. [Ephraim Cawood] Bradshaw	
	M. M. Newman	
	Rev. Broady	

The annual meeting of the Mount Horeb Sunday School was called to order by Supt. G. M. [George Mack] Lyle, March 26th 1922. After the reading of the minutes and report of the secretary the following officers were elected – John [R.] Garber superintendent, M. C. [Mac Calvin] Franklin assistant Superintendent. Grace Brotherton secretary and treasurer, with Lucille Bradshaw assistant. Miss Ruby Rankin was elected organist and Mrs. G. L. [George Lee] Brotherton [Julia] and Miss Lucille [Henry] Bradshaw assistants. The meeting adjourned to meet the last Sunday in March 1923.

Grace Brotherton, Sec.

The annual meeting of Mount H. was called to order by M. C. Franklin assistant Sup. March 27, 1923. After the reading of the minutes and report of Sec. and Treas. the following Officers were elected. M. M. [Milton Mack] Newman Supt., M. C. Stoner assist. Supt. I. D. Brotherton, Sec and Treas., Fred Franklin, Second Sec. and Treas., Lucille Bradshaw organist. All others that play asst. Org.

Adjourned until last Sunday in March 1924.

[Informal notation about offerings]

March 25, 1923, Clat p3 c16,	2.15
(April 22 c. 15 pupils)	6.20
	6.45
Contribution by [Rev.] Mr. Broady for missions	1.00

M. M. N. paid,   March 25, 1923

Sabbath School Lesson Guide

A series of small books was found in the Mount Horeb cabinet that was apparently used as a guide for the Sabbath School lessons. The hard back book measures five and a quarter tall and three and a quarter wide. "Rankin" is written on the inside cover of one. This book has 39 lessons and 133 pages. The beginning of Lesson 1 is given below. It mainly consists of a list of questions for each lesson.

UNION QUESTIONS;

OR

QUESTIONS ON SELECT PORTIONS OF SCRIPTURE,

FROM THE

OLD AND NEW TESTAMENT

Written for the American Sunday School Union, and Revised by the Committee of Publication.

Vol. III

Embracing the History of the Patriarchs

Philadelphia:

American Sunday school Union

No. 146 Chestnut Street

Copyright 1834

By Paul Beck, Jr., Treasurer

UNION QUESTIONS,

Lesson I.

The Creation

Genesis I. 1-13

What is the first book of the Bible called?

What is the meaning of the word *Genesis*?[111]

Who wrote the book of Genesis?

What other parts of the Bible were written by Moses?

What are these five books call? (*Pentateuch or Five Books*)

From whence did Moses get his knowledge of all these things 2 Tim. iii. 16.

---

[111] See the *Bible Dictionary*, published by the American Sunday School Union, words Generation and Bible, where a full explanation is given, together with an entire History of the Bible.

Chapter 6

Property Deeds

Transcribed and abstracted by Hazel Timblin Townsend, 2016

Overview

A torn and fragile paper was found in the Mount Horeb Minute Book Volume III. In places where tape had been holding it together, the words were difficult or impossible to read. It gave information about three deeds pertaining to the church and school property but it appears that this particular document was never recorded. There is no exact date or signature. Was this a summary of three deeds or a rough draft of a deed that was to be recorded? The three deeds referenced are abstracted below.

1842

Book W, p. 578-579, Courthouse, Dandridge, Jefferson County, Tennessee, 1842
Richard D. Rankin[112] & Richard Bradshaw[113] Deed to James Newman[114] Chairman
Registered 14th March A. D. 1842
This Indenture made the 26th day of February in the year of our Lord one thousand eight hundred forty two. They and Wittnesses [*sic*] Richard D. Rankin and Richard [Ammon] Bradshaw of the County of Jefferson and the State of Tennessee of the one part and James Newman Chairman of the Board of Common School Commissioners of District No. 25 and James Newman Chairman of the Board of Trustees of the Presbyterian Congregation or Church all of the County of Jefferson and State aforesaid of the other part...said Richard D. Rankin and Richard Bradshaw for and in consideration the love and esteem they have...for the encouragement and education of youth and the prosperity of Zion and the cause of Religion...convey unto the said James Newman Chairman...and their successors in office...Land for the use of said School District as a School house and for the purpose of a Meeting House...Rankin lot...from road near the School House and Meeting House Which are now one...estimated to contain two acres and twenty poles. Said Bradshaw's lot...estimated to contain Two Acres. The first described tract...including said Meeting house and school house road...Bradshaw lot is intended...for the use of a grave yard or burying ground...In Witness thereof the said Richard D. Rankin and the said Richard Bradshaw have herein set their...Seals this day &...hence. Written, signed, sealed and delivered in the presence of
Signed: Richard D. Rankin (seal)   Richard Bradshaw (seal)
...before said John N. Lunken (?) and John P. Bradshaw

---

[112] Richard Duffield Rankin (1800-1890), son of Richard Rankin (1756-1827), the settler.
[113] Richard Ammon Bradshaw (1788-1872), son of John Bradshaw (1742-1818), the settler.
[114] James Newman (1798-1879) was the son of John Newman Sr. and Nancy Franklin. The wife of James was Isabella Rankin, daughter of Thomas Rankin II and Jennet Bradshaw.

Rec'd March 11th 1842 at 2 o'clock P.M.

State of Tennessee, Jefferson County:

A Deed of Gift from Richard D. Rankin and Richard Bradshaw to James Newman Chairman of the Board of Common School Commissioners of District No. 25 and Chairman of the Board of Trustees of the Presbyterian Congregation or Church for…a lot of Land two acres and twenty poles the other lot containing two acres…this 26th day of February A. D. 1842 was presented before me Joseph Hamilton Clerk of the County Clerk of Jefferson acknowledged…Richard D. Rankin and Richard Bradshaw the Bargainers With whom I am personally acquainted and acknowledged the same to be their lot and land for the purpose therein contained Witness my hand at Office in Dandridge the 5th day of March A. D. 1842.

Joseph Hamilton, Clerk of Jefferson County, Deputy James Fieldin [sic]

1851

Book 2, page 559, 1851

R. D. Rankin & Richard Bradshaw deed to James Newman Chairman of Common School C. & Chairman of Board of Trustees of Congregation of Horeb Church for 6 acres 130 poles of land. Registered February 21, 1851

This indenture made this Seventeenth day of February in the year of our Lord One thousand eight hundred fifty one by and between Richard D. Rankin and Richard Bradshaw of the County of Jefferson and state of Tennessee of the one part and James Newman Chairman of the Board of Common School Commissioners of District 25 and…said James Newman Chairman of the Board of Trustees of the Presbyterian Congregation…at Mt. Horeb, all of the County of Jefferson….Witnessed that the said Richard D. Rankin and Richard Bradshaw…convey unto the said James Newman…and their successors…land for the use of said school and for the purpose of a meeting house for the Congregation…Estimated to contain four acres said bounds including a lot of land of two acres donated on the 26th day of February 1842. the first lot by Rankin includes the meeting house / school house where they now stand and the lot conveyed by Bradshaw includes the lot where the grave yard is situated also where it is now intended raise / build a new meeting house…In Witness thereof…Richard D. Rankin and…Richard Bradshaw have hereunto set our hands and affixed our seals the day and year first above written. (Signed) Richard D. Rankin (seal), Richard Bradshaw (seal)

Signed Sealed and delivered in the presence of us

Attest: Joseph C. Bradshaw, Joseph R. Newman

State of Tennessee, Jefferson County

Presently appearing before me James Fuller Clerk of the County Court of Jefferson Joseph C. Bradshaw and Joseph R. Newman subscribing witness to the within named Deed who being first sworn depose and say that they are acquainted with Richard D. Rankin and Richard Bradshaw, the bargainers, and that they saw them sign and Execute the same upon the day it bears. Witness my hand at office in Dandridge this 21st day of February A. D. 1851. James Fuller, Clerk of Jefferson County

Rec'd February 26th 1851 at 1 o'clock P.M.

1871

Book 10, page 702, DEED from Richard Bradshaw to John P. Bradshaw115
Registered Oct. 5, 1871

This Indenture made and entered into this 25th of September in the year of our Lord one thousand eight hundred and seventy one by and between Richard [Ammon] Bradshaw of Jefferson County Tennessee of the first part and John P. [Prigmore] Bradshaw of said County and State of the second part...Richard Bradshaw for and in Consideration of the Love and affection he hath...for the said John Bradshaw asks as the son of the said Richard Bradshaw for and...of the dutiful and filial care...and Maintenance which the said John P. hath given and extended to the said Richard who is old and unable to provide for his own support hath...convey unto the said John P. Bradshaw all the Land wherever situated not heretofore...conveyed that is included in...a consolidation Grant for eight hundred and eighty eight (888) acres of Land made to the said Richard Bradshaw by the state of Tennessee on the 31st day of August 1839 the number of acres of Land herein Conveyed...to be about fifty-five to the Same more or less. Also the said Richard Bradshaw...convey unto the Said John P. Bradshaw the Missionary intent which the said Richard hath in...a Small piece...of land heretofore Conveyed...for religious and educational purposes being the tract...where the Mount Horeb Church and School house stands...in the Mount Horeb tract of Land all of which lie in 9th Civil District of Jefferson County Tennessee adjoining the Lands of Wm. Massengill heirs Richard H. Poradsh heirs John P. Bradshaw and others the said Richard Bradshaw doth...convey unto the said J. P. Bradshaw...

And...the said Richard Bradshaw both for himself his heirs...doth covenant to and with the said John P. Bradshaw that he is Lawfully...Right to convey the same in the manner and...to the conditions and rights as here before set and the said Richard doth further Covenant to and with the said John P. Bradshaw that he and his heirs will forever defend the title to said several pieces...and the said Richard doth further agree...said John P. Bradshaw May cause the aforementioned...Land to be Surveyed shall...be...a part of this deed of conveyance...Richard Bradshaw hath hereunto affixed his signature...Richard Bradshaw

Ack 29 Sept 1871 at 11 o'clock a.m.   Attest: Benj. Zirkle, H. Tipton (?)

State of Tennessee, Jefferson County

Personally appeared before me James M. Nicholson Clerk of the County Court of said county the within named Bargain with whom I am personally acquainted who acknowledges that he executed...for the purposes therein contained

Witnessed my hand at office in Dandridge this 29 day of September 1871 Recorded in Deed Book page 812,   James M. Nicholson, Clerk

Rec'd for Registration Sept. 29 1871 at 4 o'clock pm
W. M. Hill Registrar

---

115 John Prigmore Bradshaw (1810-1896), son of Richard Ammon Bradshaw and grandson of John Bradshaw, the settler.

1889

On the 26, Feb. 1842 Richard D. Rankin[116] and Richard [Ammon] Bradshaw[117] executed a deed of dedication of a lot of land each to James Newman[118] in his two fold capacity as Chairman of the board of Common School Com. for District No. 25 and as Chairman of the board of trustees of the Presbyterian congregation or church, all of the County of Jefferson & State of Tennessee. Which deed was registered on the 14th of March 1842, in the Book W page 578. Registrar's Of. of same County. And on Feby. 17th 1851, the same parties…by joint deed conveyed to said Newman other parcels of land adjoining those of the above named deed…which was registered in same office on 27 Feby 1851, in Book No. 2, p. 559. And on 25th Sept. 1871, the said Richard Bradshaw by deed conveyed to the undersigned, John P. Bradshaw whatever interest he had in…two parcels above described, as having been conveyed by him to said James Newman in trust…in the words following: "…for religious and educational purposes, being the tract…where the Mount Horeb Church and school be situated." This deed was registered in Book No. 10 page 702 in said County's Register's office.…

And now on this (blank) day of (blank) 1889, recognizing the trusts aforesaid and wishing to perpetuate them, and to…make more permanent the objects and purposes thereof, and knowing how the property is now used and enjoyed by said Mount Horeb Presbyterian Church and congregation, and by the Common School Commissioners for educational purposes, I, John P. Bradshaw, [119] mentioned in said deed of Sept. 25, 1871 do now and hereby sell…to Thomas J. [John] Bradshaw,[120] as Chairman of the board of trustees of said Mount Horeb Presbyterian Church and also as Chairman of the Board of Common School Commissioners of the district in which said lands are located…to be held by him and his successors…for the uses…of the said Richard's two deeds of gift, and of this deed. And if said Church shall fail to appoint a successor to said Chairman of its board of trustees, and a trustee should become necessary in order to preserve its rights under this deed, the proper court is authorized to appoint one. And so, if the School Commissioners should fail to keep up a successor, the court can appoint a trustee to preserve their rights. I [unreadable word] this title against myself, my heirs and executors. Witness my hand, this (blank) day of (blank) 1889.

1986

In 1986 the Hebron Church deeded Mount Horeb Church to the Rankin Clan. The by-laws and deed were drawn up by an attorney in Jefferson City and the deed was transferred to the Rankin-Bradshaw Church Properties, Inc. Members of the board of Directors were Robert W. "Bob" Rankin, David Jones, Chris Davis, David Moore Rankin and Melanie Thomas Hodgson.

---

[116] Richard Duffield Rankin (1800-1890), son of Richard Rankin (1756-1827), the settler.

[117] Richard Ammon Bradshaw (1788-1872), son of John Bradshaw (1743-1818), the settler.

[118] James Newman (1798-1879) was the son of John Newman, Sr. and Nancy Franklin. The wife of James was Isabella Rankin, daughter of Thomas Rankin II and Jennet Bradshaw.

[119] John Prigmore Bradshaw (1810-1896), son of Richard Ammon Bradshaw.

[120] Thomas John Bradshaw (1838-1896), son of John Prigmore Bradshaw (1810-1896).

Chapter 7

Family Genealogies

Overview

The birth, marriage and death records are helpful for family genealogists. It is also of interest to discover the date of an ancestor's baptism and their involvement in church leadership.

The brief genealogies of the Rankin and Bradshaw families were included to help figure out relationships. The early families in Jefferson County were intertwined with each other and some of the same names are repeated in both genealogies. This information was found in various sources, such as birth and death records, cemetery and church records, census, deeds, wills, court files, family Bibles, family and county histories, *Ancestry.com* and *Find-a-Grave*. If you desire more detailed information about the genealogy, you may contact Hazel Townsend through the Rankin Reunion website at <http://www.Rankinreunion.org>.

Bradshaw-Rankin Family Bible (1805)
Transcribed by Hazel Timblin Townsend, 2015

The old 1805 family Bible was found by Donna Turner in 2015 in a box from the former home of Faye Rankin in Knoxville, Tennessee. She was the daughter of George Christopher Rankin, brother of Frank Walter Rankin and Harry Jay Rankin. They were the sons of Christopher Houston Rankin and Catherine Ruth Franklin Rankin of White Pine, Jefferson County, Tennessee. Houston was the son of Christopher Rankin who was the son of Thomas Rankin II and Jennet Bradshaw. In 2015 the Bible was given to Hazel Timblin Townsend of Greenville, South Carolina, a granddaughter of Frank Walter Rankin and daughter of Beulah Belle Rankin Timblin. The Bible was donated to the Calvin M. McClung Historical Collection of the East Tennessee Historical Center, 601 South Gay Street, Knoxville, Tennessee 37902.

The New Testament of Our LORD and SAVIOUR JESUS CHRIST, Translated out of the original Greek and with the former translations, diligently compared and revised by the special command of King James I. of England, eighth Philadelphia Edition, printed from the last Oxford Edition, Philadelphia, Printed by Mathew Carey, No. 122, Market Street, M.DCCC.V. [1805] (The front cover and the first 148 pages of the Bible are missing.)

Family Record

[page 677]
Marriages
Jane Conaway was married March 30th 1768 to Nathan Sellers
John [D.] Rankin was married February the 13th 1815 to Ruth McGuire.
Thomas [W.] Rankin was married March the 9th 1819 to Caroline M. T. Franklin.
Isabella Rankin was married February the 19th 1822 to James Newman
James Rankin was married to Sarah Randolph 4th Sept'm 1823.
Sinea Rankin was married to Aaron Newman Dec. 21st 1824.
Jane A. W. [Wright] Rankin was married to John P. Mathis Sept. 18th 1834
Christopher Rankin was married to Fanny Gilbraith Oct. 1st 1833.
Thomas [W.] Rankin second marriage to Sally Bare Dec. 18th 1834
Jennet Bradshaw was married February 24th 1789 to Thomas Rankin [II].[121]
Nancy Rankin to William Dunwody October 29th 1835.
William Rankin was married to Susan Kimbrough Feb. 16th 1836
Josiah E. [Emmons] Rankin was married November 22, 1838 to Mary [Emma] Gass.
Aaron Bogue Rankin was married 29th of October to Marjary [Copin] Lockhart 1840.

[Page 678]
Births
Jane Conaway born July 9th 1752
Jennet Bradshaw was born May 21st 1772
Nancy Rankin was born Sunday the 4th of April 1790.
John [D.] Rankin was born on Monday the 20th of February 1792.
Thomas [W.] Rankin was born on Monday the 6th of January 1794.
William Rankin was born on Tuesday the 2nd of August 1796.
James Rankin was born on Sunday the 7th of October 1798.
Isabella Rankin was born on Thursday the 11th of December 1800.
Conaway Rankin was born on Saturday the 6th of August 1803.
Sinea Rankin was born on Wednesday the 7th of May 1806.
Christopher Rankin was born on Thursday the 7th January 1809.
Samuel Emmons Rankin was born on Tuesday the 2nd of April 1811.
Jane [A.] Wright Rankin was born on Tuesday the 9th day of February 1813.
Josiah Emmons Rankin was born on Tuesday 12th of September 1815.
Aaron Bogue Rankin was born on Tuesday the 22nd of December 1818.
Hannah L. Adaline [Rankin] was born on March 26th 1842.

---

121 Bold print is to highlight the references to the original owners of the Bible.

[Page 679]
Births
Thomas [W.] Rankin was born on January 6th, 1794
Caroline M. T. Franklin was born February 14th 1800
Edwin C. [Clendenin] Rankin was born January 25th 1820
Creed W. [Wilson] Rankin was born September 25th 1821
Louisa G. Rankin was born March 18th 1834
Harriet E. Rankin was born February 11th 1826
Martha A. Rankin was born October 2_ 1827
Thomas C. Rankin was born September 18th 1829
Egbert E. Rankin was born June 28th 1831
Sarah Caroline [Rankin] was born October the 2nd 1835
Mary Emily [Rankin] was born 25th 1836
Katherine Jane [Rankin] was born December 24th 1834

Deaths
Samuel Emmons Rankin died on the 23rd of November 1812
Thomas Rankin [II] died August 3rd 1821 aged 57 years and 5 months
Jennett Rankin died January 14th 1824 aged 51 years and 8 months
Caroline M. T. Rankin died May 24th 1833 aged 33 y 5 m & 10 days
Sinea Rankin died 23rd March 1833
John [D.] Rankin died June 18th 1828
Nancy Dunwody [Dunwoody] died April 22nd 1842
Jane [A.] W. Mathes died September 4, 1847

[Page 680]
Deaths
Creed W. [Wilson] Rankin died May the 7th AD 1862
Thomas [W.] Rankin departed this life December the 2nd AD 1870 aged 75 years 11 monts [sic]
Christopher Rankin departed this life July the 1st 1881 aged 72 years & 5 monts [sic] 17 day

Great Bend, Kansas
Edwin C. Rankin died November the 9th 1892
Elizabeth E. Rankin departed this life April the 17th 1893
~~Edwin C. Rankin died November the 9 1892 at Great Bend, Kansas~~
~~Elizabeth E. Rankin his wife departed this life April the 17 1893~~

Chart of Descendants of Alexander Rankin
Four Generations
Hazel Timblin Townsend

Descendants of Alexander Rankin

Page 1

1-Alexander Rankin b. Cir 1628, Scotland, d. Cir 1690, Ireland
+Maria d. After 1703
    2-Alexander Rankin b. , Scotland
    2-John Rankin b. , Scotland
    2-William Rankin b. 1658, Scotland, d. 1720, Ulster, Ireland
      +Dorothy Black b. Cir 1670, Scotland, m. Scotland
        3-Jane Rankin
        3-Adam Rankin b. Jul 16, 1688, Stirlingshire, , Scotland, d. 1747, Lancaster Co., Pennsylvania, USA
          +Elizabeth Ray b. 1688, Londonderry Co., Ireland, UK, m. 1710, Ulster, Ireland, d. 1721, Philadelphia, Philadelphia, PA, USA
            4-Mary Catherine Rankin b. Cir 1705, Ireland, UK, d. 1756, Pennsylvania, USA
            4-James Rankin Sr. b. 1711, Londonderry, Londonderry Co., Ireland, UK, d. Oct 10, 1795, Montgomery Twp., Franklin Co., PA
          +Mary Steele m. Chester Co., PA, d. Sep 21, 1747, Lancaster Co., Pennsylvania, USA
            4-William Dunwoody Rankin b. 1726, Chester Co., PA, d. Nov 1792, Antrim Township, Franklin Co., Pennsylvania, USA
            4-Jeremiah Rankin b. 1733, Lancaster Co., Pennsylvania, USA, d. 1760, Lancaster Co., Pennsylvania, USA
            4-Esther Rankin b. Cir 1734, Chester Co. (later Lancaster Co.), PA, d. Bef Sep 9, 1822, Welch Run, Franklin Co., PA, USA
        3-John Rankin b. Cir 1690, Co. Donegal, Ireland, d. Jan 1749, Lancaster Co., Pennsylvania, USA
          +Jane McElwee b. 1689, Co. Derry, Ireland, m. Abt 1719, d. , Pennsylvania, USA
            4-Richard Rankin I. b. Abt 1720, Ulster, Ireland, d. Bef Dec 1792, Augusta Co., Virginia, USA
            4-Thomas Rankin I. b. Cir 1724, Londonderry, Derry Co., Ireland, d. 1812, Jefferson Co., TN
            4-Elizabeth Rankin b. Abt 1726
            4-Ann Rankin b. Abt 1728
            4-Margaret "Peggy" Rankin
            4-Catherine "Catrin" Rankin
            4-Rebecca Rankin b. Abt 1732
            4-Nancy Agnes Rankin b. Abt 1734
            4-Mary "Molly" Rankin
            4-Martha Rankin
        3-Hugh Rankin b. Abt 1692, Co. Derry, Ireland, d. Abt May 4, 1747, Lancaster Co., Pennsylvania, USA
          +Dunlap

Descendants of Alexander Rankin
Prepared by Hazel Timblin Townsend

This preceeding Rankin family chart was prepared by some unknown person. Roy M. Rankin made some additions and corrections to it over the years. However, it may still have some errors. The following chart came from my Legacy database. It might be helpful to make connections in the Rankin family. [122] *Family tradition says that Alexander Rankin was the ancestor of the Rankin settlers in East Tennessee and the Dumplin Valley area of Jefferson County but I have have found no documents to prove it. Not all of the multitude of descendants are included in this chart, mostly those associated with Jefferson County. The first three generations are in bold and underlined to make them easier to follow. The numbers represent the generation from the beginning ancestor Alexander who is 1. He is the father of 2-William, 2-Alexander and 2-John. William 2 is the father of 3-Adam, 3-John, 3-Hugh and 3-Jane. Their children are indicated with a 4. It is interesting to see the intertwining of the families.* [123]

1-**Alexander Rankin** b ca 1628 Scotland, d ca 1690 Ireland, m Maria d aft 1703
|--2-**William Rankin** b 1658 Scotland, d 1720 Ulster, Ireland, m Dorothy Black in Scotland, b ca 1670 Scotland
| |--3-**Adam Rankin** b Jul 16, 1688 Stirlingshire, Scotland, d May 4, 1747 Lancaster Co PA, m 1) 1710 Ulster, Ireland, Elizabeth Ray\May, b 1688, Derry, Ireland, d 1721 Philadelphia, PA
| | |--4- **Mary Catherine Rankin** b ca 1705 Ireland, d 1756 PA, m Joshua Cox b 1694 Ireland, d 1747 Lancaster Co, PA
| | | |--5-David Cox b 1735 Lancaster Co, PA, d 1818 Carroll Co, VA, m 1764 Augusta Co, VA, Margaret Ann McCown
, b 1742 Orange Co, VA, d 1811 Carroll Co, VA
| | | |--5-John Cox b 1735, d 1818 Ashe Co, NC
| | |--4- **James Rankin Sr.** b 1711, Derry, Ireland, d 1795 Franklin Co, PA, m Jane "Jean" Campbell, par William Campbell
| | | |--5-William Rankin b ca 1730 Lancaster Co, PA, d Franklin Co, PA, m 1774 Franklin Co, PA, Mary Stewart
| | | |--5-David Rankin b ca 1736 Lancaster Co, PA
| | | |--5-Ruth Ann Rankin b Lancaster Co, PA, d TN, m John Toole
| | | |--5-Esther Rankin b Lancaster Co, PA, m Samuel Smith
| | | |--5-Jeremiah Rankin b Lancaster Co, PA, d Franklin Co, PA
| | | |--5-James Rankin, Jr., m Mary McGinley

---

[122] Much of the information about the Jefferson County Rankin families was gathered by Reva E. Rankin Hammer who visited the Rankin families to copy Bible records during 1940-1960. She compiled a genealogy that was never published. However, much of Hammer's information was published by Hazel Timblin Townsend in *Rankin Roots in East Tennessee*. Additional information was added from various other records— Bibles, church, cemeteries, census, deeds, family records, historical books, marriage and death records, wills, *Ancestry.com* and *Find-A-Grave* online. Please be aware there may be errors in the information.

[123] Abbreviations are used to conserve space: b = born, bap = baptized, bur = buried, ca = circa, Cem = Cemetery, Ch = church, Co = county, d = died, Jeff = Jefferson, m = marriage, Mt = Mount, prob = probably, par = parents, state postal abbreviations used, sometimes birth and death dates combined with a dash, most month and day omitted to conserve space.

| | m 2) [124] Mary Steele m 1721 Chester Co, PA, d 1747 Lancaster Co, PA, par Rev. Steele

| | |--4-**William Dunwoody Rankin** b ca 1723 Chester Co, PA, d 1792 Franklin Co, PA, m ca 1742 Lancaster Co, PA, Mary Huston, b 1725 Chester Co, PA, d ca 1792 Franklin Co, PA, par. Archibald Ray Huston & Agnes Shaw

| | | |--5-William Jackson Rankin 1743-1826 PA, m 1) Elizabeth A. McGinley, m 2)[125] Susanna Huston

| | | |--5-David Rankin b ca 1745 PA d 1836 TN

| | | |--5-Betsy Rankin, m Robert Robison

| | | |--5-Jeremiah Rankin

| | | |--5- Rev. Rankin b 1762 Cumberland Co, PA d 1848 Center Co, PA, m Isabella Dundass

| | | |--5-Archibald Rankin b ca 1764 PA d 1849, m 1790 Franklin Co, PA Agnes Long 1770-1819

| | | |--5-James Rankin b 1766 Lancaster Co, PA d 1847 Lancaster Co, PA

| | | |--5-Dr. Adam Rankin, b 1770 Cumberland Co, PA d 1817 Henderson Co, KY, m 1792 Danville, Boyle Co, KY, Elizabeth Speed, b 1774 VA, d 1803 Henderson Co, KY

| | |--4-**Jeremiah Rankin** b 1733 Lancaster Co, PA, d 1760 Lancaster Co, PA, m 1754 Esther Rhoda Craig

| | | |--5- Rev. Adam Rankin b 1755 Cumberland Co, PA, d 1827 Philadelphia, PA, m 1783 Martha McPheeters, b 1763 Augusta Co, VA, d 1836 Maury Co, TN, par Alexander McPheeters & Jane Campbell

| | | |--5-William Rankin b 1757 Cumberland Co, PA, d 1798 KY, m 1783 Mary b 1765

| | | |--5-Jeremiah Rankin b ca 1758 Cumberland Co, PA, d Fayette Co, KY, m Nancy Kincaid, KY 1767-1853

| | | |--5-Thomas Rankin b 1765 Cumberland Co PA d 1808 Woodford Co, KY, m Mary "Polly" Young b 1760 Augusta Co, VA d bef 1822

| | | |--5-Mary "Polly" Rankin b Cumberland Co, PA

| | | |--5-Joseph Rankin

| | | |--5-Nancy Rankin

| | | |--5-John Rankin

| | |--4-**Esther Rankin** b ca 1734 Chester Co (later Lancaster Co) PA d bef Sep 9, 1822 Welch Run, Franklin Co PA, m 1754 William Dunwoody/Dinwiddie, Sr., Lancaster Co PA d 1796, Franklin Co PA, par James Dunwoody & Ann Barnett

| | | |--5-John Dunwoody b ca 1749 PA, m Frances

| | | |--5-William Dunwoody b ca 1750 PA, d 1776, m Agnes

| | | |--5-Joseph Dunwoody b ca 1752 PA, d 1824 Franklin Co PA

| | | |--5-Sam. Dunwoody, Lieut., b ca 1854 Cumberland Co PA d 1827 Greene Co TN, m ca 1783 Martha McClain, Cumberland Co PA b 1753 Cumberland Co PA d ca1840 Greene Co TN

| | | |--5-Mary Dunwoody b ca 1755 PA d 1794 TN, m William Baird

| | | |--5-Ann Dunwoody b ca 1760 PA d 1796 TN, m John Erwin

| | | |--5-James Dinwiddie b 1762 Franklin Co PA d 1846 Greene Co TN, m 1790 Jean Robinson, Lincoln Co NC b 1770 NC

| | | |--5-Adam Dunwoody/Dinwiddie b ca 1764, m Esther Moser

| | | |--5-Esther Dunwoody b ca 1768

| | | |--5-David Dunwoody b 1771 PA d 1856 PA, m 1798 Jane Van Lear, Franklin Co PA

---

[124] Mary Steele is the second wife of Adam Rankin.
[125] Susanna Huston is the second wife of William Jackson Rankin.

| |--3-**John Rankin** b ca 1690 Co Donegal, Ireland d 1749 Lancaster Co, PA, m ca 1719
Margaret Jane McElwee,[126] b 1689 Co Derry, Ireland, d PA.
| | |--4-**Richard Rankin I.** b ca 1720, Ulster, Ireland, d bef Dec 1792, Augusta Co, VA, m 1)
1746 Mary Agnes Douglas, b 1735, d bef 1788, m 2) Mary Duncan
| | | |--5-John Rankin b ca 1754, Cumberland Co PA, d probably Ohio, m Jemima Johnson
| | | |--5-James Rankin b ca 1756, Cumberland Co PA, d ca 1828 Rockingham Co VA, m ca
1783 Mary Kerr, Augusta Co VA, b ca 1758 Augusta Co VA, d 1808 Augusta Co VA
| | | |--5-Richard Rankin II, b ca 1757 Cumberland Co, PA, d ca 1828 Augusta Co, VA, m
1789 Mary Jane "Polly" Matthews, Augusta Co, VA, b 1767 Augusta Co, VA, d 1808
| | | |--5-Mary Rankin b ca 1758, PA, d Cumberland Co PA, m bef 1788 Thomas Johnson Sr.,
par George Johnson
5-Rachel Rankin, b ca 1765 Cumberland Co PA, m bef 1788 Richard Gilston III, PA
| | | |--5-Isaac Rankin b bef. 1766 Cumberland Co PA d Augusta Co VA, m 1789 Anne
Seawright, Augusta Co, VA
| | | |--5-Armstrong Rankin Sr. b aft 1767 Cumberland Co PA d 1804 Augusta Co VA, m 1801
Augusta Co VA, Mary "Polly" Ralston d aft 1835, par Samuel Ralston
| | | |--5-George Rankin b ca 1770 d bef Jun 19, 1792, Augusta Co, VA
| | | |--5-Joseph Rankin b ca 1772 d 1830 Augusta Co VA, m 1804 Augusta Co VA, Elizabeth
"Betsy" Cline d aft Feb 28, 1840
| | | |--5-Samuel Rankin b ca 1772 Cumberland Co PA d 1830 Augusta Co VA, m 1794
Augusta Co VA, Betty Jean Regan b ca 1771 d 1851
| | |--4-**Thomas Rankin I.** b ca 1724 Co Derry, Ireland d 1812 Jeff Co TN, bur Dandridge, Jeff
Co TN, m bef 1754 PA, Isabella Clendenin b ca 1725 PA d 1812 Jeff Co, TN, par John
Clendenin Sr. & Janet "Jane" Huston
| | | |--5-John Rankin b 1754 Cumberland Co, PA d 1829 Blount Co, TN,[127] m ca 1777 PA,
Martha Jane "Jenny" Waugh, par John Waugh
| | | | |--6-John M. Rankin b 1781 Cumberland Co PA, m 1801 Margaret "Peggy" Weir, Blount
Co TN
| | | | |--6-Isabella "Ibby" Rankin b bef 1780 TN d 1838 Blount Co TN, m Archibald Frow b
Ireland d 1829 Blount Co, TN
| | | | |--6-Jane "Jenny" Rankin, m 1820 James Duncan, Blount Co, TN
| | | | |--6-Martha "Patsy" Rankin m 1802 James Ware b 1785, d 1868 Cooper Co, MO
| | | | |--6-Samuel M. Rankin b ca 1797 PA, d 1884 Blount Co, TN, m 1824 Blount Co TN,
Mary A. Duncan d 1826 Blount Co TN, par John Duncan & Margaret Alexander
| | | | |--6-Mary "Polly" Rankin, m James Bradshaw b 1779, par John Bradshaw & Nancy
Agnes "Annie" Clendenin
| | | |--5-Richard Rankin b 1756 Allen Tp, Cumberland, PA d 1827 Jeff Co TN, m ca 1782
Jennett "Jane" Steele b 1764, prob Augusta Co, VA d 1846 Jeff Co TN, par Samuel Steele &
Margaret Campbell
| | | | |--6-Samuel Steele Rankin b 1784 TN d 1859 Adams Co, IL, m 1804 Jeff Co TN, Mary
"Polly" White 1782-1811 TN, par William White Jr. & Mary Johnson

---

[126] Some records say John Rankin's wife was Jane McElwee. In John Rankin's will, he names his wife, Margret Rinkin, and son, Thomas Rinkin, to be the executors. Did he marry twice or was her name Margaret Jane? (Dated Jan. 1, 1749, attested Feb. 25, 1749/50; *Will Book J*, Vol. 1, p. 211, Lancaster Co., Pennsylvania).
[127] Two years are given for John's death, 1825 and 1829. His will was dated Feb 10, 1826. The 1829 date was given in the *Roster of Soldiers and Patriots of the American Revolution Buried in Tennessee*, compiled by Lucy Womack Bates,1974, Tennessee Society, NSDAR.

| | | | |--6-Thomas Rankin b 1787 Jeff Co TN, d Louisville KY, m 1815 Augusta Co VA, Jane Cole

| | | | |--6-Isabella Rankin, m 1812 Alexander Biggs, Jeff Co, TN, 1789-1857

| | | | |--6-David Rankin b 1791 Jeff Co, TN, d 1814

| | | | |--6- Rev. John Thomas Rankin b 1793 Jeff Co TN d 1886 Lawrence Co, OH, m 1816 Washington Co, TN, Jane Gilfillen "Jean" Lowry, b 1795 Washington Co TN, d 1878 Osage Co, KS, par Adam Lowry & Julia Doak

| | | | |--6- Rev. William Clendenin Rankin b 1795 Jeff Co TN d 1889 Van Buren Co, Iowa, m 1815 TN, Katherine Gault 1785-1828, par. John Gault & Margery

| | | | |--6-James Gardner Rankin b 1797 Jeff Co TN d 1841 Indiana, m Sarah Gault

| | | | |--6-Richard Duffield Rankin b 1800 Jeff Co TN d 1890 Jeff Co TN, bur Mt. Horeb Cem, Jeff Co TN, m 1829 Monroe Co, TN, Nancy McClure 1811-1838

| | | | |--6-Hervey Rankin b 1802 Jeff Co, TN d ca 1802 Jeff Co, TN

| | | | |--6- Rev. Alexander Taylor Rankin b 1803 Jeff Co TN d 1885 Baltimore, MD, m 1829 Clemont Co, OH, Mary Merriweather Lowry b 1810 Washington Co TN d 1841 Fort Wayne, IN, par Adam Lowry & Julia Doak

| | | | |--6-Andrew Campbell Rankin b 1806 Jeff Co TN d 1828 Augusta Co, VA

| | | | |--6- Rev. Robert Henderson Rankin b 1810 Jeff Co TN d Montgomery Co, IN, m 1833 Ripley, Ohio, Eliza Rowe Lowry, 1808-1898, par Adam Lowry & Julia Doak

| | | |--5-Samuel Rankin b 1758 Cumberland Co, PA d 1834 Jeff Co TN, bur Mt Horeb Cem, m ca 1782 PA, Jane Isabelle "Ibby" Petty b 1764 PA d 1846 Jeff Co TN, bur Mt Horeb Cem

| | | | |--6-Lucy Rankin b 1784

| | | | |--6-Jane Isabelle "Ibbie" Rankin b 1785 VA d 1873

| | | | |--6-Elizabeth "Betsy" Rankin, m 1823 John Whittington, Jeff Co TN

| | | | |--6-Sarah Rankin b 1804 TN d 1883 Jeff Co TN, bur Mt Horeb Cem, Jeff Co TN, m John Newman Lockhart b 1802 VA d 1874 Jeff Co TN, bur Mt Horeb Cem, Jeff Co TN

| | | | |--6-Mary Rankin

| | | | |--6-John Rankin d bef 1828

| | | | |--6-Thomas Rankin d 1821, m 1821 Jeff Co TN, Sarah Elizabeth Ashmore b ca 1802

| | | |--5-William Rankin b 1759 Cumberland Co, PA d 1833 Greene Co, TN, bur Timber Ridge Ch Cem, Greene Co, TN, m 1787 Greene Co, NC/TN, Sarah L. Moore b 1763 Northampton Co, PA d 1850 Greene Co, TN, bur Timber Ridge Ch Cem, Greene Co, TN

| | | |--5-*Thomas Rankin II,* b 1764 Allen, Cumberland Co, PA d 1821 Jeff Co TN, bur Dandridge, Jeff Co TN, m 1789 Greene Co, TN, *Jennet Bradshaw*, b 1772 d 1824 Jeff Co TN, par **John Bradshaw & Nancy Agnes Clendenin**

| | | | |--6-Nancy Rankin b 1790 TN d 1842, m 1835 William Dunwoody b 1787 Greene Co d Greene Co, TN, par. Lieut. Samuel Dunwoody & Martha McClain

| | | | |--6-John D. Rankin b 1792 Jeff Co TN d 1828 Jeff Co TN, m 1815 Jeff Co TN, Ruth McGuire d ca 1827, TN, par Patrick McGuire & Catherine Prigmore

| | | | |--6-Thomas W. Rankin b 1794 NC/TN, d 1870, m 1819 Jeff Co TN, Catherine M. T. Franklin, b 1800 VA d 1833 Jeff Co TN, par Owen Franklin & Elizabeth Roper

| | | | |--6-William Rankin b 1796 Jeff Co TN d 1871 Jeff Co TN, bur Mt Horeb Cem, m 1836 Jeff Co TN, Susan Kimbrough b 1810 TN d 1876, bur Mt Horeb Cem

| | | | |--6-James Rankin b 1798 Jeff Co TN d 1824, m 1823 Sarah Randolph

| | | | |--6-Isabella Rankin, b 1800, Jeff Co, TN, d 1886, Jeff Co, TN, m 1822 Jeff Co, TN, Col. James Newman b 1798 VA d 1879 Jeff Co TN, bur Mt Horeb Cem, par John Newman Sr. & Nancy Franklin

| | | | |--6-Conway Rankin b 1803 Jeff Co, TN, d 1823

| | | | |--6-Sinea Rankin b 1806 Jeff, TN, d 1833 Jeff, TN, m 1824 Jeff, TN, Aaron Newman, b 1802 VA, d 1884 Jeff, TN, bur Mt Horeb Cem, par John Newman Sr. & Nancy Franklin

| | | | |--6-Christopher Rankin b 1809 Jeff Co, TN, d 1881 Jeff Co, TN, bur Hebron Ch Cem, m 1833 Jeff Co, TN, Frances George "Fanny" Gilbraith b 1816 Jeff Co, TN d Jeff Co, TN, bur Hebron Ch Cem, par James Gilbraith & Martha "Patsy" Hoskins

| | | | |--6-Samuel Emmons Rankin b 1811 Jeff Co, TN, d 1912

| | | | |--6-Jane A. Wright Rankin b 1813 Jeff Co, TN, d 1847, m 1834 Jeff Co, TN, Dr. John Pinckney Mathis, 1812-1870

| | | | |--6-Josiah Emmons Rankin b 1815 Jeff Co TN d 1893, bur Mt Horeb Cem, m 1838 Jeff Co TN, Mary Emma Gass b 1819 TN d 1883 Jeff Co TN, bur Mt Horeb Cem

| | | | |--6-Aaron Bogue Rankin b 1818 Jeff Co TN d 1884 Greene Co, Indiana, m 1840 Jeff Co TN, Marjary Copin Lockhart b 1820 TN d 1895 Greene Co, Indiana

| | | |--5-Jane Rankin b 1766, m William Gillespie, par John Gillespie

| | | |--5-Margaret Rankin b 1769, m 1791 Greene, TN, Samuel Harris d 1816

| | | |--5-James Rankin I, b ca 1770 Cumberland Co, PA d 1839 Morgan Co, IL, m 1799 Margaret Massey/Massie 1780-1864, par Edmund Massey/Massie and Mary Dabney Winston

| | | |--5-Ann Rankin b 1770 Allen, Cumberland Co, PA d Saint Clair Co, IL, m ca 1789 TN, Lionel Lacy b ca 1765 Buckingham Co, VA d 1816 Saint Clair Co, IL, par Elliot Lacy & Lois Brown

| | | |--5-Isabella Rankin b 1772 d ca 1807, m 1805 Jeff Co TN, Robert McCuistion b 1773 Jeff Co TN d 1834, par James McCuistion, Jr. & Catherine Jane Tennant

| | | | |--6-Thomas McCuistion b 1806 Jeff Co, TN

| | | |--5-Mary Rankin b ca 1775 d TN, bur Kingston, Roane Co, TN, m 1797 Jeff Co TN, Andrew McCuistion, b ca 1772 Jeff Co TN d 1834 Roane Co, TN, par James McCuistion, Jr. & Catherine Jane Tennant

| | | | |--6-James McCuistion b ca 1798 Jeff Co, TN, m 1818 Nellie Grace

| | | | |--6-Catherine McCuistion b 1800 Jeff Co, TN, d aft 1802, m 1830 James Kitchen, b 1778 VA

| | | | |--6-Jane McCuistion b 1802 Jeff Co, TN, d ca 1803

| | | | |--6-Thomas McCuistion b 1809 Jeff Co TN d 1895 Nacogdoches Co, TX, m 1829 McMinn Co, TN, Mary Ann Meals

| | | | |--6-Robert McCuistion b 1810 Jeff Co TN, m ca 1830 Annie Lankford, McMinn Co, TN, b ca 1811 VA

| | | | |--6-Rebecca B. McCuistion b ca 1806 Jeff Co TN, m ca 1835 Luallen Looney, b ca 1810 d ca 1845

| | | | |--6-Mary McCuistion b 1812 Jeff Co, TN, d ca 1830 McMinn Co, TN

| | | | |--6-David Rankin McCuistion b ca 1815 Jeff Co TN d ca 1883 TN, m ca 1835 McMinn Co, TN, Scythia "Cytha" Power, b ca 1817 KY d 1877 TN

| | | | |--6-Andrew J. McCuistion b 1816 Jeff Co TN d 1888 Benton Co, AR, m 1939 Roane Co, TN, Hannah S. Clapp Foust, b 1810 TN d Benton Co, AR

| | | |--5-Nancy Rankin b ca 1775 Allen, Cumberland, PA d Greene Co, TN, m 1797 Samuel White, Jeff Co TN, b ca 1775 Loudoun Co, VA, par William White Jr. & Mary Johnson

| | | | |--6-William Grant C. White b 1801 Jeff Co TN d 1870 Overton Co, TN, m ca 1820 Monroe Co, TN, Nancy Cooksey Dennis, b 1805 Caswell, NC, d 1889 Overton Co, TN

| | | | |--6-John L. White b 1804 Jeff Co TN d 1861 Morgan Co, IL, m ca 1825 Monroe Co, TN, Temperance "Tempy" Lyon, b 1810 Caswell, NC

| | |--4-**Elizabeth Rankin** b ca 1726, m Nicholson

| | |--4-**Ann Rankin** b ca 1728, m aft 1749, Samuel McClure

| | |--4-**Margaret "Peggy" Rankin,** m James Crockett
| | |--4-**Catherine "Catrin" Rankin,** m aft 1749, Hill
| | |--4-**Rebecca Rankin** b ca 1732, m aft 1749, McIntire
| | |--**4-Nancy Agnes Rankin** b ca 1734, m aft 1749, Stuart
| | |--4-**Mary "Molly" Rankin,** m bef 1849, William White, Sr. b ca 1710 PA
| | |--4-**Martha Rankin,** m John Waugh
| |--3-<u>**Hugh Rankin**</u> b ca 1692, Co Derry, Ireland, d ca 1747 Lancaster Co, PA, m Dunlap
| |--3-<u>**Jane Rankin**</u>
|--2-**Alexander Rankin** b Scotland
|--2-**John Rankin** b Scotland

Chart of Descendants of John Bradshaw

Descendants of Bradshaw

1-Bradshaw b. , Wales, Great Britain
+Unknown
    2-James Bradshaw
    2-Thomas Bradshaw
    2-John Bradshaw b. Mar 18, 1743, Wales, d. Sep 30, 1818, Jefferson Co., TN
    +Nancy Agnes "Annie" Clendenin b. May 1748, m. Cir 1773, Probably Cumberland Co., PA, d. Aug 1823, par. John
        Clendenin Sr. and Janet "Jane" Huston
        3-Eliza Beth Bradshaw b. Oct 24, 1770
        +Richard Grace
            4-Nellie Grace
            4-Sally Grace
        3-Jennet Bradshaw b. May 21, 1772, d. Jan 14, 1824, Jefferson Co., TN
        +Thomas Rankin II b. Mar 3, 1764, Allen, Cumberland, PA, USA, m. Feb 24, 1789, Greene Co.,
            Tennessee, USA, d. Aug 3, 1821, Jefferson Co., TN, USA, par. Thomas Rankin I. and Isabella
            Clendenin
            4-Nancy Rankin b. Apr 4, 1790, Tennessee, USA, d. Apr 22, 1842
            4-John D. Rankin b. Feb 20, 1792, Jefferson Co., TN, d. Jun 18, 1828, Jefferson Co., TN
            4-Thomas W. Rankin III b. Jan 6, 1794, North Carolina, USA, d. Dec 2, 1870
            4-William Rankin Sr. b. Aug 2, 1796, Jefferson Co., TN, d. Feb 24, 1871, (Mt. Horeb Cemetery,
                Jefferson Co., Tenn., USA)
            4-James Rankin b. Oct 7, 1798, Jefferson Co., TN, d. Aug 18, 1824
            4-Isabella Rankin b. Dec 11, 1800, Jefferson Co., TN, d. Dec 29, 1886, Jefferson Co., TN
            4-Conway Rankin b. Aug 6, 1803, Jefferson Co., TN, d. Dec 1823
            4-Sinea Rankin b. May 7, 1806, Jefferson Co., TN, d. Mar 23, 1833, Jefferson Co., TN
            4-Christopher Rankin b. Jan 7, 1809, Jefferson Co., TN, d. Jul 1, 1881, Jefferson Co., TN
            4-Samuel Emmons Rankin b. Apr 2, 1811, Jefferson Co., TN, d. Nov 23, 1812
            4-Jane A. Wright Rankin b. Jan 9, 1813, Jefferson Co., TN, d. Sep 4, 1847
            4-Josiah Emmons Rankin b. Sep 12, 1815, Mt. Horeb Comm., Jefferson Co., TN, USA, d. Dec
                29, 1893, (Mt. Horeb Cemetery, Jefferson Co., Tenn., USA)
            4-Aaron Bogue Rankin b. Dec 22, 1818, Jefferson Co., TN, d. May 15, 1884, Greene Co., IN
        3-John Bradshaw Jr. b. Oct 1774
        3-Francinea Bradshaw b. Aug 1775
        +McQuistion
        3-William Bradshaw b. Jan 7, 1778
        +Margaret Bingham m. Feb 6, 1797
        3-James Bradshaw b. Nov 13, 1779
        +Mary "Polly" Rankin , par. John Rankin and Martha Jane "Jenny" Waugh
        3-Samuel Bradshaw b. Sep 1, 1782
        +Dorcas Prigmore m. Aug 30, 1803, Jefferson Co., TN
        3-Christopher Bradshaw b. May 3, 1785
        +Mary Davis m. Sep 24, 1806, Jefferson Co., TN
        3-Richard Ammon Bradshaw b. Jan 15, 1788, NC (Now Jefferson Co., TN), d. Oct 3, 1872, Mt. Horeb
            Comm., Jefferson Co., TN, USA
        +Lydia Prigmore b. Oct 10, 1778, Pennsylvania, USA, m. Aug 4, 1809, Jefferson Co., TN, d. Nov 27,
            1853, (Mt. Horeb Cemetery, Jefferson Co., Tenn., USA), par. Joseph Prigmore and Ann Prigmore
            4-John Prigmore Bradshaw b. May 28, 1810, Tennessee, USA, d. Mar 15, 1896, (Mt. Horeb
                Cemetery, Jefferson Co., Tenn., USA)
            4-Joseph C. Bradshaw b. Aug 16, 1811, Tennessee, USA, d. Jul 4, 1897, Tennessee, USA

            4-Rev. Thomas Rankin "Tom" Bradshaw b. Jan 7, 1813, Tennessee, USA, d. Jul 4, 1899, (Mt.
                Horeb Cemetery, Jefferson Co., Tenn., USA)
            4-Richard Harden Bradshaw b. Mar 16, 1815, Jefferson Co., TN, d. Jan 7, 1863, Jefferson Co.,
                TN

            4-Nancy Ann Bradshaw b. May 17, 1817
        +Margaret Rawlings b. Jan 25, 1810, m. Abt 1854, d. Jan 19, 1867, (Mt. Horeb Cemetery, Jefferson Co.,
            Tenn., USA) (see Richard Ammon Bradshaw on page 1)
        3-Thomas Bradshaw b. 1793

Descendants of John Bradshaw

Compiled by Hazel Timblin Townsend

This chart may be helpful to make connections in the earlier generations of the Bradshaw family. Rankin and Bradshaw were early settlers in East Tennessee and the Dumplin Valley area of Jefferson County. Not all of the descendants are included in this chart, mainly those associated with Jefferson County. It is interesting to see the intertwining of the families.[128]

1-**John Bradshaw** b Mar 18, 1743 Wales, d Sep 30, 1818 Jefferson Co, TN, m Nancy Agnes "Annie" Clendenin b May 1748, m ca 1773 prob Cumberland Co, PA, d Aug 1823, par John Clendenin Sr. & Janet "Jane" Huston [129]

|--2-**Eliza Beth Bradshaw** b. Oct 24, 1770 m Richard Grace
| |--3-Nellie Grace m 1818 James McCuistion b ca 1798 Jeff Co, TN par Andrew McCuistion & Mary Rankin
| |--3-Sally Grace
|--2-**Jennet Bradshaw** b May 21, 1772, d Jan 14, 1824, Jeff Co, TN m Feb 24, 1789 Greene Co, TN, **Thomas Rankin II** b Mar 3, 1764 Cumberland, PA, d Aug 3, 1821, Jeff Co, TN, par Thomas Rankin I. & Isabella Clendenin
| |--3-Nancy Rankin b 1790 TN d 1842 m 1835 Wm. Dunwoody b 1787 Greene Co, NC d Greene Co, TN, par Lieut. Samuel Dunwoody & Martha McClain
| |--3-John D. Rankin b 1792 Jeff Co TN d 1828 Jeff Co TN, m Ruth McGuire 1815 Jeff Co TN d ca 1827 TN, par Patrick McGuire & Catherine Prigmore
| | |--4-Lucinda Harriet Rankin b 1815 Jeff Co TN d 1893 Jeff TN, m 1841 Jeff TN, Benjamin Francis Franklin Sr. b 1814 Jeff TN d 1876 Jeff TN, par John M. Franklin & Ann Dinwiddie
| | | |--5-John Rankin Franklin b 1842 Jeff Co, TN d 1845 Jeff Co, TN
| | | |--5-Thomas Patrick "Pad" Franklin b 1843 Jeff Co TN d 1913, m 1867 Sarah Emily Corbett 1845-1914 Jeff Co TN, par Col. Michael Montgomery Corbett & Nancy Dicky Gilbraith
| | | | |--6-Nancy Harriet "Nannie" Franklin b 1868 d 1887, bur Hebron Cem, Jeff Co, TN
| | | | |--6-Lurana Zemilee Franklin 1870-1940, bur Hebron Cem Jeff Co, TN
| | | | |--6-Ida Jane Franklin 1871-1958, bur Hebron Cem, Jeff Co, TN
| | | | |--6-Olen Howard Franklin 1873-1943, bur Hebron Cem Jeff Co, TN
| | | | |--6-Porter Estella "Stella" Franklin 1875-1936, bur Hebron Cem, Jeff Co, TN
| | | | |--6-Benjamin Francis Franklin 1878-1927
| | | | |--6-Patrick Montgomery Franklin 1880-1962, bur Mt. Horeb Cem, Jeff Co, TN
| | | | |--6-McDonald Franklin 1883-1884
| | | | |--6-Thomas Sawtell Franklin 1884-1975
| | | | |--6-John Montford Franklin 1886-1887, bur Hebron Cem, Jeff Co, TN

---

[128] Most of the information was found in the following types of records: Bibles, church, cemeteries, census, deeds, family records, historical books, wills. There could be errors in the information.

[129] Abbreviations are used to conserve space: b = born, bap = baptized, bur =buried, ca = circa, Cem = Cemetery, Ch = church, Co = county, d =died, Jeff = Jefferson, m = marriage, prob = probably, par = parents, state postal abbreviations used, birth and death years combined with a dash, month and day omitted to conserve space. Commas and periods often eliminated.

| | | |--6-Lucy Elgin Franklin 1890-1962, bur Hebron Cem, Jeff Co, TN
| | | |--5-Benjamin Francis Franklin Jr. 1845 Jeff Co, TN d 1926 bur Hebron Cem, Jeff Co, TN,
m 1867 Margaret Cordelia McMurray 1849-1929, bur Hebron Cem, Jeff Co, TN
| | | |--6-Lillie Emma Franklin 1868-1956, bur Hebron Cem, Jeff Co, TN
| | | |--6-Samuel Horace Franklin Sr. 1870-1956
| | | |--6-Charles W. [Walter] Franklin 1872-1873, bur Hebron Cem, Jeff Co, TN
| | | |--6-Hugh McCall Franklin 1874-1899, bur Hebron Cem, Jeff Co, TN
| | | |--6-Harriet Ann Franklin 1877-1958
| | | |--6-John Francis Franklin Sr. 1879-1973
| | | |--6-Howard Benjamin Franklin 1881-1964, bur Hebron Cem, Jeff Co, TN
| | | |--6-Nelle Ruth Franklin 1884-1978, bur Hebron Cem, Jeff Co, TN
| | | |--6-Nina Franklin 1886-1887, bur Hebron Cem, Jeff Co, TN
| | | |--6-Clarence McMurray Franklin b 1888
| | |--5-Nathan Hood Franklin b 1849, Jeff Co TN d 1923, bur Hebron Cem, Jeff Co TN, m 1)
1869 Sarah Jane "Jennie" Fain b 1847 Jeff Co TN d 1904, bur Hebron Cem, Jeff Co TN, par
Thomas Washington Fain & Nancy D. Rankin, m 2) 1906 Adda J. Rankin 1853-1914, bur
Hebron Cem, Jeff Co TN, par Robert L. S. Rankin & Louisa A. Devault
| | | |--6-Betty May Franklin 1874-1899, bur Hebron Cem, Jeff Co, TN
| | | |--6-Cora Washington Franklin 1876-1890, bur Hebron Cem, Jeff Co, TN
| | | |--6-Nanetta F. Franklin 1878-1879, bur Hebron Cem, Jeff Co, TN
| | | |--6-James Nicholas Ernest Franklin 1882-1961
| | | |--6-Robert Best Franklin 1885-1935, bur Hebron Cem, Jeff Co, TN
| | | |--6-Nancy Huldah "Nannie" Franklin b 1887 Jeff Co TN d 1965, bur Hebron Cem
| | |--5-Catherine Ruth "Kate" Franklin b 1852 Jeff Co TN d 1926 White Pine, Jeff Co TN, m
1874 Jeff Co TN, Christopher Houston Rankin b 1851 Jeff Co TN d 1932 White Pine, Jeff Co
TN, par Christopher Rankin & Frances George "Fanny" Gilbraith
| | |--5-George W. Franklin b 1854 Jeff Co TN d 1905 Mt. Horeb, Jeff Co TN, m 1) 1874
Julia E. Blackburn 1853-1879, par Thomas Snoddy Blackburn & Mary Louise Minnis, m 2)
1879 Sallie Ann "Sara" Bell 1859-1949, bur Hebron Cem, Jeff Co, TN
| | |--5-Lucinda Ann "Lucy" Franklin b 1857 Jeff Co TN d 1894 Cherokee, AL, m 1890 Jeff
Co TN, Wm. Martin Elgin b 1847 Jeff Co TN d 1913
| | |--5-Nancy Emma Franklin b 1859 Jeff Co TN d 1862, bur Mt. Horeb Cem, Jeff Co TN
| | |--5-Infant Franklin
| |--4-Catherine Ruth Rankin b 1817 Jeff Co TN d 1860, Dallas, TX, m ca 1836 Jeff Co TN,
George Washington Routh b 1813 Jeff Co TN d 1866 Dallas, TX
| |--4-Patrick McGuire Rankin b 1818 Jeff Co TN d 1902 Jeff Co TN, bur Mt. Horeb Cem, m
1840 Jeff Co TN, Louisa Jane Lockhart b 1822 Jeff Co TN d 1902, bur Mt. Horeb Cem, par
John Lockhart & Mary Coppock
| | |--5-John Patrick "Pad" Rankin b 1842 Jeff Co TN d 1915, bur Lebanon Cumberland Cem,
Jeff Co TN, m 1867 Jeff Co TN, Phoebe Ann Armentrout 1837-1904, bur Missouri
| | |--5-Mary Ann Rankin b 1843 Mt. Horeb Jeff Co TN d 1923 Mt. Horeb Jeff Co TN, m
1866 Jeff Co TN, Gideon W. Newman b 1839 TN d 1880 Jeff Co TN, par John "Black Jack"
Newman & Jane Kennedy Caldwell
| | |--5-Sarah Jane Rankin b 1844 Jeff Co TN d 1925, bur Hebron Cem, Jeff Co TN, m 1865
Jeff Co TN, Wm. Emmons Blackburn b 1844 Jeff Co TN d 1917, bur Hebron Cem, Jeff Co TN,
par Alexander Anderson Blackburn & Sarah Phina Biddle
| | |--5-Harriet Malinda Rankin b 1846 Jeff Co, TN d 1862 TN
| | |--5-Patrick Thomas Rankin b 1849 Jeff Co, TN, d 1862

| | | |--5-Elizabeth Harrison Rankin b 1851 Jeff Co, TN, d 1852 Jeff Co, TN
| | | |--5-Catherine Ruth Rankin b 1853 Jeff TN, m 1881 Wm. Lafayette Campbell b 1832 TX
| | | |--5-Marjorie Emmaline "Emma" Rankin b 1855 Jeff Co TN, m 1888, Dr. Henry Havelock Carson 1858-1943
| | | |--5-Susan Prudence Rankin b 1857 Jeff Co TN d 1862, bur Mt. Horeb Cem, Jeff Co TN
| | | |--5-Benjamin Caswell Rankin b 1858 Jeff Co TN d 1926, bur Mt. Horeb Cem, Jeff Co, TN, m 1884 Emma Carroll Newman b 1863 TN d 1948, bur Mt. Horeb Cem, Jeff Co TN, par Andrew Carroll Newman & Catherine Emeline "Emily" Bradshaw
| | | |--5-Helen Rankin b 1860 Jeff Co TN d 1936, bur Mt. Horeb Cem, Jeff Co TN, m 1893 Greene Co, TN, Rev. Lemuel Lee Carson 1863-1901 NC
| | | |--5-Effie Lillian Rankin b 1862 Jeff Co TN d 1937, m 1892 Miles N. Roberts 1855-1919
| | |--4-Thomas Rankin 1824-1849, bur Mt. Horeb Cem, Jeff Co, TN
| |--3-Thomas W. Rankin III, b 1794 NC d 1870, m 1819 Jeff Co, TN, Caroline M. T. Franklin b 1800 VA d 1833 Dandridge, Jeff Co TN, par Owen Franklin & Elizabeth Roper
| | |--4-Edwin Clendenin Rankin b 1820 Jeff Co, TN, d 1892
| | |--4-Col. Creed Wilson Rankin b 1821 Dandridge, Jeff Co TN d 1862 Cocke Co, TN, m 1845 Cocke Co, TN, Martha Jane Clark b ca 1826 Jeff Co TN d 1890 Gordon Co, GA
| | |--4-Louisa Jannet Rankin b 1824 Jeff Co TN d 1881, bur Tarrant Co, TX, m 1842 Jeff Co, TN, David Harvey Dunwoody b 1820 TN, d 1883 Arlington, TX, par Patrick McClain Dunwoody & Esther Bare McSpadden
| | |--4-Harriet Elizabeth Rankin b 1826 Jeff Co TN d 1889, bur Westminster Cem, White Pine, Jeff Co TN, m 1846 Jeff Co TN, Robert Harden Carson 1824-1898, bur Westminster Cem, White Pine, Jeff Co TN, par John L. Carson & Mary Snodgrass
| | |--4-Thomas Conway Rankin b 1829, d 1865 Jeff Co, TN
| | |--4-Egbert Etherton Rankin b1831
| | 2)[130] m 1834 Sarah "Sally" Bare b 1796 VA d 1888, par Bare & Barbara Halver
| | |--4-Katherine Jane "Kate" Rankin b 1834 Jeff Co TN d 1907, bur Mt. Horeb Cem, Jeff Co, TN, m 1865 P. W. Ritchleigh 1834-1905, bur Mt. Horeb Cem, Jeff Co TN
| | |--4-Sarah Caroline Rankin b 1835 Jeff Co TN d 1899, bur Dandridge, Jeff Co TN, m 1867 Cyrenus Mort b 1832 Shenandoah Co, VA d 1869 Jeff Co TN, par John T. Mort & Harriet
| | |--4-Mary Emily Rankin b 1836 Jeff Co TN d 1919, bur Shady Grove, Jeff Co TN, m 1865 Jeff Co TN, John Harrison 1835-1921, bur Shady Grove, Jeff Co TN, par Daniel Harrison & Rhoda Brown
| | |--4-Carrie E. Rankin b 1841
| | |--4-Hannah L. Adaline Rankin b 1842 Jeff Co TN d 1911 Barton Co, MO, m 1865 Jeff Co TN, Shadrack Robinson "Shade" Mitchell b 1841 Dandridge, Jeff Co TN d 1920 Jasper, MO
| |--3-Wm. Rankin Sr. b 1796 Jeff Co TN d 1871, bur Mt. Horeb Cem, Jeff Co TN, m 1836 Jeff Co TN, Susan Kimbrough 1810-1876
| | |--4-Martha Jane Rankin b 1836 Jeff Co, TN, d 1843 Jeff Co, TN
| | |--4-John McCampbell "Mack" Rankin b 1838 Jeff Co, N d 1871, bur Mt. Horeb Cem, Jeff Co TN, m 1860 Jeff Co TN, Elizabeth Catherine "Kate" Rankin b 1839 TN d 1931, bur Hebron Cem, Jeff Co TN, par James (Eaton) Rankin & Julia Ann J. Newman
| | | |--5-Leonidas Smith "Lon" Rankin 1861-1942, bur Hebron Cem, Jeff Co TN, m 1886 Josephine "Josie" Looney 1859-1940, bur Hebron Cem, Jeff Co TN
| | | |--5-Wm. Melvin "Will" Rankin 1864-1924, bur Hebron Cem, m 1892 Jeff Co TN, Martha Lea "Mattie" Davis 1869 1930 Jeff Co TN, par James Bradshaw Davis & Martha Jane Rankin

---

[130] Sarah :"Sally" Bare is the second wife of Thomas W. Rankin

| | | |--5-Mark Elby Rankin 1869-1870 TN
| | |--4-Mary Emily Rankin b 1839 Jeff Co TN d 1890, bur Hebron Cem, Jeff Co TN, m 1860 Jeff Co TN, David George Newman b 1835 TN d 1913, par John "Black Jack" Newman & Jane Kennedy Caldwell
| | | |--5-Serepta Newman, m Mont Edgar
| | | |--5-William Fletcher Newman b 1862 Jeff City, Jeff Co TN d 1930 New Market, Jeff Co TN, m 1887 Jeff Co TN, Lou Emily Douglas 1861-1904 Jeff Co TN
| | | |--5-John Newman m 1899 Harriet Isabel Newman 1870-ca 1952, par Gideon W. Newman & Mary Ann Rankin
| | | |--5-Infant Newman b and d Jan 4, 1865, bur Mt. Horeb Cem, Jeff Co, TN
| | | |--5-Infant Newman b and d Oct 19, 1872, bur Mt. Horeb Cem, Jeff Co, TN
| | | |--5-Infant Newman b and d Sep 15, 1874, bur Mt. Horeb Cem, Jeff Co, TN
| | | |--5-Infant Newman b and d Jan 12, 1876
| | | |--5-Emma G. Newman b and d May 24, 1878, bur Mt. Horeb Cem, Jeff Co, TN
| | | |--5-Infant Newman b and d Jul 28, 1880, bur Mt. Horeb Cem, Jeff Co, TN
| | | |--5-Infant Newman b and d Aug 13, 1882, bur Mt. Horeb Cem, Jeff Co, TN
| | |--4-Mark Thomas Rankin b 1841 Jeff Co TN d 1913, m 1861 Jeff Co TN, Nancy Jane Newman b 1844 TN d 1933 Charleston, Coles Co., IL, par W. Madison Newman & Mary Ann Nicholson (she m. 2nd Kelly)
| | |--4-Wm. Rankin Jr. b 1843 Jeff Co TN d 1862, bur Mt. Horeb Cem, Jeff Co TN
| | |--4-Alexander Porter "Alex" Rankin b 1845 Jeff Co TN Mary Ann McGhee b 1847 TN, m 1868 Jeff Co TN par William S. McGheeand Eliza
| | |--4-Susan Adeline Rankinb 1849 TN, m 1868 Jeff City, Jeff Co TN, George Samuel McGhee b 1849 TN
| | |--4-James Lafayette Rankin b 1854 Jeff Co TN, bur Hebron Cem, Jeff Co TN, m 1877 TN Martha Caledonia Corbett 1852-1896, par Col. Michael Montgomery Corbett & Nancy Dicky Gilbraith
| | | |--5-Ira Grace Rankin b 1877-1913 Jeff Co TN, m 1897 Jeff City, TN, Christopher Alexander "Chris" Davis 1874-1957 Jeff Co TN, par James Bradshaw Davis & Martha Jane Rankin
| | | |--5-Ida Bell Rankin b 1879 TN d 1905, bur Hebron Cem, Jeff, TN, m 1902 Horace Edmund Blackburn b 1876, bur Dandridge, Jeff, TN par Wm. Wirt Blackburn &Harriette Roxanna Miller
| | | |--5-Leota Texas Rankin b 1882 TN, m 1906 Charles G. Radke 1877-1921
| | | |--5-Nancy Eulalia Rankin b 1885, TN d 1944, m 1904 Benjamin Rule "Ben" Corbett b 1882 d Flat Gap, Jeff Co TN
| | | |--5-Rolfe Montgomery Rankin b 1892 Jeff City, Jeff Co TN, m 1) 1918 Lula Baxter Creswell 1894-1957, m 2) 1960 Martha Elizabeth Horton
| |--3-James Rankin b 1798 Jeff Co TN d 1824, m 1823 Sarah Randolph
| |--3-Isabella Rankin b 1800 Jeff Co TN d 1886 Jeff Co TN, m Col. James Newman b 1798 VA, m 1822 Jeff Co TN d 1879 Jeff Co, TN, par John Newman Sr. & Nancy Franklin
| | |--4-Joseph Reece Newman b 1824 Jeff Co TN d 1914 Bryson, Giles Co TN, m 1) Mary A. Lockhart b 1830 Jeff Co TN, m 1848 Jeff Co TN d 1863 Jeff Co TN, par John Newman Lockhart & Sarah "Sally" Rankin
| | | |--5-Sarah Isabelle Sinea Newman b 1849 Jeff Co TN, bap Mt. Horeb Ch, Jeff, TN d 1852
| | | |--5-Oliver Hood Newman b 1850 Jeff Co, TN, bap 1850 Mt. Horeb Ch, Jeff, TN
| | | |--5-Rev. Henry Harrison Newman b 1851 Mossy Creek, Jeff Co TN, bap 1852 Mt. Horeb Ch, Jeff Co TN, d 1936 Lakeland, Polk Co, FL

| | | |--5-Nancy Elizabeth "Nannie" Newman b 1853 Jeff Co TN, bap 1853 Mt. Horeb Ch, Jeff Co TN d 1888 Bryson, Giles Co TN, m Lincoln Co, TN, Wm. Samuel Gaultney b 1843 Alexander Co, NC, d 1906 Giles Co, TN, par Nathan Gwaltney & Louisa Gwaltney

| | | |--5-Infant Daughter Newman b & d 1855

| | | |--5-Archibald Blackburn "Arch" Newman b 1855, bap 1856 Mt. Horeb Ch, Jeff Co TN

| | | |--5-Lydia Jane Newman b 1857, bap 1858 Mt. Horeb, Jeff Co TN, d 1858

| | | |--5-Boyd Robinson Newman b 1859, bap 1859 Mt. Horeb Ch, Jeff Co TN

| | | |--5-Infant Son Newman b Aug 15, 1860

| | | |--5-Lee Converse Newman b 1861, bap 1862 Mt. Horeb Ch, Jeff Co, TN

| | |--m. 2)[131] Martha Ann Bradshaw b 1839 Jeff Co TN, m 1864 Jeff Co TN, d 1878, Bryson, Giles Co, TN, par Richard Harden Bradshaw & Jane P. Rawlings, (had 6 children, not listed), m 3)[132] 1879 Margaret J. "Maggie" Ralston 1830-1904 (no children)

| | |--4-Nancy C. Newman b 1825 VA d 1895 AL, m 1) ca 1859 Rev. Nathaniel Hood b 1804, Greene Co, TN d 1873 AL, m 2) James Kerr, m 3) Carter Boozer

| | |--4-James Conway Newman b 1827, Jeff Co, TN

| | |--4-Lidea Jane Newman b 1828 VA d 1857, bur Mt. Horeb Cem, Jeff Co, TN

| | |--4-Andrew Carroll Newman b 1830 VA d 1864 TN, bur Mt. Horeb Cem, Jeff Co, TN, m 1857 Jeff Co, TN, Catherine Emeline "Emily" Bradshaw 1836- 1914 TN par Joseph C. Bradshaw & Sarah Blackburn

| | | |--5-Luella May "Lula" Newman b 1861 Jeff Co, TN, bap 1862 Mt. Horeb Ch, Jeff Co, TN, d 1924 Jeff City, TN, bur Hebron Cem, Jeff, TN, m 1882 Jeff Co, TN, Isaac Anderson Coile b 1858 Dandridge, Jeff, TN, d 1938 Jeff City, TN, par John L. Coile & Mary Elizabeth Bettis

| | | |--5-Emma Carroll Newman b 1863 TN, d 1948 bur Mt. Horeb Cem, Jeff, TN m 1884 Benjamin Caswell Rankin b Jeff Co, TN, d 1926, bur Mt. Horeb Cem, Jeff Co, TN, par Patrick McGuire Rankin & Louisa Jane Lockhart

| | |--4-Rev. Charles C. Newman b 1831 Jeff Co, TN, d 1868 Talladega Co, AL, m Wallace

| | |--4-John McCampbell Newman b 1833 VA, m 1858 Mary Peck

| | | |--5-Ida Ella Newman bap 1861 Mt. Horeb Ch, Jeff Co., TN

| | | |--5-Edmond S. "Ed" Newman b 1862 TN, bap 1862 Mt. Horeb Ch, Jeff Co TN, d 1925 Knoxville, Knox, TN, m 1) Eva L. Newman 1858-1893, m 2) 1894 Lula Cassandra Rankin b 1875 Jeff Co TN d 1971 Maryville, Blount, TN, par Capt. Wm. Erskine "Will" Rankin & Nancy Elizabeth "Lizzie" Newman

| | |--4-Thomas Newman b 1834 VA d 1902, bur Mt. Horeb Cem, m 1854 Jennie H. McGhee

| | |--4-Benjamin Houston Newman b 1836

| | |--4-Mary Ann Newman 1841-1860, bur Mt. Horeb Cem, Jeff Co, TN

| | |--4-Isabelle Elizabeth Newman b 1846,VA d 1925, bur Mt. Horeb Cem, Jeff Co TN, m 1871 James M. Peck 1844-1919, bur Mt. Horeb Cem, Jeff Co, TN

| | | |--5-Lelia M. Peck 1873-1920 m 1894 Lon Fielding

| | | |--5-Florence A. Peck 1875-1955, bur Mt. Horeb Cem, m 1904 Dr. Charles N. Newman b 1856 Jeff Co TN d 1925, bur Mt. Horeb Cem, TN, par Aaron Newman & Cassandra Branner

| | | |--5-Ella Porter Peck b 1876, m 1910 John Franklin Haworth 1869-1936

| | | |--5-Howard M. Peck 1878-1919, m Clara Beaver

| | | |--5-Col. James Frank Peck 1880-1950, bur Mt. Horeb Cem, Jeff Co, TN

| | | |--5-Theodore M. Peck 1882-1888, bur Mt. Horeb Cem, Jeff Co, TN

---

[131] Martha Ann Bradshaw is the second wife of Joseph Reese Newman
[132] Margaret J. "Maggie" Ralston is the third wife of Joseph Reese Newman

| | | |--5-John Carroll Peck 1885-1943, bur Mt. Horeb Cem, Jeff Co, TN
| | | |--5-Buford Odell Peck 1886-1887, bur Mt. Horeb Cem, Jeff Co, TN
| | | |--5-Benjamin Oscar Peck 1888-1889, bur Mt. Horeb Cem, Jeff Co, TN
| | | |--5-Harry Eugene Peck Sr. 1891-1969, m 1919 Anna Pauline Mitts
| |--3-Conway Rankin b 1803 Jeff Co, TN d 1823
| |--3-Sinea Rankin b 1806 Jeff Co TN, d 1833 Jeff TN, m 1824 Jeff Co TN, Aaron Newman b
1802 VA, d 1884 Jeff Co TN, bur Mt. Horeb Cem, par John Newman Sr. & Nancy Franklin
| | |--4-Daughter Newman b ca 1825 Jeff Co, TN, d bef 1840 Jeff Co, TN
| | |--4-John Franklin Newman b 1830 Jeff Co,TN d 1921 Roane Co, TN, bur Mt. Horeb Cem,
Jeff Co TN, m 1852 Jeff Co, Martha Matilda Gilbraith b 1827 Jeff Co TN d 1860 Jeff Co TN,
bur Mt. Horeb Cem, Jeff Co TN, par James Gilbraith & Martha "Patsy" Hoskins
| | | |--5-Catherine Cole "Kate/Cate" Newman b 1853 Jeff Co TN, bap 1854 Mt. Horeb Ch, d
1920 Monroe Co, TN, bur Mt. Horeb Cem, Jeff Co TN, m 1876 Jeff Co TN, Wm. Newton
McMurray 1847-1936 Jeff Co TN, bur Mt. Horeb Cem, Jeff Co TN, par Samuel McMurray &
Mary A. "Polly" Shadden
| | | |--5-James Aaron Newman b 1855 Jeff Co TN, bap 1858 Mt. Horeb Ch, Jeff Co, TN, d
1926, m 1876 Jeff Co TN, Priscilla Ellen Palmer b 1852
| | | |--5-Mark Alexander Newman b 1857 Jeff City, Jeff Co TN, bap 1858 Mt. Horeb Ch, Jeff
Co TN, d 1937 New Market, Jeff Co TN, bur Lebanon Cumberland Cem, Jeff Co TN, m 1)
1882 Jeff Co TN, Mary Elizabeth "Mollie" Douglass b 1856 Jeff Co TN d Apr 1930, New
Market, Jeff Co TN, par Mathew D. Douglas & Martha L. Elmore, m 2) ca 1835, Sally Burnette
Hutchinson
| | | |--5-Sinea Frances Newman b 1859 Jeff Co TN, bap 1860 Mt. Horeb Ch, Jeff Co TN, d
1862, Jeff Co TN, bur Mt. Horeb Cem, Jeff Co TN
| | |--m 2)[133] 1861 Jeff Co TN, Eliza Catherine McGuire 1830-1864 Jeff Co TN, bur Mt. Horeb
Cem, Jeff Co TN, par Michael McGuire & Harriet Jacobs
| | | |--5-George Arthur Newman b 1862 Jeff Co TN d 1951, m 1) 1883 Jeff Co TN, Elizabeth
Tymanda Bradshaw b 1860 Jeff Co TN, bap 1861 Mt. Horeb Ch, Jeff Co, TN, d 1887 Jeff Co,
TN, bur Mt. Horeb Cem, Jeff Co TN, par Richard Harden Bradshaw & Jane P. Rawlings
| | | |--5-Anna Lee Newman b 1885, bap 1867 Mt. Horeb Ch, d 1973, bur Hebron Ch, Jeff TN
| | | |--5-Samuel Harvey Newman b 1887, bap 1887 Mt. Horeb Ch, d 1887, bur Mt Horeb Cem
| | | |--m 2)[134] 1889 Jeff Co, TN, Martha Parthena "Mattie" McMurray 1862-1891, bur Mt.
Horeb Cem, Jeff Co TN, par Samuel McMurray & Mary Ann "Polly" Shadden
| | | |--5-Leroy McMurray Newman 1890-1887, bur Mt Horeb Cem, Jeff Co, TN
| | | |--m 3)[135] 1892 Roane, TN, Signora Isadora Gound b 1863, TX d 1959
| | | |--5-Infant Newman b and d April 10, 1864 Jeff Co TN, bur Mt Horeb Cem, Jeff Co TN
| | m 3)[136] 1868 Jeff Co TN, Mary Jane Corbett b 1843 Jeff Co TN d 1918 Jeff Co TN, bur Mt
Horeb Cem, Jeff Co TN, par John William Corbett & Elizabeth "Betsy" Eudaily
| | | |--5-Andrew Johnson Newman b 1869 Jeff Co TN d 1919, m Lillian W. Alexander d 1902,
m 2) Florence Wallace d 1944
| | | |--5-Martha Gilbreath Newman b 1871 Jeff Co TN d 1947, m 1901 Jeff Co TN, Rev. John
Wesley McGee 1852-1926
| | | |--5-Zorada Florence Newman b 1873 Jeff Co, TN d 1913 Jeff Co TN, bur Mt Horeb Cem

---

[133] Eliza Catherine McGuire is the second wife of John Franklin Newman
[134] Martha Parthena "Mattie" McMurray is the second wife of George Arthur Newman
[135] Signora Isadora Gound is the third wife of George Arthur Newman
[136] Mary Jane Corbett is the third wife of John Franklin Newman

| | | |--5-Joseph Portrum Newman b 1875 Jeff Co TN d 1965, bur White Pine, Jeff Co TN, m 1899 Martha Miranda Blackburn, 1877-1943, bur White Pine, Jeff Co TN

| | | |--5-Daniel Hickson Newman b 1877, Jeff Co TN, d 1960 Hamblen Co, TN, bur Jarnagin Cem, Hamblen Co TN, m Lula M. Smith 1874-1953, Hamblen Co TN

| | | |--5-John Crawford Newman 1879-1951 Indianapolis, Marion, IN, bur Wooten's Ch Cem, Jeff Co TN, m 1904 Jeff Co TN, Daisy Doane 1884-1981, bur Wooten's Ch Cem, Jeff Co TN

| | | |--5-Lillie Caroline Newman b 1881 Jeff Co TN d 1949 Chattanooga, Hamilton Co, TN, m 1910 Alpha, Hamblen Co, TN, William Lloyd Manis b 1872 Sevier Co, TN d 1946, Strawberry Plains, Jeff Co TN, par Thomas D.A.F.S. Manis & Frances Amanda Bird

| | | |--5-Lula Jane Newman b 1886 Jeff Co TN d 1918 Hamblen Co, TN, m 1908 Wm Arthur Ailey b 1877 Cocke Co, TN d 1917 Jeff Co TN, par Jacob Ailey & Catherine Swann

| |--3-Christopher Rankin b 1809 Jeff Co TN d 1881 Jeff Co TN, bur Hebron Cem, Jeff Co TN, m 1833 Jeff Co TN, Frances George "Fanny" Gilbraith b 1816 Dandridge, Jeff Co TN d 1906, Jeff Co TN, bur Hebron Cem, Jeff Co TN, par James Gilbraith & Martha "Patsy" Hoskins

| | |--4-James Thomas "Jim Tom" Rankin b 1834 Jeff TN d 1901, m 1858 Jeff Co TN, Sarah Jane Frances Lockhart b 1839 Jeff Co TN d 1877, par John Newman Lockhart & Sarah "Sally" Rankin

| | | |--5-Bellvada "Belle" Victoria Rankin b 1858 d 1934 Miami, Dade Co, FL m 1893 Orville Meigs Carson b 1872

| | | |--5-Martha "Mattie" Melissa Rankin b 1861 Mossy Creek, Jeff Co TN d 1910, m 1896 Rev. John Wallace Cunningham Willoughby b 1845 d 1907 New Market, Jeff Co TN, par. John Willoughby & Mary Wallace Maxwell

| | | |--5-Sarah "Manda" Amanda Frances Rankin 1863-1867, bur Mt. Horeb Cem, Jeff Co TN

| | | |--5-John Alvin Christopher Rankin b Jan 1865 TN d May 1865, bur Mt. Horeb Cem, TN

| | | |--5-Samuel Trumbull Rankin b 1866 Mossy Creek, Jeff Co TN d 1941 Long Beach, Los Angeles, CA, bur Sunnyside Mausoleum, Long Beach, CA, m 1) 1890 Annie Eliza Bishop 1864-1928, bur Sunnyside Mausoleum, CA, m 2) 1931 Mrs. Lillian Mae Chamberlain d 1941

| | | |--5-Milton Elmer Rankin b 1868 Jeff City, Jeff Co TN d 1960 Redlands, San Bernardino Co, CA, m 1898 Jeff City, Jeff Co TN, Corrie Maurusa Bales b 1869 Jeff City, Jeff Co TN d 1959 Redlands, San Bernardino Co, CA, par Martin Bales & Rebecca Angeline Henderson

| | | |--5-Olive "Trudy" Gertrude Rankin b 1871 Jeff Co TN d 1946 San Bernardino Co, CA

| | | |--5-Rev. Benjamin Houston "Ben" Rankin b 1873 Mossy Creek, Jeff Co TN d 1924 Attica, Warren Co., IN, m 1900 Woodsfield, Monroe, OH, Minnie Estelle Neff b 1879

| | | m 2)[137] Nancy Jane Webb b 1851 Sevier Co, TN, m 1877 Jeff, TN, d Sevier Co, TN

| | | |--5-Geneva Lytle Rankin b 1878, Mossy Creek, Jeff Co, TN, m 1907, Decatur, Morgan Co, AL, Walter Lamar Penney b 1884 Decatur, Morgan Co, AL d 1957 Decatur, Morgan Co, AL

| | | |--5-Ora Ida Rankin b 1880 Mossy Creek, Jeff Co TN, d 1946, m 1914 Philadelphia, PA, Ernest Beecham Bayless

| | | |--5-Thomas Galyon Rankin b 1882 Mossy Creek, Jeff Co TN d 1919, m 1904 Laura Elizabeth Schrader b 1880

| | | |--5-William Rankin b 1883 Mossy Creek, Jeff Co TN d 1883

| | | |--5-Charles Conway Rankin b 1884 Jeff Co TN d 1954, m 1917 Helen Douglas Young

| | | |--5-Reu Raymond Rankin b 1886 Mossy Creek, Jeff Co TN d 1977 Maryville, Blount, TN, bur Grandview Cem, Blount Co, TN, m 1913 Cassville, Barry, MO, Florence Edens b 1888 Barry, MO d 1967 Comanche, TX, par Columbus Walker Edens & Tennessee Van Zandt

---

[137] Nancy Jane Webb is the second wife of James Thomas "Jim Tom" Rankin

| | | |--5-Robbie "Gusta" Augusta Rankin b 1888, Mossy Creek, Jeff Co TN d 1955, m 1916 Philadelphia, PA, William M. Baldwin 1881-1957

| | | |--5-Olen Orlena Rankin b 1890 Mossy Creek, Jeff Co TN, d 1965, m 1910, Creed Mont Yarnell b 1887

| | | |--5-Marvin Rex Rankin Sr. b 1898 Mt Horeb, Jeff Co TN d 1966, m 1918 Decatur, Morgan Co., AL, Ivy Mae Cain b 1896

| | |--4-William Marion Rankin b 1835 Jeff Co TN d 1837 Jeff Co TN, bur Hebron Ch Cem

| | |--4-Nancy Elizabeth Rankin b 1837 Jeff Co TN d 1921, TN, bur Hebron Ch Cem, m 1856 Jeff Co TN, Samuel Blair Newman b 1828 TN d 1892, bur Hebron Cem, Jeff Co TN

| | | |--5-Mary Josephine Newman b 1857, m 1885 Rev. David A. Clemens 1858-1927

| | | |--5-Mark Rufus Newman 1858-1949, m 1887 Cordelia "Cordie" Smith 1864-1918

| | | |--5-Emily Augusta Newman 1860-1953 Boise, Ada Co, ID, m 1903 Rev. David A. Clemens 1858-1927

| | | |--5-Rev. John Grant Newman D.D. b 1862 Dandridge, Jeff Co TN d 1956, m 1893 New Market, Jeff Co TN, Mary E. Minnis 1875-1901

| | | |--5-Frances Jane "Jennie" Newman b 1865 d 1953 Raymond, Pacific Co., WA, m 1892 Walter Eggleston Mountcastle Sr. b 1860 d 1951

| | | |--5-Charlotte Eglantine "Lottie" Newman 1867-1956, m 1902 John Mott 1870-1931

| | | |--5-Jonathan Houston Newman 1869-1949, m 1902 Nell May "Nellie" McReynolds, ca 1877-1962

| | | |--5-Edith Leannah Newman 1875-1961, m 1921 John Reynolds Stoffell 1869-1942

| | | |--5-Samuel Rankin Newman Sr. b 1880 Dandridge, Jeff Co TN d 1939 Dandridge, Jeff Co TN, m 1911 Delta Mallena Byerily 1879-1966, bur Dandridge, Jeff Co TN

| | | |--5-Anthony R. Newman b aft 1880 d bef 1900

| | | |--5-David Harding Newman b aft 1880 d bef 1900

| | |--4-Capt. Samuel Edwin Rankin b 1839 Jeff Co TN d 1900 Jeff Co TN, m 1867 Jeff, TN, Sarah Lorinda Lyle b 1846 Jeff Co TN d 1918, par Sam. Rogers Lyle & Miriam Alexander

| | | |--5-Rozee A. Rankin b 1867 Jeff, TN d 1955, m 1917 Dr. Wm. H. Taylor 1853-1930

| | | |--5-Sara Rankin b and d Oct 10, 1868, bur Mt. Horeb Cem, Jeff Co, TN

| | | |--5-Dr. Horace Rudolph Rankin 1869-1937, m 1903 Nettie Oliver 1883-1927

| | | |--5-Chase Rozolf Rankin Sr. 1869-1917, m 1901 Sue Keene 1873-1946

| | | |--5-Courtland Thales Rankin Sr. b 1871 Jeff Co, TN d 1956, m 1) 1900 Nora E. Maples, m 2) 1926 Lula Belle Young

| | | |--5-Samuel Hull Rankin b 1873 Gravelly Hill, Jeff Co TN d 1956 Jeff City, Jeff Co, TN, m 1922 Jeff City, Jeff Co TN, Chlorice Nevada Bible 1901-2001

| | | |--5-Frances Marian "Fannie" Rankin b 1875 Jeff Co TN d 1924, m E. Marvin Snoddy b 1877

| | | |--5-Christopher Morton Rankin b 1877 TN d 1952 Seattle, King Co, WA, m 1898 Nannie L. Banning b 1880 TN d 1958

| | | |--5-Nina Barentha Rankin 1878-1907

| | | |--5-Rev. Elmer Neil Rankin b 1880 Jeff Co, TN d 1919

| | | |--5-Herman Lyle Rankin 1882-1882, bur Hebron Ch Cem, Jeff Co, TN

| | | |--5-Denmar William Rankin Sr. b 1883 Jeff Co TN d 1963, m 1910 Martha Josephine Simmons b 1882

| | | |--5-Harriet Isabel Rankin 1888-1889, bur Hebron Ch Cem, Jeff Co, TN

| | |--4-John Fain Rankin I. b 1840 Jeff Co TN d 1917 Jeff Co TN, bur Hebron Ch Cem, m 1867 Jeff Co TN, Martha Jane "Mattie" Williams 1847-1924 Jeff Co, bur Hebron Ch Cem

| | | |--5-Emily Leannah Rankin 1868-1945, m 1891 Carl L. Hudson d 1949

| | | |--5-George Elbert Rankin b 1870 Jeff Co TN d 1951 Knoxville, Knox, TN, bur Hebron Ch Cem, TN, m 1896 Telford, Washington Co, TN, Mary Abbey "Georgia" Middleton b 1873 Jonesboro, Washington Co., TN, d 1941 Knoxville, Knox, TN, bur Hebron Ch Cem, Jeff Co TN

| | | |--5-Gordon B. Rankin 1872-1950, m 1900 Carrie Virginia "Virgie" Hudson 1881-1951

| | | |--5-Mark Roy Rankin 1875-1948, bur Hebron Ch Cem, m 1907 Jeff, TN, Nellie Margaret Blackburn 1877-1971, bur Hebron Ch Cem, par William Wirt Blackburn & Harriette R. Miller

| | | |--5-Edwin Loy Rankin 1875-1955, m 1919 Effie Dennison b 1876

| | | |--5-Joella Rankin b 1878, d 1903, bur Hebron Ch Cem, Jeff Co, TN

| | | |--5-Oscar Mcteer "Snow" Rankin 1880-1959, m 1911 Clara Elsewick b 1889

| | | |--5-Sermon Rankin b 1882 Jeff Co TN d 1882 Jeff Co TN, bur Hebron Ch Cem

| | |--4-Martha Jane Rankin b 1842 Jeff Co TN d 1918 Jeff City, Jeff Co TN, bur Hebron Ch Cem, Jeff Co TN, m 1866 Jeff, TN, James Bradshaw Davis b 1839 Jeff Co TN d 1917 Jeff, TN

| | | |--5-John Nicholas Davis b 1867 d 1914 Menominee, MI, m 1906 Omaha, Douglas, NE, Winifred Lemon

| | | |--5-Martha Lea "Mattie" Davis b 1869 d 1930 Jeff Co TN, bur Hebron Ch Cem, m 1892 Jeff Co TN, William Melvin "Will" Rankin 1864-1924, bur Hebron Ch Cem, Jeff Co TN, par John McCampbell "Mack" Rankin & Elizabeth Catherine "Kate" Rankin

| | | |--5-Mary Francis Davis b 1871 Jeff Co TN d 1947 Jeff Co TN, bur Hebron Ch Cem, m 1901 Jeff Co, TN, Lee Wilson Rankin b 1880 Jeff, TN, bap 1884 Mt Horeb Ch, d 1953 Jeff TN, bur Hebron Ch Cem, par Joseph A. H. "Andy" Rankin & Almira Jeanette "Miranna" Parrott

| | | |--5-Christopher Alexander "Chris" Davis b 1874 d 1957 Jeff Co TN, bur Hebron Ch Cem, m 1897 Jeff Co TN, Ira Grace Rankin b 1877 d 1913 Jeff Co TN, bur Hebron Ch Cem, par. James Lafayette Rankin & Martha Caledonia Corbett

| | | |--5-Lorine Clementine Davis b 1876 Jeff Co TN d 1937, m Dallas, TX, John I. Huckaby

| | | |--5-Benjamin Franklin Davis Sr. 1879-1955, Hebron Ch Cem, Jeff Co TN, m 1917 Eula Catherine "Cate" Rankin 1888-1917 d 1965, bur Hebron Ch Cem, Jeff Co TN, par. Leonidas Smith "Lon" Rankin & Josephine "Josie" Looney

| | | |--5-Dr. James Elbert Davis 1883-1922, bur Hebron Ch Cem, Jeff Co TN, m 1907 Nancy Huldah "Nannie" Franklin b 1887 Jeff Co TN d 1965, bur Hebron Ch Cem, Jeff Co TN, par Nathan Hood Franklin & Sarah Jane "Jennie" Fain

| | | |--5-Thomas Logan Davis b 1885 d 1914 Jeff Co TN, bur Hebron Ch Cem, Jeff Co, TN

| | |--4-Mary Ann Rankin b 1844 Mt. Horeb, Jeff Co TN d Mt. Horeb, Jeff Co TN

| | |--4-Sarah Malinda Rankin b 1846 Jeff Co TN, bap 1846 Mt Horeb Ch, d 1919, m 1874 Jeff Co TN, Thomas Michael Harden "Mike" Bradshaw b 1852 Jeff Co TN, bap 1852 Mt Horeb Ch, d 1919, par Richard Harden Bradshaw & Jane P. Rawlings

| | | |--5-Christopher Colvin Bradshaw 1875-1922

| | | |--5-Richard A. Bradshaw 1878-1948, m 1912 Dora J. Sturgeon

| | | |--5-John M. Bradshaw 1881-1937, m Lula Garland

| | | |--5-Martha Ella Bradshaw b 1885, m 1901 Albert J. Kidd

| | |--4-Frances Leannah "Leanna" Rankin b 1847 Jeff Co TN, bap 1848 Mt Horeb Ch, d bef 1930 Cisco, Eastland, TX, m 1868 Jeff Co TN, John Calvin Bradshaw b 1848 Jeff Co TN, bap 1848 Mt Horeb Ch, d 1939, par Joseph C. Bradshaw & Sarah Grizzle "Sally" Blackburn

| | | |--5-Wm. Edward "Ed" Bradshaw b 1870 TN d 1926, m 1894 Sue Ella Newman b 1870, bap 1878 Mt. Horeb Ch, d 1943, par Hugh A. Newman & Lydia Timantha "Tim" Bradshaw

| | | |--5-Charles Cleton "Charley" Bradshaw 1872-1956, m 1897 Bernice Entychus Gattis

| | | |--5-James Crawford "Jimmie" Bradshaw b 1874 TN, bap 1876 Mt Horeb Ch, Jeff Co TN d 1946, m 1902 Nancy Paralee Yarbough 1870-1953

| | |---5-Rev. Ernest Neal Bradshaw b 1876 TN, bap 1876 Mt Horeb Ch, Jeff Co TN, d 1955, m 1920 Jo Dahl 1884-1945

| | |---5-Flora May Bradshaw b 1878 TN d 1971 Eastland Co, TX, m 1901 John Robert "Bob" Snoddy b 1874 KY d 1949, Eastland Co, TX

| | |---5-Emma Cate "Katie" Bradshaw 1881-1946, m 1904 Arthur B. Leech b 1876

| | |---5-Ralph Rankin Bradshaw Sr. b 1883 Jeff Co TN d 1975 McCamey, Upton Co, TX, m 1910 Eastland Co, TX, Barbara Lenora Harris b 1881 Limestone Co, TX, d 1962 Upton Co, TX

| | |---5-Joseph Richard Bradshaw 1886-1887, bur Mt. Horeb Cem, Jeff Co TN

| | |---5-Mary Elgin Bradshaw b 1889, bap 1890 Mt. Horeb Ch, Jeff Co TN d 1947, m 1909 Earle Shell 1885-1958

| |---4-Charlotte Isabel Rankin b 1849 Jeff Co TN d 1925, m 1891 David George Newman b 1835 TN d 1913, par John "Black Jack" Newman & Jane Kennedy Caldwell

| |---4-Christopher Houston Rankin b 1851 Dumplin Valley, Jeff Co TN d 1932 White Pine, Jeff Co TN, m 1874 Jeff Co TN, Catherine Ruth "Kate" Franklin b 1852 Jeff Co TN d 1926 White Pine, Jeff Co TN, par Benjamin Francis Franklin Sr. & Lucinda Harriet Rankin

| | |---5-Frank Walter Rankin b 1875, Dumplin Valley, Jeff Co, TN d 1962 White Pine, Jeff Co TN, m 1899 Lula Belle Sharp b 1880 White Pine, Jeff Co TN d 1963 White Pine, Jeff Co TN, par Robert Porter Sharp II & Mary Anne Minnis "Mollie" Caldwell

| | |---5-Charles Clyde Rankin b 1877 White Pine, Jeff Co TN d 1884 White Pine, Jeff Co TN

| | |---5-Lucy May Rankin b 1881, Jeff. Co., TN, d 1913, Knoxville, Knox, TN

| | |---5-Harry Jay Rankin b 1883 Jeff Co TN d 1966 Nashville, Davidson Co, TN, m 1905 Harriet J. "Hattie" Cutts b 1879 Hamblen Co, TN d 1967 Nashville, Davidson Co, TN, par William F. Cutts & M. Amanda

| | |---5-George Christopher Rankin b 1887 White Pine, Jeff Co TN d 1956, TN, m 1915 Nannie Carson b 1887 d 1974 Knoxville, Knox, TN, par Thomas Henderson Carson & Laura D. Chilton

| |---4-Joseph Marshall Hood Rankin Sr. b 1854 Jeff Co TN, bap 1854 Mt Horeb Ch, d 1932, Knox Co., TN, m 1883 TN, Rebecca Elizabeth Stoffell b 1861 Grassy Valley, Knox, TN d 1938 par Stephen Van Resselaer Stoffell and Mary Ann M. Crawford

| | |---5-Christopher Van Rensselaer Rankin b 1884 Jeff Co TN d 1950, m 1913 Rush Co, KS Osa Fisher 1884-1959

| | |---5-Frances Roberta "Bob" Rankin b 1886, Grassy Valley, Knox, TN d 1976

| | |---5-Mary Isabel Rankin b 1888 Knoxville, Knox, TN d 1975 Knoxville, Knox, TN, m 1913 Bruce Phillip McCampbell b 1883 Knox Co, TN d 1929 Knox Co, TN

| | |---5-Joseph Marshall Rankin Jr. b 1890 Knoxville, Knox, TN d 1956, m 1916 Iowa, Sara Schneckner b 1886

| | |---5-Cina Estelle Rankin b. 1893 Knoxville, Knox, TN, m 1925 John Lawrence Perry b 1893

| | |---5-Elizabeth Louise Rankin b 1897 Knoxville, Knox, TN, m 1920 Earl Anderson Webster, Sr. 1887-1957

| | |---5-Margaret Sangster Rankin b 1900, Knoxville, Knox, TN, m 1933 Elmo E. Hundley b 1899

| | |---5-Ida McKinley Rankin b 1902 Knoxville, Knox, TN, m 1933 J. Walter Capps b 1884

| |---4-Andrew Nelson "Andy" Rankin b 1856 Jeff Co TN, bap 1858 Mt Horeb Ch, d 1927, bur Cedar Grove Cem, Athens, McMinn Co, TN, m 1886 Knox Co, TN, Martha Elizabeth "Mattie" Callen, b 1857 TN d 1930

| | |---5-Guy Callen Rankin b 1892 TN d 1964, m 1915 Frances Noeline Magill b 1894

| | |---5-Edwin Bruce Rankin b 1894 TN, d 1949, m 1925 Mamie Lee Cate 1900-1982

| | | |--5-Max Montfort Rankin b 1896, TN d 1967 Chattanooga, TN, m 1928, San Antonio, Bexar, TX, Stella Hudson b 1898 d 1978 Chattanooga, TN

| | | |--5-Reva Ethylene Rankin b 1899 Jeff Co TN d 1963 Salt Lake City, UT, m 1926 Athens, McMinn, TN, Charles Wilson "Charlie" Hammer b 1893 Jeff Co, TN, d 1979 Beaumont, Jeff Co, TX, par Melville Blackburn Hammer & Lillie Ellen McGuire

| | |--4-Huldah Iantha Rankin b 1858 Jeff Co TN d 1946 Jeff TN, bur Hebron Ch Cem, Jeff TN

| | |--4-Leah Fair Rankin b 1859 Jeff Co TN d 1860, bur Hebron Ch Cem, Jeff Co TN

| |--3-Samuel Emmons Rankin b 1811 Jeff Co TN d 1812

| |--3-Jane A. Wright Rankin b 1813 d 1847, m 1834 Jeff Co TN, Dr. John Pinckney Mathis b 1812 d 1834 Jeff Co TN, d 1870

| | |--4-Martha Jane Mathis 1835-1913, m 1860 Knoxville, Knox, TN, John Vance 1837-1905

| | |--4-Sara Mathis b 1836, d infancy, twin

| | |--4-Nancy Elizabeth Mathis b 1836, d infancy, twin

| | |--4-William Thomas Mathis 1838-1882, m Florence White

| | |--4-Harriet Louisa Mathis 1840-1907, bur Dandridge, Jeff Co TN, m 1879 Rev. Wm. Harris Lyle b 1838 Jeff TN d 1905, bur Dandridge, Jeff TN, par Samuel Rogers Lyle & Miriam Alexander

| | |--4-Sara Porter Mathis 1843-1878, bur Dandridge, Jeff Co TN, m 1864 Rev. Wm. Harris Lyle b 1838 Jeff TN, d 1905, bur Dandridge, Jeff, TN, par Samuel R. Lyle & Miriam Alexander

| | |--4-Milton Anderson Mathis 1846-1888, m 1877 Nancy Jane Tedford 1844-1903

| |--3-Josiah Emmons Rankin b 1815 Mt Horeb, Jeff Co TN d 1893, m 1838 Jeff Co TN, Mary Emma Gass b 1819 TN d 1883, bur Mt. Horeb Cem, Jeff Co TN

| | |--4-Dr. William Thomas Rankin b 1839 Jeff Co TN d 1865, bur Mt. Horeb Cem, m 1864 Jeff Co TN, Emma Jane McGuire 1838-1916, par Michael McGuire & Harriet Jacobs

| | |--4-Nancy Emily Rankin b 1841 Jeff Co TN d 1927, bur Mt. Horeb Cem, m Dr. Benjamin Franklin Brown b 1846, bap 1842 Mt. Horeb Ch, m 1868 Jeff TN, d 1922, bur Mt. Horeb Cem

| | |--4-John Gass Rankin b 1843 Jeff Co TN d 1913, bur Lebanon Cumberland Cem, Jeff Co TN, m 1) 1866 Jeff Co TN, Adiadne Jane "Adna" Lyle b 1847 Jeff Co TN d 1883, bur Lebanon Cumberland Cem, Jeff Co TN, par Samuel Rogers Lyle and Miriam Alexander, m 2) 1886 Jeff Co TN, Florence Caldwell 1859-1931, bur Lebanon Cumberland Cem, Jeff Co TN, par Isaac Anderson Caldwell & Margaret E. Chumlea

| | |--4-Ellen Leander Rankin b 1845 Jeff Co TN, bap 1849 Mt Horeb Ch, d 1912, m 1869 Jeff Co TN, David C. Snodgrass b ca 1848 Jeff Co TN, par Allen W. Snodgrass & Cassandra Gass

| | |--4-Martha Ann Rankin b 1847 Jeff Co TN, bap 1849 Mt Horeb Ch, d 1923, bur Lebanon Cumberland Cem, Jeff Co TN, m 1867 Jeff Co TN, John James Coile b 1846 Jeff TN d 1928, bur Lebanon Cumberland Cem, Jeff Co TN, par John Leonard Coile & Mary Elizabeth Bettis

| | |--4-Mary Emmons "Mollie" Rankin b 1853 Jeff Co TN, bap 1854 Mt Horeb Ch, d 1888, bur Lebanon Cumberland Cem, Jeff Co TN, m 1876 John Anderson Bettis b 1848 Jeff Co TN, d 1888 Jeff Co TN, bur Lebanon Cumberland Cem, par John W. Bettis & Isabella Henderson Lyle

| | | |--5-Clara Armenia Bettis 1877-1954, bur Lebanon Cumberland Cem, Jeff Co TN, m 1902 Dr. George Paul Zirkle b 1876, bap 1877 Mt Horeb Ch, Jeff Co TN, d 1966, bur Lebanon Cumberland Cem, Jeff Co TN, par George Adam Zirkle & Florence Obalma Wisdom

| | | |--5-Eric Thales Bettis b 1880 Jeff Co TN, d 1948 Morristown, Hamblen Co, TN, m 1908 Ida Pearl Sherwood b 1884 Morristown, Hamblen Co, TN d 1973 Morristown, TN

| | | |--5-Federick "Fred" Bettis b 1883

| | |--4-Rev. Joseph Wilson Rankin b 1856, bap 1857 Mt Horeb Ch, Jeff Co TN d 1880, bur Mt Horeb Cem, Jeff Co TN

| | |--4-Rev. Melville McElvain "Melvin" Rankin b 1861 Jeff Co TN, bap 1862 Mt Horeb Ch, Jeff Co TN d 1924, m 1889 Jean Erie Brown
| |--3-Aaron Bogue Rankin b 1818 Jeff Co TN d 1884 Koleen, Greene Co, IN, m 1840 Jeff Co TN, Marjary Copin Lockhart b 1820 TN d 1895 Koleen, Greene Co, IN
| | |--4-Mary Jannette "Jane" Rankin b 1841 TN, bap 1842 Mt Horeb Ch, d 1927 Greene Co, IN, m 1866 Jeff Co TN, Francis James Marion Titus d 1904 Joelton, Davidson Co, TN
| | |--4-Nancy Rankin b 1843 TN, bap 1843 Mt Horeb Ch, Jeff Co TN d 1850
| | |--4-Margaret Ellen Rankin b 1844 TN, m 1975 Samuel I. Caldwell 1831-1912
| | |--4-Thomas Bradley Rankin Sr. b 1850 TN, d ca 1925, m 1882 Martha Skomp d 1923
| | |--4-Harriet Melinda Rankin b 1852 Jeff Co TN d 1896 Scotland, Greene Co, IL, m 1873 Greene Co, IL, Matthew Stewart McElroy b 1845 d 1933 Fresno, CA
| | |--4-Nathaniel Hood Rankin b 1853 TN d 1931, bur Howell Cem, Koleen, Greene Co, IN
| | |--4-John Harrison "J. H." Rankin b 1855 Jeff Co TN d 1954 Orange Co, CA, m 1882 Emma Henderson b 1855
| | |--4-Oliver Smith Rankin b 1860 TN d 1926, m 1894 Carrie Rudd
|--2-**John Bradshaw** b 1774, d in infancy
|--2-**Francinea Bradshaw** b 1775, m McQuistion
|--2-**William Bradshaw** b 1778, m 1797 Margaret Bingham
|--2-**James Bradshaw** b 1779, m Mary "Polly" Rankin, par John Rankin & Martha Jane Waugh
|--2-**Samuel Bradshaw** b 1782, m 1803 Jeff Co, TN, Dorcas Prigmore
|--2-**Christopher Bradshaw** b 1785, m 1806 Jeff Co, TN, Mary Davis
|--2-**Richard Ammon Bradshaw** b 1788, NC/TN, d 1872, bur Mt. Horeb Cem, m 1) 1809 Jeff Co TN, Lydia Prigmore b 1778 PA d 1853, bur Mt. Horeb Cem, par Joseph Prigmore & Ann Prigmore, m 2) Margaret Rawlings 1810-1867, bur Mt. Horeb Cem (Margaret had no children)
| |--3-John Prigmore Bradshaw b 1810 TN d 1896, bur Mt. Horeb Cem, Jeff Co TN, m 1831 Elizabeth W. Rawlings b 1807 TN d 1860, bur Mt. Horeb Cem, Jeff Co TN, par John Rawlings & Sarah, m 2) 1862 Sarah J. Bowers b 1826 NC d 1896 Jeff Co TN, bur Mt. Horeb Cem, TN
| | |--4-Lydia Praytor Bradshaw b 1833 TN d 1890, bur Mt. Horeb Cem, Jeff Co TN, m 1853 Thomas S. Franklin 1831-1885, bur Mt. Horeb Cem, Jeff Co TN
| | |--4-Richard Rawlings Bradshaw b 1834 TN d 1863 Vicksburg, Warren, MS, m 1857 Frances Jane Berry 1832-1892, bur Mt. Horeb Cem, Jeff Co, TN
| | | |--5-John D. Bradshaw 1858-1860, bur Mt. Horeb Cem, Jeff Co, TN
| | | |--5-Elizabeth Tymanda Bradshaw b 1860 Jeff Co TN, bap 1861 Mt. Horeb Ch, d 1887 Jeff Co TN, m 1883 Jeff Co TN, George Arthur Newman b 1862 Jeff Co TN d 1951, par John Franklin Newman & Eliza Catherine McGuire
| | | | |--6-Anna Lee "Annie" Newman b 1885, bap 1887 Mt. Horeb Ch, d 1973, bur Hebron Ch Cem, Jeff Co, TN, m 1921 Howard Benjamin Franklin b 1881-1964, bur Hebron Ch Cem, par Benjamin Francis Franklin Jr. & Margaret Cordelia McMurray
| | | | |--6-Samuel Harvey Newman b Jun 1887, bap Nov 1887 Mt. Horeb Ch, d Nov 1887, bur Hebron Ch Cem, Jeff Co TN
| | | |--5-Richard Samuel Bradshaw b abt 1862 Jefferson Co, TN
| | | |--5-Rev. Harvey Smith Bradshaw b 1863 Jeff Co TN d 1939 Durham, NC, m 1857 Jeff Co TN, Frances Jane "Fanny" Berry 1832-1892
| | |--4-Stephen Roten Bradshaw b 1836 TN, d 1879, m 1859 Mary A. Boothe
| | |--4-Thomas John Bradshaw b 1838 TN, d 1896, bur Mt. Horeb Cem, m 1868 Cinderella Caldwell Bradshaw b 1839, par Joseph C. Bradshaw & Sarah Grizzle "Sally" Blackburn
| | | |--5-Bob Lea Bradshaw b 1868, bap 1874 Mt. Horeb Ch, Jeff Co, TN
| | | |--5-Frank Ashley Bradshaw b 1870 TN, m Edna H. b WI

| | | |--5-Oakley D. Bradshaw b 1871 d 1947
| | | |--5-Sally Bradshaw b 1872
| | | |--5-Infant Bradshaw b 1875 d 1875, bur Mt. Horeb Cem, Jeff Co, TN
| | | |--5-Clide Park Bradshaw b 1875
| | |--4-Sarah Elizabeth Bradshaw b 1840 TN d 1844
| | |--4-Joseph Reece Bradshaw b 1843 Jeff Co TN, bap 1844 Mt Horeb Ch, Jeff, TN, d 1844
| | |--4-Daniel Hardin Bradshaw b 1845 TN, bap 1845 Mt Horeb Ch, m 1866 Margaret E.
Routh
| | |--4-William Porter Massengil Bradshaw b 1847 TN, bap 1848 Mt Horeb Ch, d 1928 Jeff Co
TN, bur Mt Horeb Cem, m 1871 Mary Louise Lyle 1846-1936, bur Mt. Horeb Cem
| | | |--5-Arlen Weihl "Arley" Bradshaw Sr. b 1872 TN, bap 1874 Mt Horeb Ch, Jeff Co TN d
1923 MS, bur Lauderdale Cem, Lauderdale Co, MS, m 1908 Grace Neal 1885-1923
| | | |--5-Henry Lyle Bradshaw b 1875 TN, m 1926 Agnes Harris
| | | |--5-Ephriam Cawood Bradshaw b 1884, bap 1885 Mt. Horeb Ch, Jeff Co, TN, m 1906
Lillie Neal b 1883
| |--3-Joseph C. Bradshaw b 1811 TN d 1897 TN, m 1833 Sarah Grizzle "Sally" Blackburn b
1814 TN d 1860 TN, bur Mt Horeb Cem, Jeff Co, TN, par Edward Blackburn & Margaret
"Peggy" McGirk
| | |--4-Nancy Jane Bradshaw b 1834, m 1851 James H. Darr
| | |--4-Catherine Emeline "Emily" Bradshaw 1836-1914, TN, bur Mt Horeb Cem, m 1857 Jeff
Co TN, Andrew Carroll Newman b 1830 VA d 1864 TN, bur Mt Horeb Cem, par Col. James
Newman & Isabella Rankin
| | | |--5-Luella May "Lula" Newman b 1861 Jeff Co TN, bap 1862 Mt Horeb Ch, d 1924 Jeff
City, Jeff Co TN, m Jeff Co TN, Isaac Anderson Coile b 1858 Dandridge, Jeff Co TN d 1938
Jeff City, Jeff Co TN, par John Leonard Coile & Mary Elizabeth Bettis
| | | | |--6-Estella Laverge Coile b 1883 Mt. Horeb, Jeff Co TN d 1960 Okmulgee Co, OK
| | | | |--6-Roy Victor Coile b 1884 Jeff City, Jeff Co, TN d 1963 Jeff Co, TN
| | | | |--6-Dexter Rhea Coile b 1886 Jeff City, Jeff Co TN d 1903 Mt. Horeb, Jeff Co TN, bur
Hebron Cem, Jeff Co TN
| | | | |--6-Mary Emma Coile b 1888 Mt. Horeb, Jeff Co TN d 1979 Mecklenburg Co, NC
| | | | |--6-John Andrew Coile b 1894 Mt. Horeb, Jeff Co TN d 1975 Jeff City, Jeff Co TN, bur
Hebron Cem, Jeff Co TN, m Helen Nance 1899-1986 TN, bur Hebron Ch Cem
| | | | |--6-Maurice Conway Coile b 1900 Mt. Horeb, Jeff Co TN d 1901, bur Hebron Ch Cem
| | | | |--6-Marjorie Luella Coile b 1903 Mt. Horeb, Jeff Co TN d 1908 Jeff Co, TN, bur
Hebron Ch Cemetery
| | | | |--6-Carroll Anderson Coile, b 1906 Mt. Horeb, Jeff Co TN d 1992 Jeff Co TN, bur
Jarnagin Cem, Morristown, TN, m David Quince Brotherton b 1894 Greene Co, TN, bap 1923
Mt Horeb Ch d 1967 Jeff Co TN, par Richard P. Brotherton & Lillian Kidwell
| | | |--5-Emma Carroll Newman b 1863 TN d 1948, bur Mt. Horeb Cem, Jeff Co TN, m 1884
Benjamin Caswell Rankin b 1858 Jeff Co TN, bap 1859 Mt Horeb Ch, d 1926, bur Mt. Horeb
Cem, par Patrick McGuire Rankin & Louisa Jane Lockhart
| | | | |--6-Della Pearl Rankin b 1885 TN d 1925
| | | | |--6-Ruby Lillian Rankin b 1890 TN d 1941, bur Mt. Horeb Cem, Jeff Co TN
| | | | |--6-Hubert Andrew Rankin b 1892 TN d 1954 Jeff City, Jeff Co TN, bur Lebanon
Cumberland Cem, Jeff Co, TN, m 1937 Elizabeth Geneva "Dixie" Landrum 1902-1986
| | |--4-Enoch Nelson Bradshaw 1838-1870, m 1863 Victoria T. Rawlings 1842-1871
| | |--4-Cinderella Caldwell Bradshaw b 1839, m 1868 Thomas John Bradshaw b 1838 TN d
1896, bur Mt. Horeb Cem, Jeff Co, TN, par John Prigmore Bradshaw & Elizabeth W. Rawlings

| | | |--5-Bob Lea Bradshaw b 1868, bap 1874 Mt. Horeb Ch, Jeff Co, TN
| | | |--5-Frank Ashley Bradshaw b 1870 TN, m Edna H, b Wisconsin
| | | |--5-Oakley D. Bradshaw 1871-1947
| | | |--5-Sally Bradshaw b 1872
| | | |--5-Infant Bradshaw 1875-1875, bur Mt. Horeb Cem, Jeff Co, TN
| | | |--5-Clide Park Bradshaw b 1875
| | |--4-Edward Alexander Bradshaw b 1841, bap 1842 Mt. Horeb Ch, d 1863, bur Mt. Horeb Cemetery
| | |--4-William Minnis Bradshaw b 1844, bap 1845 Mt. Horeb Ch, Jeff Co TN, d 1864
| | |--4-John Calvin Bradshaw b 1848 Jeff Co, TN, bap 1848 Mt. Horeb Ch, d 1939, m 1868 Jeff Co TN, Frances Leannah "Leanna" Rankin b 1847 Jeff Co TN, d bef 1930, Cisco, Eastland, TX, par Christopher Rankin & Frances George "Fanny" Gilbraith
| | |--5-Wm. Edward "Ed" Bradshaw b 1870 TN d 1926, m 1894 Sue Ella Newman 1870-1943, bap 1878 Mt Horeb Ch, par Hugh Alexander Newman & Timantha "Tim" Bradshaw
| | | |--5-Charles Cleton "Charley" Bradshaw b 1872 TN d 1956, m 1897 Bernice Entychus Gattis d 1932
| | | |--5- James Crawford "Jimmie" Bradshaw b 1874 TN, bap 1876 Mt. Horeb Ch, d 1946, m 1902 Nancy Paralee Yarbough 1870-1953
| | | |--5-Rev. Ernest Neal Bradshaw b 1876 TN, bap 1876 Mt Horeb Ch, Jeff Co TN d 1955, m 1920 Jo Dahl 1884-1945
| | | |--5-Flora May Bradshaw b 1878 TN d 1971 Eastland Co, TX, m 1901 John Robert "Bob" Snoddy b 1874, KY d 1949 Eastland Co, TX
| | | |--5-Emma Cate "Katie" Bradshaw 1881-1946, m 1904 Arthur B. Leech b 1876
| | | |--5-Ralph Rankin Bradshaw Sr. b 1883 Jeff Co TN d 1975 McCamey, Upton Co, TX, m 1910 Eastland Co, TX, Barbara Lenora Harris b 1881 Limestone Co, TX d 1962 Upton Co,TX
| | | |--5-Joseph Richard Bradshaw 1886-1887, bur Mt. Horeb Cem, Jeff Co TN
| | | |--5-Mary Elgin Bradshaw b 1889, bap 1890 Mt. Horeb Ch, d 1947, m 1909 Earle Shell 1885-1958
| | |--4-Dr. Joseph Richard Bradshaw 1850-1975, bap 1851 Mt. Horeb Ch, bur Mt. Horeb Cem
| | |--4-Sarah Margaret Lydia Bradshaw 1856-1863, bap 1856 Mt. Horeb Ch, bur Mt. Horeb Cem
| | |--4-Andrew Thomas Hood Bradshaw 1858-1929, bap 1858 Mt. Horeb Ch, bur Mt. Horeb Cem, m 1875 Jeff Co TN, Isabelle "Belle" Tittsworth b 1855 TN, par James O. Tittsworth & Martha M. Lockhart
| |--3-Rev. Thomas Rankin Bradshaw 1813-1899, bur Mt. Horeb Cem, m 1838 Margaret Blackburn 1820-1847 Jeff Co TN, par Edward Blackburn & Margaret "Peggy" McGirk
| | |--4-Orlena Eglentine Clementine Bradshaw b 1843 Jeff Co TN, bap 1844 Mt. Horeb, Jeff Co TN d 1863, bur Mt. Horeb Cem
| |--m 2)[138] ca 1852 Martha E. Gass 1825-1853, bur Mt. Horeb Cem, Jeff Co TN
| | |--4-John R. Bradshaw *1853-1920*, bur Mt Horeb Cem, m 1) *1874* Eliza Emaline Coile b 1848 Jeff Co TN d 1930, bur Mt. Horeb Cem, par John Leonard Coile & Mary Bettis
| |--m 3)[139] 1861 Nancy Biggs, d 1883, par Alexander Biggs & Isabella Rankin
| |--3-Richard Harden Bradshaw b 1815 Jeff Co TN d 1863 Jeff Co TN, bur Mt. Horeb Cem, m Jane P. Rawlings b 1818 Jeff Co TN d 1863 Jeff Co TN, bur Mt. Horeb Cem
| | |--4-Nancy Dorthulia Bradshaw b 1838 Jeff Co TN,d 1898, bur Mt. Horeb Cem

---

[138] Martha E. Gass is the second wife of Rev. Thomas Rankin Bradshaw
[139] Nancy Biggs is the third wife of Rev. Thomas Rankin Bradshaw

| | |--4-Martha Ann Bradshaw b 1839 Jeff Co TN d 1878 Bryson, Giles, TN, m 1864 Jeff Co TN, Joseph Reece Newman b 1824 Jeff Co TN d 1914 Giles Co, TN, par Col. James Newman & Isabella Rankin

| | |--4-Unknown Child Bradshaw

| | |--4-Harriet Jane Bradshaw b 1843 Jeff Co TN, bap 1843 Mt. Horeb Ch, d 1883 Jeff Co TN, m 1880 Jeff Co TN, Elias Alexander Sr. b 1815 TN d 1891 Jeff Co TN, bur Mt. Horeb Cem

| | |--4-Unknown Child Bradshaw

| | |--4-Lydia Timantha "Tim" Bradshaw b 1844 Jeff Co TN, bap 1845 Mt. Horeb Ch, d 1896 Jeff Co, TN, bur Mt. Horeb Cem, m 1866 Hugh Alexander Newman b 1843 Jeff TN, bap 1846 Mt. Horeb Ch, d 1917, bur Mt. Horeb Cem, par Wm. M. Newman & Mahulda "Huldah" Henry

| | | |--5-Frank Adam Newman b 1867 Jeff Co TN, bap 1878 Mt Horeb Ch, m Sue Owen d 1935

| | | |--5-Sue Ella Newman 1870-1943, bap 1878 Mt Horeb Ch, m 1894 Wm. Edward "Ed" Bradshaw b 1870 TN d 1926, par John Calvin Bradshaw & Frances Leannah "Leanna" Rankin

| | | |--5-Jinnie Belle Newman b 1872, bap 1878 Mt. Horeb Ch, Jeff Co, TN

| | | |--5-Nancy Hulda Newman b 1873, bap 1878 Mt Horeb Ch, Jeff Co, TN

| | | |--5-Lizzie Kate Newman b 1874, bap 1878 Mt Horeb Ch, Jeff Co, TN

| | | |--5-Harnet Jantha Newman b 1876, bap 1878 Mt Horeb Ch, Jeff Co, TN

| | | |--5-David Pearl Newman b 1877, bap 1878 Mt Horeb Ch, Jeff Co, TN

| | | |--5-Milton Mack Newman b 1878, bap 1878 Mt Horeb Ch, Jeff Co, TN

| | | |--5-Lucy Moore Newman b 1880 TN, bap 1884 Mt Horeb Ch, m Hendrix

| | | |--5-Mattie Lee Newman b 1881 TN, bap 1884 Mt Horeb Ch, Jeff Co, TN

| | |--4-Sarah Elizabeth Bradshaw b 1846 Jeff Co TN, bap 1847 Mt. Horeb Ch

| | |--4-Unknown Child Bradshaw

| | |--4-John William Massengill Bradshaw b 1850 Jeff Co TN, bap 1850 Mt. Horeb Ch, d 1928 Jeff City, Jeff Co TN

| | |--4-Thomas Michael Harden "Mike" Bradshaw b 1852 Jeff Co TN, bap 1852 Mt. Horeb Ch, d 1919, m 1874 Jeff Co TN, Sarah Malinda Rankin b 1846 Jeff Co TN, bap 1846 Mt. Horeb Ch, d 1919, par Christopher Rankin & Frances George "Fanny" Gilbraith

| | | |--5-Christopher Colvin Bradshaw 1875-1922

| | | |--5-Richard A. Bradshaw 1878-1948, m 1912 Dora J. Sturgeon d 1964

| | | |--5-John M. Bradshaw b 1881 d 1937, m Lula Garland

| | | |--5-Martha Ella Bradshaw b 1885, m 1) 1901 Albert J. Kidd, ca 1872-1950, m 2) 1957 Washington Davis Farmer b 1877

| | |--4-Joseph Paluthiah Hood Bradshaw b 1854 Jeff Co TN, bap 1855 Mt. Horeb Ch

| | |--4-Asahel Biddle Bradshaw b 1857 Mt. Horeb, Jeff, TN, bap 1857 Mt. Horeb Ch, d 1899 Mt. Horeb, Jeff Co TN, bur Mt Horeb Cem, m 1889 Mary Bell Anderson b 1873 VA, d aft 1941

| |--3-Nancy Ann Bradshaw b 1817, m Thomas J. Alexander

|--2-**Thomas Bradshaw** b 1793

About the Author

Hazel Timblin Townsend grew up in Western Pennsylvania on a farm about 50 miles north of Pittsburgh. This was part of the 400-acre farm on which her great, great grandfather, Joseph Timblin, was the original settler around 1800. The family belonged to the Muddy Creek Presbyterian Church in Clay Township, Butler County. Joseph Timblin and his family helped to organize this church about 1804.

After attending a one-room school for eight years and graduating from a small vocational high school in West Sunbury, Hazel graduated from Maryville College, Maryville, Tennessee in 1954 with a Bachelor of Science Degree in Elementary Education. Her parents, William Cecil Timblin and Beulah Belle Rankin (of Jefferson County, TN), as well as many relatives, graduated from Maryville College. Hazel earned her Master of Education Degree in 1958 from Duke University, Durham, North Carolina.

While in college, Hazel's father was transferred to the new Veteran's Administration Hospital in Durham, North Carolina where he became Chief Engineer of the boiler house. When visiting her parents' new home, she met her future husband, D. Earle Townsend, Jr., in the church parking lot where his mother, Henrietta Covington Townsend, introduced him to the "new girl." Earle and Hazel were married in 1958 in the Mount Bethel Presbyterian Church. They spent most of their married life in Medford, New Jersey. Earle was an Electrical Engineer at RCA in Camden.

Hazel taught second and third grades for 5½ years. After becoming a stay-at-home mom with their three children—Walter, Susan and Sara—she was active in church and school activities. She served one term on the Medford Township School Board. She taught Sunday School and was ordained as an Elder in Faith Presbyterian Church. She was Director of their pre-school program, Small World, for 12 years, and a Christian Education Consultant for the West Jersey Presbytery for about ten years.

Hazel began her writing career in 1980 when she was invited by the Presbyterian Church (USA) to write a short-term Sunday School curriculum, *We Presbyterians*. This was followed in 1983 by *My Church's Story, the Presbyterian Church* for an independent publisher. Later she wrote lessons for the Sunday School series *Celebrate* and the Vacation Bible School series, *Storyteller*, both published by PCUSA.

After retiring in Greenville, South Carolina in 1994, Earle and Hazel have enjoyed traveling throughout the U.S. and Ireland. Both enjoy genealogy. Hazel's first major book in 1997 was *Rankin Roots in East Tennessee*. In 2004 she published a history of the area where she grew up, *A Town Hidden on a Hill, Queen Junction: The History of a Railroad Town, Clay Township, Butler County, Pennsylvania*. Preserving family stories continues to be her goal.

Index of Names

Overview

Every attempt has been made to index the hundreds of names from the stories and records of *Mount Horeb Church Minute Books*. Note that the members of session that are listed frequently are not indexed every time they appear. They are indexed the first and last time the individual appears in the minutes as present or absent. Also, they are indexed when that individual had a special responsibility, and when he appears elsewhere in various lists or stories.

Mary J. McCuistion · 143
Mary Jane McCuistion · 80, 84, 94, 143
Norrit · 137
Polly · 81, 97, 137
Sarah Elizabeth · 276

B

Baird
    Mary Dunwoody · 274
    William · 274
Balch
    Hezekiah, Rev. · 28
Baldwin
    Robbie "Gusta" Augusta Rankin · 287
    William M. · 287
Bales
    Corrie Maurusa · 286
    Frances M. Lyle · 143
    Martin · 286
    Rebecca Angeline Henderson · 286
Banning
    Nannie L. · 287
Baptist Board of Missions · 58
Barbee
    David · 80, 84, 85, 94, 96, 139
    Don · 6
    Edward "Eddie" · 184, 252, 259
    Harvey · 256, 258
    James A. · 81, 99, 124, 125, 139
    James C. "Jimmie" · 169, 245, 251, 253,
        257, 259
    Jennie · 259
    Katie · 258
    Mary · 258
    Mary F. · 169, 251
    Mary G. · 245, 253
    Mintie · 256, 259
    Porter A. · 184, 246, 252, 253, 259
    Samuel Edward · 246, 253
    William "Willie" · 258, 259
    William, Sr. · 259
Barby
    James A. · 89

Bare
    Sarah "Sally" (1796-1888) · 270, 282
Barnett
    Ann · 274
Bartlett
    Cora · 57
Bartley
    Richmond · 263
Bayless
    Ernest Beecham · 286
    Ora Ida Rankin · 286
Beard
    Harold · 74
Beaver
    Clara · 284
Beirut, Lebanon · 58
Bell
    George Alexander · 250, 257
    Inez · 43
    James Houston · 250
    Luther Lee · 250, 257
    Lydia Jane Zirkle · 81, 89, 99, 105, 118,
        151, 165, 243, 250
    Sallie Ann · 194, 207, 227, 247, 248,
        256, 257, 258, 259, 260, 263, 281
Bemis
    Joy Hammer · 20, 72
Berea College Appalachian Center · 75
Berry
    Frances Jane · 58, 87, 97, 109, 138, 291
Bettis
    Bradley · 256, 257, 258
    Clara (1877-1954) · 57
    Clara Armenia · 6, 48, 57, 73, 290
    Cora · 258, 260
    Daniel Lyle · 81, 90, 101, 130, 139
    Darthula Jane · 81, 89, 100
    Ebert · 257
    Ed · 73
    Edward S. · 74
    Eric Thales · 290
    Federick "Fred" · 290
    Ida Pearl Sherwood · 290
    Isabella Henderson Lyle · 34, 79, 139,
        290

D

E

G

I

J

M

R

T

Tadlock
   J. D. · 168
Talbott
   Barsheba W. · 81, 100, 150
   John · 82, 90, 102, 150
Taylor
   Rozee A. Rankin · 22, 54, 287
   William H., Dr. · 287
Tedford
   Nancy Jane · 290
Tennant
   Catherine Jane · 277
Territory South of the Ohio River · 66
Texas · 242, 243, 244
Thomas
   D. L. · 70
   Florence · 80, 86, 96, 150
   Melanie L., Dr. · 6, 21, 71, 72, 268
   Tanya · 73
   Wanda Faye Rankin · 71, 72
Thornwell Orphanage · 198, 255
Tiller
   Mary Elizabeth · 108, 156
   Sophia Emily · 108, 156
   Sophriah E. Newman · 144
Timber Ridge · 49, 65, 67, 69
Timber Ridge Cemetery · 55, 65
Timblin
   Beulah Belle Rankin · 14, 269, 295
   Hazel · 27, 45, 49, 59, 64, 68, 71, 75,
      76, 265, 269, 273, 280, 295
   Joseph · 295
   Stanley Walter · 76
   William Cecil · 295
Tipton
   H. · 267
   Henry · 78
   Henry C. · 58
   Nelle Roberts · 58
   Rebecca Catharine Massengill · 58, 78
   William Henry, Rev. · 58
Tittsworth

   Isabelle "Belle" · 164, 185, 189, 244,
      254, 257, 258, 259, 260, 261, 293
   James O. · 293
   Martha M. Lockhart · 293
   Sallie · 191
Titus
   Carol · 73
   Francis James Marion · 291
   Mary Jane Rankin · 115, 148
   Mary Jannette "Jane" Rankin · 291
Toole
   John · 273
   Ruth Ann Rankin · 273
Townsend
   Barbara Lefferts · 6
   Daniel Earle, Jr. · 6, 295
   Hazel Timblin · 27, 45, 49, 59, 64, 68,
      71, 75, 76, 265, 269, 273, 280, 295
   Henrietta Covington · 295
   Sara Elizabeth · 295
   Susan Leonora · 295
   Walter Rankin · 6, 76, 295
Transfer of the Church · 228
Trentham
   Ina Rankin · 71, 73
Trustees
   Board of · 36
Tullock
   John, Rev. · 71
Turner
   Donna · 6, 269
   R. R., Dr. · 74
Tusculum College · 28, 58, 73

U

Underwood
   Kathy · 6, 39

V

Van Lear